THE ONE, THE MANY, AND THE TRINITY

Marc A. Pugliese

THE ONE, THE MANY, AND THE TRINITY

Joseph A. Bracken and the Challenge of Process Metaphysics

THE CATHOLIC UNIVERSITY OF AMERICA PRESS
Washington, D.C.

The paper used in this publication meets the minimum
requirements of American National Standards for Information
Science—Permanence of Paper for Printed Library Materials,
ANSI Z39.48-1984.
∞

Library of Congress Cataloging-in-Publication Data
Pugliese, Marc A.
The one, the many, and the Trinity : Joseph A. Bracken and
the challenge of process metaphysics / Marc A. Pugliese.
p. cm.
Includes bibliographical references (p.) and index.
ISBN 978-0-8132-1794-9 (cloth : alk. paper)
1. Trinity—History of doctrines. 2. Bracken, Joseph A.
3. Process theology. I. Title.
BT111.3.P84 2011
231'.044—dc22 2010018858

To Laura, Dominic, and Gabriel

dulcissima dona Dei

Contents

Acknowledgments

I would like to thank all who have contributed to this project in so many ways. I owe a great debt to my colleagues and students at Brescia University, who are a constant source of intellectual inspiration. I am deeply grateful to the Lilly Endowment for a grant that partially funded this project. A special word of thanks is due to Joseph A. Bracken, S.J., for graciously reading the bulk of the manuscript. His emendations were greatly helpful. I thank Richard Viladesau for his eminently helpful input in the early stages of this project, as well as for his intellect and erudition. I am indebted to the editors at the Catholic University of America Press, especially Theresa Walker and James Kruggel.

I would further like to thank Allen S. Gehring Jr. for his help in thinking through some of the issues addressed in these pages, and for his personal and intellectual friendship: *cor ad cor loquitur.* I am also indebted to Steven P. Morrissey, a sort of personal professor of English to me from a young age: "You understand change, and you think it's essential." I would also like to thank my parents, without whose support, in innumerable ways, this and so many other things would never have come to fruition.

I thank my wife and two sons, who have been extremely supportive of my professional endeavors, and who, at times, seem to be even more convinced of my vocation as an academic than I am. They have been a source of constant encouragement during this and other arduous journeys.

And last but certainly not least, *Deo gratias.*

Introduction

Process-relational metaphysics demands careful attention. Like classical metaphysics, process metaphysics is too often quickly dismissed by those who do not understand it or fail to grasp its significance. Too often have contemporary philosophers and theologians viewed process thought as a recent curiosity that must be relegated to the memory of twentieth-century intellectual anomalies. This is because neither the questions process metaphysics addresses nor its complex and sophisticated answers are adequately understood, let alone appreciated. This work tries to treat process thought with the detail and thoroughness required to grasp its true significance. Theologians and philosophers doing metaphysics, as well those who abandon the metaphysical project, must heed the challenges and responses raised by process thought.

Process thought continues the task of systematically addressing the ultimate questions of ontology, epistemology, and axiology that never go away. It does so, however, in the context of the challenges presented to metaphysics, intellectually and practically, by the monumental happenings of the modern period. Process thinkers claim that the metaphysical project is an ineluctable one, but argue that many Occidental philosophical and theological traditions share certain common features in need of radical revision because of the theoretical and practical developments of modernity. For instance, the turn to the subject, with its prioritization of epistemology over metaphysics, is nothing short of an epochal change. The nineteenth century's turn to history burst pretensions of eternality, universality, and absoluteness by historicizing, particularizing, and relativizing everything from cultures and institutions to ideas and the great religious traditions. Process metaphysics has arguably worked most assiduously to address these challenges by beginning with subjectivity and taking temporality with the utmost seriousness.

Modern science has presented a litany of problems for theology and philosophy. The rapidity with which the scientific method has advanced our knowledge of the categorical world and the successes of technology in controlling it have led to not only naturalistic explanations of all categorical phenomena but attempts to use strictly empirical methods to answer the fundamental questions of reality and human experience traditionally handled by philosophy and theology.[1] The frequent paradigm shifts in modern science also present a unique set of challenges for philosophy and theology. Process metaphysics honestly and strenuously tries to reconcile the procedures and findings of modern science with philosophical inquiry.[2]

Process thought is an attempt to continue the ineluctable metaphysical task in the wake of modern developments. Modernity introduced an entirely different way of viewing human existence. Instead of a "vale of tears" through which we must prepare to pass into a better world, life in this world can and should be improved unhindered by the shackles of otherworldly philosophical systems and authoritarian theologies. Human existence and activity have become the preeminent concern, while God and religion have receded from the mainstream. Intellectual and practical problems for traditional religious belief have burgeoned, from the radical historicizing of scriptures and religious institutions to religion's compatibility with science to the question of the commensurability of belief in God with evil and great suffering.

Process thought contends that it is precisely certain aspects of Western metaphysical and theistic systems that cannot be reconciled with these concerns. On the other hand, the questions addressed by metaphysics and discussions of ultimate reality are valid ones that cannot be jettisoned by those who, as a result of these developments, have abandoned metaphysics and in some cases embraced modern atheism.

Process theology emerged as a reworking of Western metaphysics and monotheism. A theological school in its own right, process theology has for more than half a century influenced, directly or indirectly, countless

1. By "categorical" here and elsewhere I mean the post-Kantian distinction between the world of our experience known through our senses and whatever innate epistemic apparatus ("categories") we may have and the "transcendent" realm that refers to what is beyond such experience.

2. See Alfred North Whitehead, *Science and the Modern World: Lowell Lectures, 1925* (New York: Macmillan, 1925; reprint, New York: Free Press, 1967), 139–56, 193–94.

theologians. Even the Protestant evangelicalism often considered insular has incorporated insights from process theology in the open theism movement.

Process theologians and those influenced by them argue that much Western metaphysics and the classical theism built upon it cannot be reconciled with the many developments of the modern period. Classical theism in particular, not theism in general, precipitated modern atheism. Classical theism's authoritarian appeals to "mystery" do not preclude a rationally consistent theism according to modern epistemological standards. The ultimate metaphysical questions that will not go away can be sufficiently answered according to modern canons.

Thus process thinkers claim to justify the metaphysical project in the face of modern and postmodern criticisms; address the modern concern for scientific and rationally consistent explanations over those based on a priori religious authority, appeals to mystery, and supernatural revelation; demonstrate God's existence as a necessary condition of the possibility of ontology, epistemology, and axiology; make Christian theism relevant especially in its view of the relationship between God and the world; resolve the problem of evil for religion; reconcile religion and science; provide a theology of religions that sufficiently accounts for diversity as well as unity among traditions; provide points of contact for interreligious dialogue; and solve many enigmatic questions in the history of philosophy and theology. Classical theism, they say, fails in each of these endeavors. These claims alone merit careful attention.

A root problem of classical theism according to process theologians is how it, being heavily informed by classical Western philosophy, has privileged one set of terms in a litany of pairs of antithetical concepts. Classical theism privileges infinity over finitude, eternality over temporality, stasis over change, continuity over discontinuity, similarity over difference, unity over plurality, simplicity over complexity, the abstract over the concrete, universality over particularity, form over matter, the mental/spiritual/ideal over the physical, being over becoming, actuality over potency, objectivity over subjectivity, absoluteness over relativity, necessity over contingency, determinism over indeterminism, and causality over freedom. The prejudice in favor of the first term in each of these pairs is significantly responsible for the failure of classical theism to address the challenges posed by modernity, process theists claim.

Beginning with change and stasis in the Presocratics, these dialectical pairs frequently arise in discussions of what has come to be known as the "problem of the one and many," from ancient times up to the present.[3] Although the questions about whether ultimate reality is one or many and whether ultimate reality changes or remains the same may seem nugatory to many today, others point to the enduring nature of these questions, as well as aspects of the questions themselves, as telling against any facile dismissal of them.[4]

Indeed modern philosophy did not abandon the problem of the one and the many, and many recent philosophers and theologians have addressed it. From their precursors in the nineteenth century through Whitehead's manifesto up to contemporary process philosophers and theologians, process thinkers have addressed the problem of the one and the many time after time.[5] Whitehead claimed that the problem of how there could be incessant change or flux *(panta rhei)* as well as stasis or permanence is "the complete task of metaphysics."[6] Process thinkers repeatedly argue that process metaphysics solves the problem better than alternative solutions. Indeed Whitehead sums up his ultimate metaphysical principle in the celebrated statement: "The many become one and are increased by one."[7]

While the doctrine of the Trinity was by no means originally intended to be a solution to this problem, some theologians see it as a locus from

3. Plato mentions the one and the many as "two principles" in the *Sophist* 242: "There are Ionian, and in more recent time Sicilian, muses, who have arrived at the conclusion that to unite the two principles, is safer, and to say that being is one and many, and that these are held together by enmity and friendship, ever parting, ever meeting . . . peace and unity sometimes prevailing under the sway of Aphrodite, and then again plurality and war, by reason of a principle of strife" (Plato, *Sophist,* 242d–243a).

4. Philip Wheelwright, ed., *The Presocratics* (New York: Macmillan, 1966), 90. William James confessed that he believed the problem of the one and the many to be the most central of all philosophical problems (William James, *Pragmatism: A New Name for Some Old Ways of Thinking,* ed. Bruce Kuklick [Indianapolis: Hackett, 1981], 61–62).

5. Whitehead lists the one and the many, along with Creativity, as the three notions involved in his "category of the ultimate," which "are the ultimate notions involved in the meaning of the synonymous terms 'thing,' 'being,' 'entity'" (Alfred North Whitehead, *Process and Reality,* corrected ed., ed. David Ray Griffin and Donald W. Sherburne [New York: Free Press, 1978; originally published by Macmillan, 1929], 21–22 [pp. 31–32 in the 1929 edition]). All subsequent references to this work will reference the pagination in the corrected 1978 edition, followed by the page references in the original 1929 edition in parentheses.

6. Ibid., 208–9 (317–19).

7. Ibid., 21 (32).

which to address the problem of the one and the many. Since Whitehead did not incorporate the Trinity into his system, few process theologians explicitly integrate trinitarianism into their theologies. Some attempt a process reformulation of the Trinity, but more as an ancillary part, and not as a major feature, of their theology.

Joseph A. Bracken, S.J., is one process theologian who has made the Trinity an integral feature of his theology and has tackled the problem of the one and the many through this doctrine. Trained in both philosophy and theology and working in both disciplines his entire career, Bracken is well known and highly respected in the academy. He is currently the foremost Catholic advocate of process thought. His theology is arguably the most systematic, rigorous, and sophisticated bringing together of Christian trinitarian theism with process thought. In the doctrine of God, anthropology, Christology, ecclesiology, and eschatology, Bracken tries to harmonize distinctively Christian doctrines that process thought has traditionally had difficulty incorporating. In these ways Bracken offers the most rigorous and robust synthesis of traditional Catholic and process theology available. With eight monographs and over ninety published essays, articles, and reviews, and still publishing in semi-retirement, he has long been an important interlocutor in contemporary theology and philosophy.

In addition to developing sophisticated combinations of process metaphysics and classical trinitarianism, Bracken integrates into a Whiteheadian framework a multitude of diverse sources: Aristotelianism, Thomism, German idealism, Anglo-American idealism, social theory, existentialism, postmodern thought, contemporary philosophy of science, and a variety of thinkers whose programs often vary sharply from one another.

Although critical of many ancient, medieval, and early modern paradigms, Bracken does not shrink from drawing on them. He appropriates in revisionist ways these traditions sometimes easily dismissed by other process thinkers, but also forges ahead with the reformations of neoclassical and process metaphysics. On the whole faithful to Whiteheadian metaphysics in this prodigious integration, he modifies Whitehead in several important ways, for which there are detailed justifications and which need serious attention from other process thinkers. Drawing on tradition in engagement with our current age, Bracken is a shining example of the longstanding Catholic approach of grappling with the best philosophy at a given point in history.

Bracken provides one of the most powerful critiques by a process thinker of late-modern and postmodern abandonments of metaphysics. As he defends the ineluctability of the metaphysical task he explains why Whiteheadian thought avoids logocentrism in ways that other metaphysical systems cannot. Bracken's reinterpretation of Whitehead's relatively less developed "derivative notion" of the "structured society," which is based on texts in the Whiteheadian corpus itself, commands attention from both process philosophers and process theologians. Chief among the reasons for this is that Bracken's interpretation of the structured society is arguably the best way to redress possible atomism in Whiteheadian metaphysics. Bracken's understanding of the structured society opens up new and unexpected possibilities for moving ahead in a number of seemingly unrelated areas in systematic theology, including panentheism as a model for the God-world relationship, the doctrine of the Trinity, the traditional eschatological hope of subjective immortality, interreligious dialogue, and the location of the "causal joint" in the religion and science debates. He sees this revised Whiteheadian society as a new way to deal with the problem of the one and the many.

Process theologians should pay very careful attention to Bracken's claim that his revised Whiteheadian structured society solves certain problems that more "traditional" interpretations of Whitehead in this area leave inadequately resolved in process theology. In so many ways all types of theologians and philosophers will find insights in Bracken as they strive to address the contemporary context. To be unfamiliar with Bracken's work is to miss a great opportunity.

Process thought's project of producing a metaphysics adequate to the needs of modernity merits the careful attention of all philosophers and theologians who want to address the litany of challenges posed by modern and postmodern intellectual and practical developments. Bracken epitomizes the very best of this project.

Therefore in this book I do several things. In the first chapter I survey the genesis and historical development of process thought including the reasons for its appearance, explain the fundamentals of Whitehead's metaphysics and process theology as it emerged from Whitehead, and examine one of many contemporary theologies influenced by process theology: open theism.

In the second chapter I describe Bracken's theology, analyzing how he incorporates diverse sources into a unique synthesis. I trace how he uses and modifies Whiteheadian and classical Thomistic metaphysics as primary sources and provide a fairly comprehensive explanation of his doctrine of God. I present in detail his unique process theological construction of the Trinity, and conclude with how he addresses the problem of the one and the many.

In the third chapter I examine process solutions to the problem of the one and the many, with special attention to Bracken's solutions. There I explain why I judge them to be finally inadequate. In the fourth chapter I present a possible way to view the problem of the one and the many from a classical theistic perspective.

I end with a conclusion summarizing the contributions of process metaphysics in general, Bracken's thought in particular, and my arguments concerning the problem of the one and the many. In the end I must disagree with process solutions to the problem of the one and the many and must fault process thought for a major metaphysical shortcoming. However, process thought may very well be one of the best attempts at a metaphysics of categorical reality in light of theoretical and practical developments of the last few centuries. There has been an epochal shift and there is no going back. Contemporary theologians and philosophers have much to learn from process metaphysics. They also must better address the challenges process thought raises, as well as the challenges posed by modernity that process theology has the intrepidity to confront.

The project of this book seems very worthwhile. In philosophy nowadays process thought has been far removed from the mainstream. This is ironic because process philosophy is arguably one of the most sophisticated systems based on significant developments in philosophy during the modern period. My hope is to reintroduce Whiteheadian metaphysics into contemporary philosophical discussions.

In theology there are many currently working from within a process paradigm. Process theologians working in various Protestant traditions will be interested in Bracken's attempt at a Catholic, even Thomistic, process theology. Bracken's modifications of certain aspects of the Whiteheadian system, and his reasons for these modifications, deserve engagement from process theologians. As many process thinkers are similarly concerned with the problem of the one and the many, they will read with interest Bracken's understanding of and response to this problem. Process theologians may also be interested in reading my critiques of process metaphysics, which, if not entirely new, are presented in a new form.

In addition, many theologians who would not consider themselves process theologians are influenced by process theology and incorporate aspects of it in their own constructive theologies. In these pages they might find new insights from process thought for addressing their theologies to the contemporary world. Evangelical open theists, who share common concerns with and cull some resources from process theology, will perhaps find in these pages new insights for how to address their concerns in sophisticated ways.

Those who are engaging changes in the doctrine of God during the modern period but remain committed to certain aspects of classical theism will be interested in the challenges process thought poses to more traditional doctrines of God. Roman Catholic theologians and classical theists of all types will be interested in how Bracken works toward a synthesis of classical theism, especially Thomism, with the significant insights that process thought brings to theology in the modern and postmodern contexts.

Finally, I hope that every reader may find interesting the analysis of process thought from a more classical theistic perspective, specifically regarding the problem of the one and the many, offered at the end of the book.

THE ONE, THE MANY, AND THE TRINITY

CHAPTER 1

The Challenge of Process Thought

Considered in isolation, Whitehead's process metaphysics might seem a bizarre, unrealistic, and irrelevant eccentricity of the early twentieth century. Without understanding the issues it was addressing, one runs the risk of underestimating process thought's meaning and importance, and of easily dismissing it.[1] Therefore here I will raise some of the important questions of the last several centuries that process thought tries to address.

In one sense process thought is yet another attempt to address the perennial metaphysical problem of change and permanence,[2] and in doing so it has engaged the best philosophy and science of its day. In Western philosophy this problem goes back to the Presocratics.

1. "Whitehead seems to have a kinship with all the great thinkers in the classical philosophic tradition; his philosophy is a syncretistic absorbing, modifying, and systematizing of the finest insights in that tradition; and with all that, a joining together of recent developments in scientific and mathematical philosophy, until a structure is built into a system so vast and complex as to include not only what he regards as the actual picture of the world of circumstance but also its multitudinous and as-yet-unrealized possibilities!" (Vergilius Ferm, *First Adventures in Philosophy* [New York: Scribner's, 1936], 182)

2. "That 'all things flow' is the first vague generalization which the unsystematized, barely analysed, intuition of men has produced. . . . But there is a rival notion antithetical to the former . . . this other notion dwells on the permanence of things. . . . Accordingly we find in the first two lines of a famous hymn a full expression of the union of the two notions in one integral experience: Abide with me; Fast falls the eventide. Here the first line expresses the permanences, 'abide,' 'me' and the 'Being' addressed; and the second line sets these permanences amid the inescapable flux. Here at length we find formulated the complete problem of metaphysics" (Alfred North Whitehead, *Process and Reality*, corrected ed., ed. David Ray Griffin and Donald W. Sherburne [New York: Free Press, 1978; originally published by Macmillan, 1929], 343 [pp. 208–9 in the 1929 edition], 4). All subsequent references to this work will reference the pagination in the corrected 1978 edition, followed by the page references in the original 1929 edition in parentheses.

Process thought culls a litany of resources from the history of Western philosophy and religion. To treat all of these sources, even summarily, would beget tomes. Yet in order to catch a glimpse of what process metaphysics was really undertaking, it is necessary to trace some of the important issues raised in philosophy and science in the last several centuries. Before discussing Whitehead's metaphysics, then, in the next few sections I will summarize some important developments of modernity and how thinkers in Whitehead's time were addressing them.

The Modern Context of Process Thought

The modern period signaled a seismic shift in Western intellectual history. The numerous large-scale changes on many levels beginning in the late Middle Ages through the Renaissance and Reformation set a trajectory of irrevocable change for philosophy and theology. It is precisely some of these changes that occurred in the wake of the shift to modernity with which process metaphysical thought reckons.

The repudiation, on a spectrum of degrees, of the traditional religious authorities that had provided answers to many of the ultimate limit questions led to searches for other ways to answer these questions. Descartes's methodological doubt and turn to subject had in the long run the broad effect of prioritizing reason in answering the questions and prioritizing epistemology over ontology. The canons of human reason and rational comprehensibility would gradually displace appeals to authority, tradition, and mystery, and epistemology would preoccupy modern philosophy.

With the turn to the subject came a fervent desire to adequately ground human knowledge. Much ink would be spilled on which type of knowledge, that derived empirically through induction or that derived from the mental ideas and deduction, is superior, if not the only real form of knowledge. Epistemology would come to frequently ground metaphysics. In addition to providing an indubitably certain foundation for his own thinking, Descartes's "I think therefore I am" would come to embody the grounding of metaphysics in epistemology.[3]

3. This represents a reversal of much classical Western philosophy, which found in being and hence ontology or metaphysics the unifying and grounding element of other philosophical considerations. Regarding the relationship of epistemology and metaphysics prior to Descartes the majority approach could cursorily be described by: "I am therefore I think."

Among rationalists and empiricists alike developed an increasing distinction between the knowing or perceiving subject and what is known or perceived. In various ways and degrees, a bifurcation between subject and object appeared. This would become enshrined in Kant's celebrated distinction between phenomenal and noumenal realms.

A philosophical question directly overlapping the developments of modern science is the question of mind and matter. Many empiricists would prioritize both metaphysically and epistemologically the matter in motion studied by modern scientists. Others were pointing to the presence, in the organic world but especially in humans beings, of the center of feelings, reason, memory, and volition. These seem to transcend matter in motion in what we call "mind." Questions about the relationship between extension and mind as the two fundamental substances became pressing. How are they related? How are they different? How do they come into contact and interact, if at all? Is one prior to and the source of the other?

The metaphysical mind-matter questions also bore on pressing epistemological questions. What aspects of the world we perceive are actually inherent in the world apart from the existence and activity of the knowing subject, and which aspects of the objective world as known by the knower are relative to and dependent on the knower? Are the things unifying our experience of the world, like universals, mathematical principles, and the laws of science, inherent in the world itself or are they merely creations of human mind?

Many of these questions were essentially reembodiments of the same ancient philosophical questions in the modern context. Modern science and technology, however, represented both a break with the Middle Ages and a return to the classical posture of the ancient world. Appealing to the theology of the goodness of God's creation and humanity's viceregency over creation, Renaissance Christian humanism would argue that humanity can and should study the physical world to know and control it better. Life in this world is not only a preparation for the next life but can and should be improved through science. This increased emphasis on the goodness and importance of human existence and activity raised questions about its commensurability with the medieval theistic worldview in which God is the ultimate reality, and for which creation is not of much, if any, consequence.

Yet as scientific explanations proved successful in experimentation and in technological application, hopes for purely scientific explanations of the world grew. Some eventually concluded that scientific explanations would some day answer even the ultimate limit questions traditionally handled by philosophy and religion. Appeals to non-empirical causes like spirits, minds, the gods, or God only masked ignorance of the causal workings of nature. As knowledge of the causes of nature's happenings was increasing, spiritual explanations were decreasing. Perhaps, some said, the need for God as an explanation would eventually be eliminated.[4] Non-empirical spiritualistic explanations, appeals to mystery, or insertion of the "God of the gaps" came to be viewed with suspicion.[5]

Although the late Middle Ages witnessed criticism of Aristotelianism, modern scientists' gradual discovery of the errors in Aristotle's physics fueled rejection of Aristotelianism in toto, including its metaphysics. Concepts once used to contemplate the nature of beings in general and reality as a whole, like essences and substances, cannot be empirically perceived or scientifically verified. This move away from Aristotelianism included rejection of teleological or final causality and an almost exclusive emphasis on efficient causality. Entities and events in the world should be explained solely in terms of their prior causes as determined by science, not in terms of their purpose, goals, or meaning. Eventually this would lead to the metaphysical question of whether or not reality as a whole has any meaning or purpose. It also put the whole realm of philosophy dealing with values, axiology, into a crisis. Asking if there is any connection between what "is" (the indicative, descriptive) and what "ought" to be (the imperative, prescriptive), some would wonder what grounds ethics, or if even there is such a ground.

These philosophical and scientific developments of the modern peri-

4. Part of the rise of Deism in the Enlightenment, for instance, was due to the fact that more and more the workings of the world could be explained entirely in terms of efficient causality within the realm of nature itself, without the need for a "God of the gaps." God was no longer needed to make the grass grow, send the storm clouds, or rise up the great waves of the deep. God was relegated to the task of creating the perfect machine of the universe and then letting it run by itself. Eventually the necessity of God with respect to even the origins of the universe would be called into question.

5. Newton was initially criticized for his theory of universal gravitation, in which he was proposing gravity as some non-empirical, occult, or spiritualistic explanation for the experience of empirical phenomena in the natural world.

od would eventually feed the considerations of process metaphysics. One early modern philosopher, Leibniz, is of relatively more importance for some immediate antecedents of Whitehead, and for process thought in general. Like process thinkers, Leibniz is frequently misunderstood and not appreciated. He was trying to produce a metaphysics consistent with the science of his day. He even adumbrated relativity theory in a period that was enraptured by Newton. Leibniz realized that mathematically ordered forces, not extended matter, are the most fundamental units in the cosmos. This foreshadowed the interchangeability of matter and energy in contemporary physics, which Whitehead was also considering. It is not surprising, then, that aspects of Leibniz's metaphysics resurface in process metaphysics as it has tried to incorporate findings of science.

Leibniz begins by accepting what he calls the "popular philosophy" that there are two primary substances, Descartes's mind and matter, and that they interact. He then indicates how it is difficult if not impossible to conceive how these two discrete substances can interact. Leibniz further concluded that matter is dynamic and energetic, like mind or spirit, due to the forces of physics. He did not agree with Spinoza, however, that thought and extension are merely two attributes of the one universal substance because the empirical fact of plurality in the world discredits Spinoza's monism.

Leibniz does agree, however, with Spinoza's redefinition of "substance" as something that stands alone in complete independence of other things. Substance is what can be conceived in itself without reference to anything else.[6] Although from this Spinoza deduced one universal substance, Leib-

6. Spinoza's deduction for only one infinite substance is based on his definition of substance. He rationalistically modified the classical Aristotelian definition of substance by defining substance as that which is "in itself, and is conceived through itself: in other words, that of which a conception can be formed independently of any other conception" (Spinoza, *Ethics,* part 1, definition 3). Based on this definition substance must be infinite, otherwise we must conceive something external to it in order to impose finite limits on it. Spinoza agrees with the traditional definition of God as infinite, perfect substance (ibid., part 1, definition 6), so this one infinite substance is God. All finite beings require concepts other than themselves in order to be conceived by themselves. The concept of substance, while conceivable by itself, is required to conceive all other finite beings. Thus all finite beings are not substances according to Spinoza's definition. This means that all finite beings other than God are only accidental modifications of the one infinite substance, and are in this way like Aristotelian "accidents." Since there is no other substance other than God, this is a form of pantheism, not panentheism. Substance for Aristotle is what underlies and remains the

niz instead introduced monads to account for real plurality. Since extended material entities, like atoms, are divisible, they cannot be the most fundamental units of reality. Since the ultimate building blocks of reality are centers of force and not extended matter, they are mental points that are also indivisible. Leibniz calls monads "metaphysical points," or "beyond physical points." Without extension or size of matter, they are completely independent of each other so that they cannot be acted upon by any other monad. Inert extended matter is thus somewhat illusory, akin to a rainbow that is really composed of tiny water droplets.

Unlike mathematical points, however, monads are objective realities and not mere mathematical abstractions. Mind is real but not subject to the extension of matter. Monads, then, are infinitesimal minds with no extension and therefore indivisible. They primarily perceive and so are primarily subjects of experience. As a subject of experience, every monad is unique.

Accepting the Cartesian redefinition of "substance," Leibniz says God created each monad with an intrinsic freedom or spontaneity limited to and constitutive of its own existence and activity. At the same time God created monads so that their internal self-constitutive natures would be in harmony with the experiences of all other monads, which Leibniz calls "pre-established harmony." This explains how innumerable absolutely independent, discrete, and unrelated units can still constitute the one seemingly complex and interrelated world of our experience. Leibniz explains the organized purposeful activity of living organisms in terms of a "dominant monad."

Noting important differences, Whitehead acknowledges how his actual entities bear similarities to Leibniz's monads.[7] Whitehead's fundamental and irreducible metaphysical units are infinitesimal subjects of experience with no extension and are thus indivisible. They are primarily subjects of experience and each one is unique. When contemporaneous these units

same in an entity despite the changes it experiences across time. A substance is therefore capable of what he calls "separate existence," typically described with reference to sensible beings in terms of a composition of matter and form (Aristotle, *Metaphysics*, 1042a24–31). In another sense even matter and form independently can be considered substances because they themselves in a sense each remain the same despite experiencing adventures of change across time (ibid., 1042a33–b3 and 1043a25–27). Linguistically speaking, substance for Aristotle is "that which is neither said of a subject nor in a subject" (Aristotle, *Categories*, 2a14–15).

7. Whitehead, *Process and Reality*, 27 (40), 80 (124).

do not interact. These subjects of experience are objectively real and not abstractions in a mind (human, divine, or other). Both Leibniz and Whitehead thus exhibit a species of panpsychism, but as we will see Whitehead tries to take the physical world of matter more seriously than Leibniz.[8]

Another important development, especially in the century and a half before Whitehead, is the general turn to history. This attended to history's power to particularize, relativize, and diversify what upon first glance appeared universal, absolute, and unified. This applies to everything from human societies, cultures, and institutions to religions and the abstract concepts of philosophy itself. Coupled with this historicization, the fact that Western culture was through global exploration and trade coming into increasing contact with extremely diverse cultures and belief systems resulted in a crisis for all types of religious absoluteness. Some would soon suggest that any one religion is merely a situated, contextual, relative, and subjective but at last inadequate perspective on ultimate reality. Perhaps the absolute could be better described by philosophers doing metaphysics than by any one of the many particular religions of humanity.

Nineteenth-century attentiveness to the effects of the vicissitudes of history was tempered, however, by a belief in the notion of general progress toward the better. This belief found support in Darwin's theory of biological evolution by natural selection, Marx's historical movement toward the utopia, and the plain fact that humanity's mastery of its environment was advancing exponentially through the applications of modern science in technology. Some would even argue that the development of philosophy, religious beliefs, and religious institutions throughout history involves progress for the better, and is hence a good thing.

The nineteenth century also saw the rise of modern atheism. This arose in part as a protest against the seemingly necessary diminution, if not obliteration, of human existence and activity in order to give the classical God of Western monotheism a proper place.[9] With humanity's exponentially increasing knowledge and control of the world, many

8. "His [Leibniz's] monads are best conceived as generalizations of contemporary notions of mentality. The contemporary notions of physical bodies only enter his philosophy subordinately and derivatively. The philosophy of organism endeavours to hold the balance more evenly" (ibid., 19 [29]).

9. "To enrich God, man must become poor; that God may be all, man must become nothing" (Ludwig Feuerbach, *The Essence of Christianity,* trans. George Eliot [New York: Harper & Row, 1957], 26).

thought the belief in God once required to explain the unexplainable and frightful would eventually become unnecessary.

Immediate Antecedents of Whitehead

Whitehead's most proximate antecedents were the late-nineteenth- and early-twentieth-century philosophers and scientists who strove for a metaphysics that could incorporate the scientific and philosophical developments of modernity. These thinkers had a significant impact on Whitehead.

Modernity's matter-mind problem was exacerbated by the rapidly increasing findings of modern science. On the one hand, the scientific method was successfully explaining every entity and occurrence in the physical world in terms of efficient causality, or cause and effect. For some metaphysicians this led to determinism, as well as attempts to explain all order, including highly complex life and mental activity, in terms of matter and the laws of science alone. This is the position of "mechanistic materialism."

On the other hand, findings in biology complicated the already pressing problems of the presence in the material world of life, consciousness, purposeful value-oriented activity, and complex noetic activity. The most highly developed levels of consciousness also include memory, knowledge of the world, and complex manipulation of the material world. Biological evolution by natural selection added to these problems the question of increasing organization and complexity in the world, which did not fit neatly with the second law of thermodynamics. When physics made its quantum leap with the Einsteinian paradigm shift, the question of indeterminacy arose not only for living organisms, but also for inorganic reality. Those who saw these factors as telling against a pure mechanistic materialism are the "vitalists."

Key developments after Kant included German idealism's insistence, with strands of the great Western philosophical tradition but in a new key, that ultimate reality must be mental and spiritual. Idealism grounds existence in mentality, which can alone count for unity, order, and purpose in reality, as well as the reality of knowledge. This aggrandized the questions coming from the biological sciences about life, mind, and increasing complexity. The nineteenth century's turn to history, and the issues of the historicization of rationality itself raised by German idealism, became important factors. Of course questions about religion's possible contributions to all of these discussions entered the picture as well.

Despite sometimes explicitly repudiating metaphysics, even those of a more empirical, mechanistic, materialistic bent were wrestling with metaphysical questions: the questions of being and becoming in general, the whole of reality, and the ultimate principles of reality.[10] From a variety of allegiances and perspectives arose thinkers dealing with metaphysical questions, questions of unity and diversity, stasis and flux, absoluteness and relatedness, order and disorder, and determinism and indeterminacy, but in the light of modern philosophical and scientific developments.

Broadly speaking, mechanistic materialists said that everything necessary for understanding the whole of reality is innate in matter or "extension" alone. Others introduced additional "vital" principles, like Hans Driesch's "entelechy" or Henri Bergson's *élan vital,* to account for what they said could not be explained by matter alone. Following Hegel specifically and the older tradition of Platonic idealism generally, absolute idealists like F. H. Bradley, Bernard Bosanquet, and J. M. E. McTaggart insisted on an extra-material, mental reality as necessary for accounting for the whole of reality.

In terms of the primary and secondary qualities of the early modern philosophers, mechanistic materialists typically said that the only primary quality is extension (matter) and that everything else is a secondary quality.[11] Absolutely everything is explicable in terms of the motion of material particles, so that there is no need for an appeal to a nonmaterial, spiritual, mental, or metaphysical principle of explanation for any phenomenon. Scientific laws can explain everything without exception.[12] Consciousness and rationality are ultimately reducible to purely physical causes.[13] Logical and mathematical order resides in material reality apart from imposition by some external mind, contra idealism. This

10. Later we will see how Whitehead makes precisely this point: "By 'metaphysics' I mean the science which seeks to discover the general ideas which are indispensably relevant to the analysis of everything that happens" (Alfred North Whitehead, *Religion in the Making* [New York: Macmillan, 1926; reprint, New American Library, 1974], 82 n.).

11. Examples of mechanistic materialists would include Herbert Spencer, J. S. Haldane, Jacques Loeb, Bernardino Varisco, William Pepperell Montague, George Santayana, Walter B. Pitkin, and Wilfrid Sellars.

12. James Ward, *The Realm of Ends or Pluralism and Theism* (Cambridge: Cambridge University Press, 1911), 4.

13. Edwin B. Holt, Walter T. Marvin, William Pepperell Montague, Ralph Barton Perry,

realism affirms that order is discovered, not created, by mental activity.[14] This imperative to explain everything in terms of matter in motion directly resulted from the many new modern scientific explanations where hitherto there were none. As scientific knowledge increased, appeals to extra-physical, spiritual, occult, and even theological explanations decreased.

Essential for mechanistic materialists are the first and second laws of thermodynamics: the conservation of matter and energy and entropy. These were crucial in their criticisms of vitalism and idealism, which by introducing some principle other than matter and energy violate the first law of thermodynamics.[15] The conversion of potential energy to kinetic energy is enough to account for activity in reality. Following modernity's general lead of rejecting Aristotelian final causality, mechanistic materialists frequently said that questions of purpose or meaning are irrelevant. For the mechanist everything down to the atom is causally determined, with no spontaneity or indeterminacy whatsoever.[16] All of the phenomena pointed to by vitalists and idealists to support the need for something non-physical in order to account for reality can be explained solely by random variations of particles of matter.[17]

Regarding life, mechanistic materialists insisted that heredity explained continuity and natural selection explained diversity. Evolution, an idea used before Darwin, is the gradual unfolding of what is already in matter.[18] So there is no addition of something above and beyond what is

---

Walter B. Pitkin, and Edward Gleason Spaulding, *The New Realism: Coöperative Studies in Philosophy* (New York: Macmillan, 1912), 443–68.

14. Bernardino Varisco, *The Great Problems*, trans. R. C. Lodge (London: George Allen, 1914), 232, 243–44. See also, Holt et al., *The New Realism*, 11–154, 263–302. See also, William Pepperell Montague, "Professor Royce's Refutation of Realism," *Philosophical Review* 11 (1902): 43–55.

15. J. S. Haldane, *Mechanism, Life and Personality* (London: John Murray, 1913), 17–18, 27–28.

16. Ward, *The Realm of Ends or Pluralism and Theism*, 51.

17. Hans Driesch, *The Science and Philosophy of Organism*, 2 vols. (London: Adams and Charles and Black, 1908), 1:290.

18. For instance, an anonymous review of Jan Swammerdam's 1669 treatise on insect embryology uses the concept. (Anonymous, "Review of *Historia insectorum generalis*," *Philosophical Transactions of the Royal Society* 5 [1670]: 2078), and the eighteenth-century philosopher Johann Gottfried Herder applied an evolutionary theory to the development of universe in conjunction with Christian theism (Johann Gottfried von Herder, *Ideen zur*

physically given, which would violate the law of the conservation of matter and energy. Mentality is reducible to physiological brain states, which always parallel mental states.[19]

Vitalists claimed that diversity, activity, spontaneous indeterminacy, and the increased order in the cosmos, which contradicts entropy, refutes mechanistic materialism. In its strict causal determinism, mechanism cannot account for indeterminacy and hence the genuine plurality necessary for activity.

Some mechanists responded by arguing that the nature of material reality includes innate activity and diversity. For instance, regardless of logical inferences about the inability of matter to account for activity, there is much empirical evidence that matter inherently contains activity.[20] Others argued that diversity comes from the one being (matter) dividing itself into spontaneous centers operating in themselves in ways that are not causally predetermined. The most fundamental of these is the atom, or "monad."[21] These spontaneous centers of material activity, though indeterminate in themselves, exercise real influence on one another in a causal and mechanistic fashion. These spontaneous centers of activity in matter provide the true diversity and relationality necessary for activity. Matter-energy is the one absolute unchanging being of the universe, but always includes many indeterminate relationships due to matter's inherent indeterminacy. However, specific indeterminate relationships between the spontaneous centers of activity are never predetermined.[22]

Vitalists also contended that an observable increase in order and complexity, including life, contradicts the law of entropy. Some mechanists responded by saying that increased order and complexity in one physical location are always counterbalanced by decreased order in another location. Organization up to and including life results from differences between the causal interactions of the spontaneous centers of activity. These causal interactions result in new variations in activity different from the variations of the original spontaneous monads.[23]

Philosophie der Geschichte der Menschheit [*1784–91*], vol. 6 in *Herder Werke*, ed. Martin Bollacher et al., 10 vols. [Frankfurt am Main: Deutscher Klassiker Verlag, 1985]).

19. Henri Bergson, *Matter and Memory*, trans. Nancy Margaret Paul and W. Scott Palmer (London: Swan Sonnenschein, 1911), xi.

20. Haldane, *Mechanism, Life and Personality*, 27.

21. Varisco, *The Great Problems*, 139. The term "monad," of course, evokes Leibniz.

22. Ibid., 267.

23. Ibid., 248.

Whitehead would agree with the mechanists that in accounting for all of reality we must not introduce a distinction between matter and some non-material principle, as vitalism did. Matter and energy are an indivisible whole requiring nothing *ab extra* to account for activity. If all of matter is organic then the problem of how the universe could move from being inorganic to organic is obviated.[24] Whitehead will make the same points and refer to his system as the "philosophy of organism."[25]

That matter contains spontaneous centers of activity or monads, indeterminate in themselves but in causal relationships with one another, is also important for Whitehead. These help redeem true diversity, spontaneous indeterminacy, and hence activity. These also coalesce with some findings of early-twentieth-century physics that Whitehead was grappling with.

As mentioned, vitalists criticized mechanistic materialism for its monistic and deterministic implications. Mechanism cannot explain order in the cosmos or the fact that all potential energy has not already been converted to kinetic energy to result in a static state through entropy. Matter in motion and strict efficient causality leave little room for freedom, indeterminacy, and novelty in the form of unique events and beings. Nothing genuinely new and different can appear, and the one fundamental reality of matter seems to necessarily preclude diversity and individuality on the ultimate level. Without a real diversity of individual entities or events there are also no real relationships. Activity or becoming requires a genuine plurality in addition to unity, but mechanistic materialism's monism leads to an ultimate denial of real activity by denying fundamental diversity. In addition, some vitalists argued that the concept of time is useless if reality is monistic and causally determined.

The sciences were discovering real diversity and real unity on the level of life. Living individuals were being classified by their similarities and differences in the taxonomy of biology. Vitalists argued that life and biological evolution introduce genuine novelty beyond what is potential in matter, and so the living organism is more than a highly complex machine composed of dead matter.[26] Life also shows that activity requires diversity in the form of discrete individuals, and that activity is purpose-

24. Haldane, *Mechanism, Life and Personality,* 100.

25. See Whitehead, *Process and Reality,* 18–19 (27–29), and *passim.*

26. Driesch, *The Science and Philosophy of Organism,* 1:141–42.

ful.[27] Mechanistic materialism's monism devoid of true diversity, and its rejection of final causality in the form of goal-oriented activity, are impotent to explain the presence of genuine purposeful activity in the world.[28]

Because of its increasing order and complexity, life also seems to violate the second law of thermodynamics. Hence something other than matter alone must account for life.[29] Life's activity goes contrary to entropy's direction without completely avoiding it, and life seems to acquire energy and use it without losing it.[30] Further, the progress of biological evolution requires the interaction of individual living things that are both similar and different in order to provide the unity and plurality necessary for activity, or becoming, in general.[31]

All of this, said the vitalists, means that some principle, force, or power distinct from physical matter and energy is necessary to account for life.[32] This is the only way to account for diversity, activity, life, and teleology in the midst of dead matter. This principle must also provide true indeterminacy and diversity in order to account for the activity of nonliving material beings in general, as well as resistance to entropy. Only something other than matter can explain diversity, activity, individuality, and resistance to entropy. These vitalists made their non-physical, or "vital," principle directly active upon the material world in ways that the early modern mind-matter metaphysical dualists could not.

Agreeing on these points, vitalists differed in specifics about the vital principle. Bergson said time or history, which include activity and progress, both generate and connect the diverse individuals of reality. Time and history function as a continuum to unite, through duration, the many disconnected and discrete moments of existence, activity, and experience. Since ideas represent static entities, perhaps only raw intuition is the key to apprehending this creative, ever new, becoming, living, absolute force underneath experience. Using living things as an analogy,

27. See, for instance, Edmund Noble, *Purposive Evolution: The Link between Science and Religion* (New York: Henry Holt, 1926).

28. Ward, *The Realm of Ends or Pluralism and Theism,* 18.

29. Hans Driesch, *The Problem of Individuality* (London: Macmillan, 1914), 35–36.

30. Henri Bergson, *Creative Evolution,* trans. Arthur Mitchell (New York: Henry Holt, 1911), 260–61.

31. Ward, *The Realm of Ends or Pluralism and Theism,* 97.

32. Driesch, *The Science and Philosophy of Organism,* 2:205. Driesch called this vital principle "entelechy" and Bergson called it *élan vital.*

he argued that the feelings all life forms experience are the source of ongoing activity, even though monistic dead matter itself has no way to really be active.[33] Higher life forms even exhibit memory, which is "duration" of time and in which a unified past enters a present that is absolutely new or different.[34] Bergson would say God is the ultimate non-material source of creativity, incessant process, and life.[35] Driesch suggested that by ubiquitously containing activity, nature as whole, inclusive of its non-living aspects, operates according to a principle of "becoming."[36] Becoming in nature approximates an absolute, which can then be predicated to the many real individuals encountered in nature as a whole participating in becoming.[37]

With the vitalists, Whitehead would agree that pure mechanistic materialism is monistic, leads to determinism, and cannot account for real diversity, indeterminacy, novelty, and hence activity in reality. Activity requires both real diversity and real unity, and progress obtains only through the interaction of many discrete individuals. He would agree that whatever is ultimate must account for real, not only apparent, diversity. Time and becoming as real undermine the static implications of monistic materialism. He would further agree that becoming, time, and history as real processes contain windows into ultimate reality. The universe involves a real process of becoming, not just static being. Because all of nature participates in becoming, the reality of becoming is in a sense unified, homogenous, and continuous on the one hand, but the fact of novelty in the process of becoming, change, and diversity means there is pervasive plurality as well.

Whitehead would also agree that in addition to efficient causality there is final causality. Activity is purposeful, goal-oriented, and hence meaningful, even in what we call non-living entities. Life highlights this purposefulness, for which pure mechanistic materialism cannot account. So in addition to applying the category of "organism" to all of reality Whitehead followed the vitalists in using aspects of consciousness, like feeling, perception, duration, intentionality, and duration. He would also priori-

33. Henri Bergson, *Time and Free Will,* trans. F. L. Pogson (London: Swan Sonnenschein, 1910), 31–32.

34. Bergson, *Creative Evolution,* 210.

35. Ibid., 248.

36. Driesch, *The Problem of Individuality,* 45.

37. Driesch, *The Science and Philosophy of Organism,* 2:363.

tize direct experience, feeling, and intuition over rational mental processes. For Whitehead, then, the unique and novel events or activities necessary for diversity and activity have their origins in individual centers of experience.

Late-nineteenth- and early-twentieth-century Anglo-American absolute idealism, which developed out of German idealism, also heavily informed Whitehead. With the vitalists, these absolute idealists had a low estimate of mechanistic materialism's ability to provide unity, organization, and ultimately valid knowledge on the one hand, and true diversity and relatedness on the other hand. Yet, the absolute idealists had reservations about vitalism. With Hegel and even older strands of Platonic thought, they focused on rationality or reason in contrast to empirical experience and intuition.

The absolute idealists noted how matter appears to be a pure multiplicity of disparate events and values not implicating each other for their existence, but nonetheless involved in external relationships.[38] Reality also contains contradictions, which further threaten unity. The problem is that we comprehend the world as a unified whole, not as entirely disconnected diversity. There therefore must be a principle that provides unity to the many things in relationships without itself participating in relationships, as Hegel claimed. The absolute idealists agreed that activity and change require both unity and diversity. With its utterly disparate nature, matter cannot supply the underlying permanence needed to unify the many independent but interrelated parts of the process of becoming. Thus a nonmaterial or mental principle first supplying unity is required.[39]

With the mechanistic materialists, the absolute idealists said that what unifies the cosmos must be absolute, but judged matter to be unable to do this. Unifying scientific laws and mathematical principles are not inherent in the physical world but are imposed on it by the mind. Physical matter is pure multiplicity until mind supplies the unity. This means knowledge obtained through the senses provides only false appearances, not reality. This distrust of direct sense experience is essential in historic rationalism and idealism. Since the physical world cannot provide the

38. F. H. Bradley, *Appearance and Reality* (London: George Allen & Unwin, 1916), 30.

39. Thomas Hill Green, *Prolegomena to Ethics*, ed. A. C. Bradley (Oxford: Clarendon Press, 1883), 14, 28, 38. See also Josiah Royce, *The World and the Individual* (New York: Macmillan, 1901), and Bradley, *Appearance and Reality.*

unity that relates without itself being related, absolute unity must be *meta* (beyond) the physical.

The vitalists' time and duration is only in the mind and so cannot objectively unify reality apart from mind. Time is also relative, but the absolute principle of unity must relate without itself being in a relationship. The vitalists' vital force is still in a relationship with matter as "outside" to and "imposed" on matter, and thus cannot be what relates without itself being related. Also, since what unifies is in the mind, unity must still involve an experience, as per vitalism, but it must be mental and rational, not pre-rational, intuitive experience, which only provides false appearances.[40] With Hegel the absolute idealists would say that reality is inherently rational—"the real is the rational and the rational is the real"—and that the modern bifurcation of subject and object is a serious misstep. The *philosophia perennis* was right in its unity of knowing and being. The rationality of reality or being itself unites knower and known in a direct way.[41]

This all means that the absolute is not just an abstract mental principle related to and unifying reality from outside. Rather, the absolute must be mental but at the same time an actual concrete unity in reality itself, unifying the pluralities, diversities, complexities, and contradictions of reality. The many particularities in their relationships can only be understood with respect to their place in the whole.[42] This is because every relationship in which a particular entity is involved makes an essential difference to that entity.[43]

The God of traditional monotheism cannot provide the necessary rational unity of reality either. This God is personal, and therefore in relationships with creation and human beings, which means this God does not provide unity by relating without itself being related. The God of monotheism is too personal and related to be the absolute. This God is only an appearance of the absolute, not the real absolute. Monotheism's

40. Bradley, *Appearance and Reality*, 147.

41. Bradley, *Essays on Truth and Reality* (Oxford: Clarendon Press, 1914), 159, 200.

42. Josiah Royce, *The Religious Aspect of Philosophy: A Critique of the Bases of Conduct and of Faith* (Boston: Houghton Mifflin, 1885), 433; Bradley, *Essays on Truth and Reality*, 174; Bradley, *The Principles of Logic* (Honolulu: University Press of the Pacific, 1883), 2:623; Bernard Bosanquet, *The Essentials of Logic* (London: Macmillan, 1895), 1, 78. See also Royce, *The World and the Individual*.

43. Edward Caird, *The Evolution of Religion* (Glasgow: James Maclehose, 1893), 1:65–68; Bradley, *Essays on Truth and Reality*, 238.

God is therefore not the absolute.[44] There is a pragmatic place for the God of religion by addressing very important relationships, not the least of which are those of morality between human beings. However, at the end of the day religion and philosophy must be separated. Only philosophical metaphysics is prepared to integrate the findings of modern science with a comprehensive vision of reality as a whole.[45]

Some idealists made an effort to respond to the challenges of scientifically minded and pragmatic critics by trying to ground metaphysics more in experience of the physical world, to allow for more plurality and individuality, and to more closely unite the absolute with the physical world.[46] Metaphysics can begin with empirical experience instead of pure deduction based on ideas alone.[47] Idealism must be careful to not "swallow up" the world's many individual consciousnesses into the one absolute consciousness, so as to ultimately obliterate the many in the one.[48] Some moved away from strict metaphysical idealism toward realism by arguing that knowing the world through mental concepts does not relegate the world entirely to the realm of ideas.[49] Some of these responses represented a monistic panpsychism in which all individual, particular events and processes in reality are part of one overall process as the absolute or God.[50] Some even advocated a modified but faithful version

44. Caird, *The Evolution of Religion,* 1:140; Bradley, *Appearance and Reality,* 448; Bradley, *Essays on Truth and Reality,* 446–47; Bernard Bosanquet, *The Value and Destiny of the Individual* (London: Macmillan, 1913), 251; Andrew Seth Pringle-Pattison, *The Idea of God in the Light of Recent Philosophy* (New York: Oxford University Press, 1917), 297–320. See also Josiah Royce, Joseph LeConte, George Holmes Howison, and Sidney Edward Mezes, *The Conception of God: A Philosophical Discussion concerning the Nature of the Divine Idea as a Demonstrable Reality* (New York: Macmillan, 1897).

45. Bradley, *Essays on Truth and Reality,* 11.

46. Friedrich Paulsen, James Ward, Josiah Royce, and William Ernest Hocking are examples.

47. Ward, *The Realm of Ends or Pluralism and Theism,* 227, 409–29. See also Royce, *The World and the Individual,* and John McTaggart Ellis McTaggart, *The Nature of Existence,* 2 vols. (Cambridge: Cambridge University Press, 1921).

48. Andrew Seth Pringle-Pattison, *Hegelianism and Personality* (London: William Blackwood and Sons, 1887), 185–214. See also, Borden Parker Bowne, *Metaphysics: A Study in First Principles* (New York: Harper & Brothers, 1882); and Bowne, *Personalism* (New York: Houghton Mifflin, 1908). See also Royce, *The World and the Individual.*

49. Pringle-Pattison, *The Idea of God in the Light of Recent Philosophy,* 190–204.

50. William Ernest Hocking, *The Meaning of God in Human Experience* (New Haven, Conn.: Yale University Press, 1912), 172.

of Leibniz's monadology for metaphysics in general.[51] Others argued for an objective immorality in the absolute, but with the richest kind of individuality, for the many rational subjects upon the death of the body.[52] Perhaps the absolute even contains a temporal element in addition to it non-temporal element.[53] This stricter monistic identity of the principle of process or becoming with the physical world provided a better ontological basis for the process than when the principle of process must be introduced from outside of the material world.

Whitehead would readily appropriate aspects of idealism as well.[54] Important among these was that philosophy, not religion, must address the modern science responsible for the mechanistic materialist-vitalist debate. Process thought would become a metaphysics for the age of modern science, without presupposing the religion that had been segregated from philosophy in the modern period. Whitehead would not see the sciences as eradicating metaphysics, but requiring and providing it with new opportunities. He would borrow from the pragmatic idealists the necessity of grounding metaphysics in empirical experience.

Although agreeing with mechanistic materialists that the ultimate cannot be imposed from the outside in an external relationship to physical reality, Whitehead would deny that pure matter-energy is an adequate ultimate. Hence he agreed with the absolute idealists, against both mechanism and vitalism, that the absolute must be concrete and in reality itself. With the more pragmatic, empirical idealists, Whitehead would want to identify the mental and the physical in a more monistic and panpsychist way.

By unifying the diversity and relatedness of material reality the ultimate must include plurality and relatedness, but cannot be identical with the plurality and cannot itself be related. Whitehead would agree with the absolute idealists that cosmic activity depends on something that relates and on things that are related, but that they cannot be identical.

51. Ward, *The Realm of Ends or Pluralism and Theism,* 50–54, 61–67, 190–200, 207–11, 254–60.

52. Josiah Royce, *The Conception of Immortality* (Boston: Houghton Mifflin, 1900).

53. Pringle-Pattison, *The Idea of God in the Light of Recent Philosophy,* 363.

54. "Finally, though throughout the main body of the work I am in sharp disagreement with Bradley, the final outcome is after all not so greatly different. . . . Indeed, if this cosmology be deemed successful, it becomes natural at this point to ask whether the type of thought involved be not a transformation of some main doctrines of Absolute Idealism onto a realistic basis" (Whitehead, *Process and Reality,* xii–xiii [vii–viii]).

Corresponding to "real is the rational and the rational is the real," Whitehead would say that all of reality contains rationality. There cannot be an ultimate physical-mental dualism. The mechanistic materialists were right in saying there is only one metaphysical ultimate, but were wrong in denying that mentality is inherent in it. Epistemologically, Whitehead would also reject the modern hiatus between subject and object. Finally, although Bradley would reject any facile distinction between external and internal relations, that every relationship in which an entity finds itself is constitutive of that entity is central for Whitehead. For him as for the absolute idealists, the many particularities can be understood only with respect to their place in the whole.

In Whitehead's time, some people working broadly from within mechanistic materialism but listening to vitalist and idealist concerns rejected pure mechanistic materialism. Like the mechanists these thinkers, too, would sometimes deny they were doing metaphysics, associating it with vitalism and idealism.[55]

Samuel Alexander admitted there was orderly but novel activity in the world and that pure matter alone could not account for this.[56] He argued that reality is fundamentally composed of momentary events, not material objects related in space and time, and that space and time is the absolute relating the relative events.[57]

Vitalists had long pointed to "epigenesis," or the appearance with life of more than what is potential in matter, as evidence of a vital force.[58] Accounting for increased organization, Alexander said there are levels of increasing complexity emerging solely from the events taking place in space and time. Each level, or "nisus," has its own defining characteristic. The number of entities in each nisus progressively decreases as the levels become more complex, but each higher nisus includes each lower-level nisus. The reality of each nisus depends on its many constituent member entities. Matter emerges first as modes of space and time at a certain level of complexity in motions between the fundamental spatiotemporal events. At a higher level life emerges and at a higher level mind emerges

55. C. Lloyd Morgan, *Instinct and Experience,* 2nd ed. (London: Methuen, 1913), viii.

56. Samuel Alexander, *Space, Time, and Deity,* 2 vols. (London: Macmillan, 1920).

57. Ibid., 1:38, 60, 66.

58. Hans Driesch, *History and Theory of Vitalism,* trans. C. K. Ogden (New York: Macmillan, 1914), 39. The word "epigenesis" had long been used in the modern biological sciences, for instance by Caspar Friedrich Wolff in his 1759 *Theoria Generationis.*

with the characteristic of consciousness.[59] The highest nisus has God as its only member.[60] Emergence does not violate the first law of thermodynamics because higher levels of emergence do not create more space or time; they only organize space and time into an increasingly more complex order.

Alexander's account tries to give a fundamentally mechanistic-materialistic explanation but endeavors to explain real activity and the diversity it requires. On each level there is a balance of diversity, change, contingency, and indeterminacy with unity, stasis, necessity, and casual determination. All levels are necessary in that they were predetermined to eventually emerge out of space and time. Each level or nisus is changeless, permanent, and necessary, but the many member entities in each nisus change, are impermanent, and are contingent. In the highest nisus the deity reflects all changes occurring in the lower levels, but the fact that God is the principle of unity including and unifying the lower levels does not change. In terms of the overall cosmic process, the nisus of God becomes increasingly complex as all other entities in the lower levels are incorporated into God. Plurality and diversity are so real that every spatiotemporal event and every change is not only in space and time, but also in God.[61]

C. Lloyd Morgan similarly sought to account for true diversity, activity, and emergent complexity within a more mechanistic-materialist framework.[62] He tried to avoid any extra-material principle of unity and organization. The many momentary events of space and time occur entirely in matter.[63] Increasingly complex levels of organization, or "plans," emerge as new forms of relatedness between material events appear. The specific types of relatedness between the events on any given level and missing from lower levels define that level's complexity and order. Again, each level depends on its many constituent member entities.

The plurality of changing unique member entities at each level provides diversity. The level or plan provides unity and continuity. Morgan

59. Alexander, *Space, Time, and Deity.* 2:345.

60. Ibid., 2:345.

61. Ibid., 2:353, 365.

62. C. Lloyd Morgan, *Emergent Evolution* (London: Williams and Norgate, 1923); Morgan, *Instinct and Experience,* 2nd ed. (London: Methuen, 1913); Morgan, *Life, Mind and Spirit* (London: Williams and Norgate, 1923).

63. Morgan, *Emergent Evolution,* 24.

stressed the indeterminacy in the events themselves. Some events, for instance, are unpredictable even with a comprehensive knowledge of all prior factors.[64] Since the many individual events are indeterminate and since each level is generated by and depends on its member events, the emergent levels are not predetermined by the basic nature of space and time as they were for Alexander. This gives each unique event greater power in shaping the outcome of the process of emergence than if the actual levels of emergence were predetermined by space and time.

Believing there are no compelling proofs for God's existence, Morgan does include God to account for ultimate unity and ultimate diversity. God has two "poles." The "individuality" pole is God's uniqueness, which is absolute, unchanging, and provides unity. The "personality" pole is God's relatedness to all other events and the other levels of emergence. The personality pole is relative, always changing, and provides diversity. God is not the absolute since absoluteness is only one pole of God, and to call God the "absolute" seems to connote that God has no relationships. All of reality besides God reflects this "bipolar" structure, containing both absolute individuality and relative personality.

The ways emergent evolutionism tries to give both unity and diversity ultimate cosmic significance are important for Whitehead.[65] Only true unity and true diversity can explain activity or process. The fundamental entities in space and time are momentary events. Emerging from these spatiotemporal events are higher levels of order and complexity that represent a type of unity, permanence, and continuity in contrast to the many, diverse, unique events.[66] Yet these higher levels depend on their

64. Morgan, *Instinct and Experience,* 151.

65. He references Alexander and Morgan in his preface to *Science and the Modern World.* (Alfred North Whitehead, *Science and the Modern World* [New York: Macmillan, 1925; reprint, New York: Free Press, 1967], viii)

66. When speaking of emergent evolution and "epigenesis," the great French Jesuit scientist and philosopher Pierre Teilhard de Chardin frequently comes to mind. Even though Teilhard's career was roughly contemporaneous with Whitehead's, the two men worked independently, but within the same scientific and philosophical milieu. Teilhard remained more on the emergent evolutionist path than Whitehead. Much of Teilhard's work was not available to the English-speaking world until the 1960s but he is a witness to the metaphysical synthesizing in the light of modern science and philosophy taking place in Whitehead's day. Teilhard is especially important as one of the few Roman Catholic thinkers engaging these currents at the time, and one of the few early Catholic thinkers influenced by incipient process thought, broadly speaking.

member entities for their existence and development. The highest level of reality, God or deity, participates in unity, permanence, continuity, and absoluteness on the one hand, and diversity, change, discontinuity, and relativity on the other hand. The cosmic process itself then reflects God's nature. The cosmic process is meaningful to God as God incorporates all momentary events or entities and their relationships.

The Anglo-American pragmatism of John Dewey, Charles Sanders Peirce, and William James also influenced process thought.[67] From pragmatism came the concern for a philosophy grounded in empirical experience, not a priori rationalism or authority. William James's psychology of experience was important for Whitehead in analyzing reality's fundamental building blocks.

The Fundamentals of Whitehead's Metaphysics

Whitehead and his forerunners knew that all of the limit questions addressed by philosophy are interconnected, and so any particular philosophical answer must be related to a philosophical system as a whole. This point has arguably been lost on some in contemporary analytic philosophy, where a highly specialized question is considered in isolation from the litany of other philosophical questions bearing on it. As with many philosophers, including those in immediate propinquity to him, Whitehead undertook to create a coherent system that addresses and consistently integrates metaphysics and ontology with epistemology and axiology.

Whitehead viewed his speculative cosmology in part as an attempt to reconcile religion with science and the modern world. He embraced the findings of modern science but urged that science be based on a proper cosmology. The questions addressed by metaphysics are real and valid, and in fact every science presupposes a tacit metaphysics.[68]

Whitehead maintained that philosophy, not religion, must undertake the task of metaphysics in the light of modern science and the philosophical developments of modernity. Distinguishing religion from science, he says: "The difference is that religion is the longing of the spirit

67. Whitehead mentions his debt to James and Dewey in his preface (*Process and Reality,* xii [vii]). See also, Brown, Reeves, and James, "Preface," v, and Reeves and Brown, "The Development of Process Theology," 27.

68. See Alfred North Whitehead, *Adventures of Ideas* (New York: Macmillan, 1933; reprint, New York: Free Press, 1967), 163–64; and Whitehead, *Religion in the Making* (New York: Macmillan, 1926; reprint, New York: New American Library, 1974), 76, 83.

that the facts of existence should find their justification in the nature of existence."[69] Conversely, he makes his program more congenial to the modern scientific mind by referring to metaphysics as a "science,"[70] and makes philosophy the handmaiden of science.

Whitehead took seriously the relativity and quantum-theory paradigm shift in physics for constructing a metaphysics that reckons seriously with chance and contingency, instead of strict efficient causality, in the realm of matter and energy.[71] Accordingly, physical energy is an abstraction of a more complex energy found in every event.[72] Concordant with new scientific data, he abandoned "the notion that simple location is the primary way in which things are involved in space-time."[73]

Similar to his nineteenth-century predecessors, to replace scientific materialism Whitehead offered a system of "organic mechanism" based on the analogies with living organisms and making room for indeterminacy.[74] The existence of life presents unique problems not the least of which is activity, which must always include unity and diversity.[75] Pure mechanistic materialism is wrong in saying that matter and the scientific laws alone can account for activity. Mind is necessary for activity. Whitehead denies, however, that some non-material vital principle or absolute must be imposed *ab extra* on what is physically given in order to account for activity. So on the analogy of living organisms, especially conscious ones, *all* matter, inorganic as well as organic, has an element of freedom and subjectivity. Matter and life are not separate entities, however, but are fused together as what constitutes the fundamental aspect of reality.[76] Thus he borrows from vitalism and calls his system "the philosophy of organism," but does not introduce a dualism between matter and life in the way vitalism does.

69. Whitehead, *Religion in the Making,* 83.

70. "By 'metaphysics' I mean the science which seeks to discover the general ideas which are indispensably relevant to the analysis of everything that happens" (Whitehead, *Religion in the Making,* 82 n.). "It is the task of philosophic speculation to conceive the happenings of the universe so as to render understandable the outlook of science" (Alfred North Whitehead, *Modes of Thought* [Cambridge: Cambridge University Press, 1938], 223).

71. Whitehead, *Science and the Modern World,* 113–56.

72. Whitehead, *Adventures of Ideas,* 186.

73. Whitehead, *Science and the Modern World,* 91.

74. Ibid., 79–80, 107.

75. Alfred North Whitehead, *Nature and Life* (Cambridge: Cambridge University Press, 1934), 53; Whitehead, *Modes of Thought,* 202.

76. Whitehead, *Nature and Life,* 57.

Whitehead categorizes himself as early modern and pre-Kantian in the tradition of Descartes and Hume because he begins with subjectivity as his starting point.[77] He aligns himself with modern philosophy's turn to the subject and commencement with epistemology and the experience of the subject for discovering the first metaphysical principles. Yet, like Alexander and Morgan, he strongly opposes the gap between appearance and reality epitomized by Kant and evident in post-Kantian idealism. Instead, he opts for early modern, pre-critical realism, which essentially sees direct continuity between the knowing subject and the objectively known.[78] Doubting the correspondence between subjective mental representation and what is objectively known has no basis in our experience of nature nor in the pragmatic way minds find their way in the world.[79] It is thus an egregious error to bifurcate the individual subject's experience and the external world. In fact, the only form of unity is the unity coming through the experience of the knowing (or feeling) subject.[80]

For Whitehead modernity's "turn to the subject" is the "subjectivist principle," and the necessary thoroughgoing application of this principle to all of reality involves the "reformed subjectivist principle." Whitehead calls Descartes's turn to the subject a "halfway house" because it was not applied to all of reality. Interrelated subjectivity applies to all of reality, inorganic as well as organic, which means all of reality is causally related and interdependent.[81] In addition to faulting Kant's subject-object disjunction, Whitehead criticizes Kant for adopting the subjectivist position when he saw the temporal world as merely experienced by the subject but failing to conclude from this that the temporal world itself is an expe-

77. Whitehead, *Process and Reality,* xi (v).

78. Ibid., xi (v), 71–72 (111), 79–80 (123); Whitehead, *Symbolism, Its Meaning and Effect* (New York: Macmillan, 1927), 10. Whitehead's repeated references to "appearance" and "reality," as well as the title of his magnum opus, *Process and Reality,* are probably evocations of Bradley's *Appearance and Reality.*

79. Alfred North Whitehead, *Modes of Thought* (Cambridge: Cambridge University Press, 1938), 156.

80. "The consideration of experiential togetherness raises the final metaphysical question: whether there is any other meaning of 'togetherness.' The denial of any alternative meaning, that is to say, of any meaning not abstracted from the experiential meaning, is the 'subjectivist' doctrine. This reformed version of the subjectivist doctrine is the doctrine of the philosophy of organism" (Whitehead, *Process and Reality,* 189 [288]).

81. See Whitehead, *Process and Reality,* 48–51 (76–80), 67–69, (105–7); and *Science and the Modern World,* 141, 194–95.

riencing subject.[82] A fundamental problem with all of modern philosophy, says Whitehead, is that having accepted the subjectivist principle it still employs categories of the older metaphysics.[83]

The priority of ubiquitous subjectivity and thus total interdependence led Whitehead to formulate his "reformed subjectivist principle." This says that the experiences of subjects are fundamental for the reality of "beings" or "entities": "apart from the experiences of subjects there is nothing, nothing, nothing, bare nothingness."[84] Borrowing from Williams James's psychology, Whitehead describes the subject's experience as the irreducible unification of numerous momentary and discrete pulses of experiences of the radical heterogeneous bits of data, or "a bloomin' buzzin' mess."[85] Although we can divide abstractly the various component parts of a subject's experience, there is no real division in the one unified experience.[86] On the analogy of the living organism, momentary events of experience constitute the unity traditionally associated with being amidst the flux of becoming.[87] Whitehead also agrees with the absolute idealists who say events always occur in a mind. He there identifies being with subjective experience. The one experiencing subject must enter relationships with experienced objects, which introduces both the elements of event and relationships into subjective experience. All of this led Whitehead to conclude that the numerous infinitesimal subjects of experience as events called "actual entities" are the only real beings that exist.

For modern physics the fundamental building blocks of enduring material objects are particles of activity or energy, in the form of electrons and their partner protons, which themselves are a form of the irreducible

82. Whitehead, *Process and Reality,* 190 (289).

83. Ibid., 167 (253).

84. Ibid., 167 (254). He says: "The subjectivist principle is that the whole universe consists of elements disclosed in the analysis of the experience of subjects. Process is the becoming of experience" (*Process and Reality,* 166 [252]).

85. "Either your experience is of no content, of no change, or it is of a perceptible amount of content or change. Your acquaintance with reality grows literally by buds or drops of perception. Intellectually and on reflection you can divide these into components, but as immediately given, they come totally or not at all" (William James, *Problems of Philosophy,* chap. 10, quoted in Whitehead, *Process and Reality,* 68 [105–6]). See also, ibid., xii–xiii (vii), 50 (78).

86. Whitehead, *Symbolism Its Meaning and Effect,* 14–16.

87. In classical Western metaphysics the transcendental predicates of being are one, true, good, and beautiful.

unity characteristic of beings or entities.[88] These are similar to Varisco's centers of activity or events, which by themselves lack the mental organization to avoid pure random chaos. Modern physics sees subatomic particles as the fundamental units of energy, but there is no mental basis for their unity and organization.

Thus Whitehead says the fundamental, irreducible, indivisible building blocks of reality are submicroscopic entities, similar to Democritus's "atoms" and Leibniz's "monads,"[89] which he calls "actual occasions" or "actual entities," and which are complex, interdependent drops of experience. These "particulars" are the building blocks of reality beyond which there is nothing else, and "the ultimate agents of stubborn fact."[90] Infinitesimal physical events of experience and perpetual activity are the *fundamental* from which everything else, including matter, emerges. This corresponds to the nineteenth-century emergent evolutionists. As genus or type all actual entities, including God, are essentially identical, but as unique instances of experience no specific actual entities are the same.[91]

For Whitehead, and distinct from Leibniz, actual entities do not move and do not change. An actual entity's "concrescence" or process of self-constitution is instantaneous, not occurring in "physical time," although it can be notionally divided into its constituent parts.[92] On the level of sense perception we perceive the extensive relations between space and time, but these do not apply on the level of the actual entity.[93] Whitehead describes the space-time continuum as a "physical field" and a nexus of actual entities, each actual entity of which is comparable to a "region of space" that cannot move.[94]

Constituted by the totality of its relationships and perishing at the mo-

88. Whitehead, *Science and the Modern World*, 35–36, 79–80, 185.

89. Leibniz's monads are likewise indivisible. He explicitly characterizes his theory as a "theory of monads" along the lines of Leibniz's, but while Leibniz's monads change, Whitehead's monads only *become*. (Whitehead, *Process and Reality*, 80 [124]). See also ibid., 18 (27–28).

90. Ibid., 27–28 (18), 80 (124), 128–29 (196), 245 (374–75). He also says actual entities are "Final Realities" or "*Rēs Verae*" (ibid., 22 [32]).

91. Ibid., 18 (27–28), 110 (168). Cf. Leibniz's "identity of indiscernibles."

92. Whitehead, *Process and Reality*, 283 (433–34). See also, ibid., 22–26 (33–39). For a further discussion of this, see Bowman C. Clarke's article, "God and Time in Whitehead," *Journal of the American Academy of Religion* 48, no. 4 (1980): 563–79.

93. Whitehead, *Process and Reality*, 61 (95).

94. Ibid., 70–73 (108–14). For Newton a region of space could not move.

ment of its appearance, the actual entity can have only an "internal adventure of becoming," not "external adventures of becoming" in the way that nexūs, societies, and eternal objects can through their multiple temporal instantiations.[95] The event-like character of the actual entity is specified by the term "actual occasion," which refers to an actual entity in its aspect of temporal or spatial extension.[96]

Since only what is actual is real, only an actual entity can be a "reason" or "cause": "that actual entities are the only *reasons;* so that to search for a *reason* is to search for one or more actual entities."[97] The "ontological principle" means that only experiencing subjects are actual or real, and so only actual entities can be the efficient causes or reasons for anything else.[98] The ontological principle maintains "the general Aristotelian principle" that "apart from things that are actual, there is nothing—nothing either in fact or in efficacy."[99] It is also the general principle of which Descartes's statement that every attribute requires a substance is a particular example.[100]

The ontological principle reduces all beings to the decisions of one or more actual entities, where "decision" means the "cutting off" of possibilities resulting in any actuality or existent.[101] Whitehead includes indeterminacy and novelty in the "decisions" of these finite subjects of experience. Form limits or determines infinite potentiality or prime matter

95. Ibid., 80 (124–25). See also Whitehead, *Adventures of Ideas,* 204.

96. Whitehead, *Process and Reality,* 22 (33), 77 (119), 73 (113).

97. Ibid., 24 (36–37), 40 (64), 43 (68–69). He says: "It is a contradiction in terms to assume that some explanatory fact can float into the world out of nonentity. Nonentity is nothingness. Every explanatory fact refers to the decision and to the efficacy of an actual thing" (ibid., 46 [73]).

98. "The 'ontological principle' broadens and extends a general principle laid down by John Locke in his *Essay* (Bk. II, Ch. XXIII, Sect. 7), when he asserts that 'power' is 'a great part of our complex ideas of substances.' The notion of 'substance' is transformed into that of 'actual entity'; and the notion of 'power' is transformed into the principle that the reasons for things are always to be found in the composite nature of definite actual entities—in the nature of God for reasons of the highest absoluteness, and in the nature of definite temporal actual entities for reasons which refer to a particular environment. The ontological principle can be summarized as: no actual entity, then no reason" (Whitehead, *Process and Reality,* 18–19 [28]). See also ibid., 24 (36–37), 43 (68–69)).

99. Ibid., 40 (64). See also 46 (73).

100. Ibid., 78 (123).

101. Ibid., 19 (28), 23 (36–37), 32 (48), 40 (64–65), 43 (68–69), 46 (73), 244 (373), 256 (392). Etymologically *de-cido* means to "cut off."

to produce determination or actuality in Aristotelian hylomorphism. So, too, the decisions of finite subjects in their experiences limit or determine potentiality, thereby creating actual beings or entities, and these decisions are not causal adjuncts but the very essence of actual entities.[102] The "givenness" or actuality of actual entities consists precisely in their decisions of limitation.[103] By its self-constitution or concrescence the actual entity is the cause of its own existence or *causa sui,* precisely because there is no going beyond the decisions for a reason for the actual entity, and this decision is identical with the entity itself.[104] Thus freedom or indeterminacy is essential to being. That every actual entity, God or finite, uniquely constitutes itself in virtue of creativity is the meaning of "transcendence" for Whitehead. The entity's freedom "transcends" the mechanistic, deterministic causality latent in all previously given actuality.[105]

Whitehead does give other reasons or causes for the final constitution of the actual entity insofar as the indivisible entity can be abstractly analyzed in terms of parts. These causes include: (1) "feelings" from all other actual entities having completed their concrescence or "superjects"; (2) the initial aim that God provides for the actual entity; and (3) "eternal objects," which correspond to Platonic Forms.

The relatedness of each newly concrescing actual occasion entity to the actual entities of the antecedent universe is "prehension."[106] The current entity's activity of consciousness is viewed as a felt relationship between subject and object.[107] Concordant with the prioritization of subjectivity over objectivity, these relations are not impassive material facts but instead insisting "feelings."[108] In prehension the present entity experiences as a datum a "simple physical feeling" of a past entity. The past entity precipitating the physical feeling is a "cause" and the present entity experiencing the physical feeling is an "effect."[109] Whitehead uses the term

102. Ibid., 42–43 (68–69).

103. Ibid., 45–46 (72).

104. Ibid., 88 (135), 150 (228), 221–22 (338–39).

105. Ibid., 88 (135), 93–94 (143), 222 (378).

106. See Whitehead, *Adventures of Ideas,* 176, 180, 226, 230–34; *Science and the Modern World,* 69, 148; and *Process and Reality,* 18–20 (28–29), 22 (32), 23–24 (35), 52 (82), 235–80 (358–428).

107. Whitehead, *Process and Reality,* 56–57 (87–89).

108. "There is nothing in the real world which is merely an inert fact. Every reality is there for feeling: it promotes feeling; and it is felt" (ibid., 310 [472]).

109. Ibid., 236 (362).

"felt" to describe the subject's response to the "ingression" of an object and conveys the causal element of feelings by calling them "vectors": they feel what is "there" and transform it into "here."[110]

The initial phase of an actual entity's concrescence is simply passive reception of physical feelings from the universe as a given actuality in terms of past actual entities.[111] Prehension insures continuity with the past through causality and preserves novelty through the new entity's freedom to accept and reject any given prehension.

Generally when Whitehead speaks of "feelings" he means "positive prehensions," or those feelings accepted and incorporated by the entity into its self-constitution.[112] "Negative prehensions" are feelings the entity rejects and does not allow to become part of its self-constitution.[113] A negative prehension is a purely formal prehension of an antecedent entity without its having any impact on the new entity's concrescence;[114] it occurs when a new actual occasion dismisses a datum from a past entity as irrelevant to its self-constitution.[115] Through negative prehensions the actual entity can stymie the causal influence of the past. The entity's freedom for negative prehension avoids mechanistic determinism and preserves the genuine indeterminacy necessary for individuality, diversity, and activity. This avoids a mechanistic determinism limited to what is already given.

Whitehead distinguishes between levels of subjectivity. Most actual entities have a negligible "depth of subjectivity." This means that most of the time the causal determination of the past is so influential that there is virtually no novelty resulting from the actual entity's freedom.[116] The simple physical feelings that are the most primitive acts of perception take place on a very low level of subjectivity, devoid of consciousness. They act in al-

110. Ibid., 87 (133).

111. Ibid., 219 (335).

112. Ibid., 220–21 (337).

113. Ibid., 23–24 (35), 41–42 (66), 83 (128), 106 (162), 220–35 (337–60), 237 (362), 345 (524).

114. Ibid., 41 (66).

115. Ibid., 23–24 (35), 41 (66), 83 (127–28), 106 (162), 221–35 (338–60), 362 (237), 345 (524).

116. Ibid., 245 (374–75). The "transfer of energy" spoken of in the natural sciences is really only an abstraction of the inherited habits of selection of physical prehensions among low-level, simple actual entities in Whitehead's scheme. See Victor Lowe, "Whitehead's Metaphysical System," in *Process Philosophy and Christian Thought*, ed. Delwin Brown, Ralph E. James Jr., and Gene Reeves, 3–20 (New York: Bobbs-Merrill, 1971), 14–15.

most a strictly causal fashion. Yet he insists that despite their improbability, contrary options do exist, and this is confirmed by the recent findings of physics and quantum theory, which must allow for this.[117]

Whitehead associates "consciousness" with the higher functioning of complex minds having "knowledge." He speaks of "four grades" of actual occasions, only some of which possess consciousness. In humans, for example, only higher transmuted feelings appear to the consciousness, and never the "simple physical feelings." Therefore his panpsychism says "feeling," not "consciousness," is characteristic of all of reality.[118]

Whitehead also distinguishes between "physical" and "conceptual" prehensions. The former are feelings from past actual entities, now superject. The latter are goals for what the entity will actually become. Whitehead warns against confusing, as Hume does, conceptual feelings with perceptual feelings. Although we can *conceive* only in terms of universals, many stretch this truism to the false idea that we can also *feel* only in terms of universals.[119]

God's initial aim is another causal factor in the actual entity's constitution. God posits an initial aim as the desired end result for the outcome of the entity's concrescence. As the source of the initial aim beginning the entity's concrescence into a definite concrete entity, God is the "principle of concretion." By introducing a goal from among the infinite possibilities to strive for in actuality God is also the source of order and purpose in the universe.[120] As the "appropriate goal" the initial aim becomes a moral judgment for the actual entity.[121]

Whitehead also interprets the doctrine of God as "creator" to mean God supplies each actual entity's initial aim at the incipience of its concrescence.[122] God is not creator in the classical sense that God creates *ex nihilo* by an act of volition. When God supplies a formal cause for the actual entity to aim at, this is similar to Aristotle's Prime Mover. Referencing Aristotle, Whitehead says an "Unmoved Mover" is possible just as the object of desire and thought moves the entity moved without itself moving.[123]

117. Whitehead, *Process and Reality*, 254 (389).
118. Ibid., 177–78 (269–70); 236 (362); 160–62 (243–46), 166 (252), 308 (470).
119. Ibid., 230 (351).
120. Ibid., 244 (373); 244 (374), 345 (523); 83–84 (127–28), 88 (135).
121. Whitehead, *Religion in the Making*, 114.
122. Whitehead, *Process and Reality*, 225 (343).
123. Ibid., 344 (522).

In the course of its self-constitution the actual entity transforms this conceptually prehended initial aim into its own subjective aim for its actuality. The entity's subjective aim becomes its very own in virtue of its radical freedom, and can differ from God's initial aim. This subjective aim constitutes the actual entity as a unique actual entity. As the source of physical feelings the objectifications of past actual entities, or superjects, are "efficient causes," and the subjective aim is the "final cause" because it is the entity's self-determined purpose. Whitehead argues that Aristotelian final causation and atomism are interconnected because the entity's subjective aim is what constitutes the actual entity as such.[124]

Whitehead sees all aesthetic experience as feeling arising out of contrast under identity.[125] Hence he calls positive prehensions "adversions," a liking or taste, and calls negative prehensions "aversions," a disliking or distaste. This means the entity's conceptual feelings are all mutually determined by being joint elements in the satisfaction aimed at by the subject entity. Here the aesthetic adaptation for achieving an end or goal is the formative condition in the pre-established harmony spoken of in "subjective harmony."[126]

Another determining factor in the actual entity's concrescence is "eternal objects." They are eternal because finite actual entities prehend them from the non-temporal actual entity of God and not from other temporal actual entities, their integrity is maintained before and after their unity with the subject, they are uncreated, and they are never novel.[127] Eternal objects are purely potential forms of definiteness that any given temporal actuality can assume in the perpetual process of becoming, and correspond to the Platonic Forms of which transient material actualities are instantiations.[128] The temporal realm of change, then, is the description of the adventures of eternal objects in the evolving temporal universe of actual things.[129] As with physical prehensions from superjects and the

124. Ibid., 244–45 (373–75); 244 (373); 108 (164), 150 (228); 19 (29).

125. Whitehead, *Religion in the Making*, 111.

126. Whitehead, *Process and Reality*, 234 (358), 253–54 (388). Ibid., 252–55 (389–90).

127. Ibid., 22 (33), 31 (46), 43–44 (69–70), 46 (73), 257 (392).

128. Whitehead, *Religion in the Making*, 87–88; Whitehead, *Process and Reality*, 22 (33), 23 (34), 39–40 (63–64), 44 (70), 60 (73), 184 (280), 188 (287), 214 (326), 290–91 (445–46).

129. "The abrupt synthesis of eternal objects in each occasion is the inclusion in actuality of the analytical character of the realm of eternality" (Whitehead, *Science and the Modern World*, 176). "The things which are temporal arise by their participation in the things which

conceptual prehension of God's initial aim, the actual entity in concrescence makes decisions regarding the integration of eternal objects into its own self-constitution.[130] All eternal objects are available to, and the same for, every knowing subject.

According to Whitehead's ontological principle the efficacy of any cause or reason depends on actuality, which in turn depends on a knowing subject. Since everything must be "somewhere," or in an actual entity, even the general potentiality from which actual entities draw in their processes of concrescence must be located in actual entity. This actual entity is the non-temporal actual entity of God. Although eternal objects are pure potentials and not actualities, they are conceptually prehended by God in God's primordial nature, and then actualized in finite actual entities.[131]

Like Morgan's, Whitehead's metaphysics is "dipolar" with respect to all actual entities, including God. Instead of prioritizing either the mental or the physical at the expense of the other, Whitehead says all entities have both.[132] An actual entity's concrescence is dipolar because of the two different types of prehensions it experiences. Physical prehensions correspond to the actual entity's "physical pole" and conceptual prehensions correspond to its "mental pole."[133] In "objectification" the actualities of superject past entities in God's consequent nature supply the possibilities felt as physical prehensions in the actual entity's physical pole.[134] As the objectifications of all prior actual entities the physical pole supplies the data for the actual entity in concrescence, which become its efficient causes.[135] Only past actual entities can be efficient causes, as an actual en-

are eternal" (Whitehead, *Process and Reality,* 40 [63]). See also ibid., 35 (52), 55–56 (86–88). This is also alluded to in the title of Whitehead's book *Adventures of Ideas.*

130. Whitehead, *Process and Reality,* 185 (281–82).

131. Whitehead, *Religion in the Making,* 147–48; *Process and Reality,* 46 (73). God is the source of possibilities or essences for Leibniz's monads (Leibniz, *Monadology,* 43–44). This roughly corresponds to the classical theistic doctrine of the Divine Ideas, which itself goes back to the Middle Platonist reinterpretation of the Platonic Forms as ideas in a Supreme, Divine Mind. See for instance, Albinus, *Epitome* 9.

132. Whitehead, *Religion in the Making,* 114; *Process and Reality,* 108 (165), 239 (366), 244 (374), 277 (423), 344–45 (523–24).

133. Whitehead, *Process and Reality,* 45 (72), 108 (165), 239 (366).

134. Ibid., 23 (34), 245 (374). Here, as elsewhere, Whitehead's grounding of possibility on prior actuality seems to assume the Aristotelian maxim that actuality precedes potentiality, which, interestingly enough, some later process theologians explicitly deny.

135. Ibid., 87 (134), 150 (228). Whitehead uses "efficient" and "final" causes in the Aristotelian sense.

tity never prehends its contemporaries. This is because contemporaneous entities in concrescence are not yet actual and are therefore unable to be causes or reasons. This means contemporary events occur independently of each other.[136]

As lures of feeling for what could actually be in the future, conceptual prehensions in the actual entity's mental pole begin with God's initial aim and the eternal objects. These are then registered according to the entity's own subjective aim.[137] The mental pole begins with a "conceptual registration" of the physical pole, which contains "values" for the future and moves into the subjective operation of the actual entity by which it determines its own ideal outcome for itself in reference to the eternal objects.[138] The subjective aim is the entity's self-determined final form, the direction in which its feeling is lured, for its final entitative reality.[139]

"Concrescence" integrates the actual entity's physical and mental poles into a "unity of experience."[140] This is also a movement from the possibilities of the mental pole, derived from prior actualities in the physical pole, to a new actual entity once concrescence is completed. This also means the actual entity moves from subject to object. Once it obtains its subjective aim or "satisfaction" the objective actual entity becomes "superject," or a datum for successive generations of actual entities.[141] The entity thus moves from a "private" function of concrescence independent of its contemporaries to a "public" function available to newly concrescent entities.[142] Thus there is a constant movement from subject to object in the becoming, actuality, and perishing of every actual entity. White-

136. Ibid., 61 (95), 318 (484).

137. Ibid., 26 (40), 224 (343) 239–40 (366), 244 (373).

138. Ibid., 248 (379–80). Here Whitehead criticizes Kant and Hume for making conceptual registration of the physical data the *only* datum of experience, and not allowing direct contact with the physical data in the physical pole.

139. Ibid., 25 (37).

140. Ibid.

141. Ibid., 22 (33), 45 (72); 25–26 (38), 220 (337); 29 (43), 44–45 (71), 58 (191), 84 (129), 87–88 (134), 289 (443).

142. Whitehead sees the individual concrescence of the actual entity, or its subjective state, as totally self-contained and therefore "private," while its objective state as superject brings it into contact, through feelings, with successive generations of actual occasions, and thereby makes it "public" (ibid., 151 [229], 289–90 [443–45]). The private function of the entity in concrescence has commerce only with God in whose consequent nature all superject entities reside, which is similar to Leibniz's windowless monads in contact with God alone.

head emphasizes this movement by calling the actual entity a "subject-superject."[143]

Once superject, the entity obtains objective, not subjective, immortality in God's consequent nature. Subjective concrescence is entirely private and ceases at the moment of objective satisfaction. There is no continuation of subjectivity beyond satisfaction, because no entity can be conscious of its own satisfaction. Such knowledge would itself be a prehension in the process, thereby possibly altering the satisfaction. Objective immorality in God's consequent nature is what constitutes the "everlastingness" spoken of in the various religions, and solves the problem of perpetual perishing. Despite reality's processive, constantly changing nature, nothing is eternally lost but all is eternally saved in God's consequent nature.[144]

The actual entity and its concrescence show how Whitehead's metaphysics is carefully framed to address the problems of continuity vs. discontinuity and causality vs. freedom. The causal influence of all past entities in the universe on the new actual entity preserves continuity. The new actual entity's freedom to make decisions about its own self-constitution preserves discontinuity.[145] The irreducible unity of the actual entity is fundamental but at the same time the multiplicity of actual entities maintains diversity and multiplicity. Now we will turn to a problem that the fundamental units of Whitehead's metaphysics pose, and how Whitehead addresses it.

Nexūs and Societies

For Whitehead the many discrete actual entities are the "building blocks of reality," and unity only ever obtains at the end of an individual entity's concrescence.[146] Thus some characterize Whitehead's funda-

143. Ibid., 29 (43), 44–45 (71), 84 (129), 87–88 (134), 289 (443).

144. Ibid., 29 (44), 347 (527); 85 (130); 347 (527).

145. "The birth of a new aesthetic experience depends on the maintenance of two principles by the creative purpose: 1. The novel consequent must be graded in relevance so as to preserve some identity of character with the ground. 2. The novel consequent must be graded in relevance so as to preserve some contrast with the ground in respect to that same identity of character. These two principles are derived from the doctrine that an actual fact is a fact of aesthetic experience. All aesthetic experience is feeling arising out of the realization of contrast under identity" (Whitehead, *Religion in the Making*, 111). See also Whitehead, *Process and Reality*, 150 (228).

146. Whitehead, *Process and Reality*, 18 (27–28), 35 (52–53), 62–63 (98), 80 (124), 227

mental metaphysical stance as atomistic, saying Whitehead's thought is challenged in insuring continuity among successive actual occasions over time and across space.[147] In classical metaphysics this is the problem addressed by the concept of an enduring "substance." Later process thinkers have seen atomism as a problem and have tried to redress it.[148]

In his mature thought Whitehead himself dealt with the question of macroscopic temporal and spatial continuity with the ideas of "nexūs" and "societies."[149] The apparent world of multifarious "things" is essentially groupings of actual entities. A nexus is an aggregate of actual entities just as "real, individual, and particular" and "factual" as individual actual entities themselves.[150] It is a "public matter of fact" as opposed to the "private matter of fact" of the subjective form of an individual actual entity in concrescence.[151] Just as an entity's final form corresponds to an eternal object, the nexus's form corresponds to a "complex eternal object."[152] Like superject actual entities and eternal objects, nexūs are also data or objects for the prehension of actual entities undergoing concrescence.[153]

---

(347), 245 (374–75). In describing his view of living organisms Whitehead focuses on living things as composites of individual discrete parts, and sees the problem as not dissociation of parts but of unifying the whole (ibid., [108], 165).

147. Whitehead says: "Thus the ultimate metaphysical truth is atomism. The creatures are atomic" (Whitehead, *Process and Reality,* 35 [53]). Victor Lowe characterizes Whitehead's system as pluralistic rather than monistic, but finds it difficult to fit into traditional generalizations beyond that (Lowe, "Whitehead's Metaphysical System," 3–20). See also John B. Cobb Jr., *God and the World* (Philadelphia: Westminster Press, 1969), 70; Marjorie Hewitt Suchocki, *The Fall to Violence: Original Sin in Relational Theology* (New York: Continuum, 1999), 56; and Donna Bowman, *The Divine Decision: A Process Doctrine of Election* (Louisville, Ky.: Westminster/John Knox Press, 2002), 108.

148. See, for instance, Lewis S. Ford, "Inclusive Occasions," in *Process in Context: Essays in Post-Whiteheadian Perspectives,* ed. Ernest Wolf-Gazo (Bern: Peter Lang, 1988), 107–36; Bradford Wallack, *The Epochal Nature of Process in Whitehead's Metaphysics* (Albany: State University of New York Press, 1980), 7; and Judith A. Jones, *Intensity: An Essay in Whiteheadian Ontology* (Nashville: Vanderbilt University Press, 1998), 3, 8–10.

149. Whitehead, *Process and Reality,* 34–35 (50–51), 55 (86), 55–57 (87–88), 72 (112), 83–84 (128), 89–109 (136–67), 110–11 (169), 129 (197), 192 (293), 244 (373). I will follow Whitehead's spelling of the plural form of "nexus" as "nexūs," the plural of the Latin fourth declension.

150. Whitehead, *Process and Reality,* 20 (29–30); Whitehead, *Adventures of Ideas,* 203–5.

151. Whitehead, *Process and Reality,* 22 (32).

152. Ibid., 24 (35–36), 250 (383), 251 (385), 252–53 (386). Every mutual relation between actual entities in a given nexus is also an eternal object (ibid., 194 [295]).

153. "There are four main types of objects, namely 'eternal objects,' 'propositions,' 'objectified' actual entities, and nexūs" (ibid., 52 [82]).

While "nexus" is one of the "eight categories of existence" for Whitehead, "society" is a "derivative of the general notion of order" that the "nexus" represents.[154] A society is essentially a nexus perduring across time due to a "defining characteristic" or "common element of form" perpetuated by each of the society's member actual entities and imposed on new actual entities in the society.[155] There is a unilateral, serial, or sequential relationship between the society's antecedent and later entities, and the latter inherit the common element of form from the former.[156] Nexūs can be purely coincidental, with no principle of continuity, but nexūs that are societies have a "common element of form" over space and time as their defining characteristic.

Societies also differ from other nexūs in that they are self-sustaining and are "their own reasons."[157] A society's order is self-perpetuating in and through the successive generations of its actual entities. There is a mutual dependence of society and member entities, since the society's members exist only by the laws dominating the society, but these laws come into being only through the analogous characters of the member entities. The laws determining the reproduction of a given society come into dominance, have a stage of endurance, and then pass out of existence, at which point the society decays and ceases to exist.[158]

Prehending the conditions in the society's past member entities, each newly arising member entity obtains the society's "common element of form," and the prehensions impose a condition of reproduction of this form in the new member entity. The members impose on each other conditions leading to their similarity. The "common element of form" corresponds to a complex of eternal objects that becomes the society's defining characteristic. The actual entities in the society do not create this complex of eternal objects. In their processes of objectification the society's member entities in concrescence positively and negatively prehend the eternal objects in their societal predecessors, and through a process called "transmutation" make them the eternal object suitable for the society as a whole.[159]

154. Ibid., 22 (31); 34–35 (50–52), 89 (136); Whitehead, *Adventures of Ideas,* 203–4.
155. Whitehead, *Process and Reality,* 34 (50–51), 89 (137).
156. Ibid., 34–35 (51–52).
157. Ibid., 89 (137); Whitehead, *Adventures of Ideas,* 203.
158. Ibid., 90–91 (139).
159. Ibid., 25 (38), 27 (40), 34 (50–51), 41–42 (66), 58 (91–92), 89 (137), 92 (140).

Embodying a genetic character across successive generations of actual occasions, societies constitute what common sense refers to as "enduring objects."[160] Enduring across time necessarily involves change. An actual entity's concrescence is puncticular, involving no change, so the entity does not endure.[161] Thus, according to Whitehead's definition, only societies "endure" but actual entities do not.[162]

Relativity, Internal Relations, and Event Ontology

In the light of modern philosophical reflection and recent scientific developments Whitehead formulated his "principle of relativity." This means the ontological constitution of an actual entity is related to every other actual entity, which obviates the classical distinction between the universal and the particulars.[163] In contrast to the classical idea that a substance has purely external relations not constitutive of its being, Whitehead says all entities have "internal relations" so that every entity in the world becomes part of the formation of every other actual entity in the world.[164] Through prehensions of predecessor entities relatedness becomes part of the self-constitution of every actual entity. Universal rela-

160. Ibid., 35 (52), 109 (166). It is important to note, however, "form" and not "substance" is what unifies Whiteheadian societies over time (Lowe, "Whitehead's Metaphysical System," 10).

161. Whitehead, *Process and Reality,* 73, (113), 124–26 (189–92).

162. Whitehead, *Adventures of Ideas,* 204.

163. "The ontological principle, and the wider doctrine of the universal relativity on which the present discussions is founded, blur the sharp distinction between what is universal and what is particular. The notion of a universal is of that which can enter into the description of many particulars; whereas the notion of a particular is that it is described by universals, and does not itself enter into the description of any other particular. According to the doctrine of relativity which is the basis of the metaphysical system of the present lectures, both these notions involve a misconception. An actual entity cannot be described, even inadequately, by universals; because other actual entities do enter into the description of any one particular entity. Thus every so-called 'universal' is particular in the sense of being just what it is, diverse from everything else; and every so-called 'particular' is universal in the sense of entering into the constitutions of other actual entities" (Whitehead, *Process and Reality,* 48 [76]).

164. "When we understand the essences of these things, we thereby know their mutual relations to one another" (Whitehead, *Adventures of Ideas,* 112). See also, Whitehead, *Process and Reality,* 22 (33), 59–60 (92–93). Leibniz said something similar about the essence of every monad being dependent on its relations to all other monads. With internal relations and universal relativity Whitehead does not deny external relations (ibid., 309 [470–71]).

tivity is also a reason why actual entities cannot change. Eternal objects incarnated in time experience change but actual entities are constituted by pure relations at any given moment.[165] That no entity can be abstracted from the entire cosmic process by which it is essentially and internally related to all other entities also provides a form of unity for the whole cosmic process, and this does not require the imposition of something from the outside, such as a vital principle or ideas. This addresses the mechanists' and emergent evolutionists' concerns for one world process without the introduction of some qualitatively other category or principle in order to account for unity.

Of a piece with this relational ontology is Whitehead's revision of substance. Nothing exists on its own but is determined by all other entities. This differs from the view of much modern philosophy that a substance is independent and its own reason. For Whitehead "events" (activity) rather than "objects" (substance) make up reality,[166] and the category of creativity or process replaces substance.[167] The idea of enduring substance with persistent qualities, either essentially or accidentally, is pragmatically useful but is metaphysically wrong if predicated to reality.[168] Ideas of "objects" are merely abstractions from events, and eternal objects or forms, not substances, are what are permanent.[169]

Creativity

Central to Whitehead's metaphysics is "creativity," the principle of novelty, activity, or process.[170] Along with "many" and "one," creativity completes what he calls the "category of the ultimate."[171] Creativity is

165. Ibid., 58–59 (92).

166. "My own view is a belief in the relational theory both of space and time, and of disbelief in the current form of the relational theory of space which exhibits bits of matter as the *relata* for spatial relations. The true *relata* are events" (Alfred North Whitehead, *The Concept of Nature* [Cambridge: Cambridge University Press, 1920], 24). See also, ibid., 14–15. Cf. Alexander, *Space, Time, and Deity.*

167. Whitehead, *Process and Reality,* 21 (32), 80 (123).

168. Ibid., 79 (122).

169. Whitehead, *The Concept of Nature,* 125; *Process and Reality,* 29 (44).

170. John Cobb explains how in early works like *Science and the Modern World* Whitehead simply uses "activity" to describe what he later refers to as "creativity." See John B. Cobb Jr., *A Christian Natural Theology* (Philadelphia: Westminster Press, 1965), 148–49.

171. "'Creativity,' 'many,' 'one' are the ultimate notions involved in the meaning of the synonymous terms 'thing,' 'being,' 'entity.' These three notions complete the Category of the

an abstraction from the concrete facts of new actual entities continually coming into existence. New entities perpetually form a complex unity or "one" as an entity or being emerges out of the "many" or world of many antecedent actual entities now superject.[172] Creativity connects unity or the one with plurality or the many for Whitehead. Creativity is the principle of novelty seen in the perpetual appearance of new actual entities.[173]

The ultimate metaphysical principle is the creative advance from plurality to unity, as, in every new moment, "the many become one and are increased by one." This metaphysical principle of creativity is as fundamental for Whitehead as "substance" was for Aristotle and later in Spinoza.[174] Creativity is like classical "primary substance" because it is that which produces all things in the world through its own power and because it never ceases to exist. It is not an actual existent like a substance. As indeterminacy and infinite possibility, creativity is infinite; as determination or the limitation of possibility, all actuality is finite. There cannot, therefore, be an infinite actuality.[175]

Whitehead also reverses the classical relationship between form and matter. He identifies creativity with Aristotelian matter and reverses its role as passive receptor of form to active principle of advance. As the active principle of advance, creativity is the always stable element of divine ordering. But it does not have a character of its own, just as Aristotelian prime matter does not have a character of its own. It is formless and undetermined.[176]

Related to this is how creativity has no "existence" apart from the entities in which it instantiated. The ultimate of any philosophy is only ever

Ultimate and are presupposed in all the more special categories" (Whitehead, *Process and Reality,* 21 [31]).

172. "'Creativity' is the universal of universals characterizing ultimate matter of fact. It is that ultimate principle by which the many, which are the universe disjunctively, become the one actual occasion, which is the universe conjunctively. It lies in the nature of things that the many enter into complex unity" (ibid.) See also ibid., 57 (89).

173. "'Creativity' is the principle of *novelty.* An actual occasion is a novel entity diverse from any entity in the 'many' which it unifies. Thus 'creativity' introduces novelty into the content of the many, which are the universe disjunctively. The 'creative advance' is the application of this ultimate principle of creativity to each novel situation which it originates" (ibid., 21 [31–32]).

174. Ibid., 7 (10), 21 (32).

175. Whitehead, *Adventures of Ideas,* 259.

176. Whitehead, *Process and Reality,* 31 (46–47).

actual in virtue of its accidental embodiments and never by itself.[177] Creativity is just the ongoing activity of novel togetherness. We cannot know creativity through rational analysis because such analysis results in mere abstraction with no reality apart from the concrete processes of concrescence of the innumerable actual entities. Thus creativity is ultimate in the sense that it is cannot be accounted for and described by something or things more fundamental than itself.[178] Having no independent existence, creativity or process is ubiquitous in everything, and the entire perpetual activity taken as a whole is what is real or actual.[179] Process or activity, not factuality, which is always based in an entity, is ultimate.

God in Whitehead

In some ways, Whitehead introduces the concept of God to account for unity in reality. Reality is unified because: (1) all entities share the common principle of creativity; (2) God as eternal actual entity is the primordial instantiation of creativity providing an ontological basis for the fact of creativity; and (3) there is a common past retained in God's consequent nature. God provides unity as the actual entity that mediates the past to the future, thus maintaining continuity between the previous world and each newly emerging world in the process. Without this continuity time would be entirely inconsistent and probability alone, or indeterminism, would rule. There would be no guarantee of any continuity between the newly emerging universe in the present and the universe of immediate past.

177. Ibid., 7 (10–11), 81 (125). These actual embodiments of creativity correlate to Spinoza's modes of the primary substance. See also, Whitehead, *Science and the Modern World,* 177.

178. Whitehead, *Process and Reality,* 7 (10), 21–21 (32).

179. "This creative principle is everywhere, in animate and so-called inanimate matter, in the ether, water, earth, human hearts. But this creation is a continuing process and 'the process is itself the actuality', since no sooner do you arrive than you start on a fresh journey" (Whitehead, *Dialogues of Alfred North Whitehead as Recorded by Lucien Prince* [New York: Mentor Books, 1956], 297). Most Whiteheadians interpret creativity as a general name for all empirical, concrete instances of concrescence (William Christian, *An Interpretation of Whitehead's Metaphysics* [New Haven, Conn.: Yale University Press, 1959], 403; John B. Cobb Jr. "A Whiteheadian Doctrine of God," in *Process Theology and Christian Thought,* ed. Delwin Brown, Ralph E. James Jr., and Gene Reeves, 215–43 [New York: Bobbs-Merrill, 1971], 239–40), however some argue creativity has a sort of ontological independence (John R. Wilcox, "A Monistic Interpretation of Whitehead's Creativity," *Process Studies* 20, no. 3 [Fall 1991], 162–74).

For some, like Morgan, overall unity and organization means a decrease in the multiplicity of entities, but for Whitehead this organizational unity means an increase in multiplicity. Many vitalists introduced a type of energy beyond what is already given in order to account for activity, but this violates the first law of thermodynamics. Whitehead argues that unity itself must be seen in terms of true multiplicity; otherwise the emergent unity is different from the plurality from which it arises. That what emerges cannot be different from what is given is also part of the ontological principle.[180] Thus every organization must have continuity with less organized states.[181] For many, such as Morgan and Teilhard, process ultimately eliminates diversity. By not assigning exhaustive concrete content or actuality to the ultimate unifying principle, creativity or process, Whitehead avoids final monism and determinism. His formulation allows for permanence without determining the cosmos or eliminating the individuality of actual discrete entities. Organization intensifies rather than reduces individuality and diversity.[182]

In Whitehead's scheme, since the only real things are actual entities, God too is an actual entity.[183] With many moderns Whitehead is adamant that God must not be outside of the principles applicable to all of reality in order to account for what those principles alone cannot explain.[184] Thus he formulates his famous axiom that provides the starting point for much later process theology: "God is not to be treated as an exception to all metaphysical principles, invoked to save their collapse. He is their chief exemplification."[185] Ontologically God is an entity among

180. Whitehead, *Process and Reality,* 19 (28), 23 (36–37), 32 (48), 35–36 (52–55), 40 (64–65), 43 (68), 46 (73), 244 (373), 256 (392).

181. Whitehead, *Adventures of Ideas,* 185–86.

182. "Here is the phase of perfected actuality, in which the many are one everlastingly, without the qualification of any loss either of individual identity or of completeness of unity. In everlastingness, immediacy is reconciled with objective immortality" (ibid., 350–51 [532]). See also Whitehead, *Adventures of Ideas,* 67.

183. Whitehead, *Process and Reality,* 27–28 (30), 87–88 (134–35), 345 (523–24).

184. For example, he criticizes some early modern philosophers for invoking God to explain human knowledge: " . . . recourse to a pious dependence upon God. This principle was invoked by Descartes and by Leibniz, in order to help out their epistemology. It is a device very repugnant to consistent rationality. The very possibility of knowledge should not be an accident of God's goodness; it should depend on the interwoven nature of things. After all, God's knowledge has equally to be explained" (Whitehead, *Process and Reality,* 190 [289]).

185. Ibid., 343 (521).

other entities insofar as God's "Being" is understood univocally with finite beings.

Although there is only one genus of being, the actual entity applying equally to God and creatures, there are key distinctions between God and all other actual entities. For instance, God is the primordial entity or the sum total of the world process incorporating all finite actual entities, and God's concrescence is never finished.[186] God is also an eternal, or non-temporal, entity in perpetual concrescence.[187]

One reason God is eternal or non-temporal is the ontological principle that everything of consequence must exist in some actual entity. This means the general potentiality of the universe must be somewhere since it is a cause of actual entities in their self-realization. Whitehead places this "proximate relevance" of the universe's potentiality in God's primordial nature.[188] Likewise, for eternal objects, which are non-temporal, to be efficient causes in the concrescence of actual entities they must exist in some actual entity. This is God, who is eternal and non-temporal.[189]

However, since God is immanent in every cosmic epoch as well as transcendent of it, God experiences process, and "before" and "after" are valid terms for God. God's being is also affected by temporal events, just as God affects temporal events.[190] New events incorporated into God's consequent nature change God's concrete content, but primordially with reference to the eternal objects God remains the same across time.

Like all actual entities God is dipolar, consisting of a primordial and a consequent nature corresponding to the mental and physical poles of an actual entity. These also correspond to a "private function" or subjective side and a "public nature" or objective side. God's primordial nature or mental pole "is the unlimited conceptual realization of the absolute wealth of potentiality." This is a gathering together of all conceptual feelings including all eternal objects, directed by God's subjective aim. God's subjective aim is the increased "order with contrasts" producing "intensity of feeling," but not with regard to particular actual entities that do not yet exist, nor with regard to novelty per se, nor preservation.[191] God's

186. Ibid., 75 (116), 110 (143).

187. Ibid., 7 (10–11), 46 (73), 93 (143).

188. Ibid., 46 (73).

189. Ibid., 31–32 (46–48).

190. Ibid., 350–51 (532–33).

191. Ibid., 345 (524). See also 31 (46), 87–88 (134–35), 105 (160–61), 244 (373–74), 249 (381), 342–51 (519–33), 343 (521).

primordial nature has the highest absoluteness among actual entities because it contains all past relationships, each of which God participates in, in an ever-increasing unity and organization. God's primordial nature, then, is the repository of all potentiality or possibility.

The conceptual realization of the eternal objects in God's primordial nature also involves a valuation of the relevance of the various eternal objects for each particular occasion coming into existence, based on God's overriding subjective aim. God's primordial nature supplies possibility and novelty by mediating the eternal possibilities to temporal actualities via God as the requisite actual entity, according to the ontological principle. Ordering possibilities and providing an initial aim for every entity, God is the source of novelty for the world.[192]

As discussed earlier, God provides every actual entity with an initial aim at the start of its concrescence in the form of a lure or desire. The initial aim is in a very real sense God's initiating the individual identity of the actual occasion. God's initial aim is contextual in that it is custom-tailored for each particular entity given its uniquely individual situation. This is the "relevance" of each initial aim for each actual occasion. To receive God's initial aim the actual entity physically feels the eternal object through God's conceptual prehension of that eternal object in a "hybrid physical prehension."[193]

Like all other entities, in addition to a mental pole God has a physical pole or consequent nature. God's consequent nature resolves two intricately related and inseparable problems: (1) the perpetual perishing and fluency in the world, without everlasting permanence; and (2) the introduction of temporality and fluency into God, who is ultimately permanence and eternality.[194] All completed actual entities become part of God's consequent nature, and thereby God becomes "really actual," instead of having only a "conceptual actuality." This bears on the conceptual actuality of the eternal objects of God's primordial nature because God's consequent nature provides the actuality required for any cause or reason. God's consequent nature is continually growing and ever-enlarging

192. Ibid., 87–88 (134), 224–25 (343), 344 (522); 40 (63–64). See also Whitehead, *Science and the Modern World*, 176–77; *Process and Reality*, 108 (164).

193. Ibid., 84 (128), 87–88 (134), 105 (161), 207 (315), 244 (374), 246–47 (377), 344 (522). He speaks of "particular providence for particular occasions" (351 [523]).

194. Ibid., 347–48 (527–29).

as new entities come into actuality. The entities received into God's consequent nature are no longer temporal, however, but are transmuted into an almost eternal, ever-present fact.[195]

As when finite actual entities move from being subjects to become objective data for newly emerging entities, God, in God's role of providing data for new actual entities through initial aims, has a "superject" nature. Like all past actual entities, God is a superject to all finite actual entities. Every new actual entity prehends God in God's superjective nature in an internal feeling, just as it prehends finite superject entities.[196]

God as dipolar plays a role in guaranteeing genuine freedom, novelty, and indeterminacy in the cosmos. There must be some limitation of the infinite possibilities in order for there to be decision. Freedom, and hence novelty, requires some principle of limitation. Creativity itself offers infinite possibilities for activity, but finite consciousnesses cannot function apart from some limitation of these infinite possibilities.[197] Although the free decision of an infinitesimal subject constitutes an actual entity, prior determining causes are necessary because infinite possibility must be limited. The data from the past actuality of superjective entities in God's consequent nature limits the infinite possibilities for a new actual entity currently. This data narrows down the possible options for the actual entity's self-constitution. The initial aim for each new entity derived from God's primordial nature also acts as a principle of limitation. By limiting the infinite possibilities so that actual entities can freely constitute themselves as entities, God as dipolar is the "principle of concretion" for the realization of actualities.[198]

Like every other actual entity, God undergoes concrescence. God's concrescence, however, is the opposite of the concrescence of finite actual entities. Prehending all past superject entities, a finite actual entity begins with the plural data in its physical pole and moves in its concrescence to a unity of satisfaction in its mental pole. God, however, begins concrescence with the unity of the mental pole or primordial nature, and moves through concrescence to the physical pole or consequent nature with its plurality of innumerable completed actual entities.[199] One reason

195. Ibid., 349–50 (530–31).

196. Ibid., 88 (135).

197. Ibid., 110 (168), 164 (248), 244 (374).

198. Ibid., 31 (46), 110 (168), 133 (202), 164 (248), 244 (374).

199. Ibid., 34 (51), 345 (524), 348 (528).

for this reversal is that God, being non-temporal, does not have a past from which to prehend physical data.[200] Another reason is that only an eternal actuality can explain the eternal objects as genuine possibilities, which are the causes of novelty in the process of the universe.

That God and the world are converse to each other in their respective processes is related to the problem of the one and the many for Whitehead. God is primordial unity, emerging into consequent plurality, while actual entities move from plurality to unity in their satisfaction—yet there is at all times both unity and plurality.[201] The world of actual entities is plurality for God in God's unitary primordial pole and God's consequent nature, representing plurality, is constituted of actual entities each of which has the unity of being.[202] Whitehead also speaks of God's consequent nature, in which "everlastingness" is obtained, as the locus of the reconciliation of unity and plurality.[203] God for Whitehead is the locus of a litany of pairs of opposites frequently associated with the problem of the one and the many.[204]

200. Ibid., 87 (134), 345 (524). 201. Ibid., 348–49 (529).

202. "In every respect God and the World move conversely to each other in respect to their process. God is primordially one, namely, he is the primordial unity of relevance of the many potential forms: in the process he acquires a consequent multiplicity, which the primordial character absorbs into its unity. The World is primordially many, namely, the many actual occasions with their physical finitude; in the process it acquires a consequent unity, which is a novel occasion and is absorbed into the multiplicity of the primordial character. Thus God is to be conceived as one and as many in the converse sense in which the World is to be conceived as many and as one. The theme of Cosmology, which is the basis of all religions, is the story of the dynamic effort of the World passing into everlasting unity, and of the static majesty of God's vision, accomplishing its purpose of completion by absorption of the World's multiplicity of effort" (ibid., 349 [529–30]).

203. "Thus the consequent nature of God is composed of a multiplicity of elements with individual self-realization. It is just as much a multiplicity as it is a unity; it is just as much one immediate fact as it is an unresting advance beyond itself. Thus the actuality of God must also be understood as a multiplicity of actual components in process of creation. This is God in his function of the kingdom of heaven" (ibid., 350 [531]). "In this later phase, the many actualities are one actuality, and the one actuality is many actualities" (349 [530]). "Creation achieves the reconciliation of permanence and flux when it has reached its final term which is everlastingness—the Apotheosis of the World" (348 [529]). "Thirdly, there is the phase of perfected actuality, in which the many are one everlastingly, without the qualification of any loss either of individual identity or of completeness of unity" (350–51 [532]). See also 34 (51).

204. "Thus the universe is to be conceived as attaining the active self-expression of its own variety of opposites—of its own freedom and its own necessity, of its own multi-

God and Creativity

An important question is God's relationship to creativity. There is much agreement that creativity is the ultimate in Whitehead's metaphysics, even above and beyond God, who is a "creature" of creativity, along with all other actual entities.[205] While in *Science and the Modern World* Whitehead explicitly acknowledges two metaphysical absolutes, namely God and creativity, [206] in the later *Process and Reality* he seems to make creativity transcendent of even God, and thus in some way more metaphysically ultimate.[207]

Whitehead is clear that creativity, or process, is the ultimate metaphysical principle, and speaks of creativity as "mediating" between God and the world.[208] A distinction between God and creativity seems necessary for dipolarity. If creativity is identical with God as an actual entity then there would be a concrete unity not only of superject actual entities but also of creativity as ultimate reality in God's physical pole. This would make the pole of unity, absoluteness, and concreteness truly ultimate, and plurality, relativity, and indeterminate activity merely secondary. The ultimate fact is not a concrete actual entity but the process itself.

As creativity never exists by itself but only in and through instantiation in actual entities, God is the primordial instantiation of creativity, and creativity sustains both God and the world of finite entities from moment to moment. Along with all other actual entities, God is "in the grip" of creativity and a "creature" of creativity, but is, as God, the "aboriginal instance of creativity."[209]

The idea that God is a "creature of creativity" became an issue for

---

plicity and its own unity, of its own imperfection and its own perfection. All the 'opposites' are elements in the nature of things, and are incorrigibly there. The concept of 'God' is the way in which we understand this incredible fact—that what cannot be, yet is" (ibid., 350 [531]).

205. See Reeves and Brown, "The Development of Process Theology," 24.

206. Whitehead, *Science and the Modern World,* 173–79.

207. "This is the conception of God, according to which he is considered as the outcome of creativity . . . it is also to be noted that every actual entity, including God, is a creature transcended by the creativity which it qualifies" (Whitehead, *Process and Reality,* 88 [135]); "God is the aboriginal instance of this creativity, and is therefore the aboriginal condition which qualifies its action" (225 [344]).

208. Ibid., 21 (31–32), 348 (528).

209. Ibid., 7 (11), 31 (47), 88 (135), 225 (344), 244 (374), 348–49 (529).

some later process theologians, who would equate creativity more strictly with God in order to theologically have God as the sole creator and philosophically to have one unified concrete explanatory principle for everything else. Having investigated the rudiments of Whitehead's metaphysics, we will now turn to the twentieth-century process theology that developed out of Whitehead's metaphysics.

Process Theology

Although God is a "derivative notion" for Whitehead, God has become a central concern of process theologians who appropriate Whitehead. Theologians seeing the real challenges modern science and philosophy pose for the doctrine of God employ, to some degree or other, aspects of Whitehead's metaphysics to address these challenges. Whitehead's dipolar understanding of God is essential to process theology as developed by Hartshorne and others,[210] even though it is ultimately only an analytical tool.[211] Charles Hartshorne is widely recognized as the father of process theology, but many theologians have appropriated Whitehead and Hartshorne to revise not only the doctrine of God but the whole spectrum of Christian theology.[212]

210. See Charles Hartshorne, "The Dipolar Conception of Deity," *The Review of Metaphysics* 21, no. 2 (December 1967): 273–89; Hartshorne, *Creative Synthesis and the Philosophic Method* (LaSalle, Ill.: Open Court, 1970), 99–130; Hartshorne, "Philosophical and Religious Uses of 'God,'" in *Process Theology,* ed. Ewert H. Cousins (New York: Newman Press, 1971), 101–19; W. Norman Pittenger, *God in Process* (London: SCM Press, 1967), 100; Lewis Ford, *The Lure of God: A Biblical Background for Process Theism* (Philadelphia: Fortress Press, 1978), 82–84; and Donna Bowman, *The Divine Decision: A Process Doctrine of Election* (Louisville, Ky.: Westminster/John Knox Press, 2002), 98.

211. Whitehead refers to God's two poles as "distinctions of reason" (*Process and Reality,* 344 [522]). Reeves and Brown indicate that Whitehead's dipolar God is only one God, with both concrete individual and abstract primordial aspects ("The Development of Process Theology," 31). Lewis Ford warns against the danger of seeing the two poles or natures in God as operating independently of one another, and running the risk of reifying God as two different actual entities (*The Lure of God,* 105, 111 n. 12). See also, Victor Lowe, "Whitehead's Metaphysical System," 9 n. 5.

212. Some other key figures include: Lionel Thornton, Daniel Day Williams, John B. Cobb Jr., Norman Pittenger, Schubert M. Ogden, Marjorie Hewitt Suchocki, Catherine Keller, David Ray Griffin, Donald Sherburne, Bernard Meland, Bernard Lee, Joseph A. Bracken, S.J., Bruce G. Epperly, Stephen T. Franklin, C. Robert Mesle, Phillip Clayton, Roland Faber, and Donna Bowman. Jewish process theologians include William E. Kaufman and Alvin J. Reines.

Process theology constructs a new doctrine of God in juxtaposition to classical theism. Classical theism developed and became constitutive of traditional Christian theology starting with the patristic era, going through the Reformation, and continuing to exist in prominent contemporary theologians.[213] It involves, but is not limited to, the ideas that God is pure act, eternal, independent, unsurpassable, immutable, impassible, absolute, really unrelated to creatures, omnipotent, omnipresent, omniscient, and ultimately the source of everything that comes to pass.[214] According to process theologians or "neo-classical theists," this view is based on a philosophically inconsistent, outdated, and irrelevant metaphysics, is unscriptural, and is irrelevant practically to religious persons.[215] In fact, it has directly resulted in modern atheism.

God's incommunicable attributes in classical theism make God "monopolar," and so this list of divine attributes "is in need of a very thorough revision, or at the least of a very careful reinterpretation."[216] Hartshorne does

213. With widespread usage by "classical theism" I mean views of God that, while differing in specific details, affirm a transcendent personal God with a nature and attributes distinguishing God as ultimate reality from the rest of reality in fundamental metaphysical ways. Classical theism includes the idea that there is only one God numerically *(unitas singularitatis),* who is infinitely transcendent of finite beings, can only be discussed or thought of by analogy to finite beings, possesses self-existence or aseity, is simple or not composed of some things more metaphysically fundamental, is necessary, independent, perfect, infinite, eternal, immutable, impassible, omnipotent, omniscient, omnipresent, omnibenevolent, personal, and is the Creator and Sustainer of all reality that is distinct from, and dependent upon, Him, while He is not dependent in any way upon this rest of reality. In many presentations these attributes also include creation out of nothing, the claim that God's necessary existence can be expressed by saying God's essence is existence, and the belief that God is pure actuality with no admixture of potentiality, or *actus purus.* Oft-cited examples of classical theists include Philo, Augustine, Maimonides, Thomas Aquinas and Thomism, Calvin, Spinoza and Leibniz, German idealism, Josiah Royce, Paul Tillich, Judaism, Islam, and even types of Hinduism.

214. Charles Hartshorne, *Man's Vision of God and the Logic of Theism,* 2nd ed. (Hamden, Conn.: Archon Books, 1964), 5, 24, 37, 41–44, 95–97, 114, 121–22; Cobb, *God and the World,* 45.

215. The process or neoclassical critique of classical theism has also influenced many other contemporary theologians who would not necessarily identify themselves as process or neoclassical theists. See, for example, David Tracy, *Blessed Rage for Order: The New Pluralism in Theology* (New York: Seabury Press, 1975), 147.

216. Hartshorne, *Creative Synthesis,* 52–53, 82–84, 167–70; Schubert M. Ogden, *The Reality of God and Other Essays* (New York: Harper & Row, 1966), 49–50. Pittenger, *God in Process,* 14–15.

not reject the older philosophical theology entirely, but wants to transform it. Neoclassical theism heartily accepts many tenets of classical theism, but they must be subjected to drastic and scarcely traditional qualifications. Most of traditional theology is acceptable, but only as the "A" (absolute) pole of the God who is AR (absolute and relative). We should not discard what is good in classical theism just because it denies the importance of change, growth, possibility, increase, suffering, and sociality in God. Hartshorne wants to balance this imbalance by focusing just as much on the *relative* ("R") pole of God.[217] A monopolar deity leads to insuperable philosophical problems that have led in extreme cases to modern atheism.

Classical theism is the God of ancient philosophy, not of "religious sentiment," according to process theists.[218] It embodies the "impossible attempt to synthesize the personalistic view of the God of Holy Scripture with the substance ontology of classical Greek philosophy." "Being" or *esse* is its starting point, instead of "Becoming," which it sees as grossly inferior.[219] By taking seriously God's temporality, passibility, limitations, personality, and relatedness to creation and humans, process theology is much more faithful to the scriptural picture of God than classical theism.[220] Process theism's God is the "Living God" of the Bible, while the static, perfect, immutable, unrelated, and impassible God of classical theism is not.[221]

The Greek philosophical traditions that influenced nascent Christian-

217. Hartshorne, *Man's Vision of God,* xii, xv, 17.

218. "As we all know, the God of the philosophers is not the same as the God of Abraham, Isaac, and Jacob" (Ford, *The Lure of God,* 25). See also, Hartshorne, *Man's Vision of God,* 95–97; Hartshorne, *Creative Synthesis,* 243.

219. Ogden, *The Reality of God,* 174. See also, Cobb, *God and the World,* 27–31; Pittenger, *God in Process,* 90. John F. Haught, *God After Darwin: A Theology of Evolution* (Boulder, Colo.: Westview Press, 2000), 83–84.

220. Charles Hartshorne, *A Natural Theology for Our Time* (LaSalle, Ill.: Open Court, 1967), 18–19; Hartshorne, "Is Whitehead's God the God of Religion?" *Ethics* 53, no. 3 (April 1943): 219–27; Cobb, *God and the World,* 42, 68, 82; Schubert M. Ogden, "Theology and Philosophy: A New Phase of the Discussion," *Journal of Religion* 44, no. 1 (January 1964): 1–16; Eulalio R. Baltazar, *God within Process* (New York: Newman Press, 1970), 110–14, 127, 130; Ogden, *The Reality of God,* 66–67, 121–22; Pittenger, *God in Process,* 17, 90, 99, 101; Ford, *The Lure of God,* x; Haught, *God After Darwin,* 187, 189; Bowman, *The Divine Decision,* 125, 167–68, 173; Tracy, *Blessed Rage for Order,* 160–61, 174, 177, 179, 180–84, 189, 200 n. 89. See also George Allan, "The Aims of Societies and the Aims of God," in *Process Philosophy and Christian Thought,* ed. Delwin Brown, Ralph E. James Jr., and Gene Reeves, 464–74 (Indianapolis: Bobbs-Merrill, 1971).

221. Daniel Day Williams, *God's Grace and Man's Hope* (New York: Harper & Brothers,

ity had long argued that change and temporality and possibility are imperfections, because time and change involve corruption or the loss of being. This implies a defect in all of creation and the realm of human activity, which are replete with time and change. Process theists say perfection involves the capability of infinite enrichment, so that time and change are positive, not negative.[222] This implies that the realms of creation and human activity are good and free from inherent imperfection.

Despite classical theism's claim to a personal God, it ultimately must hold that God *in se*, apart from human expressions of divine experience, is really abstract, absolute, unrelated, independent, and thus devoid of genuine personality.[223] If the ultimate reality responsible for all that exists is itself impersonal, there is no explanation for the phenomenon of personality. There are also many deleterious practical consequences for religious believers if God is ultimately impersonal.

Process theologians urge that if God is really personal, is in real relationships, and can change, then creation in general and human existence and human effort have real ultimate meaning. In classical theism they do not. This is of great significance for many moderns who cannot reconcile the bona fide existence and activity of creation and humanity with the God of classical theism. A particular species of classical theism arose in the late Middle Ages, continued through the Renaissance and Reformation, and into modernity and late modernity. This view frequently leads to a forced decision to affirm either God or man, which are seen as mutually exclusive. Part of modern atheism was an option for the latter: "In order to enrich God, man must become poor; that God may be all in all, man must be nothing";[224] "theism removes man from his humanity and alienates him from his freedom, his joy and his true being. 'If man is free,

---

1949; revised edition, 1965), 42; Pittenger, *God in Process*, 14, 15, 18, 99, 104, 108; Bowman, *The Divine Decision*, 171.

222. Ford, *The Lure of God*, 11. See also, Hartshorne, *A Natural Theology for Our Time*, 18; and Tracy, *Blessed Rage for Order*, 178. Gilkey relates this classical derogation of change and temporality: "Temporality is itself a mark of dependence and contingency, and as such is impossible for the independent and necessary source of all being"(Langdon Gilkey, *Maker of Heaven and Earth: The Christian Doctrine of Creation in Light of Modern Knowledge* [Garden City, N.Y.: Anchor Books, 1965], 88).

223. Hartshorne, *Man's Vision of God*, 41–42.

224. Ludwig Feuerbach, *The Essence of Christianity*, trans. George Eliot (New York: Harper & Row, 1957), 26. At the incipience of the Protestant Reformations, Huldrych Zwingli

then there is no such God; if there is such a God, then man is not free.'"[225]

The general question of whether divine and created existence and activity are compatible or mutually exclusive bears on a particular question in Christian theology. This is the soteriological debate over God's sovereignty and human freedom. It is no surprise that many process theologians work from the Arminian-Wesleyan traditions instead of from the Reformed-Calvinistic traditions.[226] The former sees God's essence as infinite, unlimited love, while the latter sees God's essence as unfettered freedom and power. The former focuses on human freedom, synergism in salvation, and God's universal salvific will. The latter deemphasizes or even denies human freedom, while focusing on monergism in salvation, and God's restricted electing love. Intimately related to everything, process theism's God is Charles Wesley's "pure unbounded love," fully respecting creaturely freedom.[227] Some nineteenth-century Wesleyan theologians even argued, independently of proto-process currents, for what would become aspects of process theology, such as denying that divine omniscience includes future contingencies.[228]

---

wrote: "In this entire chapter I have been aiming to prove that since all things have their being, existence, life, movement and activity from One and in One, that One is the only real cause of all things, and those nearer things which we call causes, are not properly causes, but the agents and instruments with which the eternal mind works, and in which it manifests itself to be enjoyed" (*On Providence and Other Essays*, ed. William John Hinke [Philadelphia: Heidelberg Press, 1922; reprint, Eugene Ore.: Wipf & Stock, 1999], 157–58.

225. Jürgen Moltmann, *The Crucified God: The Cross of Christ as the Foundation and Criticism of Christian Theology*, trans. R.A. Wilson and John Bowden (San Francisco: Harper & Row, 1974), 250.

226. Hartshorne writes: "When Charles Wesley, who must have known something of religious values, wrote: 'Father, thou art all compassion, Pure unbounded love thou art,' he was not distinguishing God by denying relativity or passivity to him" (*The Divine Relativity: A Social Conception of God* [New Haven, Conn.: Yale University Press, 1967], 36); and Ogden specifically applies Wesley's statement that God is "pure unbounded love" to the process-relational view of God. (*The Reality of God*, 177). For the many connections between process theology and Wesleyan theology, see *Thy Nature and Thy Name Is Love: Wesleyan and Process Theologies in Dialogue*, ed. Bryan P. Stone and Thomas Jay Oord (Nashville: Kingswood Books, 2001). Process theology is also popular among those working from the Anglican traditions (e.g., Norman Pittenger), from which Methodism emerged.

227. Hartshorne says the only predicate of God's whole nature is "love" (*Man's Vision of God*, 111), and says this essential attribute of God is contradicted by the older philosophical theologies (ibid., ix; Hartshorne, *A Natural Theology for Our Time*, 14). See also Pittenger, *God in Process*, 108.

228. See, for instance, Lorenzo D. McCabe, *Divine Nescience of Future Contingencies a*

Viewed from certain perspectives, classical Christian theism makes God out to be a monster. From St. Augustine through St. Thomas through the Magisterial Protestant Reformers, classical theism emphasized divine providence to the point of affirming divine election and reprobation of individuals in salvation. As Arminian theology perhaps drawn to its consistent logical conclusions, process theology emphasizes creaturely freedom so much that election in salvation essentially becomes a general call to all creatures, which choose salvation for themselves.[229] Some process theologians working from traditionally Reformed Protestant backgrounds have even formulated a divine election along these lines.[230]

Process theologians redefine many of God's incommunicable attributes. Immutability is not the unchangeable divine substance, but becomes God's unchanging character and fidelity in keeping promises. Because life always involves change, biblical references to the "Living God" deny God's essential immutability, not to mention the ways God changes in scripture. In fact, mutability is a virtue if it involves change for the better. God is always changing, but only and ever for the better. The self-contrasting, self-surpassing being will only ever contrast with itself through increase, and never through decrease. Ultimate reality encompassing all real events is an ever-growing whole. It surpasses all other beings since as other beings bring new being and value the whole process acquires new value but loses none. God increases but never decreases. Because it is improvement and never diminishment, change for God is positive and therefore a perfection, not a weakness or inferiority. In these ways process theologians argue there is an aspect of God that is mutable, contra classical theism.[231]

Necessity (New York: Philips and Hung, 1882), and *The Foreknowledge of God* (Cincinnati: Cranston and Stowe, 1887).

229. "God calls every man, but some like Abraham respond more fully to that call" (Ford, *The Lure of God,* 75).

230. Bowman, *The Divine Decision,* 77,110–11, 153, 162, 185, 197, 208. Bowman says this view is more biblical (ibid., 216). The Reformed tradition, after all, should always be reformed by the Word of God: *Ecclesia reformata semper reformanda secundum verbum Dei.* In the end, however, she explicitly and consciously denies the unconditional election of the Reformed heritage, averring that election is conditional (ibid., 137–39).

231. Hartshorne, *Man's Vision of God,* 15, 109–13, 117–18, 129–30, 159; Hartshorne, *Reality as Social Process: Studies in Metaphysics and Religion* (Glencoe, Ill.: Free Press, 1953), 118–19; Ogden, *The Reality of God,* 59–60; Joseph A. Bracken, *What Are They Saying about the Trinity?* (New York: Paulist Press, 1979), 46; Bowman, *The Divine Decision,* 167–68.

For process theologians the immutability intuition is correct insofar as perpetually eminent becoming itself constitutes an element of immutability. The fact that God is ever-changing never changes.[232] By accounting for both divine mutability and immutability, dipolar theism balances the two poles of absolute ("A") and relative ("R") in contrast to monopolar theism. This is similar to process theism's revision of divine simplicity. As Whitehead's God tries to consistently maximize unity and diversity, process theism says God is complex in the relative pole ("R") but the unity of God's absolute pole ("A") constitutes a type of simplicity.[233]

Related to immutability is impassibility.[234] Process theologians indicate how, in the Greek philosophy informing classical theism, divine immutability requires impassibility. For process theists, in God is eminent passibility as well as eminent mutability. Related to everything, God is affected by everything. While humans are unaffected by the joys and griefs of much of the world, God shares in the wealth and burdens of every aspect of the world. God's perfection thus lies in "omnipassibility," not impassibility. Soteriologically, God's love is manifest in God's suffering. If God neither changes nor suffers then Jesus' incarnation and suffering make no sense as the communication of God's love to humanity. Scripturally, God's passibility is more consistent with a prima facie reading of the Bible than impassibility.

With their implications for human existence and activity, and their pragmatic relevance for human suffering, process theism's reconstruals of divine immutability and impassibility have impacted contemporary theologians.[235] God as "the fellow-sufferer who understands" seems more im-

232. Hartshorne, *Man's Vision of God,* 110, 29; Ogden, *The Reality of God,* 59–60.

233. Hartshorne, *Man's Vision of God,* 182.

234. Ibid., 196–98; Hartshorne, *Reality as Social Process,* 24; Williams, *The Spirit and the Forms of Love,* 166–67, 183; Pittenger, *God in Process,* 16, 46–47, 57, 61, 81; Cobb, *God and the World,* 37–38, 96–97; Ford, *The Lure of God,* 11, 82–92; Marjorie Hewitt Suchocki, *God, Christ, Church: A Practical Guide to Process Theology* (New York: Crossroad, 1982), 152–53; Bracken, *What Are They Saying about the Trinity?* 41–42; Bowman, *The Divine Decision,* 166–68, 173–74. Haught, *God After Darwin,* 46–49, 112–13.

235. Those who evidence such influence, on a wide spectrum of degrees, are too many to list, but some include: Gordon D. Kaufman, *Systematic Theology: A Historicist Perspective* (New York: Scribner's, 1968); John J. O'Donnell, S.J., *Trinity and Temporality: The Christian Doctrine of God in the Light of Process Theology and the Theology of Hope* (Oxford: Oxford University Press, 1983); Warren McWilliams, *The Passion of God: Divine Suffering in Contemporary Protestant Theology* (Macon, Ga.: Mercer University Press, 1985); Paul S. Fiddes,

mediately relevant in the face of evil and suffering than classical theism's immutable, impassible God.[236] The horrendous evils of the Second World War led Moltmann to emphasize God's suffering in ways similar to process theology.[237] Moltmann's crucified God is also a response to modern atheism, which he believes is in part a reaction to the idea that God's perfection means God is impervious to pain and suffering.

Process theology also undertakes to reinterpret the classical theistic "omni-" predicates of God: omniscience, omnipresence, and omnipotence. Divine omniscience for process theologians includes foreknowledge of the future that is not exhaustive in the classical theistic sense. Contingency in the cosmos is not merely unpredictability due to lack of causal knowledge. It is genuine indeterminacy. God's foreknowledge cannot include future contingents because if God knows them now they would be necessary, not really contingent.[238] Similarly, genuine contingency means some future events cannot be deduced from antecedent causes. In addition, because only what is actual or real can be a cause or reason, as of yet unrealized possibilities cannot cause knowledge in a subject and so cannot be presently known.[239] There is no actual future to know. An increase in God's knowledge comes with the appearance of new actualities, and this increase in knowledge is another way God is mutable, but only for the better.[240]

God is omniscient, then, by knowing all that can be known, or all actualities. Because the same metaphysical principles apply to God and

---

The Creative Suffering of God (Oxford: Clarendon Press, 1988); Joseph M. Hallman, *The Descent of God: Divine Suffering in History and Theology* (Minneapolis: Fortress Press, 1991); Wilfrid J. Harrington, *The Tears of God: Our Benevolent Creator and Human Suffering* (Collegeville, Minn.: Liturgical Press, 1992); Alan G. Padgett, *God, Eternity and the Nature of Time* (New York: St. Martins Press, 1992); Ted Peters, *God as Trinity: Relationality and Temporality in the Divine Life* (Louisville, Ky.: Westminster/John Knox Press, 1993); and Michael Welker, *Creation and Reality* (Minneapolis: Fortress Press, 1999).

236. Whitehead, *Process and Reality*, 351 (532).

237. "The God of theism is poor. He cannot love nor can he suffer. . . . 'God is the great companion—the fellow-suffer, who understands'" (Moltmann, *The Crucified God*, 253, 255).

238. Hartshorne, *Man's Vision of God*, 159; Ford, *The Lure of God*, 11; Baltazar, *God Within Process*, 169–70; Bowman, *The Divine Decision*, 128. This old argument antedates process thought but clearly follows from it.

239. Hartshorne, *Man's Vision of God*, 13–14, 98–99; Ford, *The Lure of God*, 11–12, 37; Bowman, *The Divine Decision*, 169, 178.

240. Hartshorne, "The Dipolar Conception of Deity," 277–78; Ford, *The Lure of God*, 109; Bowman, *The Divine Decision*, 179.

creatures, the difference between God's knowledge and rational creatures' knowledge is one of degree, not kind. It is quantitative, not qualitative. Finite minds have knowledge of some past and present actualities, but God knows them all.[241] Also, because of the possibilities in God's primordial nature God knows all future possibilities as possibilities, not actualities, but finite minds know a limited set of the future possibilities.[242]

Process reconstructions of omnipresence are often variations on Hartshorne's panentheism. Classical theism distinguishes God from the world in essential, qualitative terms. Pantheism identifies God with the world in similarly essential, qualitative terms. Panentheism sees the world as being "within God."[243] God is eminently related to but in some sense independent of the world.[244] The perfection of omnipresence subsists not in utter independence from all finite realities, but in both including those realities and surpassing them.[245]

In contrast to substance ontology, a process-event-relational ontology allows two entities to occupy the same time and space. An actual entity's unique individuality consists in its subjective immediacy or subjective event, not in being in a particular space-time region. Thus more than one entity can be in the same spatio-temporal location without the individuality of either being lost.[246] This also explains how God is omnipresent in every spatiotemporal location without being the "whole" of which all other entities are merely "parts."

Hartshorne's panentheism lends itself to understanding the God-world relationship as similar to the soul-body relationship. The world is the

241. Charles Hartshorne, "Redefining God," *The New Humanist* 7 (July–August 1934): 8–15.

242. Bowman, *The Divine Decision,* 205.

243. "Many follow Whitehead in insisting . . . that the concept of omnipresence needs to be stated in terms which guarantee that all things are present to him precisely because all things occur 'within' him—the panentheistic position, which of course needs to be distinguished very sharply from pantheism" (Pittenger, *God in Process,* 100). See also ibid., 17, 19–20, 25, 27, 90.

244. "'Panentheism' is an appropriate term for the view that deity is in some real aspect distinguishable from and independent of any and all relative items, and yet, taken as an actual whole, includes all relative terms" (Hartshorne, *The Divine Relativity,* 89).

245. Hartshorne, *A Natural Theology for Our Time,* 8–9, 12.

246. Cobb, *A Christian Natural Theology,* 82–91; Cobb, "A Whiteheadian Doctrine of God," 227–29; Cobb, *God and the World,* 78–80; Cobb, "Response to Ted Peters," *Dialog* 30 (Summer 1991): 243; Ford, *The Lure of God,* 102.

"Body of God."[247] The philosophy of organism that denies mind-matter dualism easily leads to this analogy. The soul is a personally ordered society giving coherence and unity to the various nexūs of living and nonliving actual occasions in the human body. So, too, God is a transcendent society of living occasions giving coherence and unity to the many societies constituting the world.[248] As the soul is present to the body to coordinate the activities of both, even more so is God intimately present to all finite actual entities in the world, coordinating all activity.[249]

For Christian theology the analogy of the world as God's body corresponds with the doctrine of the Incarnation, making the Incarnation a guiding principle inclusive even of the doctrine of creation.[250] Thus others who would not necessarily identify themselves as process theologians have readily used Hartshorne's panentheism and the world-as-God's-body analogy.[251]

Hartshorne's soul-body analogy points to an important difference from Whitehead. Hartshorne's analogy arose as part of a response to the problem that in the succession from one actual entity to the next something is always lost. A standard interpretation of Whitehead is that God is single eternally concrescent actual entity, not a society, but immune to the possibility of loss.[252] Hartshorne and others argue, however, that since the category of "subjective perishing" applies to all entities including God, not even God is immune to the possibility of loss.[253] For White-

247. Hartshorne, *Man's Vision of God,* 174–211; Hartshorne, *The Logic of Perfection,* 191–215, Hartshorne, *The Divine Relativity,* 89; Hartshorne, *Reality as Social Process,* 120; Hartshorne, *A Natural Theology for Our Time,* 8–9, 12; Hartshorne, "The Compound Individual," 218–20; Ogden, *The Reality of God,* 58–60, 178–79; Cobb, *A Christian Natural Theology,* 82–91, 192–96; Bowman, *The Divine Decision,* 106, 108.

248. Hartshorne, "The Compound Individual," 218–20; *Man's Vision of God,* 174–211.

249. Hartshorne, *Man's Vision of God,* 174–211; *The Logic of Perfection,* 191–215.

250. Pittenger, *God in Process,* 19.

251. For instance: Jürgen Moltmann, *God in Creation: A New Theology of Creation and the Spirit of God,* trans. Margaret Kohl (Minneapolis: Fortress Press, 1993), 103; Tracy, *Blessed Rage for Order,* 181; Sallie McFague, *The Body of God: An Ecological Theology* (Minneapolis: Fortress Press, 1993).

252. Christian, *An Interpretation of Whitehead's Metaphysics,* 393; Lewis Ford, "Boethius and Whitehead," *International Philosophical Quarterly* 8, no. 1 (March 1968): 63–67. Cf. Whitehead, *Process and Reality,* 31–32 (47), 36 (54), 350 (531).

253. Hartshorne, "Whitehead's Novel Intuition," 23; Ivor Leclerc, "Review of *An Interpretation of Whitehead's Metaphysics,* by W. A. Christian," *Journal of Philosophy* 57, no. 4 (1960): 138–43; Cobb, *A Christian Natural Theology,* 188–92.

head "society" provides endurance, so God is a temporally organized personal society of actual occasions.[254] Hartshorne's panentheism and body-of-God analogy are also conducive to seeing God in more personal terms than Whitehead does.[255]

As for omnipotence, Whitehead poignantly related the abuses in religious belief and practice that viewing God as the sovereign omnipotent heavenly tyrant has led to. For Whitehead, God saves the world through tenderness, patience, and harmonization, not destructive force.[256] Classical theism cannot adequately address the problem of evil and suffering, leading to the agnosticisms and atheisms of modernity. In the view of many, evil and suffering mean that if God exists God cannot be both omnipotent and omnibenevolent in the classical theistic senses. Classically understood, omnipotence also seems to make God ultimately responsible for not only natural evil, but even moral evil and horrendous evil.[257]

If omnipotence and omnibenevolence classically conceived are incommensurable with evil and suffering, and if God does exist, then God can have only one of these attributes at best. Gnosticism opts for power over goodness, but process theology opts for God's goodness over an exhaus-

254. Hartshorne, "The Compound Individual," 218–20.

255. See ibid., and Cobb, "A Whiteheadian Doctrine of God," 224–25, 241–42. Cobb tries to reconcile Whitehead and Hartshorne by distinguishing between "time" and "non-temporality." Since God's consequent and primordial natures are eternal, there is a sense in which God never perishes and is a single non-temporal entity. Yet, in view of God's past and future, God is a society of successive divine occasions of experience—Cobb uses the human person as an analogy for God here. He argues that becoming in God's consequent nature must be like the time or becoming between successive actual entities and not the division of components of a single actual entity. This is because Whitehead holds that the internal process of becoming of the actual entity has no efficacy for other actual entities than itself. So if there is no sense in which God is a succession of actual entities, then God would have no effect on the events in the world. It is here that Whitehead would benefit, in Cobb's view, by construing God more in terms of human personhood. See ibid., 222–25.

256. "This worship of glory arising from power is not only dangerous: it arises from a barbaric conception of God. I suppose that even the world itself could not contain the bones of those slaughtered because of men intoxicated by its attraction. This view of the universe, in the guise of an Eastern empire ruled by a glorious tyrant, may have served its purpose. . . . The glorification of power has broken more hearts than it has healed" (Whitehead, *Religion in the Making,* 54–55); see also ibid., 56–57, 72, 73; and Whitehead, *Process and Reality,* 342 (519–20). See, further, Whitehead, *Process and Reality,* 346 (525–26).

257. Pittenger, *God in Process,* 14; Ford, *The Lure of God,* 20; Haught, *God After Darwin,* 111–14, 130, 184.

tive understanding of God's power. In the process universe genuine indeterminacy, not only in the free wills of rational creatures but in all actual entities, allows for contrariness to God's will both morally and naturally. God's initial aim as an "appropriate goal" also becomes a moral judgment for each entity.[258] Morally, an entity's deviation from God's initial aim could be construed as the meaning of "sin."[259]

In the view of many, true creaturely freedom or indeterminacy rules out a priori the classical theistic understanding of omnipotence. For classical theists, God is ultimately responsible for the existence and activity of every created being, enables each free being to exercise its freedom, and acts through every free subject to determine its choices in some sense. This makes finite and ultimate causation coincide, which is impossible if there is true creaturely freedom.[260] Assuming libertarian free will and denying compatibilist views of free will, genuine freedom is necessarily incompatible with all types of determinism including divine determinism.[261] Incorporating genuine indeterminacy into a mechanistically deterministic universe was a central concern of early process thinkers, so the actual entity's freedom has to be incompatibilist and libertarian. Regarding human persons' self-determination and relationships with God, uncoerced personal freedom is a sine qua non for these relationships.[262]

Process theologians, then, redefine the classical notion of God's om-

258. Whitehead, *Religion in the Making,* 114.

259. John B. Cobb Jr., "Whitehead's Philosophy and a Christian Doctrine of Man," *The Journal of Bible and Religion* 32, no. 3 (July 1964): 210–15; Pittenger, *God in Process,* 107; and Ford, *The Lure of God,* 22.

260. Hartshorne, *Man's Vision of God,* 30; Ford, *The Lure of God,* 18–19.

261. In contemporary philosophy libertarian freedom involves the beliefs that free will is incompatible with any type of causal determinism, free will is real, and therefore causal determinism is false. That is, there are no causes or reasons that determine a free subject's choice. Compatibilism holds that free will is compatible with causal determinism by defining freedom as possessing the power to choose to the contrary and being free from external constraints forbidding contrary choice. This does not preclude determining causes or reasons internal to the free subject (e.g., feelings, ideas, desires) determining the free agent's choice. There are different species of libertarianism and compatibilism, as well as indeterminism and determinism, all of which bear on the question of what free will is. This discussion involves many others, not the least of which is the question of responsibility. For a very good navigation of the complexities of free will questions in contemporary philosophy, see Robert Kane, *A Contemporary Introduction to Free Will* (New York: Oxford University Press, 2005).

262. Hartshorne, *Man's Vision of God,* 36.

nipotence.[263] They see God's power and action upon the world in terms of persuasion and goals instead of force and efficient causality. The Greek philosophy used by the early Church included the idea that God acts by persuasion, but Christian philosophers and theologians did not readily employ this. They stressed God's efficient and formal causality, not God's teleological causality. The process persuasion view seems closer to Aristotle's view than many trajectories of later Christian thought, because he understood God's acting in terms of teleological causality, as a lure or desire. St. Thomas and the scholastics would later understand creation and providence in terms of an ultimate efficient causality.[264] Envisioning omnipotence as irresistible force actually degrades God's power, because when there is no competing power omnipotence means very little.[265] Power to influence others in their own individual exercises of power is of greater value than an indomitable force, which ironically becomes a form of powerlessness. God's power as persuasion also remediates the classical theistic inability to adequately address the problem of evil and suffering due to efficient divine causality.[266] Divine power must be understood as the power to influence the exercise of power by others.

Scripturally speaking, commandments, admonitions, and even threats are forms of persuasion. Some process thinkers have said that we must abandon, however, the biblical depictions of God as a monarch because

263. In its most sophisticated and least understood forms, classical theism holds that humans have libertarian, not compatibilist, free will, and even allows for indeterminacy concomitantly with exhaustive divine providence and omnipotence as classically conceived. St. Thomas himself said: "It is not the function of divine providence to impose necessity on things ruled by it" (*Summa contra gentiles* 3.72.7). See Piet Schoonenberg, "God or Man: A False Dilemma," in his *The Christ,* trans. D. Couling (New York: Seabury, 1971), 13–49; Elizabeth Johnson, "Does God Play Dice?" *Theological Studies* 57 (1996): 2–18; Robert Masson, "Analogy and Metaphoric Process," *Theological Studies* 62 (September 2001): 571–96; and Eleonore Stump, *Aquinas,* new ed. (New York: Routledge, 2005), 277–306, 389–404. For an explanation of the Thomistic position on how there is unconditional divine election and efficacious grace along with libertarian freedom, see Reginald Garrigou-Lagrange, O.P., *Predestination,* trans. Dom Bede Rose, O.S.B., D.D. (Rockford, Ill.: Tan Books and Publishers, 1998; originally published as *La prédestination des saints et la grace*). Eulalio Baltazar, a process theologian more influenced by Thomism than many process thinkers, evidences this robust view of divine providence and omnipotence on the one hand, and libertarian freedom on the creaturely level on the other hand (Baltazar, *God Within Process,* 167–68).

264. Ford, *The Lure of God,* 10, 12, 15, 17–20, 123.

265. Cobb, *God and the World,* 88–90.

266. See ibid., 87, 88–89; Ford, *The Lure of God,* 20, 23, 29.

they are incompatible with viewing God's power as persuasion.[267] Others say we can reinterpret this common biblical metaphor to mean God is the "sovereign ruler," *pantocrator,* or ruler over everything, just not by coercion.[268] Some even question whether omnipotence as the power to do absolutely anything is really a scriptural theme, saying instead that scripture portrays God's omnipotence as "the power to accomplish that which he purposes."[269]

While God's initial aim for every entity universalizes God's power as persuasion, perhaps an even more all-encompassing way to see omnipotence in process terms is "empowerment."[270] As the primordial instantiation of the creativity in which all actual entities participate, there is a sense in which God empowers all entities.

Thus God's omnipotence is the superlative to persuade and empower.[271] While we can still use the word "omnipotence," we must realize that in all of these cases its meaning is quite altered from traditional usage.[272] The process reconstruction of God's power as persuasion and empowerment has also influenced recent feminist theologians who likewise see serious problems with the sovereign monarchical view, and want to extirpate it.[273]

In addition to theology proper, Christian process theologians have applied process categories to virtually every locus of systematic theology. In many instances they have argued that process categories solve longstand-

267. Ford, *The Lure of God,* 27, 30–31. The Bible has very diverse views of God, such as how on the one hand the prophetic genre demonstrates God's power as "persuasive" while the apocalyptic genre demonstrates God's power as deterministic, with the certain triumph over evil in the end. These diverse views must be adjudicated (ibid., 24, 31).

268. Pittenger, *God in Process,* 15.

269. Ibid. See also 46, 92–95. Since God accomplishes his purposes, however, eschatological triumph of God is guaranteed: "Purposes cannot in the long run be defeated, however much evil and sin there may be in the world as at present we see and experience it" (ibid., 16).

270. Cobb, "Response to Ted Peters," 242.

271. Williams, *The Spirit and the Forms of Love,* 120–27; Cobb, *God and the World,* 88–90; Cobb, "Response to Ted Peters," 242; Bowman, *The Divine Decision,* 113, 177; Haught, *God After Darwin,* 41–42, 47–48.

272. Cobb, *God and the World,* 88–90.

273. Elizabeth A. Johnson, *She Who Is: The Mystery of God in Feminist Theological Discourse,* 2nd ed. (New York: Crossroad, 1997), 269–70; Anna Case-Winters, *God's Power: Traditional Understandings and Contemporary Challenges* (Louisville, Ky.: Westminster/John Knox Press, 1990.

ing theological difficulties. For example, replacing substance ontology with an event-relational ontology makes some inveterate difficulties more rationally comprehensible: the identity of the trinitarian persons with the divine nature but not with each other, the union of the divine and human natures in the one person of Jesus Christ, and transubstantiation. I have already touched upon ways process theology can speak to traditional questions about soteriology, grace and free will, human responsibility, and the origins of evil and suffering.[274]

Process theology has also proved fruitful in interreligious dialogue and in moving toward a robustly pluralistic theology of religion.[275] In the religion and science dialogue, process theology has proven itself more effective than classical theism in some cases. In the wider theological world process theology has had a pervasive influence, to varying degrees, on a number of contemporary theologians who would not identify themselves as process theologians.[276]

274. Even a brief survey of how process theologians treat the systematic theological *loci* would take up much time and space. For process treatments of the different areas of Christian theology I refer the reader to the theologians referenced in this section and to the bibliography. For a good summary, see John B. Cobb Jr., and David Ray Griffin, *Process Theology: An Introductory Exposition* (Louisville, Ky.: Westminster/John Knox Press, 1976).

275. John B. Cobb Jr., *Beyond Dialogue: Toward a Mutual Transformation of Christianity and Buddhism* (Philadelphia: Fortress Press, 1982); John B. Cobb Jr. and Christopher Ives, eds., *The Emptying God: A Buddhist-Jewish-Christian Conversation* (Maryknoll, N.Y.: Orbis, 1990); John B. Cobb Jr., *Transforming Christianity and the World: A Way beyond Absolutism and Relativism,* ed. Paul F. Knitter (Maryknoll, N.Y: Orbis, 1999); Marjorie Hewitt Suchocki, *Divinity and Diversity: A Christian Affirmation of Religious Pluralism* (Nashville: Abingdon Press, 2003); David Ray Griffin, *Deep Religious Pluralism* (Louisville, Ky.: Westminster/John Knox Press, 2005). Charles Hartshorne also parallels the event-like character of actuality and personality in process metaphysics to Buddhism (*A Natural Theology for Our Time*, 22–23, 25).

276. We even see a process vaguely describing the concrescence of a Whiteheadian actual entity, with a reference to Whitehead, in a prominent twentieth-century occultist: "Infinite space is called the goddess NUIT, while the infinitely small and atomic yet omnipresent point is called HADIT. These are unmanifest. One conjunction of these infinites is called RA-HOOR-KHUIT, a unity which includes and heads all things. . . . I present this theory in a very simple form. I cannot even explain (for instance) that an idea may not refer to Being at all, but to Going. . . . The basis of theology is given in Liber CCXX . . . Here I can only outline the matter in a very crude way; it would require a separate treatise to discuss even the true meaning of the terms employed, and to show how The Book of the Law anticipates the recent discoveries of Frege, Cantor, Pointcaré, Russell, Whitehead, Einstein and others. . . . All advance in understanding demands the acquisition of a new point-of-

Evangelical Open Theism

Process theology's influence has been felt even in regions of conservative evangelical theology in the "open theism" movement.[277] Recently some prominent evangelical Protestant theologians have revised the classical theism typically held by evangelicals, not without criticism from other evangelicals.[278] Not wanting to associate themselves too closely with process theology, they indicate key differences between open theism and process theology. Open theism does bear similarities with aspects of process theology, though, and open theists acknowledge this.[279]

As evangelicals, open theists are concerned that their view of God come from scripture. They argue with process theologians that classical theism's monopolar God, who is independent, unrelated, timeless, immu-

---

view. Modern conceptions of Mathematics, Chemistry, and Physics are sheer paradox to the 'plain man' who thinks of Matter as something that one can knock up against" (Aleister Crowley, *Magick in Theory and Practice,* in *Magick: Book 4, Liber Aba,* 2d rev. ed., ed. Mary Desti, Leila Waddell, and Hymenaeus Beta, 137 and 137 nn. (Newburyport, Mass.: Weiser Books, 1998).

277. The term "open theism" seems to have originated with Richard Rice's 1979 publication, *The Openness of God: The Relationship of Divine Foreknowledge and Human Free Will* (Nashville: Review & Herald Publishers, 1979). Sometimes open theism is referred to as "free will theism" because of the centrality of libertarian free will, which drives many of its theological and philosophical concerns. The following brief comparison of evangelical open theism with process theology is based on the following works: Clark Pinnock, Richard Rice, John Sanders, William Hasker, and David Basinger, *The Openness of God: A Biblical Challenge to the Traditional Understanding of God* (Downers Grove, Ill.: InterVarsity Press, 1994); William Hasker, *God, Time, and Knowledge* (Ithaca, N.Y.: Cornell University Press, 1989); David Basinger, *The Case for Free Will Theism: A Philosophical Assessment* (Downers Grove, Ill.: InterVarsity Press, 1996); John Sanders, *The God Who Risks: A Theology of Providence* (Downers Grove, Ill.: InterVarsity Press, 1998); Gregory A. Boyd. *God of the Possible: A Biblical Introduction to the Open View of God* (Grand Rapids, Mich.: Baker, 2000); Clark H. Pinnock, *Most Moved Mover: A Theology of God's Openness* (Grand Rapids, Mich.: Paternoster/Baker Academic, 2001); and William Hasker, *Providence, Evil and the Openness of God* (New York: Routledge, 2004).

278. Perhaps the most famous evangelical open theist is Clark Pinnock, but other evangelicals, both philosophers and theologians, are working with this model. These include Gregory A. Boyd, John Sanders, William Hasker, David Basinger, Richard Rice, and Thomas Jay Oord. Evangelical opponents of open theism include D. A. Carson, Norman Geisler, Roger Nicole, Bruce A. Ware, Robert A. Morey, and John Frame.

279. See, for instance, John B. Cobb Jr. and Clark H. Pinnock, *Searching for an Adequate God: A Dialogue between Process and Free Will Theists* (Grand Rapids, Mich.: Eerdmans, 2000).

table, and impassible and who is purely actual is not scripture's vision of God. They point to many biblical passages where, prima facie, God dynamically interacts with creation in ways that imply change; is limited by time; is affected by and responds to the world and humans; experiences frustration of will; has emotions; changes his mind and, in short, exhibits predicates of dipolar theism's relative pole. Open theists even argue from scripture that God does not possess exhaustive divine foreknowledge inclusive of future contingent events.[280]

As conservative Protestants, open theists grant a place, although a fallible one, to tradition in theology and thus appeal to historical theology.[281] They admit that key aspects of their view do not appear until very late in the Christian tradition, but do point to a few historically who seem to have held to something like the open view.[282] From the baroque Catholic debates on grace and free will, they sometimes draw on Molinism but modify it to deny exhaustive divine foreknowledge that includes future contingencies.[283] Like process theologians, open theists often come from the Arminian-Wesleyan traditions that stress God's universal salvific will, libertarian human free will, and soteriological synergism. With impressive knowledge of both traditions they argue the Reformed-Calvinist tradition is scripturally, philosophically, and experientially unsound.

Open theists do take issue, however, with classical Arminian "simple foreknowledge." This view says that, although God does not in any way determine creatures' free choices, God does exhaustively know the future, including these genuinely contingent choices. With process theologians and as explained above, they argue that exhaustive divine foreknowledge and truly contingent free choices are incompatible. Open theists thus claim that simple foreknowledge undercuts the puissance of indeterminacy and libertarian freedom for Arminians. They also adduce support

280. See, for example, Pinnock et al., *The Openness of God,* 11–58; Sanders, *The God Who Risks,* 38–139; and Boyd, *God of the Possible,* 53–112, 157–69.

281. Pinnock et al., *The Openness of God,* 59–100; Sanders, *The God Who Risks,* 140–72.

282. They frequently cite Calcidius, the somewhat obscure fourth-century Christian philosopher who translated some of Plato into Latin, for support.

283. See, for example, Greg Boyd, "Neo-Molinism and the Infinite Intelligence of God" (2002) at http://www.gregboyd.org/essays/warning-egghead-essays/neomolonism-and-the-infinite-intelligence-of-god/; Sanders, *The God Who Risks,* 188 n. 39; and Richard Rice, "Divine Foreknowledge and Free-Will Theism," in *The Grace of God and the Will of Man,* ed. Clark H. Pinnock, 121–39 (Minneapolis: Bethany House, 1989), 124, 127.

from some nineteenth-century Arminian theologians, working independently of proto-process currents, who urged classical Arminianism's inconsistency in this regard.[284]

Open theists do believe reason and philosophy are necessary in theology, but try to avoid so heavy a reliance on them that they take precedence over the Bible. In fact, in debates with evangelical interlocutors they argue that the classical theism embraced by most evangelicals is the product of the synthesis of Greek philosophy and biblical faith, which is a bad, not a good, thing. They will similarly charge process theology with too heavy a reliance on philosophy, in this case modern instead of ancient Greek.[285]

At the same time, open theists acknowledge what they regard as strong points of process thought, and indicate how open theism coalesces philosophically and metaphysically with process theology.[286] Both open and process theism argue that classical theism is inconsistent, irrational, and an ultimately untenable position. Open theists admit process theism presents a viable alternative to classical theism in many ways. Process theology: (1) makes room for genuine contingency in creation, especially in the form of libertarian free will; (2) demonstrates metaphysically that God cannot possess exhaustive divine foreknowledge inclusive of future contingencies; (3) demonstrates that the future is partially settled and partially open; (4) argues that God's power is persuasive, not an infallibly efficacious monergism; and (5) addresses the problem of evil and suffering better than classical theism.[287] So, in addition to relying on scriptural proofs much open theistic argumentation is philosophical, in some cases directly borrowing directly from process thinkers.[288]

Perhaps the central way open theists revise classical theism is by saying the future is really "open."[289] This is because creatures, specifically free rational creatures, have libertarian free will incompatible with any

284. Early Methodist theologian, Adam Clarke, and the late-nineteenth-century Methodist theologian Lorenzo D. McCabe, are examples.

285. Pinnock et al., *The Openness of God*, 138–40, 140, 196 n. 27.

286. Greg Boyd's doctoral dissertation at Princeton was on Hartshorne, and has been published as *Trinity and Process: A Critical Evaluation and Reconstruction of Hartshorne's Di-polar Theism towards a Trinitarian Metaphysics* (New York: Peter Lang, 1992).

287. Pinnock et al., *The Openness of God*, 138–39; Boyd, *God of the Possible*, 32–33, 42–44.

288. Pinnock et al., *The Openness of God*, 126–54; Pinnock, *Most Moved Mover*, 113–51; Sanders, *The God Who Risks*, 173–248; Boyd, *God of the Possible*, 53–88.

289. This is where the "open" in "open theism" comes from.

kind of divine determination. Libertarian free will is crucial to preserve the real existence and activity of creatures vis-à-vis God, is necessary for true moral responsibility, and avoids God's being the ultimate source of evil, sin, and suffering.

Metaphysically for open theists actualities alone are knowable, so unrealized possibilities of the future that are genuinely contingent cannot be known. This means God knows only the past and present, because they are actual, not undetermined aspects of the future. God knows with certainty any future possibilities that will necessarily be actual due to deterministic causation of past and present actualities. God cannot know the contingent aspects of the future because they do not yet exist, and when they will exist as actual, it is not God who confers actuality upon them. Libertarian free will means rational free creatures help "create" the future with God as they confer actuality upon possibilities by determining them with their wills, and this is incompatible with the classical view that God simultaneously confers being, existence, or *esse* on these actualities.[290] With process metaphysics, then, open theists say that God's omniscience is knowing all that can be known, which excludes future contingencies. By knowing all that can be known exhaustively in the present God might have the best knowledge of what might *probably* happen in the future. Nevertheless, God cannot know this probability with absolute certainty. This is all very similar to the indeterministic view of actual entities in process metaphysics. A key difference, however, is that open theists typically limit this indeterminate freedom to free rational creatures like humans and spirits, but do not grant it to fundamental metaphysical units.

Open theists also argue that indeterminate, libertarian freedom is necessary to exculpate God from evil. If God exhaustively determines all choices and hence actualities, then God is responsible for what is lacking as privation in reality and for the evil choices of rational free creatures. Both process theists and open theists limit God's power but retain God's goodness in order to avoid the problem of evil and suffering for classical theism.[291]

290. Pinnock et al., *The Openness of God,* 16, 37–38, 56, 116, 117–18, 123, 133, 178; Boyd, *God of the Possible,* 16–17, 53–54, 58, 60–61, 63, 64, 65–66, 96, 97, 147; John E. Sanders, "God as Personal," in *The Grace of God and the Will of Man,* ed. Clark H. Pinnock, 165–80 (Minneapolis: Bethany House, 1989), 176, 178; Rice, "Divine Foreknowledge and Free-Will Theism," 130–31; and Greg Boyd, *Letters from a Skeptic: A Son Wrestles with His Father's Questions about Christianity* (Colorado Springs: Chariot Victor, 1994), 30.

291. By applying indeterminancy exhaustively to all of reality, process theologians also

Open theists also similarly make experiential arguments based on the practical situation of a religious believer.[292] Religion presupposes that what humans do matters to God, humans have relationships with God, and humans can even change God. Prayer is only an illusion if God is immutable and has foreordained everything. Believers in the God of classical theism are faced with the gruesome prospect that God is responsible for all of the suffering in the world, including their own. Open theists argue that believers in classical theism must in the final analysis admit they have no say in their ultimate destiny. The genuine human freedom of the open view, however, allows humans to make choices regarding where they would like to spend eternity.

Despite these important similarities there are key differences between process theology and open theism.[293] Open theists strongly maintain the doctrine of creation *ex nihilo,* that God does not need the world, and that creation was free. God's relationship to the world, which resembles the God-world relationship in process theology, was God's choice and is not a metaphysical necessity. Apparently in order to ultimately preserve what seems *dignum Deo* from a more classical perspective, open theists say God's current relationship to creation resulted from an act of divine "self-limitation."[294] So, in analyzing the evangelical open theist movement it is important to realize that while there are many similarities between open theism and process theology, there are some key differences.

---

have a ready response to the problem of natural evils. Because they are concerned chiefly with human freedom, open theists, although providing a satisfactory response for the problem of moral evil, still have difficulties explaining natural evil. Pinnock tries to avoid this by saying natural evils are the consequences of the moral evils of free rational creatures (Pinnock, *Most Moved Mover,* 46–47).

292. Pinnock et al., *The Openness of God,* 155–76; Pinnock, *Most Moved Mover,* 153–78; Sanders, *The God Who Risks,* 249–88; Boyd, *God of the Possible,* 89–112.

293. Pinnock et al., *The Openness of God,* 103–112, 133, 138, 180 n. 68; Boyd, *God of the Possible,* 147–49.

294. Pinnock et al., *The Openness of God,* 111–13, 133, 115, 117; Boyd, *God of the Possible,* 147–48. Metaphysically this seems similar to the Jewish kabbalistic doctrine of *zimsum,* in which God makes space for creatures, and which was appealed to by Jürgen Moltmann in his 1984 Gifford Lectures (*God in Creation,* 86–93). The logical distinction also bears very general similarities with the late medieval distinction between the "absolute power" and the "ordained power" of God *(potentia Dei absoluta et ordinata).*

Conclusion

Process thought undertakes the seemingly unavoidable project of metaphysics in light of the developments of modern philosophy and science. Whitehead did not appear in a vacuum, and any sound understanding of Whitehead's metaphysics requires some familiarity with the general trends of modernity informing his project, and the issues that occupied his immediate predecessors.

Process theology began with the work of a philosopher of religion, Charles Hartshorne, which served as a transition for Christian theologians to appropriate Whitehead's metaphysics. Beginning with the doctrine of God, process theologians reenvisioned every facet of Christian theology from within a process metaphysical framework. Process theologians present their theology as better meeting the challenges of modernity and the needs of contemporary humanity.

Process theology has influenced to various degrees theologians who would probably not identify themselves as process theologians. Even evangelical Protestant theology, sometimes viewed as self-consciously removed from the rest of the theological world, has opened its doors to insights from process theology in the evangelical open theism movement.

Having surveyed the predecessors, aspects, and importance of process metaphysics in this first chapter, we now turn our attention to perhaps the most important Catholic process thinker, Joseph A. Bracken, S.J.

CHAPTER 2

The Philosophical Process Theology of Joseph A. Bracken

Joseph A. Bracken, S.J., is a process thinker of unique importance. As one of the few process theologians working from within the Catholic tradition, Bracken has produced an unparalleled synthesis of the Catholic tradition and modern process metaphysics. In doing so, he is a living exemplar of how historically the best Catholic philosophers and theologians have seriously engaged the intellectual currents of their day. Bracken is important for Catholics thinkers because he makes a well-informed case that process metaphysics must not be rashly dismissed but seriously considered as a necessary rethinking of metaphysics in our day.

Bracken is also important for process thinkers because, by drawing not only on the great Catholic tradition but also on a litany of non-process theological and philosophical sources, he makes informed and nuanced modifications to process metaphysics in order to address some of its inherent difficulties. He argues that certain strands latent in Whitehead must be developed in order to take process metaphysics to its logical and consistent conclusions. By doing so, process thought can overcome some challenges it faces and even better fulfill the goals of its original project. Also, if those using more traditional metaphysics too rashly dismiss process metaphysics, process thinkers frequently dismiss classical metaphysics too quickly. Like Leibniz before him, Bracken argues there is still much truth and goodness in aspects of classical metaphysics to be used by modern philosophy and theology, even if these must appropriated in a revisionist way.[1]

Bracken is of importance for Christian process theologians specifically

1. "I have long meditated upon the modern philosophy . . . these studies made me recognize that our moderns do not give enough credit to Saint Thomas and to the other great men of his time and that there is much more solidity than one imagines in the opinions of

because he is very much concerned with thinking through the specifics of traditional Christian systematic theology in process categories. Handling virtually every locus of systematic theology at some point, Bracken produces perhaps the most thoroughgoing combination of classical trinitarianism and process metaphysics. As a *Christian* process theologian he, like Barth before him, wants to make the Trinity the starting point of theology. Accomplishing this from within a process metaphysical framework is no mean task. This attempt alone merits sustained and careful attention.

Compared with contemporary process thinkers, Bracken perhaps spends the most time addressing the problem of the one and the many. His system is intrinsically bound up with both the problem and various solutions. His solutions involve both common process attempts to resolve the problem as well his own unique contributions.

This chapter, then, examines in some detail Bracken's philosophical process theology. In doing so it tries to show how Bracken uses his manifold sources, process, traditional, and other, noting key similarities and key differences.

Analogical Predication and Models in Bracken's Theology

Bracken sees metaphysical and theological systems as analogical models, not privileged univocal descriptions of the objective realities they describe. Embracing Whitehead's axiom that "God is not to be treated as an exception to all metaphysical principles, invoked to save their collapse. He is their chief exemplification," Bracken also retains aspects of Thomistic analogical predication.[2] He describes metaphysical language as inevitably metaphorical and analogical.[3]

---

the Scholastic philosophers and theologians, provided that they are used appropriately and in their proper place" (G. W. Leibniz, *Discourse on Metaphysics*, 11).

2. See Joseph A. Bracken, *The One in the Many: A Contemporary Reconstruction of the God-World Relationship* (Grand Rapids, Mich.: Eerdmans, 2001), 42 n. 80; and Bracken, "Images of God within Systematic Theology," *Theological Studies* 63, no. 2 (June 2002): 362, where he quotes this axiom in agreement with Whitehead. He also agrees with Whitehead's criticism of the Cappadocian Fathers for not applying the same metaphysical categories to both God and the world. See in Bracken, *The One in the Many*, 184; Bracken, *God: Three Who Are One* (Collegeville, Minn.: Liturgical Press, 2008), 24; Bracken, "Trinity: Economic and Immanent," *Horizons* 25 (Spring 1998): 13, 13 n. 13. See also Bracken, *The One in the Many*, 204; and Bracken, review of *The History of the Triune God: Contributions to Trinitarian Theology*, by Jürgen Moltmann, *Theological Studies* 53 (December 1992): 766.

3. Bracken, *The One in the Many*, 165; Bracken, *Christianity and Process Thought: Spiri-*

Yet his understanding of analogies and models differs somewhat from traditional understandings. He does not entirely rule out apophaticism, yet he transfers analogical predication from statements about God to entire metaphysical systems.[4] St. Thomas knew that any concept of God is analogical but did not take the further step of seeing his entire system as an analogical model.[5] Entire metaphysical systems are analogical models.

According to Whitehead's axiom, however, individual concepts in a metaphysical system must be predicated univocally to God and other entities.[6] This does not mean the system's categories are univocal with God objectively, but that categories apply to God and all other elements univocally within the system. In this regard he says there is an essential univocal aspect to being when predicated to both God and to creatures.[7]

Bracken's emphasis on how entire systems are analogical while the terms within those systems are univocal has led him to embrace a models approach to systematic theology, which borrows from contemporary philosophy of science.[8] Theology becomes counterproductive if its limits as an extended metaphor of the God-world relationship are not recognized.[9] Even Whitehead did not see his metaphysics as a bare description of the way "things are," but as an extended metaphor or model for understanding reality in terms of human subjectivity.[10]

---

tuality for a Changing World (Philadelphia: Templeton Foundation Press, 2006), 3–5, 11, 104, 138.

4. Bracken, "Images of God," 363.

5. Ibid., 363–64.

6. See Bracken, *The One in the Many,* 204, 204 n. 87; Bracken, "Images of God," 363; Bracken, "Trinity: Economic and Immanent," 13.

7. Joseph A. Bracken, "Response to Elizabeth Johnson's 'Does God Play Dice?'" *Theological Studies* 57 (December 1996): 721–22. See also Bracken, "The Theology of God of Elizabeth A. Johnson," in *Things New and Old: Essays on the Theology of Elizabeth A. Johnson,* ed. Phyllis Zagano and Terrence W. Tilley, 21–38 (New York: Crossroad, 1999): 25–27.

8. Joseph A. Bracken, review of *God for Us: The Trinity and Christian Life,* by Catherine Mowry LaCugna, *Theological Studies* 53 (September 1992): 558.

9. Bracken, "Images of God," 373. Cf. Bracken, *God: Three Who Are One,* 105.

10. See Joseph A. Bracken, *Society and Spirit: A Trinitarian Cosmology* (London: Associated University Press; Selinsgrove, Pa.: Susquehanna University Press, 1991), 33–34. See Alfred North Whitehead, *Process and Reality: An Essay in Cosmology,* corrected ed., ed. David Ray Griffin and Donald W. Sherburne (New York: Free Press, 1978; originally published Macmillan, 1929), 343 (p. 522 in the 1929 edition), 4. All subsequent references to this work will reference the pagination in the corrected 1978 edition, followed by the page references in the original 1929 edition in parentheses. See also Bracken, *The One in the Many,* 204 n. 87.

With Barbour and echoing Niebuhr, Bracken says models "should be taken seriously but not literally."[11] This "critical realism" differs from "classical realism" and "instrumentalism." Classical realism is the "mirror of nature" approach, seeing theories as literal descriptions. Instrumentalism uses models to merely correlate and predicate observations within experience. Critical realism "claims that there are entities in the world something like those postulated in models," and is a dominant view in philosophy of science.[12] Because of the veritable ontological claims made by models, some models are really better than others.[13] Critical realism realizes the provisional nature of knowledge but believes any model gains credibility in a scholarly community as it reflects the reality it seeks to understand.[14]

Sources of Bracken's Philosophical Theology

Bracken represents a complex mix of different systems, but Whiteheadian and Thomistic metaphysics are his primary sources. He speaks of his model for the God-world relationship as a "conscious blend" of, and "midway between the basic presuppositions of," classical Thomism and Whitehead's process-relational metaphysics.[15]

11. Niebuhr was speaking of scripture, but Barbour is speaking of entire models. See Reinhold Niebuhr, *The Nature and Destiny of Man,* 2 vols. (New York: Scribner's, 1941–43), 50, 289; and Reinhold Niebuhr, *Faith and History: A Comparison of Christian and Modern Views of History* (New York: Scribner's, 1949), 237. See Ian G. Barbour, *Religion and Science: Historical and Contemporary Issues* (San Francisco: Harper, 1997), 117, quoted in Bracken, *The One in the Many,* 37 n. 63; Bracken, *Christianity and Process Thought,* 5; and Ian G. Barbour, *Myths, Models, and Paradigms: A Comparative Study in Science and Religion* (New York: Harper & Row, 1974), 47–48, cited in Bracken, "The Theology of God of Elizabeth A. Johnson," 25. See also Bracken, *Society and Spirit,* 33; Bracken, *The Divine Matrix: Creativity as Link Between East and West* (Maryknoll, N.Y.: Orbis, 1995), 5; Bracken, "Trinity: Economic and Immanent," 10; Bracken, "Images of God," 364; Bracken, "Non-Duality and the Concept of Ultimate Reality," *Ultimate Reality and Meaning* 19 (1996): 145; Bracken, review of *God For Us,* 558. At points he says that "seriously but not literally" means that models are only symbolic representations of reality, and not pictures or photographs of ultimate reality. See Bracken, *The Divine Matrix,* 4–5; Bracken, "Non-Duality," 145–46.

12. Barbour, *Religion and Science,* 117, cited in Bracken, "Images of God," 365.

13. See Bracken, *Christianity and Process Thought,* 4; Bracken, "Images of God," 365, 373; Bracken, review of *God For Us,* 559.

14. Bracken, "Trinity: Economic and Immanent," 10.

15. Joseph A. Bracken, "Subsistent Relation: Mediating Concept for a New Synthesis?" *Journal of Religion* 64 (April 1984): 199; and Bracken, "Toward a New Philosophical The-

Similarities between Bracken and Whitehead

Bracken vigorously strives to be faithful to Whitehead even when proposing interpretations that vary from standard commentaries. His system is essentially Whiteheadian except for the conscious modifications discussed in the next section.

Bracken strongly embraces Whitehead's "reformed subjectivist" and "ontological" principles.[16] Except for minor revisions in the nature, concrescence, and prehensions of actual entities, Bracken's descriptions of these are identical to Whitehead's.[17] Modernity's turn to the subject was indeed a "halfway house" because it did not apply subjectivity to *all* of reality. Subjectivity grounds objectivity, so ontology must be grounded in the experience of subjects.[18]

Idealism thus became a key source for Bracken. Schelling provided him an entrée into process thought, and Royce's social ontology and intersubjective epistemology later proved useful.[19]

Both Schelling and Whitehead make human subjectivity the starting point for metaphysics.[20] Schelling also paved the way for a more dynamic

---

ology Based on Intersubjectivity," *Theological Studies* 59 (1998): 704 n. 2. See also Bracken, "Response to Elizabeth Johnson's 'Does God Play Dice?'" 725; and Bracken, review of *Omnipotence and Other Theological Mistakes,* by Charles A. Hartshorne, *Horizons* 12 (Spring 1985): 181.

16. Joseph A. Bracken, "The Two Process Theologies: A Reappraisal," *Theological Studies* 46 (1985): 122–24.

17. See, for instance, Joseph A. Bracken, *The Triune Symbol. Persons, Process and Community* (Lanham, Md.: University Press of America, 1985), 39–42, 63; and 7, 15–16, 66, 74, 105–6. See chapter 1 for a detailed discussion of Whitehead's "reformed subjectivist principle."

18. Joseph A. Bracken, "Essential and Existential Truth," *Philosophy Today* 23 (Spring 1984): 72. See also Bracken, "The Two Process Theologies," 123; Bracken, *The Triune Symbol,* 2–3, 12 n. 5; Bracken, *Society and Spirit,* 32–33; Bracken, *Christianity and Process Thought,* 7, 15–16, 66, 71, 74, 105–6; Bracken, *God: Three Who Are One,* 63.

19. See Bracken's work on divine and human freedom in Schelling: *Freiheit und Kausalität bei. Schelling Symposion; philosophische Schriftenreihe,* 38 (Freiburg i. Br.: Alber Verlag, 1972). Bracken discussed these topics in an interview with me on November 22, 2003, in Atlanta at the annual meeting of the American Academy of Religion/Society of Biblical Literature.

20. "The reflections of Schelling on the nature of human subjectivity illuminate Whitehead's notion of an actual occasion as a self-constituting subject of experience" (Bracken, *Society and Spirit,* 14).

understanding of being when he understood human subjectivity as primarily activity *(ein Tun)* rather than a substantial agent *(ein Tätiges)*. Following Fichte, Schelling went beyond Kant by making the subject's freedom in determining the categories of its experience determinative of the objects of its experience, which become exclusively the products of the synthesizing activity of the transcendental human ego. Subjects are not passive recipients of objectivity but active subjects creating their own knowledge and experiences. This is a more dynamic understanding of beings as the objects of experience.[21]

Bracken thus concludes with Whitehead that the only source of being is the experiencing subject. The numerous infinitesimal subjects of experience, or actual entities, are the only real beings that exist. Further, since only the actual is real and therefore of consequence, only the actual can be a "reason" or "cause." Actual entities are the only real reasons for, or causes of, anything. Everything must be "somewhere," or reduced to an actual entity. Even the general potentiality actual entities use in their concrescence must be "located" in an actual entity, which is God. Thus agreeing with the ontological principle, Bracken tries to locate *all* explanatory reasons, facts, and causes in actual existents, never in mental or spiritual abstractions or ideas.[22]

For Bracken as for Whitehead process or becoming is ultimate reality. The ultimate metaphysical principle is the creative advance into novelty. Creativity, or process, replaces the primary category of substance. Creativity or the "principle of novelty" is the "universal of universals" and thus the ultimate metaphysical principle.

Bracken's reading of Schelling proved a ready resource here. For Schelling everything is transient, perpetually perishing and reproduced anew from moment to moment so that to the human senses there is only an *appearance* of permanence. This parallels the perpetual coming to be and perishing of actual entities. For Schelling, nature fundamentally considered is unified in the constant that everything is pure unending activity. Nature then divides itself into opposing forces whose synthesis and

21. Ibid., 27.

22. Bracken, *The Divine Matrix*, 59, 67, 110; Bracken, *Christianity and Process Thought*, 66, 74; and Bracken, "Revising Process Metaphysics in Response to Ian Barbour's Critique," *Zygon* 33 (September 1998): 411. For a discussion of Whitehead's "ontological principle," see the first chapter.

reunification at various levels constitutes the world of natural entities. Thus the process is an *undifferentiated unity,* out of which arises a *duality,* which then forms a *differentiated unity.*[23] Bracken likens the mixture of physical and conceptual prehensions in the actual entity to the dynamic principle of balance *(Gleichgewichtsprinzip)* in Schelling; in both the dialectical duality is overcome in a higher synthesis.[24]

Every metaphysician is concerned with understanding either "why things change" or "why they remain basically the same."[25] Like Whitehead, Bracken criticizes substance ontology and prioritizes becoming, creativity, and novelty.[26] Quoting the axiom *agere sequitur esse,* he notes how, for Aristotle, Aquinas, and much Western thought, "things" or essences are prior to processes. Bracken proposes that *esse sequitur agere,* thus positing process or activity, not substance, as the first category of being.[27] Only interrelated processes ultimately exist. Event ontology must replace substance ontology.[28]

While classical metaphysics made static being ultimately real, process thinkers reverse this priority by making "becoming" ultimately real and being just "any given moment" in the overall process of becoming. One could argue that in Aristotelian and Thomistic philosophy substance is

23. Bracken, *Society and Spirit,* 28. The dialectic of thesis, antithesis, and synthesis originated with Fichte, Schelling's teacher, not Hegel.

24. Bracken, *Society and Spirit,* 100. He also compares physical prehensions to Schelling's "will of the Ground." Both represent raw feelings in need of being shaped and ordered prior to the moment of decision by Whitehead's conceptual prehensions, or by Schelling's rational will. He does warn, however, against overdrawing the similarities between Schelling and Whitehead.

25. Bracken, *The One in the Many,* 180.

26. Bracken, *The Triune Symbol,* 5, 16, 20, 32 n. 1; Bracken, *The Divine Matrix,* 11; Bracken, *Society and Spirit,* 22, 32; Bracken, *The One in the Many,* 180; Bracken, *Christianity and Process Thought,* 23; Bracken, *God: Three Who Are One,* 73–74, 83–85; Bracken, "Images of God," 368; Bracken, "Trinity: Economic and Immanent," 7–9; and Bracken, "Process Philosophy and Trinitarian Theology," *Process Studies* 8 (Winter 1978): 222–23.

27. Bracken, *The Divine Matrix,* 11, 143 n. 4. See also, Bracken, *The Triune Symbol,* 5, 20; Bracken, "Trinity: Economic and Immanent," 17; Bracken, *The One in the Many,* 25; Bracken, *God: Three Who Are One,* 84.

28. Joseph A. Bracken, review of *The Reality of Time and the Existence of God: The Project of Proving God's Existence,* by David Braine, *Theological Studies* 50 (March 1989): 175–76; Bracken, *The Triune Symbol,* 20–21, 41, 133 n. 25; Bracken, *God: Three Who Are One,* 76, 85–86; Bracken, "Energy Events and Fields," *Process Studies* 18 (Fall 1989): 153. Cf. Whitehead, *Process and Reality,* 18 (27).

subordinate to essence, and essence is processive because it has dynamism to achieve the end for which it exists. Bracken says Whitehead's philosophy better grounds ontology in process because new entities and combinations of actual entities emerge afresh each moment. Likewise, unity must not be grounded in substance but rather in the process. Because actual entities come and go while creativity never ceases, creativity is ultimate reality and primary substance.[29]

Bracken goes on to compare the underlying ontological activity out of which actual entities arise to Spinoza's single, infinite "substance," insofar as it is that which produces all things in the world through the power of its own nature or essence.[30] Yet he makes the important distinction that for Whitehead this ontological activity is not "that which exists," or the one enduring ontological reality in the world, as it is for Spinoza. Instead, it is a "general activity" that is individualized and comes into being in the process of self-constitution for every actual occasion coming to be. So this activity is a "substantial activity," but only in and through the entities or occasions that it empowers to exist.[31]

To address postmodern anti-metaphysicalism Bracken uses the process values of intersubjectivity, otherness, contrast, and difference (alterity), positive values in postmodern thought. The actual entity's concrescence is an intersubjective affair where negative prehensions introduce difference and contrast. Metaphysics is an unavoidable project, but Whitehead makes otherness, contrast, and difference metaphysically essential.[32]

For Bracken and Whiteheadian metaphysics, radical freedom is at the heart of reality. As he embraced subjectivity as metaphysics' starting point, Bracken increased his awareness of freedom and contingency by studying Schelling: "The alpha and omega of all philosophy is—free-

29. Bracken, *The Triune Symbol,* 32 n. 1; Bracken, *Christianity and Process Thought,* 80; Bracken, "Essential and Existential Truth," 72. Joseph A. Bracken, "Philosophical Foundations of Human Rights: A Process Approach," *Cogito* 1, no. 1 (March 1983): 69; Bracken, "Process Philosophy and Trinitarian Theology," 222–23. Joseph A. Bracken, "Creativity and the Extensive Continuum as the Ultimate Ground in Alfred North Whitehead's Philosophy of Becoming," *Ultimate Reality and Meaning* 16 (March–June 1993): 112.

30. Bracken, "Creativity," 111. Bracken cites Spinoza, *The Ethics*, prop. XIV–XVII.

31. Bracken, *The Divine Matrix*, 52; Bracken, "Creativity," 111, 114.

32. Bracken, *The One in the Many,* 73–74. Cf. Bracken, *God: Three Who Are One,* 72, 120–21.

dom!"[33] A central concern of both Schelling and process thinkers is freedom as its own ground, generating being. Freedom is not grounded in an antecedent being. For both Whitehead and Schelling human subjectivity is not grounded in God as First Cause of every existent. Rather, it is grounded in its own power of radical self-constitution.[34]

Reading Schelling, Heidegger, and Wolfgang Wieland, Bracken concludes that human selfhood is grounded in decision. There is not first a substantial individual that then makes a decision. The individual becomes a subject precisely through making the decision. Wieland and Whitehead thus avoid what Heidegger calls *Willensmetaphysik*. For both, an entity is not the substrate for decision; rather the entity exists as a subject only in virtue of the decision-making process.[35]

The idea that radical freedom, contingency, and indeterminacy are prior to and the ground of being, not vice versa, is essential to existentialism as well. Heidegger said Schelling captured being quintessentially when he said there is no other being than willing, or being is will.[36] The middle and later Schelling focused on will and decision, rather than mind and thinking, as the implicit paradigm for interpreting reality.[37] Schelling went even further than Fichte by characterizing the fundamental reality of nature or objective being as pure activity, not just limiting this to the fundamental reality of the transcendental ego.

Bracken's Modifications of Actual Entities

Bracken does depart in some ways from those who appropriate Whitehead more strictly. Although pervasively influenced by Whitehead, Bracken self-consciously extends Whitehead in new directions. These are compatible with Whitehead's philosophy although Whitehead never envisioned them. Thus Bracken uses words like "modified," "revised," "neo-

33. F. W. J. Schelling, "Letter to Hegel, February 4, 1795," in *Sämtliche Werke,* 14 vols., ed. K. F. A. Schelling (Stuttgart, 1856), 1:177, quoted in Bracken "Freedom and Causality in the Philosophy of Schelling," *New Scholasticism* 50 (Spring 1976): 164. See also, Bracken, *The Triune Symbol,* 62.

34. Bracken, *Society and Spirit,* 101.

35. Ibid., 99–100, citing Wolfgang Wieland, *Schellings Lehre von der Zeit* (Heidelberg: Winter Verlag, 1956), 42.

36. Martin Heidegger, "Who Is Nietzsche's Zarathustra?" in *Nietzsche,* ed. and trans. David Farrell Krell, 211–32 (San Francisco: HarperCollins, 1991), 222.

37. Joseph A. Bracken, review of *Bruno or On the Natural and the Divine Principle of Things,* by Friedrich von Schelling, *Process Studies* 15, no. 1 (Spring 1986): 70.

Whiteheadian," and "unorthodox" in reference to his own metaphysics.[38] According to Bracken, standard interpretations of concrescence, "societies," and the God-world relationship need revision. Bracken also differs from most orthodox Whiteheadians by advocating a trinitarian understanding of God and the God-world relationship.

Mostly agreeing with Whitehead, Bracken slightly modifies the concrescence and destiny of actual entities. One difference is the claim that actual entities in concomitant concrescence influence each other. As discussed in the first chapter, for Whitehead, actual entities can prehend only past actual entities. Agreeing with Jorge Nobo, Bracken argues that the "extensive continuum" allows contemporary actual entities to influence each other as "they anticipate one another's place within the extensive continuum and thereby one another's concrete actualization as this or that physical reality here and now."[39] In addition to the common world of their predecessors and their interrelatedness in societies, actual entities may indirectly feel other entities in concrescence as members of a common emerging world.[40] Since societies alone endure, a society's common element of form is a medium through which contemporary actual entities simultaneously in concrescence can influence each other.[41] Bracken believes that Leclerc objects to Whiteheadian societies because

38. Bracken, *The Triune Symbol,* 6; Bracken, *The One in the Many,* 157, 165; Bracken, "Trinity: Economic and Immanent," 16; Bracken, "Supervenience: Two Proposals / Supervenience and Basic Christian Beliefs," *Zygon* 36 (2001): 143–44; Bracken, "Testimony and Intersubjectivity: A Process-oriented Approach to Revelation," *Philosophy and Theology* 2 (Fall 1987): 39; Bracken, "The Issue of Panentheism in the Dialogue with the Non-believer," *Studies in Religion/Sciences-religieuses* 21, no. 2 (1992): 217; Bracken, "Intersubjectivity and the Coming of God," *Journal of Religion* 83, no. 3 (July 2003): 388, 396, 398 n. 44; 399 n. 45; Bracken, review of *The Three-Personed God: The Trinity as a Mystery of Salvation,* by William J. Hill, *Journal of Religion* 65 (July 1985): 427; Bracken, "Panentheism from a Trinitarian Perspective," *Horizons* 22 (Spring 1995): 14; Bracken, "*Ipsum Esse Subsistens:* A Subsistent Being or Subsistent Activity? A Search for URAM in Systematic Theology," *Ultimate Reality and Meaning* 14 (December 1991): 290; Bracken, "Philosophical Foundations," 56, 58, 66; Bracken, "Response to Elizabeth Johnson's 'Does God Play Dice?'" 729; Bracken, "Intersubjectivity," 392; and Bracken, "Revising Process Metaphysics," 405–6, 413; Bracken, *The One in the Many,* 149 n. 45, 167.

39. Bracken, *The One in the Many,* 122.

40. Joseph A. Bracken, "Spirit and Society: A Study of Two Concepts," *Process Studies* 15 (Winter 1986): 249, 255 n. 2.

41. Joseph A. Bracken, "Substance—Society—Natural System: A Creative Rethinking of Whitehead's Cosmology," *International Philosophical Quarterly* 25 (1985): 7; Bracken, "Intersubjectivity and the Coming of God," 389.

contemporary actual entities cannot causally influence one another.[42]

Bracken also differs from Whitehead on subjective immortality. Whitehead held only to the objective immortality of actual entities, not their subjective immortality. With Marjorie Hewitt Suchocki and contra Whitehead and Hartshorne, Bracken maintains the subjective immortality of actual entities.[43] The concern for subjective immortality is, for Bracken and Suchocki, of a piece with the Christian doctrine of the subjective immortality of human persons beyond death.[44]

Suchocki modifies Whitehead's categoreal scheme to allow actual occasions to enjoy subjective immortality in God's consequent nature.[45] She posits a *tertium quid* for the actual entity between its subjective and superjective phases called "enjoyment," in which an occasion is both a determinate actuality able to be prehended by God, and yet a subject of experience "enjoying" the fulfillment of its subjective aim. This means God prehends actual occasions in their full subjectivity when they are superject, not merely objectively. If God prehends an entity when it is subject and superject, and in its entirety with no negative prehensions, then God prehends it in its subjective immediacy and preserves it as such in God's consequent nature.

Bracken accepts Suchocki's revision of Whitehead's categoreal scheme, paralleling it with how the successive actual occasions of human consciousness prehend their predecessors.[46] Because "materiality" is only the

42. Bracken, "Substance—Society—Natural System," 6–7

43. See, Bracken, *The One in the Many,* 157–78; Bracken, *Christianity and Process Thought,* 108–9; Bracken, *God: Three Who Are One,* 119, 125; Bracken, "Supervenience," 149; Bracken, review of *Omnipotence and Other Theological Mistakes,* 181.

44. Marjorie Hewitt Suchocki, *The End of Evil: Process Eschatology in Historical Context* (Albany: State University of New York Press, 1988), 81–82; Bracken, "Intersubjectivity," 396; Bracken, *Society and Spirit,* 143–44.

45. Suchocki, *The End of Evil,* 88, 92–114.

46. See Bracken, *Society and Spirit,* 141; Bracken, *The Divine Matrix,* 64–65. He cites Whitehead, *Process and Reality,* 161 (244), and combines this with Cobb's view that the present occasions constitutive of human temporal consciousness identify the mental poles of their predecessors with their own previous experiences. (John B. Cobb Jr., *A Christian Natural Theology* [Philadelphia: Westminster Press, 1965], 74–79, cited in Bracken, *Society and Spirit,* 179 n. 2). See also Bracken, *The One in the Many,* 175–76; Bracken, "Supervenience," 149–50; Bracken, *The Divine Matrix,* 64–65, 66; Bracken, "Proposals for Overcoming the Atomism within Process-Relational Metaphysics," *Process Studies* 23 (Spring 1994): 18; Bracken, "Intersubjectivity," 396–98.

way later occasions prehend earlier ones, subjective immortality does not mean finite actual occasions endure materially, or physically occupy space and time.[47] For individual eschatology this means that the complex structured field of activity a person has constructed over a lifetime, not his or her soul and body, objectively endures in God.[48]

Bracken's Modification of "Societies"

A central, if not *the* central, modification Bracken makes to Whitehead's metaphysics is his reconstruction of the Whiteheadian "society." Bracken believes Whitehead does not adequately address the problem of continuity despite discreteness, even with nexūs and societies. Whitehead's implicit atomism is an obstacle to the fully articulated social ontology for which Whitehead aimed.[49] His focus in *Process and Reality* on actual entities prevented Whitehead from developing societies as self-perpetuating aggregates of actual entities. Since Whitehead could not return to substance without undermining his whole system, he conceived societies as aggregates of actual occasions. But since the entire membership of these aggregates is changing there is no principle of continuity.[50] Also, the non-contiguous nature of successive actual entities must be reconciled with the basic assumption that nothing exists in isolation.[51]

Bracken claims his revised view of societies: (1) appeals to trinitarian Whiteheadians; (2) allows for a societal interpretation of reality deeper than Whitehead envisioned; and (3) offers a better solution to the prob-

47. Bracken, *Society and Spirit,* 141. As do all actual occasions, however, these occasions can still be prehended in terms of their "objectifications" in God's consequent nature, and therefore, in a sense, do not lose "materiality" altogether.

48. See, Bracken, *Society and Spirit,* 147; Bracken, *The One in the Many,* 175–77; Bracken, *Christianity and Process Thought,* 108–9; Bracken, *God: Three Who Are One,* 118–20, 125; Bracken, "Supervenience," 149–50; Bracken, "Intersubjectivity," 397, 398 n. 43; and Bracken, "Prehending God in and through the World," *Process Studies* 29 (2000): 8. Cf. Suchocki, *The End of Evil,* 81–96.

49. See Joseph A. Bracken, *What Are They Saying about the Trinity?* (New York: Paulist Press, 1979), 82–83; Bracken, *The Triune Symbol,* 20; Bracken, *Society and Spirit,* 48–49; Bracken, *The Divine Matrix,* 151–52 n. 8; Bracken, *The One in the Many,* 98–99, 132–33; Bracken, *Christianity and Process Thought,* 106; Bracken, "Proposals for Overcoming the Atomism," 10; Bracken, "The Two Process Theologies," 126.

50. Bracken, "Prehending God," 12 n. 3; Bracken, *God: Three Who Are One,* 66–67, 113–14.

51. Bracken, *The One in the Many,* 153–54. Bracken cites Whitehead, *Process and Reality,* 28 (42).

lem of the one and the many.[52] Bracken's social understanding roots fundamental theology in social processes rather than substances and corresponds better to humanity's social nature, salvation's communal nature, and God as a society of divine persons.[53]

Bracken attributes to societies a greater ontological reality and a quasi-independent agency akin to the agency of actual entities.[54] This would seem to violate Whitehead's ontological principle that actual entities are the only reasons. Yet this objection does not adequately account for how Whitehead: calls nexūs "real, individual, and particular"; says they are as "factual" as actual entities; refers to them as "public matters of fact"; says they each correspond to a "complex" eternal object; and says that along with superject entities, propositions, and eternal objects, nexūs are also objects for the prehensions of new actual entities. In these ways Bracken's argument that societies hold a greater ontological place for Whitehead than is often assumed is based on what Whitehead says about nexūs, of which societies are a type.

Societies as "Structured Fields of Activity"

Thus Bracken reconciles the discontinuity of successive generations of actual occasions with Whitehead's assumption that everything in the universe is connected by saying a society is not just an aggregate of loosely connected occasions but an enduring structured field of activity for those occasions.[55] Using Hocking, Bracken says the raison d'être of a society's individuals is bigger than the individuals themselves.[56] Hocking suggests that in addition to singular entities in nature there are "fields" giving individual entities unity and interrelatedness. Fields never exist abstractly in separation from their member entities, but they do possess their own reality distinguishable from nothingness. Fields themselves exist to some degree as "complex" entities.[57]

52. Joseph A. Bracken, "Process Philosophy and Trinitarian Theology—II," *Process Studies* 11 (Summer 1981): 93.

53. Bracken, *The Triune Symbol,* 6.

54. Bracken, *Society and Spirit,* 14.

55. Bracken, *The One in the Many,* 154; Bracken, *Christianity and Process Thought,* 106.

56. Bracken, *The Triune Symbol,* 5, 12 n. 13.

57. William Ernest Hocking, "Fact, Field, and Destiny: Inductive Elements of Metaphysics," *The Review of Metaphysics* 11 (1957–58): 531–34, cited in Bracken, *The Triune Symbol,* 13 n. 14.

Applying field-theory, Bracken says: "The ultimate constituents of material reality are Whiteheadian actual occasions, momentary subjects of experience, or, in the language of natural science, localized energy-events that objectify themselves to their successors as wave-patterns of energy within a common field of activity."[58] Societies are environments or contexts for their member actual entities, providing an ongoing "form" or pattern characterizing the society as such, and transmitting this principle of continuity from one generation of occasions to the next. Human societies are analogues for a continuing field: the community preserves the community's basic historical character and identity while the members come and go over time.[59]

Whiteheadian societies, accordingly, are "structured environments or unified fields of activity for the emergence of successive generations of actual entities."[60] The absence of the word "field" in the Whiteheadian corpus does not preclude societies from being equivalent to what others have dubbed "energy fields."[61] Comparing Hegel and process philosophy, he sees Hegel's "objective Spirit" as Whitehead's "structured field of activity" or society.[62]

58. Bracken, *Society and Spirit,* 58.

59. Ibid, 44, 70; Bracken, *Christianity and Process Thought,* 9.

60. Joseph A. Bracken, "The World or Field of Cosmic Activity?" in *Charles Hartshorne's Concept of God,* ed. Santiago Sia, 89–102 (Dordrecht, Netherlands: Kluwer Academic Publishers, 1990), 91, 93–94. See also, Bracken, *Society and Spirit,* 55, 58, 61–63, 68–69, 129, 149; Bracken, *The Divine Matrix,* 52–69; Bracken, *The One in the Many,* 147, 148–50, 167; Bracken, *Christianity and Process Thought,* 17, 57–58, 107; Bracken, *God: Three Who Are One,* 66–67, 77–78; Bracken, "Trinity: Economic and Immanent," 15 n. 15; Bracken, "Ecclesiology and the Problem of the One and the Many," *Theological Studies* 43 (June 1982): 306; Bracken, "Prehending God," 6; Bracken, "Proposals for Overcoming the Atomism," 11, 19–20; Bracken, "Supervenience," 143–44; Bracken, "The Issue of Panentheism," 213; Bracken, "Images of God," 369; Bracken, "Intersubjectivity," 390; Bracken, "Revising Process Metaphysics," 407, 408; Bracken, "Toward a New Philosophical Theology," 718, 718 n. 55; Bracken, "Energy Events and Fields," 154; and Bracken, "Panentheism from a Process Perspective," in *Trinity in Process: A Relational Theology of God,* ed. Joseph A. Bracken, S.J., and Marjorie Hewitt Suchocki, 95–113 (New York: Continuum, 1997), 99.

61. He references Whitehead, *Process and Reality,* 80 (123), where Whitehead refers to the extensive continuum as the "physical field." He also cites various places in ibid., 89–92 (137–42), 103 (157), in an attempt to show the similarities between societies and fields. See, Bracken, *Society and Spirit,* 44–45, Bracken, *The Divine Matrix,* 62; Bracken, "Energy Events and Fields," 153–54; Bracken, "Proposals for Overcoming the Atomism," 11.

62. Bracken, *Society and Spirit,* 105–9, 123. He says the Hegelian *Begriff* or "concept" is equivalent to the Whiteheadian concept of a "society," and governs both Hegel's and White

One reason to view a society as a field and not merely an aggregate of actual entities with a common form is that a field, unlike an aggregate, endures over time with successive generations of actual entities but aggregates disappear with their members.[63] Another reason is that the new physics Whitehead drew upon sees entities as activities, not merely spatiotemporal coordinates. Allowing Whiteheadians to retain the emphasis on an ultimate event-ontology by speaking of actual occasions as indeed "occasions," or events in a given environment of activity, field-theory better explains perduring compound entities and organisms than more common discussions of Whiteheadian societies.[64]

For theology, seeing Whiteheadian societies as unified fields of activity makes clear: (1) how the three divine persons by their intentional relations co-constitute the ultimate field of their activity, or their reality as one God; (2) how creation is a very large but still finite field of activity subsumed within the larger society of God; and (3) how Jesus' human and divine consciousnesses interpenetrate so that they co-constitute the unified field of activity of his single person.[65] Viewing the problems of the mind-body and God-world relationships as vestiges of classical metaphysics, Bracken advances this field-oriented understanding of Whiteheadian societies as a possible way to overcome these problems.[66]

"Creativity" and "Form" in Societies

If societies are also energy fields then they not only give structure to successive generations of entities but also transmit creativity, the poten-

head's organismic view of reality. This "concept" or "society" means that each of the member actual entities is both itself and the greater reality of the society at the same time, since its own internal constitution includes the common element of form defining and constituting the society as a whole (Bracken, "Ecclesiology," 303).

63. Bracken, *The One in the Many,* 148; Bracken, *Christianity and Process Thought,* 106–7; Bracken, *God: Three Who Are One,* 66–67; Bracken, "Revising Process Metaphysics," 408; Bracken, "Intersubjectivity," 391.

64. Bracken, *The One in the Many,* 149; Bracken, "Energy Events and Fields," 154. By no means does he, however, deny the spatiotemporal character of societies or structured fields of activity. At one point he defines a society as the "spatiotemporal field for the interrelatedness of actual occasions in virtue of a common element of form" (Bracken, *Society and Spirit,* 105).

65. Bracken, *The Triune Symbol,* 189.

66. Bracken, *The One in the Many,* 11, 161–76; Bracken, *God: Three Who Are One,* 77–79, 116–18; Bracken, "Supervenience," 137–38, 143–51; Bracken, "Proposals for Overcoming the Atomism," 20.

tiality for new actual entities, from one set of entities to another. While Whitehead is clear that creativity is transmitted from one set of entities to another, he is unclear as to how this happens, especially since predecessor entities pass out of existence before the successor entities appear.[67] Creativity energizes the self-constitution of actual entities in each new generation. For Bracken, creativity does not come directly from the primordial ontogenetic matrix but "enters" the society, resides in the society, and the society itself accounts for the transmission of creativity to each new generation of its member entities.[68]

Societies also transmit the structure or formal intelligibility characteristic of the society, or societal "form," from one generation of occasions to the next.[69] The form is a limiting, law-like context so that the creativity situated in the society is limited and does not produce a random nexus, but rather one more or less faithful to the pattern of the antecedent occasions.[70]

How the Member Entities Determine the Society

Whitehead addressed the society's continuity over time in a common element of form with his doctrine of "objectification." Bracken strives to adhere closely to Whitehead here. The society's form is maintained from moment to moment only through the many member entities' prehensions of the societal form in predecessor entities, member entities embody the complex eternal object corresponding to the society's form, and the society itself exists only in virtue of the dynamic interrelatedness of its constituent actual entities.[71] The member entities perpetuate the soci-

67. Bracken, *The One in the Many,* 149, 150, 150 n. 47. He cites Whitehead, *Process and Reality,* 19–20 (29), 43 (68–69), 85 (130).

68. Bracken, *The One in the Many,* 150. The "ontogenetic matrix" is, for Bracken (and Jorge Nobo), a combination of Whitehead's "extensive continuum" and primordial creativity. I will discuss this later.

69. Bracken, Christianity and Process Thought, 17, 107; Bracken, "Revising Process Metaphysics," 407; Bracken, "The Issue of Panentheism," 213; Bracken, "Prehending God," 8; Bracken, "Proposals for Overcoming the Atomism," 11–12; Bracken, "Substance—Society—Natural System," 7; Bracken, "Philosophical Foundations," 54.

70. Bracken, "Philosophical Foundations," 54; Bracken, "Ecclesiology: The One and the Many," 306; Bracken, *The One in the Many,* 150; Bracken, *Christianity and Process Thought,* 58.

71. Bracken, *The Triune Symbol,* 189; Bracken, *The Divine Matrix,* 61; Bracken, *Christianity and Process Thought,* 107; Bracken, *God: Three Who Are One,* 78, 114. Bracken, "An Example of Western Theology Taking Modernity Seriously: 'Process Theology,'" in *Different*

ety by imposing its common form on successive generations of actual entities.[72]

However, by sharing in the common element of form differently from its contemporaries, each societal occasion only imperfectly embodies the society's common element of form.[73] The actual entity's subjective aim still guides its self-constitution. Therefore the collective feelings of interrelatedness between the actual entities only "indirectly" perpetuate the society. Each actual entity is only "directly" interested in its own concrescence. The collective feeling of interrelatedness and the common element of form are the "unintended" products of the individual processes of concrescence of all the actual entities at given moment.[74]

Hence the actual entities are the causes of the society, which depends on its members for its existence. As Whitehead says, the society's common element of form comes into existence and perishes with successive generations of actual entities.[75] Since new actual entities prehend and reproduce the society's form, they alter it from moment to moment. The causal laws of the society even change the form through the member entities' self-constituting decisions. While real, this change is gradual and often imperceptible.[76]

How the Society Determines the Member Entities

While stressing the priority of actual entities in maintaining the society, Bracken does assign it a quasi-independence and says the society in toto determines successive generations of its members. If member enti-

Theologies, Common Responsibility: Babel or Pentecost? ed. Clause Geffré, Gustavo Gutiérrez, and Virgil Elizondo, 40–45, *Concilium* 171 (Edinburgh: T & T Clark, 1984), 42; Bracken, "Revising Process Metaphysics," 407; Bracken, "Ecclesiology," 302, 303, 306; Bracken, "Supervenience," 143–44; Bracken, "Substance—Society—Natural System," 7, 8.

72. Whitehead, *Process and Reality,* 89 (137), quoted in Bracken, "The World," 92.

73. See Bracken, "Supervenience," 143; Bracken, "Authentic Subjectivity and Genuine Objectivity," *Horizons* 11 (Fall 1984): 295, 295 n. 14; Bracken, "Energy Events and Fields," 161; Bracken, "Intersubjectivity," 390, 392; Bracken, "Philosophical Foundations," 59.

74. Bracken, "Spirit and Society," 249.

75. Bracken, *Society and Spirit,* 54–55, 61–62, 69, 111–12; Bracken, "Supervenience," 144; Bracken, *The One in the Many,* 131, 133, 134; Bracken, "Substance—Society—Natural System," 7, 8; Bracken, "An Example of Western Theology," 42.

76. Bracken, *Society and Spirit,* 44–45, 62, 69, 111, 149; Bracken, *The Divine Matrix,* 61, 62; Bracken, *The One in the Many,* 103, 131–34, 148–49, 166; Bracken, *God: Three Who Are One,* 114; Bracken, "Prehending God," 6; Bracken, "The World," 92–93; Bracken, "Intersubjectivity," 390–91; Bracken, "Philosophical Foundations," 54.

ties are all momentary subjects of experience, then the perduring societal form cannot exist in them alone.[77] Thus there must be continuity independent of the momentary actual entities. Also, since each member entity embodies the form differently from its contemporaries, there is no specific identity for them as a group unless the form is somehow embodied in the objective structure of the society or field itself.[78]

Christian argued that the societal form exists in the consequent nature of God.[79] Bracken interprets Whitehead as allowing for an objective reality irreducible to the member entities. The form exists in the society as an enduring structured field of activity for its constituent occasions. One need not appeal to a *deus ex machina,* as Christian does, to save causal objectification from the logical inconsistency entailed by too atomistic an interpretation of the ontological principle.[80]

Because they are "reasons" for their self-perpetuation, societies must be more than bare forms. They must exist in some sense. This cannot be in their member entities alone, since each entity embodies the form differently in its own unique subjectivity, and the entities perish each moment.[81] So for Bracken, the society is an independent ontological reality in its own right.

Bracken looks for this ontological independence of societies in Whitehead's "causal laws" of societies. Whitehead says the causal laws dominating a society arise from the member entities. These laws come into existence through the decisions of the first set of member occasions and are subsequently modified by the decisions of later generations. Yet, the causal laws regulate the activity of their member actual entities.[82] This makes the society a quasi-independent reality as a real cause, affecting successive generations of its member entities so they become members of *that* society.[83] A society's causal laws are "derivative from its constitu-

77. Bracken, "Proposals for Overcoming Atomism," 22 n. 3.

78. Ibid., 12.

79. William Christian, *An Interpretation of Whitehead's Metaphysics* (New Haven, Conn.: Yale University Press, 1959), 319–30.

80. Bracken, "Proposals for Overcoming the Atomism," 12, 22 n. 3.

81. Bracken, "Intersubjectivity," 392; Bracken, "The Issue of Panentheism," 213. Whitehead claims that form, and not substance, is the metaphysical principle of continuity: *Process and Reality,* 29 (44).

82. Bracken, "Spirit and Society," 247. Bracken references Whitehead, *Process and Reality,* 90 (139).

83. See Bracken, *Society and Spirit,* 44–45, 52, 61–63, 64–65, 68–70, 111–12, 149; Bracken,

ent occasions and yet independent of them at the same time."[84] Also, although a society's form suffers change as the member entities produce the form moment by moment, these changes are negligible.[85] A society endures across time, despite the perpetual perishing of its actual entities: "The individual members of societies (actual occasions) come and go, but the field endures."[86] This view that a society's causal laws and endurance apart from its members make it more ontologically real than a form diverges from most interpretations of Whitehead.

The Mutual Determination of Actual Entities and Societies

There is therefore a mutual determination of societies and their members, which even Whitehead intimates.[87] Society and members have a reciprocal relationship and mutually condition each other, as the society is "a context for the interaction of entities which is itself somehow structured by the interplay of those same entities."[88] The society is both the "effect" of its current members and the "cause" of its next generation of members.[89] Both society and actual entities, then, are equally important and therefore in a sense equally primordial.[90]

The Divine Matrix, 61, 62; Bracken, *The One in the Many,* 7, 148–49; Bracken, *God: Three Who Are One,* 67–68, 78, 114; Bracken, "Trinity: Economic and Immanent," 15 n. 15; Bracken, "Prehending God," 6; Bracken, "The Issue of Panentheism," 213; Bracken, "Images of God," 370; Bracken, "Intersubjectivity," 390–91; Bracken, "Philosophical Foundations," 54; Bracken, "Energy Events and Fields," 154, 161.

84. Bracken, "Proposals for Overcoming the Atomism," 12.

85. Bracken, *Society and Spirit,* 66; Bracken, *The Divine Matrix,* 62; Bracken, *Christianity and Process Thought,* 106. He cites Whitehead, *Process and Reality,* 90–91 (139).

86. Bracken, *Society and Spirit,* 70; Bracken, *The One in the Many,* 131, 133, 134; Bracken, *Christianity and Process Thought,* 7, 16–17, 57–58, 107; Bracken, *God: Three Who Are One,* 67; Bracken, "Intersubjectivity," 389, 391; Bracken, "Philosophical Foundations," 52, 61–62; Bracken, "Revising Process Metaphysics," 408; Bracken, "Whitehead and the Critique of Logocentrism," in *Process and Difference: Between Cosmological and Poststructuralist Postmodernisms,* ed. Catherine Keller, 91–110 (Albany: State University of New York Press, 2002), 94. In support, he cites Whitehead, *Adventures of Ideas,* 204.

87. Whitehead, *Process and Reality,* 90–91 (139), quoted in Bracken, *Society and Spirit,* 44, 69; Bracken, *The One in the Many,* 148; Bracken, "Intersubjectivity," 39; Bracken, "Panentheism from a Process Perspective," 99; and Bracken, "Proposals for Overcoming Atomism," 12.

88. Bracken, "The Issue of Panentheism," 213; Bracken, "Images of God," 370; Bracken, "Intersubjectivity," 390–92.

89. Bracken, *The Divine Matrix,* 61.

90. Bracken, "Philosophical Foundations," 54; Bracken, "The World," 93; Bracken, "Images of God," 369–70; Bracken, "Intersubjectivity," 391–92; Bracken, "Philosophical Foundations," 54; Bracken, *The One in the Many,* 148–59.

Here Bracken incorporates Royce, who complements Whitehead.[91] For both Royce and Whitehead the idea of being is based on the model of the human individual, and since the human individual is intrinsically related and social, being is intrinsically related and social.[92] Royce says human communities and individuals mutually constitute one another, which has implications for the relationships between actual entities and societies on every level of reality.[93]

Other Aspects of Bracken's Reconstruction of Society

Bracken's view of the Whiteheadian society as a structured field and quasi-independent actuality results in further differences from standard interpretations of Whitehead. Whitehead seems to say that successive member entities prehend the societal form from their predecessors, now superject. Bracken says member entities prehend the form directly from the society as an objective ontological reality in its own right. The society's continuity is insured by how member occasions prehend the whole societal form directly, not the form embodied in previous members, which prehended the form in a different way from their contemporaries.[94]

Bracken still adheres closely to the priority of actual entities, saying member entities can never prehend the field or society itself since it never exists by itself. An entity in concrescence prehends the field together with its constituent occasions. The difference between Bracken and more orthodox Whiteheadians is that the entity need not prehend all constituent occasions individually. It prehends the other occasions as a group with a specific identity as such, members of that society.[95] In an early draft of the Gifford lectures, Whitehead says concrescence starts with a

91. Private interview with Joseph A. Bracken, November 22, 2003.

92. "Theoretically speaking, I cannot find or even define the truth in terms of my individual experience, without taking account of my relation to the community of those who know. This community, then, is real whatever is real. . . . My life means nothing, either theoretically or practically, unless I am a member of a community" (Josiah Royce, *The Problem of Christianity* [New York: Macmillan, 1918; reprint, Chicago: University of Chicago Press, 1968], 357). See also, Josiah Royce, *The World and the Individual* (New York: Macmillan, 1901), 261.

93. Bracken, *What Are They Saying about the Trinity?* 70.

94. Bracken, "Proposals for Overcoming the Atomism," 13; Bracken, "An Example of Western Theology," 42; Bracken, "Energy Events and Fields," 161; Bracken, "Substance—Society—Natural System," 7, 8; Bracken, "Revising Process Metaphysics," 408–9; Bracken, "Philosophical Foundations," 59; Bracken, "Authentic Subjectivity," 291–95; Bracken, "Prehending God," 6.

95. Bracken, "Proposals for Overcoming Atomism," 13.

single unified datum, the entire past world as a whole, instead of a multiplicity of initial data.[96]

The typical explanation is that actual entities obtain their pattern from their predecessors through objectification. In objectification, entities in concrescence positively and negatively prehend the eternal objects *in their predecessors within the same society,* and through transmutation convert them into an eternal object for the society as a whole.[97] Member entities prehend previous members in which they attain the societal form, not the society directly.

Arguing that a more parsimonious explanation is better, Bracken responds by saying the process would be simpler if entities directly prehend the structure of the field in which they originate.[98] The typical explanation is "cumbersome," a "laborious process."[99] If member entities *directly* prehend the nexus instead of *indirectly* through an elaborate analysis and comparison of the structure proper to the individual parts, the end result would be the same but the transmission would be more objective and reliable. Whitehead himself says in transmutation "the actual world is felt as a community, and is so felt in virtue of its prevalent order."[100]

The Ontological Status and Equiprimordiality of Societies

For many Whiteheadians, the ontological unity of being is only possible in the actual entity's subjective unity. Arguing for an ambivalence in Whitehead's view of societies, Bracken says it is unclear whether societies are ultimately reducible to their actual occasions or whether they in some way are an objective reality over and above their members.[101] On the one hand "societies" are "derivative notions" for Whitehead, but on the other hand nexūs or aggregates of actual occasions are one of the eight "catego-

96. This is related by Ford, *The Emergence of Whitehead's Metaphysics,* 188, and referenced by Bracken in "Proposals for Overcoming Atomism," 23 n. 6.

97. Whitehead, *Process and Reality,* 25 (38), 27 (40), 41–42 (66).

98. Bracken, "Prehending God," 7; Bracken, "Proposals for Overcoming the Atomism," 12–13; Bracken, "Intersubjectivity," 391 n. 29; Bracken, "Revising Process Metaphysics," 408–9.

99. Bracken, "Revising Process Metaphysics," 409; Bracken, *The One in the Many,* 149.

100. Bracken, "Proposals for Overcoming the Atomism," 13. The quotation is from Whitehead, *Process and Reality,* 251 (383).

101. Bracken, "Images of God," 369; Bracken, *The Triune Symbol,* 42; Bracken, "Substance—Society—Natural System," 5; Bracken, "Spirit and Society," 247; Bracken, "Whitehead," 103–4; Bracken, *The One in the Many,* 3 n. 5, 7, 99.

ries of existence" along with actual entities.[102] In a later statement Whitehead says:

> The real actual things that endure are all societies. They are not actual occasions [actual entities] . . . . A society has an essential character, whereby it is the society that it is, and it has also accidental qualities, which vary as circumstances alter . . . . Thus a society, as a complete existence and as retaining the same metaphysical status, enjoys a history expressing its changing reactions to changing circumstances. But an actual occasion has no such history. It never changes. It only becomes and perishes.[103]

Even though "the ultimate metaphysical truth is atomism," this refers only to the ultimate constituents of reality, not the materialistic proposition that the apparent ontological totality of a reality is merely the sustained interaction of its parts. Whitehead also says: "A society is more than a set of entities to which the same class-name applies."[104] Thus for Whitehead not actual entities but societies are, if not the final real things, at least the conventional things of which the world is composed, and so "ontological realities" or "nonfactual entities."[105]

Bracken adduces Aristotle's *Politics* and Ervin Laszlo's systems theory as examples of theories showing, by analogy with human societies, that through a process like "supervenience" in contemporary philosophy of mind a community has a level of being and activity above its members. A society is ontologically real even though it depends on the mutual interaction of its members for ongoing existence.[106] Royce also claimed that individuals in community transcend their individuality to achieve a

102. Whitehead, *Process and Reality,* 31–36 (46–54), cited in Bracken, *The One in the Many,* 3.

103. Whitehead, *Adventures of Ideas,* 204, quoted in Bracken, "Substance—Society—Natural System," 5. He also references this passage in Bracken, "Images of God," 369; Bracken, "Revising Process Metaphysics," 407–8; Bracken, *The One in the Many,* 131, 133; Bracken, "Intersubjectivity," 389; Bracken, "Whitehead," 94; Bracken, "Philosophical Foundations," 52; Bracken, "The Two Process Theologies," 126 n. 29.

104. Whitehead, *Process and Reality,* 89 (137), quoted in Bracken, "Spirit and Society," 247. See also Bracken, "The World," 93–94; Bracken, *Society and Spirit,* 110.

105. Bracken, *Society and Spirit,* 44; Bracken, "Intersubjectivity," 395.

106. Ervin Laszlo, *The Systems View of the World: The Natural Philosophy of the New Developments in the Sciences* (New York: Braziller, 1972), 29, quoted in Bracken, *The One in the Many,* 136. He cites Aristotle in Joseph A. Bracken, "Toward a Grammar of Dissent," *Theological Studies* 31 (September 1970): 447. See also, Bracken, *Society and Spirit,* 49–52; Bracken, "Supervenience," 144.

higher level of existence or ontological reality.[107] Gestalt psychology expresses supervenience in saying "the whole is greater than the sum of the parts."[108]

Bracken also again appeals to German idealism, especially Hegel.[109] Though Hegel and Whitehead give different answers to the problem of the one and the many, they both assume the same metaphysical principle that the whole is greater than the sum of the parts. This principle distinguishes the organismic-idealistic view of reality from the mechanistic-materialistic view, which sees the whole as nothing more than the sum of the parts. Hegel's philosophy assumes, says Bracken, that truth and being exist foremost in the totality and only in parts insofar as they are integrated into the whole. Hegel's central distinction between concrete and abstract universals assumes that the actuality proper to any concrete individual considered as a unitary whole is greater than the actuality proper to the parts, or the many abstract universals signifying different dimensions of the one concrete reality. Even Whitehead assumes, says Bracken, that "the whole is greater than the sum of its parts," because saying a society is merely the sum of its members commits Whitehead's "genetic fallacy." Thus a society is not merely a cluster or aggregate of actual entities in spatiotemporal contiguity, as Charles Hartshorne seems to hold.[110]

107. Royce, *The Problem of Christianity,* 122, quoted in Bracken, *The Triune Symbol,* 22, and in *What Are They Saying about the Trinity?* 68; and Royce, *The Problem of Christianity,* 80, quoted in Bracken, *The Triune Symbol,* 22, and in "Process Philosophy and Trinitarian Theology," 225.

108. Bracken, *The Triune Symbol,* 18–19; Bracken, *The Divine Matrix,* 61; Bracken, *The One in the Many,* 167; Bracken, "The Holy Trinity as a Community of Divine Persons, Part I," *Heythrop Journal* 15 (1974): 171, 179; "The Holy Trinity as a Community of Divine Persons, Part II," *Heythrop Journal* 15 (1974): 259, 269; Bracken, "Supervenience," 144; Bracken, "Intersubjectivity," 392; Bracken, "Process Philosophy and Trinitarian Theology," 223; Bracken, "Toward a Grammar of Dissent," 439, 442, 447; Bracken, "Revising Process Metaphysics," 407–8; Bracken, "Whitehead," 104.

109. Bracken, *Society and Spirit,* 106, 108–111.

110. Bracken, "The World," 91, 93, 101 n. 17; Bracken, "Spirit and Society," 247, 250; Bracken, "Intersubjectivity," 392; Bracken, "Revising Process Metaphysics," 409; Bracken, "Philosophical Foundations," 55; Bracken, "Toward a Grammar of Dissent," 442, 447; Bracken, "Energy Events and Fields," 153. Independently of Bracken and on other grounds, George Allan has similarly argued that Whiteheadian societies have an independent ontological reality apart from their constituent actual occasions. He differs from Bracken, however, in essentially giving the society the same ontological status as the actual entity (George Allan, "The Aims of Societies and the Aims of God," in *Process Philosophy and Christian*

Yet Bracken is careful to guard the principle that a society can only exist in and through the ongoing interrelation of its parts. "Objectivity follows upon subjectivity" so that subjectivities of actual entities precede and establish their consequent objectivity, which applies to the objectivity of societies as well.[111] Although societies come into existence and are sustained only by the interrelated activity of member entities, the actual occasions bring into being an objective reality distinct from the actual entities as interrelated subjects of experience.[112]

Bracken does, however, maintain the strict Whiteheadian affirmation that actual entities are the final real things of which the world is composed.[113] While Wallack seems to confound "actual entity" and "nexus," Bracken says they must remain distinct.[114] A society is not a higher-level actual entity, since it does not undergo concrescence ending in a self-constituting decision.[115] Royce runs the danger of reverting to "substantialist" categories when he sees a community as a supraindividual with a mind and a purpose of its own.[116] Hegelian "Spirit" is ontologically real but is not reducible to physicality or materiality, and so only exists through the interrelation of its constituent entities, which are alone really actual.[117]

Society for Bracken, then, is as primordial as the actual entity and not just a derivative notion.[118] Although societies are not actual entities, Whitehead's inner logic demands that society be an elemental concept

Thought, ed. Delwin Brown, Ralph E. James Jr., and Gene Reeves, 464–74 [Indianapolis: Bobbs-Merrill, 1971], 464–74).

111. Bracken, *The Triune Symbol*, 103; Bracken, "Toward a New Philosophical Theology," 705–6; Bracken, "Authentic Subjectivity," 295, 295 n. 14.

112. Bracken, *The One in the Many*, 167.

113. Whitehead, *Process and Reality*, 18 (27–28). Bracken, *Society and Spirit*, 44; Bracken, *Christianity and Process Thought*, 15; Bracken, "Spirit and Society," 246, 250; Bracken, "Ecclesiology," 301, 304; Bracken, "The Issue of Panentheism," 214; Bracken, "The World," 92; Bracken, "Revising Process Metaphysics," 407; Bracken, "Energy Events and Fields," 153.

114. Bradford Wallack, *The Epochal Nature of Process in Whitehead's Metaphysics* (Albany: State University of New York Press, 1980), 7–8.

115. Bracken, "Spirit and Society," 247; Bracken, "Proposals for Overcoming the Atomism," 11, 23 n. 6; Bracken, *Christianity and Process Thought*, 106.

116. Bracken, *The Triune Symbol*, 23–24; Bracken, "Toward a Grammar of Dissent," 442; Bracken, "Process Philosophy and Trinitarian Theology," 225.

117. Bracken, "Spirit and Society," 250–51.

118. Bracken, *The One in the Many*, 3, 5; Bracken, "Proposals for Overcoming the Atomism," 14; Bracken, "Substance—Society—Natural System," 11; Bracken, "Spirit and Society," 247; Bracken, "Intersubjectivity," 395.

coequal in importance with the actual entity. Whitehead's statement that societies are self-sustaining realities with a raison d'être proper to their own level of being and activity is very close to how he speaks of actual entities.[119]

A Thoroughgoing "Social Ontology"

Whitehead was concerned to develop a social-relational ontology, as seen when he makes the patristic category of *perichoresis* in the Trinity a metaphysical fundamental.[120] At times Bracken's emphasis on societies leads him to say the "basic units of reality" are not individual entities but rather social groupings of entities.[121] A thoroughgoing social-relational metaphysics must realize that entities are themselves heavily conditioned by their societies. Indeed, individual entities only have meaning and value in terms of their societies. No entity comes into existence on its own but depends on the coexistence of other entities to which it is dynamically related.[122]

Following many process thinkers, Bracken faults classical metaphysics for having an isolationistic view of being and substance.[123] Society must become the foundational category in a new social-relational cosmology, as fundamental as substance was in classical metaphysics.[124] Classical metaphysics made communities or societies secondary or derivative. A genuinely social ontology gives coequal status to social totalities and their constituent members.

119. Bracken, *Society and Spirit,* 51. He cites Whitehead, *Process and Reality,* 89 (137). See also Bracken, "Substance—Society—Natural System," 11; Bracken, "Spirit and Society," 247; Bracken, "The World," 93–94.

120. Whitehead said *perichoresis* is an advance of the Greek Church Fathers over Plato but faults them for never incorporating it into their overall metaphysical schemes so as to apply the same metaphysical categories to God and the world (Whitehead, *Adventures of Ideas,* 168–69).

121. Bracken, *Society and Spirit,* 49; Bracken, *The One in the Many,* 5; Bracken, "Subsistent Relation," 190.

122. Bracken, "The Theology of God of Elizabeth A. Johnson," 31.

123. See, Bracken, *The Triune Symbol,* 5–6, 16, 32 n. 1; Bracken, *The Divine Matrix,* 11; Bracken, *God: Three Who Are One,* 11–12, 20–21, 24, 69, 74, 84–85; Bracken, "Images of God," 368.

124. Bracken, *Society and Spirit,* 48, 55; Bracken, *The One in the Many,* 3; Bracken, *Christianity and Process Thought,* 60; Bracken, "Subsistent Relation," 190; Bracken, "Images of God," 368.

Society and Substance

If societies are enduring structured fields of activity for successive generations of actual occasions, then we have an analogy for the classical notion of substance without its attendant problems.[125] Societal form is what endures, not substance. Raising the question of a societal form's location, Bracken says a society bears affinities with a substance even though it fundamentally differs from a substance.

In classical metaphysics substance explains ontological endurance across time while accidents explain change, and society has the same function in Whitehead's system, including accidental changes.[126] Like Aristotelian substances, societies are the principle of continuity for accidental changes taking place in them. Even though its members and common element of form are constantly changing, a society does exhibit relative stability across space and time, which is what the classical notion of substance conveys.[127] Finally, societies also embody ontological potentiality for further actualization in new actual occasions because they transmit a structure of formal intelligibility. Like Aristotelian substances, they represent actuality on the order of existence and potentiality on the order of operation.

There are important differences between societies and substances, however. Agreeing with Leclerc that a society is a quasi-independent reality beyond the collection of its members, Bracken disagrees with his virtual equation of society with substance. Many analogues to societies like macroscopic environments and human societies are recalcitrant to the imposition of a unity from a substantial form divesting its parts of their individuality.[128]

Whiteheadian societies also lack the extreme included in the idea of

125. Bracken, *The One in the Many,* 165; Bracken, "Supervenience," 143; Bracken, "Panentheism from a Trinitarian Perspective," 11 n. 14.

126. "The real actual things that endure are all societies. . . . A society has an essential character, whereby it is the society that it is, and it has also accidental qualities which vary as circumstances alter" (Whitehead, *Adventures of Ideas,* 204).

127. Bracken, *Christianity and Process Thought,* 16; Bracken, *God: Three Who Are One,* 114; Bracken, "Substance—Society—Natural System," 5; Bracken, "Revising Process Metaphysics," 407–9; Bracken, "Spirit and Society," 249.

128. Bracken, *The Triune Symbol,* 42–43, 59 n. 18; Bracken, *Society and Spirit,* 39; Bracken, "Substance—Society—Natural System," 3, 8–9; Bracken, "Spirit and Society," 250–51.

substance.[129] Also, by definition a society is a relational reality but a substance is essentially unrelated, existing in and for itself in terms of its being and activity. A society's unity is also less cohesive than a substance's because ultimate unity obtains only in the actual entity's self-constitution.[130]

Another difference lies in a reversal of the priority of whole and parts. Aristotle's hylomorphism sees the compound entity as more than an aggregate of material elements *(stoicheia)*. It is a new reality by reason of its immaterial cause or form. An element "is that into which a thing is divided and which is present in its matter." In contrast, substantial form is not another element among the material elements but rather an immaterial principle. Though immanent in the material elements the form is the primary cause of the coming to be of the compound being. The substantial form never comes to be and never perishes.[131]

In process metaphysics the material elements or actual entities have ontological priority over the form governing their interrelatedness. Through their interrelations the parts produce the form from moment to moment. The constituent entities are constantly changing, so the society's common element of form is changing, even if ever so slightly. Prime matter, energy, or creativity is the active principle and the form is passive, which is the opposite of the form-matter relationship in classical hylomorphism.[132] Also, unity is democratic and horizontal, not hierarchical and vertical. The unity of substance is a higher-level form's relationship to lower-level matter, but a society's unity arises from the interrelationships of equal entities.[133]

Bracken argues that the Whiteheadian society includes what is meant by Aristotelian substance, but not vice versa. A substance reduces its compo-

129. Bracken, "Spirit and Society," 249; Bracken, "Revising Process Metaphysics," 408.

130. Bracken, "Substance—Society—Natural System," 9; Bracken, "Prehending God," 12 n. 3; Bracken, "Energy Events and Fields," 153.

131. Aristotle *Metaphysics* 1041b, 25–31; 1051b, 29–30.

132. Bracken, *Society and Spirit,* 54, 112; Bracken, "Substance—Society—Natural System," 8–9; Bracken, "Trinity: Economic and Immanent," 17 n. 22; Bracken, "Process Philosophy and Trinitarian Theology—II," 89; Bracken, "Response to Elizabeth Johnson's 'Does God Play Dice?'" 725; Bracken, *God: Three Who Are One,* 114. Book Z of Aristotle's *Metaphysics* admits of an interpretation of substantial form where the form comes into being as it unifies the material elements into an organic whole, which differs from a competing Platonic view where form preexists and communicates unity from the outside (Ernst Tugendhat, *Ti kata tinos: eine Untersuchung zu Struktur und Ursprung aristotelicher Grundbegriffe* [Freiberg i. Br.: Karl Alber Verlag, 1958], 67–20, cited in Bracken, "Spirit and Society," 245).

133. Bracken, "Philosophical Foundations," 55.

nent parts to nothing more than accidental modifications of the substantial whole. In contrast to substance, a society preserves the ontological integrity and individuality of its parts. The parts do create something bigger than themselves, but they must remain fully actual in order to do so. The constituent parts of a substance are not actual in their own right so long as they remain parts of still another substance. Since society accounts for the whole but does not rob the parts of their distinct identities, society, not substance, should be the first category in contemporary cosmology.[134]

The Agency of Whiteheadian "Societies"

For Bracken, societies also exercise agency.[135] He believes that Whitehead's statement that agency belongs exclusively to actual occasions is not wrong but incomplete. Whitehead did not draw the logical conclusion that these individual agencies fuse into a collective agency.[136] When speaking of living organisms, Whitehead does approach corporate agency in regnant nexūs in living structured societies. Like humans, societies act as unitary wholes.[137] Such unified agency must apply to all societies, including simpler inorganic ones. Passages where Whitehead seems to ascribe ontological but non-factual reality to societies lend support to this conclusion.[138]

Adhering closely to the axiom that agency is exclusive to actual occasions, Bracken says societies exercise agency indirectly through the collective agency of their actual entities.[139] Since a society's causal laws are operative *in and through* its members, a society exercises agency through its members. There is a "collective agency," even a "fusion," coming from

134. Bracken, *Society and Spirit,* 39, 48; Bracken, "Substance—Society—Natural System," 3, 8–10; Bracken, "Spirit and Society," 251; Bracken, "Process Philosophy and Trinitarian Theology," 223; Bracken, "Proposals for Overcoming the Atomism," 23 n. 6.

135. Whitehead says that "agency belongs exclusively to actual occasions" (Whitehead, *Process and Reality,* 31 [46]).

136. Bracken, *Society and Spirit,* 56. See also, Bracken, "The World," 93; Bracken, "Revising Process Metaphysics," 409–10.

137. Whitehead, *Process and Reality,* 103 (157); cited in Bracken, "Energy Events and Fields," 157, and *Society and Spirit,* 45–46. See also Bracken, "Spirit and Society," 248.

138. Whitehead, *Process and Reality,* 90–91 (139). Bracken, *Society and Spirit,* 56; Bracken, "Spirit and Society," 248–49; Bracken, "Energy Events and Fields," 156; Bracken, "Panentheism from a Process Perspective," 97; Bracken, "Process Philosophy and Trinitarian Theology," 220; Bracken, "Revising Process Metaphysics," 409.

139. Bracken, *Society and Spirit,* 14; Bracken, *The Divine Matrix,* 61; Bracken, *The One in the Many,* 100, 134; Bracken, "Energy Events and Fields," 156.

the coordination of the members' individual agencies.[140] Societal agency comes from the "bottom up" or "from below," without any "top-down" causation.[141] Therefore, despite being ontological unities in their own right, societies can exercise agency only in and through their subsocieties and their actual occasions.[142] As the complexity of societies increases, so does their agency, which is "proper to their own level of existence and activity."[143] Like its common element of form, a society's agency once generated perdures across time.[144] However, societies do not make self-constituting decisions. Only actual occasions can do this because only they are subjects of experience.[145] Similarly, although they exercise agency, societies do not have self-awareness.[146]

The common process understanding, based on agency observed in complex organisms, is that agency happens in the "dominant" or "regnant" actual occasion.[147] Agency involves individuality, and individuality is only present where there is a self-constituting actual occasion. This means that if a society acts as a whole this must be due to a single higher-order actual occasion present exercising agency for all of the contemporary actual occasions in the nexus.

Hartshorne distinguished between "compound individuals" and "com-

140. Bracken, "Revising Process Metaphysics," 409; Bracken, *Society and Spirit,* 14, 43–44, 45, 48, 51–52; Bracken, *The Divine Matrix,* 61; Bracken, *The One in the Many,* 100, 134; Bracken, "Substance—Society—Natural System," 11–12; Bracken, "The Issue of Panentheism," 213; Bracken, "The World," 93–94, 95–96; Bracken, "Whitehead," 104; Bracken, review of *Process Catholicism: An Exercise in Ecclesial Imagination,* by Robert L. Kinast, *Process Studies* 29, no. 1 (Spring–Summer 2000): 179; Bracken, "Energy Events and Fields," 156. Cf. Whitehead, *Process and Reality,* 90–91 (139).

141. Bracken, *Society and Spirit,* 52. The "from below" specifically regards the society's *agency,* not the formal causality of the societal form. Bracken is clear that the society's common element of form, once generated by the occasions, does exercise top-down causality as an organizing principle (Joseph A. Bracken, private correspondence with the author, June 6, 2005).

142. Bracken, *The One in the Many,* 100.

143. Bracken, "Revising Process Metaphysics," 410; Bracken, *Society and Spirit,* 46–47; Bracken, "Panentheism from a Process Perspective," 98; Bracken, "Spirit and Society," 249, 253; Bracken, *The One in the Many,* 134–35, 136.

144. Bracken, *The Divine Matrix,* 61.

145. Bracken, *Society and Spirit,* 43; Bracken, "The World," 91–93; Bracken, "The Issue of Panentheism," 213.

146. Bracken, "Revising Process Metaphysics," 409; Bracken, review of *Process Catholicism,* 179.

147. Whitehead, *Process and Reality,* 109 (166–67).

posite individuals."[148] The latter are "democratically organized societies" with no regnant subsociety of actual occasions, or "soul." These are "virtual aggregates" of actual occasions equally affecting the whole, and include inanimate macroscopic objects like rocks. The former are "monarchically organized societies" governed by a regnant subsociety of actual occasions, like the animating principle of living organisms. Through its latest dominant actual occasion this regnant subsociety objectively unifies all other subsocieties in the overall structured society, and is the compound individual at the level of common-sense experience. Other process theologians have followed Hartshorne in claiming that a dominant regnant society enables a structured society to exercise an agency, in some cases even applying this scheme to inorganic societies.[149]

Affirming that societies exercise their own collective agencies through the agencies of their members, Bracken disagrees with the regnant occasion theory.[150] A dominant subsociety might heavily influence the collective agency of the whole society, but it always exists for the sake of whole, and its agency is still exercised in and through the society's collective agency. Bracken says his view is more democratic and egalitarian than Hartshorne's monarchical model, and says most societies do not possess a regnant subsociety. Hartshorne's theory ignores the fact that the overwhelming majority of Whiteheadian structured societies are not monarchically organized; most are inorganic or supraorganic and therefore have no animating principle.[151]

A more democratic view of societal agency also accounts better for a society's endurance over time. Hartshorne's theory explains the spatial to-

148. Charles A. Hartshorne, "The Compound Individual," in *Philosophical Essay for Alfred North Whitehead,* ed. F. S. C. Northrop, 193–220 (New York: Russell & Russell, 1936).

149. John B. Cobb Jr., *The Structure of Christian Existence* (Philadelphia: Westminster Press, 1967), 33–34; Cobb, "Overcoming Reductionism," in *Existence and Actuality: Conversations with Charles Hartshorne,* ed. John Cobb and Franklin Gamwell (Chicago: University of Chicago Press, 1984), 149–64; David Ray Griffin, "Whitehead's Philosophy and Some General Notions of Physics and Biology," in *Mind in Nature. Essays on the Interface of Science and Philosophy,* ed. John B. Cobb Jr. and David Ray Griffin, 122–34 (Washington, D.C.: University Press of America, 1977), 133.

150. Bracken, *Society and Spirit,* 43; Bracken, *The Divine Matrix,* 61; Bracken, "The World," 93; Bracken, "Philosophical Foundations," 63; Bracken, "Panentheism from a Process Perspective," 100.

151. Bracken, *The Divine Matrix,* 61; Bracken, *The One in the Many,* 100, 135–36, 167; Bracken, "Proposals for Overcoming the Atomism," 11; Bracken, "Whitehead," 104.

getherness of societal members at any moment, but cannot explain endurance over time.[152] Also, Hartshorne's view does not agree with the evolutionary worldview because it has a top-down unity.[153] Because of its hierarchical bent, Hartshorne's view contains remnants of logocentrism.[154]

In his own self-understanding, Bracken's theory of societal agency falls between Hartshorne's and Leclerc's, which sees societal agency as that of a new existent, because for Leclerc societies are like substances.[155]

Systems Theory and "Layers of Social Order"

In addition to having a tendency toward atomism, much Whiteheadian metaphysics does not analyze the interrelationships of societies. It fails to significantly account for the interplay of societies with one another. Only by combining Whitehead's thought with a systems theory such as Laszlo's will an adequate social ontology and philosophy of intersubjectivity result.[156]

Laszlo defines a "natural system" as a "nonrandom accumulation of matter-energy, in a region of physical space-time, which is non-randomly organized into coacting interrelated subsystems or components."[157] For Laszlo, aggregates composed of otherwise self-sufficient entities, like human societies or ecological systems, are as much systems as organic compounds and substances are. The universe is a megasystem composed of smaller subsystems like galaxies, composed of smaller systems like solar systems, composed of smaller systems like planets, composed of smaller systems like ecological systems, all the way down to very basic systems like atoms. Reality is an ontological unity in the highest sense, but a unity comprised of increasingly smaller systems in hierarchy.[158]

152. Bracken, *Society and Spirit,* 42–49; Bracken, "Trinity: Economic and Immanent," 15 n. 17; Bracken, "Panentheism from a Process Perspective," 98; Bracken, "Proposals for Overcoming the Atomism," 11.

153. Bracken, "Revising Process Metaphysics," 411.

154. Bracken, *The One in the Many,* 104; Bracken, "Whitehead," 100–101, 104–5.

155. Bracken, *The Triune Symbol,* 42–43; Bracken, *Society and Spirit,* 43–44, 45, 48–49, 56; Bracken, "Substance—Society—Natural System," 11–12.

156. Bracken, *The One in the Many,* 135, 137, 139–40; Bracken, "Substance—Society—Natural System," 10–11; Bracken, "The Theology of God of Elizabeth A. Johnson," 32 n. 31; Bracken, "Revising Process Metaphysics," 413.

157. Ervin Laszlo, *An Introduction to Systems Philosophy: Toward a New Paradigm of Contemporary Thought* (New York: Gordon & Breach, 1972), 30.

158. Laszlo, *An Introduction to Systems Philosophy,* 25–30, 97–117.

Whiteheadian societies can be viewed as hierarchically integrated systems. Any given society is always found in a context including other actual entities not in that society but which also contribute objectively to the self-constitution of the actual entities in that society: "But there is no society in isolation . . . . The environment, together with the society in question, must form a larger society in respect to more general characters than those defining the society from which we started. Thus we arrive at the principle that every society requires a social background, of which it is itself a part."[159] The society and its environment together comprise a larger, different society, for which the defining characteristic is more general. For Whitehead as for Laszlo, primitive societies are grouped into larger societies, which are grouped into ever-increasing larger societies, culminating in the unity of the entire world process.[160]

Bracken takes Whitehead's comments to imply that there are "fields within fields," and that actual entities as members of more specialized fields must also conform to the laws governing the behavior of actual entities in more comprehensive fields.[161] Societies exist in dynamic interrelation as "environments" and "layers of social order."[162] Subordinate societies retain a distinctive self-identity even when a larger structured society of which they are a part dissolves.

While Laszlo's systems theory attenuates an imbalance in Whiteheadian thought, Laszlo's theory by itself is also imbalanced, needing correction from process metaphysics. Similarities between Whitehead and Laszlo include how: (1) both reject substance-oriented metaphysics that emphasizes individuals; (2) both society and "natural system" are non-random organizations of matter-energy across space and time; and (3) both societies and systems apply not only to organisms, but also to social groups like human communities and ecological environments, thus being superior to the classical idea of substance.[163]

Yet there are also marked differences. Actual entities as momentary subjects of experience do not possess the latent capacity for further self-

159. Whitehead, *Process and Reality,* 90 (138). See also ibid., 89–92 (136–41).

160. Bracken, *Society and Spirit,* 50; Bracken, "Substance—Society—Natural System," 10; Bracken, *Christianity and Process Thought,* 9–10, 107.

161. Bracken, *Society and Spirit,* 68; Bracken, *God: Three Who Are One,* 116.

162. Bracken, *The One in the Many,* 147.

163. Ibid., 133; Bracken, "Substance—Society—Natural System," 10; Bracken, "Spirit and Society," 255 n. 3.

development beyond what they need for their self-constitution, as do Laszlo's atoms. Laszlo believes only systems exist, but for Whitehead actual entities are the final real things. For Laszlo constituent parts are always subsystems, so atoms are just subsystems. There is no fundamental constituent of reality like an actual entity. Whitehead holds that the *ultimate* parts of various fields of activity are momentary subjects of experience.[164]

Bracken and Laszlo agree against Whitehead that the basic components of material reality are social realities or systems, that only natural systems or societies exist long enough to make a difference, and that natural systems or societies exercise agency. Bracken follows Whitehead, not Laszlo, in seeing the ultimate components of natural systems as actual occasions that are context-dependent for their own internal structure and organization. Thus actual occasions are ultimately real but do not possess latent capacities for self-development beyond their own self-constitution. While Laszlo says that systems exercise agency by their own internal structure and organization, Bracken says they exercise agency indirectly through the collective agency of their interrelated entities, striving to maintain the axiom that only actual occasions exercise agency.[165]

Laszlo's idea that only systems exist is problematic because systems presuppose constituent parts. If we are to avoid a *regressus ad infinitum* we must posit final and ultimate parts qualitatively different from systems. As systems theory can emend Whiteheadian metaphysics by stressing the equiprimordiality of societies and actual entities and stressing interrelationships between societies, systems philosophers must ask themselves if they need a category of actual entity to describe the constituent parts of natural systems.[166]

Bracken's Revision of Classical Thomistic Metaphysics

So far we have seen how Bracken uses and modifies Whiteheadian process metaphysics. Another essential part of Bracken's thought is Thomistic metaphysics. Unlike many process theologians who easily dismiss

164. Bracken, "Substance—Society—Natural System," 11. See also, Bracken, *Society and Spirit,* 51; Bracken, *The One in the Many,* 151.

165. Bracken, *Society and Spirit,* 51–52 ; Bracken, *The One in the Many,* 133–34, 137.

166. Bracken, *The One in the Many,* 135; Bracken, "Substance—Society—Natural System," 11.

Thomism, Bracken seeks to reappropriate aspects of Thomism in a revisionist way. He does, however, agree that classical theism is in need of radical revision.[167]

Revisionist Use of Aristotle: Activity and Potentiality as Ultimate

Desiring to reverse the traditional prioritization of being over becoming, Bracken reverses the perennial axiom *agere sequitur esse* to *esse sequitur agere.* He argues from Aristotle that the ultimate metaphysical principle is infinite potentiality in processive activity, not substance, and that there cannot be an actual infinite substance. For Aristotle substance is the first category of being since only an individual substance can subsist in itself. Substance takes ontological priority over the other nine categories because they all depend on substance for their being and intelligibility. The principle of unity in a substance is substantial form.[168]

Bracken argues, however, that substance cannot be infinite and the ultimate metaphysical principle, even on Aristotle's own terms. For Aristotle nothing in actual existence can have an infinite number of parts. The sum of the parts must be finite if the parts are finite, which they must be if they are parts. Actual beings, which Aristotle generally conceives of spatially, can always increase in spatial magnitude and decrease in magnitude or be divided. Since there is no limit to adding, subtracting, or dividing, every actual being is finite. Every instance of being is a finite determination of infinite potentiality while infinity is without limits and is therefore indeterminate. The infinite is not an entity or an attribute of an entity since every entity is determinate, but is a process of potentiality not yet fully actual and is therefore unbounded. Aristotle considered prime matter as infinite since it has no specification or determination through form; it is pure possibility.[169] Whitehead clearly and explicitly equates creativity with Aristotle's prime matter.[170] Bracken concludes, then, that for Aristotle substance or actuality cannot be infinite, but only potentiality, prime matter, or creativity can be infinite.[171]

167. Bracken, review of *Omnipotence and Other Theological Mistakes,* 181.

168. Aristotle, *Metaphysics* 1028a10–30, 1029a–1032a.

169. Aristotle, *Physics* 204b5–9, 204a20–28. See Aristotle's discussion in Book III of *Physics.*

170. See the discussion in the first chapter on creativity in Whitehead.

171. Bracken, *The Divine Matrix,* 6, 12–13, 142–43 n. 4; Bracken, "Non-Duality," 143, and

There is also a priority of activity over stasis in Aristotle, similarly based on the infinite nature of activity. Aristotle defines activity as "the fulfillment of what exists potentially, insofar as it exists potentially."[172] He distinguishes between movements terminating in some extrinsic goal, like building a house, and movements that contain their own end, like seeing, whose object is only the act of seeing. A self-contained activity terminating in its own end Aristotle calls an *actuality,* in distinction from a *potentiality.*[173] From this Bracken says that for Aristotle movement is always a partially realized actuality en route to further actualization.[174]

Bracken aligns Aristotle's idea of activity with his idea of potentiality as infinite potentiality. For Aristotle motion is presupposed in moving from rest to movement, and from motion to rest. So there can never be an absolute beginning or terminus of motion; it must be eternal or without limits.[175] Bracken concludes that motion is infinite, complete, and self-sufficient, with no beginning or end. Static beings are finite because they are separated from one another, and motion links all static beings together. If process or activity is infinite and substance is finite for Aristotle, then process is the ultimate metaphysical principle.[176]

Aristotle's "Unmoved Mover" is also the eternal activity of potentiality moving to actuality. Whatever is moved is moved by another, and Aristotle always asks for the antecedent mover. Even in things that move themselves one part of the entity moves and the other part is moved. The part doing the moving is moved by an outside agent in order to move from potency to act. Since every temporal movement is itself moved when it moves something else, there must be a primary, eternal movement that moves but is itself unmoved.[177] This Unmoved Mover moves other things by being the fixed object of thought and desire for all other beings.[178] Aristotle thus postulates an ontological hierarchy of moved movers, ending

---

"Response to Elizabeth A. Johnson's 'Does God Play Dice?'" 727; Bracken, "Trinity: Economic and Immanent," 17, 17 n. 22; Bracken, "Process Philosophy and Trinitarian Theology—II," 89.

172. Aristotle, *Physics* 201a10.

173. Aristotle, *Metaphysics* 1048b18–34.

174. Bracken, "The Issue of Panentheism," 214–15, 214–15, n. 22.

175. Aristotle, *Physics* 250b11–252b7.

176. Bracken, *The Divine Matrix*, 5–6, 22, 142 n. 12.

177. Aristotle, *Physics* 202a4ff, 254b8–258b9.

178. Aristotle, *Metaphysics* 1072a19–1072b29.

in an eternal Unmoved Mover that moves other entities, but is not itself moved.[179]

Bracken argues that through his perpetual inquiry into the antecedent cause of a motion, Aristotle distances himself from his own dictum that motion is self-perpetuating or an ongoing, eternal reality. In using the Unmoved Mover to explain eternally continuous motion, Aristotle implies that the Unmoved Mover is both an activity and a fixed entity, because it is also in full actuality with no admixture of potentiality.[180] Aristotle describes the Unmoved Mover as "thinking on thinking" but argues that the activity of the Unmoved Mover must be "unchanging" because change would be for the worse.[181] "Thinking on thinking" is an activity. Bracken asks whether ultimate reality for Aristotle is an entity in actuality or whether it is an underlying universal activity in perpetual movement from potency to actuality. If as a self-contained activity "thinking on thinking" is not an entity or fixed determinate reality, then the Unmoved Mover must be self-actualizing or in continual movement from potentiality to actuality. If the Unmoved Mover is less a fixed actuality and more a hypostasized activity, then its being or *ousia* is self-actualizing activity. Aristotle's ultimate metaphysical principle seems to be activity.[182]

An important point Bracken draws from this is that God as person(s) is distinct from the divine nature. In their causal relations individual entities are ontologically distinct from each other. However, since the ontological ground of an entity is the entity's interior principle of existence or activity, the ontological ground cannot be an entity ontologically distinct from the entity it empowers to exist. Yet, as the source of the entity's existence, the ontological ground is ontologically prior to the existent entity. Therefore, although it is not caused by another entity, the Unmoved Mover is still an instantiation of the prior principle of motion or activity. The Unmoved Mover is not the cause of motion but the primordial instantiation of motion, and motion is the primordial reality.[183]

Bracken makes another point here bearing on his own understanding

179. Aristotle, *Physics* 256b8–258b9.

180. Bracken, *The Divine Matrix*, 20, 115, 144 n. 26; Bracken, *The One in the Many*, 19.

181. Aristotle, *Metaphysics* 1074b27, 1074b34.

182. Bracken, *The Divine Matrix*, 17, 21, 32–33.

183. Ibid., 14, 21–22, 32–33, 144 n. 41.

of God. For Aristotle actuality is equivalent to entity or determination and thus finitude or limitation. There are no actual infinites but only potential infinites.[184] On the other hand, Aristotle calls any self-contained activity an *actuality* in distinction from a *potentiality.*[185] Since there is no intrinsic reason why a self-contained activity like seeing should not be continued indefinitely, perhaps an eternally self-contained activity could be actually infinite, not as an entity, but as an activity that never terminates in a final product but only achieves successive stages of actualization. A self-contained activity is actual, and if the Unmoved Mover's activity of "thinking on thinking" goes on forever, there must be an actual infinite, albeit not an entity.[186]

Aristotle acknowledges the ontological reality of supersensible principles like form and matter, which are not entities. Bracken thus argues that motion as a universal phenomenon should be granted the status of an actual reality, although not the status of an "entity." This is especially true if motion is identical with matter for Aristotle. Indeed, matter-motion is even "more real" than the finite entities in which it is embodied, since those entities come to exist and perish, but matter-motion endures.[187]

Bracken's Revisionist Use of St. Thomas Aquinas

As with Aristotle, Bracken reappropriates St. Thomas in revisionist ways. As a process thinker he finds St. Thomas's logical rigor attractive even when he disagrees with Thomas's content and conclusions. Never implying that St. Thomas was a process thinker, Bracken says however that the antecedents of process philosophy are already present in St. Thomas.[188]

Bracken begins by comparing St. Thomas with Aristotle, indicating similarities and differences. Both focus on the individual concrete existent, not in terms of its individual particularity.[189] Both are heirs to Plato's idealism, because both implicitly define being in terms of thinking and the objects of thought. Both use a view of cause and effect that seems to imply that God or the Unmoved Mover is formally conceived not as a

184. Aristotle, *Physics* 213b30–216b22.

185. Aristotle, *Metaphysics* 1048b18–34.

186. Bracken, *The Divine Matrix,* 12–14, 21–22, 32–33, 144 n. 41.

187. Ibid., 23–24.

188. Bracken, "The Theology of God of Elizabeth A. Johnson," 24; Bracken, "The Issue of Panentheism," 216.

189. Bracken, *Society and Spirit,* 24.

subject of experience but as a fixed object of thought. The same applies to entities in the world. Related to each other in objective cause-effect relationships, they are not so much subjects of experience as objects.[190]

Perhaps more important are the ways in which Aristotle and St. Thomas differ. Aristotle considered prime matter infinite. Because it has no specification or determination through form, it is pure possibility. Thomas on the other hand said matter and potency are limiting principles whereas abstract form and actuality are infinite. Undetermined by the conditions of matter and potentiality, God is fully determinate or actual yet infinite form or essence.[191]

Aristotle would question how Thomas applies "essence" and "existence" to God. For Aristotle the relationship between existence and essence is not parallel to the relationship between actuality and potentiality. Actuality is always definite and determinate, but existence is indeterminate because it can be predicated of everything that exists simply because it is there. For Aristotle existence cannot be the essence of any specific being, even the Supreme Being, since it says nothing about the nature or basic intelligibility of the being.[192]

After comparing Aristotle and Thomas, Bracken focuses on being and its relationship to God. Thomas was not wrong in identifying being with God, in a qualified sense, but Heidegger was right that Thomas did not inquire far enough into the nature of being. Identifying God with being does not answer the deeper question of what being means.[193] For Bracken, being is an activity rather than an entity. God as the Supreme Being is therefore supreme, eternal, eminent activity. God's nature is being, the act of existence, defined as perpetual activity or continuous passage from potency to act.[194] Thomas said that "everything acts according as it is actual," so God is an always active but immaterial entity, and thus hypostasized activity.[195] This movement is fully actual at every moment since as an entelechy or self-contained activity it has already achieved its essen-

190. Bracken, *Society and Spirit,* 24; Bracken, *The One in the Many,* 19, 21; Bracken, *God: Three Who Are One,* 62–63.

191. Bracken, *The Divine Matrix,* 142–43 n. 4, 145 n. 8.

192. Ibid., 28.

193. Bracken, *"Ipsum Esse Subsistens,"* 283; Bracken, *The Divine Matrix,* 28–29.

194. Bracken, *The Divine Matrix,* 29, 31–33, 36; Bracken, *God: Three Who Are One,* 73–74, 83–84.

195. St. Thomas Aquinas, *ST* 1a.50.5.

tial perfection or form, even as it continues to attain that perfection in its successive stages of actualization. God requires no extrinsic mover, but rather moves God's self from potency to actuality in virtue of God's own intrinsic dynamism.[196] Following other process theologians, Bracken says this view is more faithful to the biblical idea of the "Living God" compared to classical theism.[197]

As mentioned, Bracken argues that since being is the ontological ground of an entity and its interior principle of existence and activity, being cannot be an entity ontologically distinct from the entities it empowers to exist. Thus being as activity never exists except as instantiated in an entity as the subject of that activity. This, coupled with Aristotle's claim that all determinate, actual beings must be limited and therefore finite, means Thomas wrongly said the Supreme Being is an actual determinate entity and infinite at the same time. Thomas wrongly conflated the divine nature or eternal activity, which is infinite, and the entitative reality of God, the Supreme Being, or more accurately the three divine persons.[198]

Thus Bracken distinguishes between the divine nature as the act of existence, and the divine persons as the instantiations of the Act of Being. The Act of Being grounds the entitative reality of God without a distinction between the Act of Being and the entitative reality of God, because the distinction between cause and effect only ever applies to two different entities.[199] Hence God is Subsistent Being (Subsistent Activity) as the primordial subject of the activity of existing. While finite entities are also subsistent activities, they eventually terminate their acts of self-constitution, and become superjects. God is the actual entity whose self-development process never ends. God never becomes an entity in the classical sense, or a fixed objective reality, but always remains the subject of ongoing activity. God as Subsistent Activity is always in act.[200]

Bracken also revises, along the same lines as other process theolo-

196. Bracken, *The Divine Matrix,* 32.

197. Ibid.; Bracken, *Christianity and Process Thought,* 23.

198. Bracken, *The Divine Matrix,* 21, 29–33, 37, 43, 56–67, 105, 138–40, 145 n. 8; Bracken, *The One in the Many,* 205; Bracken, *Christianity and Process Thought,* 19, 63; Bracken, *God: Three Who Are One,* 105 n. 33; Bracken, "*Ipsum Esse Subsistens,*" 283–84; Bracken, "The Issue of Panentheism," 216; Bracken, "Creativity," 118; Bracken, "An Example of Western Theology," 43.

199. Bracken, *The Divine Matrix,* 33; Bracken, *God: Three Who Are One,* 33–34, 89–90.

200. Bracken, *The Divine Matrix,* 29–30, 56–57; Bracken, "*Ipsum Esse Subsistens,*" 283–85.

gians, St. Thomas's treatment of God's incommunicable attributes of perfection, infinity, immutability, and eternity. Continually including actualizations of potentialities previously unrealized, God's perfection increases but never decreases.[201] Continuous overlap of potentiality and actuality from one stage in the divine life to the next constitutes a type of immutability.[202] As Aristotle defined the present as the extremity of the past and of the future, or their common boundary, the moments of divine acts of existence successively flow into each other so there is no sense of before and after as separate moments. This togetherness of the past, present, and future is God's eternity.[203] God as the enduring subject of the activity of endless conversion of potentiality to actuality is God's infinity, because this process ceases for all finite entities.[204]

The Relationship between Creativity and God

For Bracken, Whiteheadian creativity as infinite motion is the divine nature. As discussed in the first chapter, many Whiteheadians say creativity is an empirical generalization from what de facto occurs in the concrescence of actual entities. Bracken does hold that creativity never exists apart from actual entities, thus avoiding the fallacy of misplaced concreteness. However he does not believe creativity is merely a generalization. It is an ontological reality in its own right. If creativity were simply a descriptive principle it would not explain why such a perpetual process should exist in the first place. Creativity is not a higher-level entity but an activity instantiated in actual entities. It is not an entity itself but only exists in and through the entities it empowers. As such, it is the divine nature as the "Act of Being" in classical theistic parlance.[205]

In terms of the one and the many, creativity is the one. Individual actual entities come and go but creativity never ceases. It is thus both the one ultimate reality and Aristotle's primary substance. In order to be on-

201. Bracken, *The Divine Matrix*, 29–31; Bracken, *Christianity and Process Thought*, 20; Bracken, *Three Who Are One*, 11–12.

202. Bracken, *The Divine Matrix*, 31–32.

203. Bracken, *The Divine Matrix*, 34; Bracken, *Christianity and Process Thought*, 78, 82, 111.

204. Bracken, *The Divine Matrix*, 33–34.

205. Bracken, *The Divine Matrix*, 58; Bracken, *Christianity and Process Thought*, 19, 23; Bracken, *Three Who Are One*, 84; Bracken, "Non-Duality," 141; Bracken, "Creativity," 112, 114; Bracken, "Process Philosophy and Trinitarian Theology—II," 86; Bracken, "Trinity: Economic and Immanent," 21.

going, creativity must be numerically one rather than many. It must be the single foundational activity at work in all self-constituting actual occasions rather than simply a descriptive term for many, discrete, particular activities of self-constitution. Creativity is the "One *in* the Many."[206]

Bracken agrees with many that there is an ambiguity in Whitehead's discussion of God's relation to creativity. Whitehead too sharply distinguishes between God and creativity, to the point of making God as much "creature" of creativity as are finite entities.[207] With many other commentators Bracken concludes that for Whitehead creativity is metaphysically ultimate beyond God, and that thus creativity is Whitehead's "Absolute."[208]

Bracken believes Whitehead sharply distinguishes between God and creativity to exculpate God from being ultimately responsible for all evil. Creativity is impersonal and non-rational, the vital source for everything that happens, both good and evil. God is an entity whose very nature is the setting of limits to productive creativity, thus dividing the good from the evil.[209]

Since God is the aboriginal instance of creativity or aboriginal condition that qualifies action, Bracken says creativity is God's essence, what makes God to be God.[210] Creativity or the divine nature only exists in actual entities, and God as person or persons is the primordial or archetypal instantiation of creativity. This avoids positing two metaphysical ultimates. Whitehead erred by making creativity and the extensive con-

206. Bracken, *The One in the Many,* 123; Bracken, "Creativity," 112.

207. Bracken, *The Triune Symbol,* 59 n. 24; Bracken, *Society and Spirit,* 127; Bracken, *The Divine Matrix,* 54; Bracken, *The One in the Many,* 8; Bracken, *Christianity and Process Thought,* 14, 18, 22; Bracken, *Three Who Are One,* 62; Bracken, "Creativity," 113, 115; Bracken, "Trinity: Economic and Immanent," 20 n. 26.

208. Bracken, "Creativity," 112. "Absolute" here is Bracken's term. For reasons discussed in the first chapter, Whitehead would probably take issue with calling what is metaphysically ultimate "absolute," be that ultimate creativity, God, or something else.

209. Bracken, *Society and Spirit,* 132; Bracken, *Christianity and Process Thought,* 14, 18–19; Bracken, "Creativity," 111. For many classical theists evil is the privation of being, which is good, and hence not a being or entity in itself.

210. Bracken, *Society and Spirit,* 132; Bracken, *The Divine Matrix,* 3–4, 55–56, 65, 110; Bracken, *The One in the Many,* 205; Bracken, *Christianity and Process Thought,* 19; Bracken, "Trinity: Economic and Immanent," 19–21; Bracken, "Prehending God," 13 n. 6; Bracken, "An Example of Western Theology," 42–43; Bracken, "The Issue of Panentheism," 215–16; Bracken, "Non-Duality," 141, 144–45; Bracken, "Whitehead," 94; Bracken, "Creativity," 111–17.

tinuum "metaphysical givens." He should have anchored them in God as co-constituents of the divine nature, the ontological ground for God's own existence, and by derivation that for all creatures.[211]

Creativity is thus the divine nature and not something transcendent to, prior to, before, or "above" God. At the same time God's nature as the principle of being or creativity is distinct from God as the Supreme Being.[212] So, according to Bracken, we must say that the word "God" can denote two different things: the divine nature, or the Supreme Being. Although grounding the three divine persons, creativity as the Godhead does not exist "first" with the persons emerging from this transcendent ground of being.[213] Again, the one divine nature, infinite activity or creativity, does not exist in itself but only in the entities it empowers to exist. The divine nature can only exist in and through the divine persons.

Bracken exonerates God from evil by construing God in tripersonal rather than unipersonal terms. If creativity is God's underlying nature it is morally neutral but always employed for good by the divine persons. The Act of Being is Whitehead's "substantial activity," which is morally neutral. The three persons, though, effect good in creation and reduce, if not eliminate, evil by encouraging actual occasions to concur with and participate in the Son in the divine goodness.[214]

God as the "Act of Being"

Bracken's reconstruction of the divine nature leads him to a similar reframing of Thomistic participated being. If God is pure actuality without any potentiality, then God is purely objective, the supreme object of thought. God is an idea of reason instead of a living person. God as the principle of potentiality allows us to also think of God as a subject of experience. As a subject God is in the perpetual process of further actual-

211. Bracken, *The Divine Matrix,* 57; Bracken, *The One in the Many,* 84, 126–27; Bracken, *Christianity and Process Thought,* 19–20; Bracken, "Whitehead," 94; Bracken, "Creativity," 111; Bracken, "Response to Elizabeth Johnson's 'Does God Play Dice?'" 725 n. 14; Bracken, "Panentheism from a Trinitarian Perspective," 15, 17; Bracken, "The Issue of Panentheism," 216.

212. Bracken, *The Divine Matrix,* 56, 152 n. 22; Bracken, *Christianity and Process Thought,* 19, 63; Bracken, "Non-Duality," 141; Bracken, "The Issue of Panentheism," 210, 216.

213. Bracken, "Non-Duality," 144–45.

214. Bracken, *Society and Spirit,* 132, 178 n. 24; Bracken, "Process Philosophy and Trinitarian Theology—II," 90–91.

ization. If God were fully actualized then God would cease to be a subject of experience and become an object of thought.[215]

For much classical theism, the Act of Being is the principle whereby entities exist. Finite beings participate in the Act of Being in a contingent and limited way but God as the sole infinite being exists necessarily and without limitation. God's essence is coextensive with the Act of Being in its fullness.[216] Bracken agrees with this trajectory but makes two qualifications.

First, the Act of Being involves interrelating. Creativity is the principle by which all entities, including God, prehend their predecessors in the world, and which unifies them into individual self-consciousnesses.[217] In addition to being the ontological principle of self-constitution for individual entities, creativity is the principle whereby those entities in and through concrescence also co-constitute the societies to which they belong. Empowering actual occasions to become themselves, creativity also empowers them to be related to one another in various societal configurations up to and including the whole universe. Creativity is best understood as the principle of intersubjectivity by which actual entities, both finite and infinite, come into existence and relate to each other in various societal configurations. The Trinity is the archetype, where the activity of interrelating is coextensive with the Act of Being in its fullness.[218]

Second, the Act of Being as interrelating creativity is not a static, but a dynamic reality instantiated in new concrete entities each moment. Therefore the Act of Being is not an infinitely actual being or entity, but exists in its instantiations only.

The Act of Being is also a processive reality since it is instantiated differently each new moment of existence. It is not eternally unchanging. The Act of Being is an activity that: (1) is renewed moment by moment in the three divine persons; (2) exists in each entity as interrelated to all others, which are thus also subsistent relations by virtue of the same Act of

215. Bracken, "Response to Elizabeth Johnson's 'Does God Play Dice?'" 725–28. Cf. Bracken, *God: Three Who Are One,* 105 n. 33.

216. St. Thomas Aquinas, *ST* 1a.3.4.

217. Bracken, "The Issue of Panentheism," 215, 216–17.

218. Bracken, *The Triune Symbol,* 45–46; Bracken, *God: Three Who Are One,* 77–78, 84; Bracken, "The Issue of Panentheism," 215; Bracken, "Panentheism from a Process Perspective," 105; Bracken, "Process Philosophy and Trinitarian Theology—II," 86.

Being; and (3) is never the same from moment to moment, since the activity of interrelating is ever-new.[219] God is in process.

Bracken's Whiteheadian understanding of the Act of Being as subjective interrelating creativity is both similar to and different from the traditional Thomistic Act of Being. Both are formless and both are the principles of existence and activity for the entities in which they are embodied.[220] Thomas saw the Act of Being as actuality, however, while here it is potentiality. Creativity actively imparts existence and activity but the Thomistic *actus purus* experiences no movement from potency to act in its "activity" of imparting existence and activity. Thomas also strictly identifies God as entity with God as the Act of Being, while here there is a distinction.[221]

"Participated Being" in Bracken's Philosophical Theology

With this view of the Act of Being, Bracken reshapes the traditional doctrine that creatures possess their being through participation in the divine being. For St. Thomas God is the first efficient cause of all that exists by providing the being or existence *(esse)* of all that exists. God acts upon creatures through the divine essence or nature, which is being or existence *(esse)*. God is present to creatures by communicating to them the act of existence, which is a share in the divine Act of Being proportionate to their finite essences. The act of existence of finite beings properly belongs to these finite beings, even as this act participates in the unlimited act of existence proper to God alone.[222]

For Bracken participated being means all entities, including the divine persons, derive the creativity for their self-constitution from the divine nature. The unity of being obtains not in God's relation to all finite beings but in how all beings, including God as the Supreme Being, share a common principle or act of existence.[223] Creativity or the divine nature

219. Bracken, "Subsistent Relation," 194 n. 17; Bracken, "Process Philosophy and Trinitarian Theology—II," 86.

220. Bracken, "Trinity: Economic and Immanent," 17 n. 22; Bracken, "Process Philosophy and Trinitarian Theology—II," 89; Bracken, "Response to Elizabeth Johnson's 'Does God Play Dice?'" 725, 725 n. 14.

221. Bracken, "Response to Elizabeth Johnson's 'Does God Play Dice?'" 725; Bracken, "Panentheism from a Trinitarian Perspective," 15 n. 23, 17.

222. See St. Thomas Aquinas, *ST* 1a.2.3; 1a.8.1, 4; 1a.44.1.

223. Bracken, "The Issue of Panentheism," 215–16.

empowers actual occasions to constitute themselves and to be related in various societal configurations.[224] It is like a field from which all entities, including the divine persons, borrow existence. As the ground of being this energy field is like the classical divine substance in which both the divine persons and all finite entities share. It is the vital source of their existence and activity.[225] All created beings share in the divine being as the underlying nature of God, but they do not share in the concrete entitative reality of God as the supreme actual being.[226]

In addition to denying that creativity transcends God, Bracken differs from Whitehead in *how* God's nature provides being for every new actual entity. For Whitehead, God's role is summed up in the provision of the initial aim and the realm of possibilities in God's primordial nature. For Bracken, God actually imparts God's self, the divine nature, to every new actual entity. Communication of creativity from God's nature is what "participated being" means.[227]

Bracken criticizes the traditional view of participated being for making created entities accidental modifications of the divine substance with no real existence in their own right. Without at least a formal distinction between God as the primordial instantiation of the Act of Being and the Act of Being itself, all finite beings would become accidental modifications of the one divine entity, and a universe like Spinoza's results.[228]

According to the ontological principle, creativity must exist in some actual entity if it is to be a reason or cause. The creative ground of the universe must be located somewhere. It exists in God as the primordial existent from which "location" all finite occasions derive existence.[229] These finite entities are ontologically distinct from God, yet they are grounded in God because of the divine nature.[230] By God's free decision creativity

224. Bracken, *Christianity and Process Thought*, 20–21; Bracken, "The Issue of Panentheism," 215; Bracken, "Creativity," 114–15.

225. Bracken, "Panentheism from a Trinitarian Perspective," 16–17; Bracken, *God: Three Who Are One*, 53, 77–78.

226. Bracken, "*Ipsum Esse Subsistens*," 283.

227. Bracken, *The Triune Symbol*, 59 n. 24; Bracken, "Response to Elizabeth Johnson's 'Does God Play Dice?'" 729.

228. Bracken, *The Triune Symbol*, 47; Bracken, *Society and Spirit*, 138, 141, 148, 178 n. 32; Bracken, *Christianity and Process Thought*, 4, 8; Bracken, "Subsistent Relation," 196.

229. Bracken, *The Divine Matrix*, 29, 33, 55, 67, 110.

230. Bracken, "Creativity," 114.

becomes the principle of activity for all creatures.[231] In this way the creation exists "in God" and "through the power of God."[232] Since God's nature is the activity of creativity, activity, not entity, is the dynamic principle or ground of the divine being, and as such is the ground of all finite beings.

Participated being for Bracken is also a participation in the trinitarian divine life. God shares God's life with creatures by granting them the radical power of self-constituting freedom as the incipience of their concrescence. This synthesizes the traditional confession of God as the "Creator of heaven and earth" without compromising the point that actual entities come into being by a radical power of self-constitution. Being the divine nature in which we participate, freedom is mysterious to us.[233]

This creative power for self-constitution communicated to creatures is itself an image of the creative freedom for self-constitution of the divine persons. Participated being is also a participation in the principle of divine intersubjectivity. This divine intersubjectivity is how creatures come to share in the intra-trinitarian life, and how the three divine persons recreate the divine community in each new moment.[234]

Creativity and the "Void"

Bracken likens his understanding of the divine nature as creativity, potentiality, and activity to "emptiness," or *śūnyatā* in strands of philosophical Buddhism. Bracken dialogues with Keiji Nishitani, who says Absolute Nothingness "is at bottom one with being, even as being is at bottom one with emptiness" and a "field of force by virtue of which all things as they are in themselves gather themselves together into one: the field of possibility for the world."[235] For Nishitani, all "given things" gather themselves out of this field of possibility.[236]

231. Bracken, "Whitehead," 94; Bracken, "Non-Duality," 141.

232. Bracken, "Non-Duality," 141–42.

233. Bracken, *The Triune Symbol,* 46, 64–65, 70; Bracken, *Society and Spirit,* 128–29, 132; Bracken, *The Divine Matrix,* 29; Bracken, *The One in the Many,* 201; Bracken, "Trinity: Economic and Immanent," 19–21; Bracken, "Prehending God," 13 n. 6; Bracken, "An Example of Western Theology," 42; Bracken, "Non-Duality," 141–42; Bracken, "Creativity," 111–17.

234. Bracken, *The Triune Symbol,* 46, 64; Bracken, *The Divine Matrix,* 67; Bracken, *God: Three Who Are One,* 79, 104.

235. Keiji Nishitani, *Religion and Nothingness,* trans. Jan Van Bragt (Berkeley: University of California Press, 1982), 123.

236. Nishitani, *Religion and Nothingness,* 150–51.

Bracken takes a step many Buddhists would not take: identifying *śūnyatā* with the divine nature.[237] He proposes that God's underlying nature is the Whiteheadian extensive continuum plus the principle of creativity, which he says is very similar to Nishitani's "Void," or *śūnyatā* in Buddhism. He likens the "awakening" to reality of this divine matrix to Buddhist enlightenment, in which one becomes aware of one's own identification with Absolute Nothingness. Admitting incommensurabilities between his theism and much Buddhist philosophy, Bracken sees the commonalties between process metaphysics and Buddhism as potentially fruitful for interreligious dialogue.[238]

In discussing the Void, Bracken also introduces the intersubjectivity aspect of process metaphysics. Only infinite activity, not finite actuality, can be the ontological ground of divine and human subjectivity. Borrowing from Buber and Levinas, Bracken says the *activity* of intersubjectivity is a key part of infinity and transcendence. In addressing another human subject as Thou, the "I" is intuitively aware of the co-presence of the divine "Thous" as an enabling transcendent reality. The infinite is the matrix out of which all subjects emerge and interrelate, be they finite created subjects or the three divine subjects of the Trinity.[239]

From this he identifies the "vertical" dimension of the metaphysics of intersubjectivity with Nishida's "place of nothingness," the ontological matrix for the appearance of all entities, including the triune Creator God and all created entities. Absolute Nothingness, then, is the matrix from which all actual entities emerge and subjectively interrelate. The infinite ground of all entities as subjects is thus the infinite activity of intersubjectivity.[240]

237. Bracken, *The Divine Matrix,* 4; Bracken, *Society and Spirit,* 163–64, 181 n. 10; Bracken, *The One in the Many,* 124–25.

238. While lauded for his attempt at interreligious dialogue, Bracken's generalizations about Eastern traditions in order to arrive at a universal conception of ultimate reality have been criticized for ignoring the radical particularity of those traditions. See Leo D. Lefebure, review of *The Divine Matrix: Creativity as Link between East and West: Creativity of East and West,* by Joseph Bracken, *New Theology Review* 10, no. 1 (1997): 121; James L. Fredericks, review of *The Divine Matrix, Theological Studies* 57 (March 1996): 189; Anonymous, review of *The Divine Matrix, Irénikon* 68, no. 3 (1995): 444.

239. Bracken, *The Divine Matrix,* 39, 130; Bracken, *The One in the Many,* 16–17, 124; Bracken, "Prehending God," 13 n. 6; Bracken, "Intersubjectivity," 383, 397.

240. Bracken, *The Divine Matrix,* 107–8, 109, 110, 130, 132; Bracken, *The One in the Many,* 8, 10, 15–16, 113–14, 123–25, 146, 149, 172; Bracken, "The Issue of Panentheism," 210–11; Bracken, "Intersubjectivity," 393, 399; Bracken, "Non-Duality," 145.

Creativity, the Extensive Continuum, and the "Ontogenetic Matrix"

The connections between intersubjectivity, relationality, and activity lead Bracken to describe an extensive continuum as a complex of entities united by their relationships with one another. For Whitehead, *the* extensive continuum underlies the whole world, past, present, and future, providing a relational complex in which all entities, actual and potential, have their own place or standpoint. It is the "physical field" for the actual world.[241]

Bracken unites the extensive continuum with creativity as God's mode of activity in the world. He believes the extensive continuum implies that the God-world relationship is a joint field of activity for God and creatures. Christian calls creativity and the extensive continuum "two differentiable, but inseparable, aspects of the ultimate ground of the organic universe."[242] Nobo explicitly links the extensive continuum with creativity in what he calls the "ontogenetic matrix," as the ultimate field of activity and source of both God and creatures.[243] Bracken says this conjunction is necessary.[244] Nobo says that, for Whitehead,

> creativity and extension are indissoluble aspects of one ultimate reality—a reality underlying the becoming, the being and the solidarity of all actual entities . . . two differentiable, but inseparable, aspects of the ultimate ground of the organic universe. This ultimate ground has no name of its own, other than the names used to designate its two indissoluble aspects.[245]

Although creativity is the principle by which the "many become one and are increased by one," the extensive continuum is the reason why actual occasions are not just externally contiguous but are internally related.[246] As the whereby of all becoming it is termed "creativity," but as the where-

241. Whitehead, *Process and Reality,* 66 (103); 80 (123).

242. Christian, *An Interpretation of Whitehead's Metaphysics,* 395–96.

243. Jorge Luis Nobo, "Experience, Eternity, and Primordiality," *Process Studies* 26 (1997): 190–94.

244. Bracken, *The One in the Many,* 12, 123–25, 146, 149, 172, 205 n. 91; 172–73; Bracken, "Supervenience," 147.

245. Jorge Luis Nobo, *Whitehead's Metaphysics of Extension and Solidarity* (Albany: State University of New York Press, 1986), 255–56.

246. Bracken, "Proposals for Overcoming the Atomism," 23 n. 7.

in of all interconnected existence it is "extension." Without creativity the finite actual entity would lack the power of self-constitution, and without the extensive continuum it would not exist in the solidarity with other actual entities, which is necessary for its prehensions. The extensive continuum is just as much an ontological ground for actual entities as creativity.[247]

Like creativity, the extensive continuum is not an entity but is the necessary presupposition for entities. As entities presuppose a principle of activity for their activities of self-constitution, they also presuppose an ongoing context or structure in which they all coexist in dynamic interrelation.[248] Like Aristotelian prime matter, neither creativity nor the extensive continuum exists as an entity apart from the actual entities in which they are instantiated.[249]

Bracken agrees with Schelling and Heidegger that the ontological ground of a being cannot itself be a being without needing to be grounded by still another being. Thus the ontological ground of a being is not another being but a hidden dimension of that being. This ground is real but not fully actual (determinate) because without the ground the existent could never come to actually exist.[250] The determinate actuality is an entity's character as existent and what emerges out of the real but indeterminate extensive continuum as its ground. Like creativity and societies, the extensive continuum has ontological reality but is not an entity.

The extensive continuum cannot be a metaphysical given apart from the reality of God, as it is in Whitehead. With creativity it should be identified with the divine nature. Since the extensive continuum, like creativity, is not an actual entity but the condition of the possibility of the dynamic interrelation of actual entities, it, too, must be in the first place the ground and vital principle for the divine being.[251] This is in God's self as the divine nature but not completely identical with God as an entity or existent.

Once again, the ontological principle dictates that the ground of the

247. Bracken, *The Divine Matrix,* 3, 58–59; Bracken, "Creativity," 114–15.

248. Bracken, *The Divine Matrix,* 3.

249. Bracken, "Creativity," 114, 115.

250. Bracken, *The Divine Matrix,* 66–67; Bracken, "Trinity: Economic and Immanent," 20.

251. Bracken, *Society and Spirit,* 123–39; Bracken, "Panentheism from a Trinitarian Perspective," 15 n. 24, 16; Bracken, "Trinity: Economic and Immanent," 20.

universe as its "reason" must be located in an actual entity. Since it can be located only in an actual existent, it must be located in God as the primordial existent. From this "location" "in God" all finite occasions exist and have their activity. Since neither creativity nor the extensive continuum are entities but only instantiations, they subsist primordially in God and secondarily in finite entities.[252] The extensive continuum and creativity are together the all-encompassing divine field of activity out of which all finite occasions and the three divine persons originate.[253]

The Ontogenetic Matrix as All-Encompassing "Field"

If creativity and the extensive continuum are "differentiable, but inseparable, aspects of the ultimate ground of the organic universe," then we can picture them as both constituting a "force field" of unlimited proportions over which God as the sole infinite actual entity presides and in which all finite entities continually emerge.[254] One can infer the idea of a common field of activity for God and the world from Hartshorne's idea that God is a personally ordered society of actual occasions much like the human soul in relationship to the human body, which is comparable to Pannenberg's understanding of the underlying nature of God as a "force field."[255]

Like societies and their members, the extensive field and its members mutually co-constitute each other. The God-world relationship is an all-comprehensive field of activity constituted first by the three divine persons and secondly by the world of created entities. Yet this field is simultaneously the context for the origination of all entities, including the three divine persons.[256]

252. Bracken, *The Divine Matrix,* 59, 67; Bracken, "Panentheism from a Process Perspective," 106; Bracken, "Creativity," 115.

253. Bracken, "Intersubjectivity," 393, 399; Bracken, "Creativity," 114–18; Bracken, "Panentheism from a Process Perspective," 103–5, 106; Bracken, "Proposals for Overcoming the Atomism," 17, 19.

254. Bracken, *The Divine Matrix,* 60; Bracken, *Christianity and Process Thought,* 8–10; Bracken, *God: Three Who Are One,* 78–79; Bracken, "Creativity," 116.

255. Bracken, *The One in the Many,* 173; Bracken, *God: Three Who Are One,* 53, 77–78; Bracken, "Supervenience," 148; Bracken, *The Divine Matrix,* 153 n. 36.

256. Bracken, *The Divine Matrix,* 60, 65; Bracken, *The One in the Many,* 11; Bracken, *Christianity and Process Thought,* 8–10; Bracken, *God: Three Who Are One,* 76, 78–80, 103–4, 115, 188, 125.

Bracken's Critiques of "Rational" and "Empirical" Process Panentheisms

Bracken's "ontogenetic matrix" grounds his unique version of panentheism. Panentheism means all created entities exist "in and through" God while remaining ontologically distinct from God.[257] Agreeing with other process theologians, he says process thought is inherently panentheistic. In Whitehead's universe, every entity, including God, has internal relationships with all other entities through its prehensions and internal relationships. Every entity's very being is constituted by its relationships with other entities. This is a truly relational ontology.

Bracken's system is panentheistic because creatures literally exist "in" the divine nature, or ontogenetic matrix. Creatures are ontologically distinct from God because the divine persons emerge from the energy field as distinct not only from each other but from all other finite entities.[258] Creatures exist "in" God in the divine nature, but "apart from" God as personal entity.

Bracken takes issue with much process panentheism. For most process panentheists, either (1) "God" is just the collective name for all the things that currently exist, so God and the world are identical; or (2) finite beings participate in God's act of existence proper only by reduction to accidental modifications of the divine being.[259]

Whitehead says God's consequent nature is the realization of the actual world in the unity of God's nature. If this means God's consequent nature is the one world process then it is Aristotelian. The unity of the many actual occasions is grounded in the quasi-substantial reality of the one sole transcendent actual entity, God.[260] The world is ultimately transient and ephemeral compared to the reality of God. This does not really solve the "problem of the perpetual perishing" of the world because in the end only God survives. Once finite entities are actualized, they pass into

257. Bracken, *Society and Spirit,* 123; Bracken, *Society and Spirit,* 159; Bracken, *God: Three Who Are One,* 79; Bracken, "The Issue of Panentheism," 209; Bracken, "Intersubjectivity," 393; Bracken, "Panentheism from a Trinitarian Perspective," 7 n. 2.

258. Bracken, *The Divine Matrix,* 58–59; Bracken, *Christianity and Process Thought,* 8–9; 55–56, 60; Bracken, *God: Three Who Are One,* 78–79, 103, 118; Bracken, "Panentheism from a Trinitarian Perspective," 19.

259. Bracken, *The Divine Matrix,* 28.

260. Bracken, "Subsistent Relation," 192; Bracken, "Philosophical Foundations," 56–57.

God and never exist independently of God, as panentheism requires.[261]

This betrays vestiges of the Aristotelian mindset. It implicitly conceives of God as a transcendent substance that at every moment incorporates finite actual entities as its latest accidental modification. The superject entities in God's consequent nature are ultimately only accidental modifications of the one substantial reality of God. The only other option is Bracken's view of ultimate reality as a cosmic society. Bracken thinks this flows from Whitehead's decision to understand God as an individual actual entity instead of a community of persons who constitute an all-embracing field of activity.[262]

Bracken finds similar difficulties with Hartshorne's world as the "body of God" model. Hartshorne's panentheism makes the world an ontological necessity because God needs a body. This cannot support the Christian doctrine of God's freedom in creation.[263] Hartshorne's view gives the world a spatial unity but not temporal unity from moment to moment, since there is no enduring society that exists over time.[264] It also forgets that when the human body perishes, so does the soul, which raises the problem of how God can endure in the death and reconstitution of every puncticular world from moment to moment.[265] This model is not conducive to the specifically Christian doctrine of God as triune, because if God relates to the world in the same way a human soul relates to the human body, then that makes God unipersonal, not tripersonal.[266]

Perhaps Bracken's most important criticism gets to the crux of what he sees as the essence of panentheism. In the final analysis it is not clear from the soul-body analogy how creatures have ontological independence from God.[267] Hartshorne's model is problematic because organisms are conventionally regarded as substances mutually excluding one another. One substance cannot appropriate another substance without

261. Bracken, *Society and Spirit*, 135–36, 137–38, 141, 159–60.

262. Ibid., 138, 148, 178 n. 32.

263. Bracken, *Christianity and Process Thought*, 5–8; Bracken, *God: Three Who Are One*, 79; Bracken, "Intersubjectivity," 394.

264. Bracken, "Proposals for Overcoming Atomism," 16.

265. Bracken, *Society and Spirit*, 139, 141, 148; Bracken, "Panentheism from a Process Perspective," 95.

266. Bracken, "The World," 90, 100 n. 8; Bracken, "Intersubjectivity," 394; Bracken, "Images of God," 364.

267. Bracken, "The Issue of Panentheism," 211–12.

reducing the other to an accidental modification of itself. This means we must either regard God and the world as one composite substance or revert to a strict ontological dualism; either way the intention of panentheism is defeated.[268]

This soul-body analogy's failure to account for the genuine independence of creatures is related to an imbalanced view of societies among Hartshornean rationalists. The organismic model implies the parts are subordinate to the whole organism, while a true societal model presupposes the parts retain their individual identity as they constitute something bigger.[269]

While rationalistic process theologians fall into a type of pantheism, more empirical Whiteheadians like Meland and Loomer fall into a pancosmism. As radical empiricists, Meland and Loomer make the experiential realm the only final reality. Thus they tend to collapse the reality of God here and now into the enduring reality of the world.[270]

Bracken's Panentheism

Bracken's view deserves more attention from process theologians because it might resolve some difficulties connected with panentheism. Some in fact judge Bracken's panentheism to be one of the best statements and defenses of the position.[271] Seeing pantheism in many process panentheists, Bracken claims to offer genuine panentheism in his field-oriented interpretation of Whiteheadian societies.[272]

In the field-oriented view larger fields can contain smaller fields still governed by their own laws or patterns of activity. Unlike substances, fields or societies can be layered within one another without losing the ontological independence of the lower-level fields and their constituent

268. Bracken, *The Divine Matrix,* 91; Bracken, *Society and Spirit,* 148; Bracken, *Christianity and Process Thought,* 5–8; Bracken, "Images of God," 372.

269. Bracken, "The World," 90; Bracken, "Images of God," 368.

270. Bracken, *Society and Spirit,* 15; Bracken, "Panentheism from a Process Perspective," 95, 96 n.6; Bracken, "Non-Duality," 144.

271. Philip Clayton says Bracken provides "the most sophisticated defense yet of what I have called the Panentheistic Analogy" (Philip Clayton, foreword to *The One in the Many,* xi). Bracken himself notes how "panentheism as a model for the God-world relationship is easier endorsed than explained" ("A. N. Whitehead and My Search for a Fully Consistent Social Ontology," unpublished manuscript, 2009, p. 8).

272. Bracken, "Images of God," 370; Bracken, *Society and Spirit,* 140.

actual occasions. Every subfield is governed by its own laws and has relative autonomy, but at the same time it contributes to the larger field of activity in which it is contained. God and finite realities can coexist in the same "place" at the same "time," while they each retain their ontological independence.[273] Since Bracken's "divine matrix" is a "dynamic context" instead of "substance-in-place," it can inform a finite entity and be copresent with it as that entity's principle of existence and activity without removing the entity's status of ontological independence.[274] Creation is a functioning totality as a field, with its own relative autonomous existence in the larger field of activity proper to the divine persons.[275] This also accounts for how non-theists can interpret their experience of the world as a self-sufficient totality of interrelated causes and effects, while theists can interpret their experience as evidence that the world is a quasi-autonomous reality with God working in and through the world.[276]

True panentheism obtains only if one understands the God-world relationship as interpenetrating fields of activity with the creation field contained within the larger divine field without damage to the relative autonomy and mode of operation of the creatures.[277] Bracken does not deny, however, that God has a privileged status in the society of all existents through a providential role in the ongoing direction of the universe.[278]

Bracken also contends that his version of panentheism comports with St. Thomas's understanding of the God-world relationship. Because creatures exist in and through the power of God yet retain their own ontological or separate identities, St. Thomas's view seems panentheistic.[279]

Bracken says panentheism must incorporate his distinction between the divine essence and the divine persons, which he says is of a piece with the classical distinction between being *(esse)* and beings *(essentiae)*. Creatures exist "in" God where "God" designates the divine nature or essence. The divine nature is the pure Act of Being in and through the power of which both God as entity and creatures as entities are empowered to ex-

273. Bracken, *Society and Spirit,* 123, 140; Bracken, *Christianity and Process Thought,* 55–56, 60; Bracken, *God: Three Who Are One,* 68, 74, 116; Bracken, "Images of God," 370, 372.

274. Bracken, *The One in the Many,* 124–25.

275. Bracken, *Society and Spirit,* 154.

276. Bracken, "The Issue of Panentheism," 207, 209, 217.

277. Bracken, *Society and Spirit,* 137, 159.

278. Bracken, "Subsistent Relation," 192 n. 13.

279. Bracken, "The Issue of Panentheism," 210–11, 216.

ist. Creatures cannot exist in God where "God" refers to the divine "being" as *a* being or entitative reality, because then creatures would only be absorbed into the reality of God, becoming accidental modifications of God.[280]

The Objective Unity of the World Apart from God

Noting there are different interpretations, Bracken believes Whitehead locates the world's unity in God's consequent nature. Actual entities unify their physical and conceptual data, but the actual worlds perceived by these entities are "perspectival" due to their finite subjectivity. The only possible location for a non-perspectival vision of the world is God's primordial nature, and the only possible location for an objective unity of the world is God's non-perspectival physical prehension of all of the events taking place in the world.[281] If this interpretation is correct, then this is an example of how in the West *ontology* has been subtly confused with *onto-theo-logy*, as Heidegger says. Bracken describes *onto-theology* as the mistaken belief that ontological objectivity is synonymous with God's understanding of reality.[282] Those who follow Hartshorne's "body of God" analogy fall into logocentrism because all truth and value are legitimated only in reference to God as the world's principle of unity and order.[283]

Bracken points out how, when Whitehead speaks of the extensive continuum, he speaks as if the universe were an ontological totality in its own right.[284] However, since God's experience of the world's unity and objectivity is a prehension now of the world's unity and objectivity a moment ago, God's experience does not establish the world's unity and objectivity but only reflects it. What constitutes the unity and objectivity

280. Ibid., 210–11.

281. Bracken, "Whitehead," 102–3; Bracken, *The One in the Many*, 95–97.

282. Bracken, "Authentic Subjectivity," 296–97. Westphal says for Heidegger *onto-theology* occurs when philosophy, Christian or other, tries to render the whole of being intelligible with reference to God, who is also thus rendered intelligible. He further argues that classical Christian theism is *not* an instance of *onto-theology*. See Merold Westphal, "Overcoming Onto-Theology," in *Overcoming Onto-theology: Toward a Postmodern Christian Faith* (New York: Fordham University Press, 2001), 1–28.

283. Bracken, *The One in the Many*, 199; Bracken, "Whitehead," 105.

284. Bracken, "Proposals for Overcoming the Atomism," 15. See also Bracken, "Testimony and Intersubjectivity," 40; Bracken, "Authentic Subjectivity," 296–97; Bracken, "Philosophical Foundations," 57.

of world process is the same as with any society: the self-constitution of all actual entities in virtue of the common element of form derived from their joint prehension of their predecessors in the same society a moment ago. The objective universe's common element of form, not God's experience of it an instant later, is the basis of the world's unity and objectivity.[285]

Bracken adds that his modified interpretation of societies is also of help in maintaining God's freedom in the act of creation in addition to maintaining the world's objective unity. The divine society is prior to all actual occasions, which preserves divine freedom in creation.[286]

Bracken's Distinctive Process Trinitarianism

A central feature of Bracken's theology distinguishing it from other process theologies is his trinitarianism. Most process theologians devote little if any time to the doctrine of the Trinity, though some have developed tentative constructions. Some even say process thought and trinitarianism are incommensurable.[287] A perfunctory look at process trinitarian proposals reveals a diversity, betraying the difficulty of constructing a process doctrine of the Trinity.[288]

285. Bracken, "Authentic Subjectivity," 296–97.

286. Bracken, *The Divine Matrix,* 61; Bracken, *The One in the Many,* 101; Bracken, *God: Three Who Are One,* 68, 78–80, 104, 105 n. 33; Bracken, "Proposals for Overcoming the Atomism," 16–19; Bracken, "Creativity," 115, 116.

287. Samuel M. Powell, "A Trinitarian Alternative to Process Theism," in *Thy Nature & Thy Name Is Love: Wesleyan and Process Theologies in Dialogue,* ed. Bryan P. Stone and Thomas Jay Oord (Nashville: Abingdon Press, 2001), 143–67.

288. For variegated process theological constructions of the Trinity, see, for instance: Lionel Thornton, *The Incarnate Lord* (London: Longmans Green, 1928), 40–46, 271–73, 396, 415–17; Daniel Day Williams, *The Spirit and the Forms of Love* (London: James Nisbet, 1968), 121, 126, 166, 183; Schubert M. Ogden, "On the Trinity," *Theology* 83 (1980): 97–102; Norman Pittenger, *The Divine Triunity* (Philadelphia: United Church Press, 1977); Norman Pittenger, *God in Process* (London: SCM Press, 1967), 107; Lewis S. Ford, *The Lure of God: A Biblical Background for Process Theism* (Philadelphia: Fortress Press, 1978), 28, 40, 45, 47, 48, 63–65, 83, 91, 94–95, 100–105, 110 n. 8, 124–25, 128; Norman Pittenger, *The Holy Spirit* (Philadelphia: Pilgrim Press, 1974), 122–24; John B. Cobb Jr., "The Relativization of the Trinity," in *Trinity in Process: A Relational Theology of God,* ed. Joseph A. Bracken, S.J., and Marjorie Hewitt Suchocki (New York: Continuum, 1997), 1–22; Cobb, "Response to Ted Peters," *Dialog* 30 (Summer 1991): 243–44; David Ray Griffin, "A Naturalistic Trinity," in *Trinity in Process,* 23–40; Marjorie Hewitt Suchocki, *God, Christ, Church: A Practical Guide to Process Theology* (New York: Crossroad, 1982), 215–16; Suchocki, "Spirit in and through the World,"

Bracken grounds his entire system in the Trinity. Like Barth before him, he argues that a theological interpretation of reality fundamentally depends on God, who in Christianity is a Trinity.[289] Pointing to how there are few process formulations of the Trinity, Bracken thinks that Whitehead's system inherently resists trinitarianism.[290] At the same time he finds classical trinitarianism wanting because the fourth-century Fathers did not have an adequate metaphysical basis for their discussions of the Trinity and Incarnation, and because the classical view sacrifices the personal nature of the three divine persons for the sake of intellectual intelligibility.[291] Bracken concludes that many contemporary theologians commit the same errors.[292]

Bracken on the Trinity as a Society

Because metaphysics must be grounded on social processes rather than individual entities, Bracken says God is a structured society in which societies and occasions are equiprimordial.[293] God's unity subsists in a struc-

---

in *Trinity in Process,* 173–90; Lewis S. Ford, "Process Trinitarianism," *Journal of the American Academy of Religion* 43, no. 2 (June 1975): 199–213; Ford, "Contingent Trinitarianism," in *Trinity in Process,* 41–68; Gregory A. Boyd, "The Self-Sufficient Sociality of God: A Trinitarian Revision of Hartshorne's Metaphysics," in *Trinity in Process,* 73–94; Boyd, *Trinity and Process: A Critical Evaluation and Reconstruction of Hartshorne's Dipolar Theism Towards a Trinitarian Metaphysics* (New York: Peter Lang, 1992); Donna Bowman, *The Divine Decision: A Process Doctrine of Election* (Louisville, Ky.: Westminster/John Knox Press, 2002), 182–85, 189, 263 n. 46; Philip Clayton, "Pluralism, Idealism, Romanticism: Untapped Resources for a Trinity in Process," in *Trinity in Process,* 117–45; Roland Faber, "Trinity, Analogy, and Coherence," in *Trinity in Process,* 14–71; Bernard J. Lee, S.M., "An 'Other' Trinity," in *Trinity in Process,* 191–214; William L. Power, "The Doctrine of the Trinity in Whitehead's Metaphysics," *Encounter* 45, no. 4 (Fall 1984): 287–302. For a revision of Hartshorne toward a trinitarian construction from an open theistic perspective, see Boyd, *Trinity and Process.*

289. Bracken, *The Triune Symbol,* 15 ; Bracken, *God: Three Who Are One,* 20–21, 24, 84–85, 124; Bracken, "Philosophical Foundations," 52–53.

290. Bracken, *What Are They Saying About the Trinity?* 30–32; Bracken, *Society and Spirit,* 124; Bracken, "Revising Process Metaphysics," 411–12; Bracken, "The World," 99, 102 n. 30.

291. Bracken, *The Triune Symbol,* 17; Bracken, *God: Three Who Are One,* 21–22, 24, 27, 47, 49–50; Bracken, review of *The Trinitarian Faith: The Evangelical Theology of the Ancient Catholic Church,* by Thomas F. Torrance, *Theological Studies* 51 (September 1990): 523–24.

292. See, for instance, his criticisms of Jüngel and Mühlen in Bracken, *The Triune Symbol,* 16, 46, 50–51, 60, 70–71. See also, Bracken, *God: Three Who Are One,* 46.

293. Bracken, "The World," 96–97; Bracken, *The Triune Symbol,* 6–7, 36–47; Bracken, *Society and Spirit,* 128; Bracken, *The Divine Matrix,* 36, 62; Bracken, "Proposals for Overcoming the Atomism," 17; Bracken, "The World," 96–97; Bracken, "Philosophical Founda-

tured society composed of the three divine persons, which is then the corporate subject of the divine act of existence as a "divine community." There is a strict reciprocity of the terms "person" and "community" in the Trinity. To be a person is to be member of a community and vice versa, so that the divine persons would cease to be God individually if they were not a part of a community, and without the persons the divine society would cease to be.[294]

In some ways this is a move toward Hartshorne and away from Whitehead. As discussed in the first chapter, Hartshorne sees God as a transcendent, personally ordered society of occasions occurring in temporal succession rather than the one single, non-temporal, actual entity in perpetual concrescence. Bracken accepts Hartshorne's and Cobb's reformulation of God as a personally ordered society of actual occasions instead of a non-temporal actual entity.[295] Bracken differs from Hartshorne, however, by saying God is tripersonal. God is a society of three divine persons, each of whom is a subsociety of actual occasions. So we must expand Hartshorne's view to include God as "a society of societies."

Not only is God a structured society, but the divine persons are three personally ordered subsocieties of actual occasions. God is a society of three subsocieties. In Whiteheadian terms God is a democratically organized, structured society composed of three personally ordered societies, the divine persons.[296]

Since the actual occasions constituting the divine persons perish from moment to moment, what endures in the divine persons are their respective societies or structured fields of activity. Each person is an enduring subject of the divine act of existence so that the Father, Son, and Holy Spirit exist not just for the moment but for all time. As personally or-

---

tions," 62; Bracken, "Process Philosophy and Trinitarian Theology—II," 95; Bracken, "Subsistent Relation," 193–94; Bracken, *"Ipsum Esse Subsistens,"* 289–90.

294. Bracken, *The Triune Symbol,* 27.

295. Bracken, "Subsistent Relation," 193 n. 15.

296. Bracken, *The Triune Symbol,* 44, 160; Bracken, *Society and Spirit,* 124, 129; Bracken, *The Divine Matrix,* 36, 62, 154 n. 45; Bracken, *The One in the Many,* 174; Bracken, "Supervenience," 148; Bracken, "The Issue of Panentheism," 213; Bracken, "Revising Process Metaphysics," 412; Bracken, "Process Philosophy and Trinitarian Theology," 221; Bracken, "Process Philosophy and Trinitarian Theology—II," 83; Bracken, "Subsistent Relation," 193–94; Bracken, "Authentic Subjectivity," 297–98; Bracken, "Panentheism from a Process Perspective," 100, 106; Bracken, *"Ipsum Esse Subsistens,"* 290; Bracken, "Intersubjectivity," 393; Bracken, "Philosophical Foundations," 62.

dered societies these momentary actualizations of the divine act of existence flowing into one another successively constitute an ongoing personalized subject of the divine act of existence for each person.[297] The Trinity, then, is a community of coequal persons in process.[298]

Bracken cites Pannenberg here, who comes to the same conclusion as Bracken but for different reasons.[299] Because in field-oriented metaphysics societies are "structured fields of activity," the divine society is a structured field of activity with three separate foci, corresponding to the three persons.[300] Pannenberg says God's essence is an unbounded field of activity constituted by the three divine persons in dynamic interrelation, and that it is a "force field" for the three divine persons.[301] Like Pannenberg, Bracken says creation is a field within the all-encompassing field of activity proper to the triune God.[302] Both speak of the divine nature as a "force field" grounding both the divine being and creation.

Bracken's Unique Social Trinitarianism

Bracken's doctrine of the Trinity is clearly one of the many new "social" views of the Trinity. He claims that using substantialist categories to understand God and the Trinity stymied a full understanding of the social nature of the Trinity. Defining a divine "person" as a "subsistent relation" or a "distinct way of being," Thomas and others gave the doctrine of the Trinity philosophical respectability. This hindered, however, the faithful from experiencing the practical psychological reality of the three divine persons. Bracken agrees with Rahner that despite their orthodox confession, most Christians are mere "monotheists" in their practical lives.[303]

Citing the frequent claim that Western trinitarianism tends toward

297. Bracken, "*Ipsum Esse Subsistens,*" 290.

298. Bracken, "Process Philosophy and Trinitarian Theology," 221.

299. Bracken, "Panentheism from a Process Perspective," 101 n. 14; Bracken, "Revising Process Metaphysics," 412–13; Bracken, review of *Systematic Theology, Volume 1,* by Wolfhart Pannenberg, *Horizons* 20 (Fall 1993): 355–56; Bracken, "Panentheism from a Trinitarian Perspective," 18; Bracken, *God: Three Who Are One,* 57, 77–78.

300. Joseph A. Bracken, review of *In Search of Deity: An Essay in Dialectical Theism,* by John Macquarrie, *Theological Studies* 46 (December 1985): 721.

301. Wolfhart Pannenberg, *Systematic Theology,* 3 vols., trans. Geoffrey W. Bromiley (Grand Rapids, Mich.: Eerdmans, 1991–98), 1:382–84, 2:79–102.

302. Bracken, "Panentheism from a Process Perspective," 101 n. 14; Bracken, "Panentheism from a Trinitarian Perspective," 17–19.

303. Bracken, *What Are They Saying about the Trinity?* 1–3; Bracken, *The Triune Symbol,*

unity and Eastern trinitarianism tends toward plurality, Bracken says the West has tended toward modalism in an attempt to avoid tritheism.[304] Echoing the sentiments of others, Bracken judges the twentieth-century revival of trinitarian theology as "neo-modal" in its incipience in Barth and Rahner.[305] Substituting "distinct manners of subsisting" for "persons" to specify what is plural in God is dangerously close to Sabellianism, or modalistic Monarchianism, say Bracken.[306] Rahner also subordinates the persons to the divine nature as the ontological source. A corollary to these problems is Rahner's and Lonergan's allowing only a monadic consciousness in God. Bracken, by contrast, says we may speak of three consciousnesses in God.[307]

At the same time Bracken sees problems with the new social trinitarianism.[308] Many social trinitarians obscure God's reality as interpersonal process by still identifying the Holy Spirit as the bond of love between Father and Son, which confuses *person* and *nature* and does not do justice to the Holy Spirit's subjectivity. Discussing Mühlen and Jüngel, Bracken says we must associate the divine nature with process, action, and dynamism, not the individual person of the Holy Spirit, who must be understood in personal terms just like the Father and Son. All three are subjects in interrelation and intercommunication.

31; Bracken, *God: Three Who Are One,* 27, 46–60; Bracken, "The Theology of God of Elizabeth A. Johnson," 31.

304. Bracken, *God: Three Who Are One,* 17, 20, 26, 123; Bracken, "The World," 99.

305. See, for instance, Jürgen Moltmann, *The Trinity and the Kingdom: The Doctrine of God,* trans. Margaret Kohl (Minneapolis: Fortress Press, 1993), 14–48; Catherine Mowry LaCugna, *God for Us: The Trinity and the Christian Life* (San Francisco: HarperCollins, 1991), 222–24, 253–54; Engelbert Gutwenger, S.J., *"Zur Trinitätslehre von Mysterium Salutis II,"* in *Zeitschrift für katholische Theologie* 90 (1968): 325–28; William J. Hill, O.P., *The Three-Personed God: The Trinity as a Mystery of Salvation* (Washington, D.C.: The Catholic University of America Press, 1982), 144–45, 145 n. 82, 179, 215, 254–55; Walter Kasper, *The God of Jesus Christ,* trans. Matthew J. O'Connell (New York: Crossroad, 1984), 288, 302–3; Gregory Havrilak, "Karl Rahner and the Greek Trinity," *St. Vladimir's Seminary Theological Quarterly* 34 (1990): 61–77.

306. Bracken, *What Are They Saying About the Trinity?* 12–13; Bracken, "The Holy Trinity, Part II," 258, 260; Bracken, "The Holy Trinity, Part I," 167 n. 1; Bracken, review of *The Three-Personed God,* 426.

307. Bracken, *The Triune Symbol,* 25.

308. Bracken, *What Are They Saying about the Trinity?* 51, 60–61; Bracken, *The Triune Symbol,* 16; Bracken, "Images of God," 371; Bracken, "Process Philosophy and Trinitarian Theology," 219, 220.

Bracken on the Three Divine Subjects

So for Bracken the divine persons are unique centers of subjectivity similar to "personalities" as connoted by the modern word "person."[309] "Tripersonal" means three interrelated centers of consciousness, mind, and will. At the same time, however, they all think and will the same thing in virtue of the perfect harmony of love which they are as a community.

St. Thomas makes knowing and loving specifications of the divine act of existence instead of aspects of God as personal. God exists as knowing and loving, first knowing and willing the divine being itself, and then knowing and loving all creatures in and through the divine being.[310] Bracken would rather say the activities of knowing and willing pertain not to the divine nature alone but also to the persons. Elsewhere partly rejecting the view that person and nature in God are only notionally distinct but really identical, Bracken does appeal to this point to attribute the personal faculties of knowing and willing to each of the divine persons.[311]

With other social trinitarians Bracken commends the social model for its egalitarian view of power in contrast to the classical hierarchical view. Thomas Parker rightly says that by failing to see the political implications of seeing God as a community of three coequal persons early Christians abandoned early charismatic leadership and moved toward a hierarchical pattern of government, with attendant negative consequences historical-

309. Bracken, *The Triune Symbol,* 25; Bracken, *The Divine Matrix,* 29, 35–36, 62, 157 n. 40; Bracken, *The One in the Many,* 127; Bracken, *God: Three Who Are One,* xi, 3–4; Bracken, "The Holy Trinity, Part I," 180–81; Bracken, "The Issue of Panentheism," 214; Bracken, "Panentheism from a Process Perspective," 101.

310. St. Thomas Aquinas, *ST* 1a.14.6 and 1a.19.2. Thomas equates the divine intellect and the divine will (or the activities of knowing and willing) with the divine being or the divine act of existence, since there is no multiplicity in God (God's simplicity). For Thomas the proper object of the divine activities of knowing and loving is the divine nature, and the divine nature or essence is coterminous with the divine act of existence (ibid., 1.14.4 and 1.19.1).

311. Bracken, *The Divine Matrix,* 35; Bracken, *"Ipsum Esse Subsistens,"* 289; Bracken, "Spirit and Society," 246; Bracken, "The World," 99. Elsewhere he says "person and nature are rationally distinct in God according to Aquinas," but then criticizes Thomas for not distinguishing between God as entity and divine nature. Bracken says the rational distinction must have a "foundation in reality" (Bracken, "The Issue of Panentheism," 210–11).

ly and politically.[312] The divine persons are a "group of friends" and each exists to serve the other two.[313]

The Analogy of Divine Personhood to Human Personhood

There are similarities and differences between divine and human subjectivity. Defining a "person" as one who desires to know and love everything that exists, Bracken says human personhood is continuous with, but an imperfect realization of, divine personhood.[314]

Applying to the divine persons the principles Ricoeur believes are operative in human persons, Bracken says each of the three has these principles, but only one principle is dominant in each divine person. All three possess vitality, rationality, and the property of being a mediating principle; but the Father is primarily vitality, the Son primarily rationality, and the Spirit primarily the mediating principle.[315] The divine persons are also like human persons as subjects engaging in interpretation. Using Royce's communities of interpretation, Bracken describes the divine persons as "three individual processes of interpretation."[316] The chief common factor between the divine and human persons, indeed between divine subjects and *all* finite entities as subjects, however, is the possession of free agency for self-constitution.[317]

Noting these similarities, Bracken also carefully notes differences in order to maintain the Creator-creature distinction. The divine persons *objectively* possess all the perfections of their creatures but cannot *subjectively* exercise them as the creatures do. This is because being is subjectivity, so equating divine and creaturely subjectivities would identify God and creatures.[318]

Referencing Whitehead's "four grades" of actual occasions, only some of which possess consciousness, Bracken says the divine persons are "be-

312. Thomas Parker, "The Political Meaning of the Doctrine of the Trinity: Some Theses," *Journal of Religion* 60 (1980): 165–84, cited in Bracken, *The Triune Symbol*, 107 n. 19. See also, Bracken, *God: Three Who Are One*, 83–86, 90–92.

313. Bracken, "Subsistent Relation," 197.

314. Bracken, *The Triune Symbol*, 49.

315. Bracken, "Subsistent Relation," 197 n. 22. He cites Paul Ricoeur, *Fallible Man* (Chicago: Regnery, 1965), 161–64, 191–202.

316. Bracken, *The Triune Symbol*, 24.

317. Bracken, "The Theology of God of Elizabeth A. Johnson," 33 n. 32.

318. Bracken, *The Divine Matrix*, 147 n. 40.

yond all these 'grades' among finite subjects of experience."[319] God infinitely transcends human personhood. Human personhood is constrained by life in the body while divine personhood is exercised by an individual whose sphere of activity is coterminous with being as such.[320] Additionally, while self-constitution is the greatest similarity between the divine subject and created subjects, the mutual immanence of the divine subjects, or their *perichoresis,* makes their collaborative agency far more unified and collective than that of any finite subjects in collaboration.[321]

Bracken and the Tritheism Critique

A criticism of social trinitarianism, including Bracken's, is that it reduces to tritheism.[322] Bracken is aware of this critique and admits with Rahner that three separate personal consciousnesses in God would lead to the heretical doctrine of three gods.[323]

He first replies that all attempts to deal with the mystery of the Trinity inevitably approach one of the trinitarian heresies. Different theories of the Trinity and/or the God-world relationship invariably presuppose an antecedent understanding of the relationship between the one and the many. Depending on the model, tritheism, modalism, or subordinationism ensues. Those who charge social trinitarians with tritheism are themselves either modalists or subordinationists.[324]

Second, Bracken says critics wrongly think a community can be reduced to a network of relationships between discrete individuals who are first and foremost individuals, and only secondarily a community. This view is based on the Aristotelian and Thomistic worldviews in which only individual entities ultimately exist, so God is an individual entity

319. Bracken, "The Theology of God of Elizabeth A. Johnson," 33 n. 32. Cf. Whitehead, *Process and Reality,* 177–78 (269–70).

320. Bracken, review of *In Search of Deity,* 721.

321. Bracken, "The Theology of God of Elizabeth A. Johnson," 33 n. 32.

322. Elizabeth A. Johnson, *She Who Is: The Mystery of God in Feminist Theological Discourse,* 2nd ed. (Crossroad: New York, 1992; reprint 1997), 209; John O'Donnell, "The Trinity as Divine Community: A Critical Reflection upon Recent Theological Developments," *Gregorianum* 69, no. 1 (1988): 29.

323. Bracken, *The Triune Symbol,* 24–25, citing Karl Rahner, *The Trinity,* tr. Joseph Donceel (New York: Herder and Herder), 106–9.

324. Bracken, *God: Three Who Are One,* 14, 70; Bracken, "Panentheism from a Trinitarian Perspective," 24–27.

first and foremost.[325] Only by introducing a foreign substance ontology can one charge Bracken with tritheism, since his metaphysics presupposes societies are equiprimordial with actual entities.[326]

Third, the critique assumes the divine persons first exist individually and subsequently relate in a community so that their unity is only secondary. Since actual entities and their respective societies come into existence "at the same time," there is no temporal logical priority of persons over community or community over persons, as there must be in classical metaphysics.[327]

Fourth, we must consider the qualitative difference between God and creatures. Bracken resorts to an analogical understanding of the divine society and creaturely societies. St. Thomas's real equation of person and nature, so that each person has no reality proper to itself distinct from the divine nature, shows how the persons cannot be abstracted from the community.[328] Although creaturely societies are separate from each other because their fields are distinct no matter how much they overlap, the divine persons have "nothing personal which is not communal" so that nothing belongs to one person without belonging to the other persons.[329]

In fact, the three divine subsocieties are infinite, which means there is no actual distinction between them. They are three infinite fields of activity that are really one and the same infinite society shared equally by each person.[330] They possess a unanimity that cannot obtain between finite entities and societies. They could never separate themselves in consciousness, knowing, willing, and loving.[331] All that they are is common to all three persons, so they are one, not three.

As a social trinitarian predicating three personalities to the persons,

325. Bracken, *The Triune Symbol,* 16.

326. Bracken, *The One in the Many,* 44 n. 86.

327. Bracken, *The Triune Symbol,* 46; Bracken, *God: Three Who Are One,* 78; Bracken, "Intersubjectivity," 393.

328. Bracken, "The Holy Trinity, Part I," 180. Cf. St. Thomas Aquinas, *ST* 1a.29.4.

329. Bracken, *The Divine Matrix,* 62–63.

330. Bracken, "The Issue of Panentheism," 213–14; Bracken, *Society and Spirit,* 130; Bracken, "Intersubjectivity," 393; Bracken, review of *The Promise of Trinitarian Theology,* by Colin E. Gunton, *Horizons* 19 (Fall 1992): 322; Bracken, "Panentheism from a Process Perspective," 100; Bracken, "Revising Process Metaphysics," 412.

331. Bracken, *The One in the Many,* 174; Bracken, *Christianity and Process Thought,* 55–57, 60; Bracken, "Supervenience," 148; Bracken, "Intersubjectivity," 393.

Bracken is clear that discrete persons cannot share the same subjectivities.[332] In the process worldview subjectivity is the principle of ontology so that it is entirely private to each entity. While God as the indeterminate subject of the divine act of existence may possibly be conceived as infinite, the three persons are clearly limited by reason of their relations to one another. The reality of each person is really something other than the reality of the other persons so that they are not ontologically and really identical, as in the logical principle of identity.

This distinction between the divine subjectivities means knowing and willing pertain not only to the divine nature, but also to the persons. Classically all of God's essential incommunicable attributes (e.g., simplicity, perfection, infinity, immutability) pertain not only to the divine nature but also to each person.[333] Although each person's knowledge is infinite, each knows reality from a "different perspective" because of its discrete personality.[334] Being infinite, however, the persons prehend not only the structural objectifications of their own past occasions but also those of the other two. In every moment each person appropriates not only the objectification of its own past decisions but also those of the other two persons. Therefore each person has an unlimited knowledge and understanding of the subjectivities of the other two persons.[335]

Bracken does say each person's subjectivity must be identified with its own subjectivity in a way more complete than with the other two subjectivities.[336] The only difference between the persons is that each appropriates its own subjectivity differently from the way it appropriates those of the others. Each person *objectively* knows and identifies with the subjectivities of other persons in every way but does not *subjectively* identify with them.[337]

Referencing Cousins, who contrasts divine and human subjectivity, Bracken at this point again invokes the creature-Creator distinction to avoid suspicions of tritheism. Despite having distinct minds and wills,

332. Bracken, *The Divine Matrix,* 129–30; Bracken, "*Ipsum Esse Subsistens,*" 289.

333. Bracken, "The Holy Trinity, Part I," 180; Bracken, "*Ipsum Esse Subsistens,*" 289. Cf. St. Thomas Aquinas, *ST* 1a.29.4.

334. Bracken, *Christianity and Process Thought,* 69; Bracken, "Authentic Subjectivity," 297.

335. Bracken, *Society and Spirit,* 130, 157.

336. Bracken, "Proposals for Overcoming the Atomism," 17; Bracken, *Society and Spirit,* 130.

337. Bracken, *The Divine Matrix,* 35–36, 65–66, 153–54 n. 43.

the divine persons are completely unified in thought and action. The divine persons, by virtue of their perfection, have perfect unanimity in their minds and wills, and their corporate agency is greater than finite collaborative corporate agency, and much more unified.[338]

Human persons are discrete individuals despite existing in the same group, family, community, or society, because their fields of activity do not perfectly coincide and they can operate individually. They have unique personal histories or fields of activity distinct from the societal or group history. Because their infinite fields of activity are identical the divine persons have personal histories identical with the corporate history of the divine community, and they exercise identical agency in virtue of their comprising a unanimous society.[339] Each person's intentionality encompasses that of the other two and is identical with those of the other two.[340]

The situation is similar with the divine persons' knowledge. Finite persons realize that other people see the world differently and therefore dialogue with others. Possessing infinite knowledge of being, the divine persons reduce knowledge's perspectival aspect to an absolute minimum and therefore have a shared consciousness, which is practically only one.[341]

The Unity of God Subsists in a Society

Bracken bases the Godhead's unity on his revised Whiteheadian societies, which replace how substance unifies God in classical trinitarianism. The fact that societies possess both an ontological unity appropriate to their own level of existence and activity, as well as a collective agency, preserves the unity of one God if God is a society of three subsocieties.[342] The equiprimordiality of society and members precludes the temporal or logical priority of either. God has no ontological objectivity apart from

338. Ewert Cousins, "A Theology of Interpersonal Relations," *Thought* 45 (1970): 69–70, quoted in Bracken, "The Holy Trinity, Part I," 180–81. See also, Bracken, *The Triune Symbol,* 25–26; Bracken, "The Theology of God of Elizabeth A. Johnson," 33 n. 32.

339. Bracken, "Process Philosophy and Trinitarian Theology—II," 83; Bracken, "The World," 97.

340. Bracken, *The Triune Symbol,* 38; Bracken, "The World," 97.

341. Bracken, *The Triune Symbol,* 25.

342. Bracken, "The Holy Trinity, Part I," 179, 182; Bracken, "Intersubjectivity," 392; Bracken, "Subsistent Relation," 194; Bracken, "Process Philosophy and Trinitarian Theology," 226; Bracken, "Revising Process Metaphysics," 412.

the three persons' prehending the society as their joint reality from moment to moment. As Royce said, "The persons constitute the process and the process, in turn, constitutes, the persons (at least as members of this particular community)."[343]

The Role of the Divine "Essence" or "Substance" in the Trinity

In classical Western theology, the divine substance often forms the basis of the Trinity's unity. St. Thomas says each person is identical with the nature so that each is fully the one God. God is God's nature, so by the principle of unity God is both "God" as well as "*this* God."[344] The plurality of persons possessing the divine nature is intelligible because of the plurality of operations of the one divine nature. If the spiritual operations of knowing and loving are proper to the divine nature, then one can see the divine persons in terms of these two operations. The spiritual operations of knowing and loving, corresponding to the second and third persons of the Trinity, presuppose the one divine nature possessing these operations. The operation of knowing has a term or end and the operation of loving has a term or end.[345] The plurality of the Godhead emerges from the unity of the substance in the two *opera ad intra* of knowing and loving.

As already discussed, Bracken redefines the divine substance in dynamic process terms instead of traditional static terms. "Being," as distinct from "beings," is a verb or activity, not a noun or a substance. Reviewing Rahner, Lonergan, and Mühlen, Bracken concludes that although each presents a coherent understanding of the Trinity none seriously entertains the idea of redefining "nature" instead of redefining "person" as they approach the problems associated with traditional trinitarianism. He takes Rahner's assertion that our terms "person" and "nature" in trinitarian dogma are logical rather than strictly ontological categories to mean these terms can be replaced, and then says that the "next logical step" in developing an adequate view of the Trinity is redefining the traditional understanding of the divine nature.[346]

343. Bracken, *What Are They Saying about the Trinity?* 70.

344. St. Thomas Aquinas, *ST* 1a.11.3.

345. Ibid., 1a.28.1 and 1a.41.3.

346. Bracken, *What Are They Saying about the Trinity?* 13–14, 24; Bracken, "The Holy Trinity, Part II," 259–60, 269. Cf. Rahner, *The Trinity*, 54, 56.

Bracken believes his view that societies constitute a higher level of being and intelligibility than individual substances could be the new concept for understanding God's nature or substance, which Rahner admits is, at least in theory, possible. The divine nature would be an interpersonal process and a society instead of a static substance, and the product of the persons' interrelations from moment to moment.[347] God's nature would not be static but the activity of interrelating based on the traditional scholastic understanding of the persons as subsistent relations. Each person exists distinctly only by reason of its relation to the other two.[348]

Despite these revisions, the Western intuition of grounding God's unity in the divine essence is correct over and against the Eastern tendency to ground unity in the Father. Grounding unity in the essence guarantees the basic equality of the divine persons. Making the Father the source of the Trinity's unity continues the Greek Fathers' subordinationism, which the Cappadocians corrected with *perichoresis.* Greek Orthodox theologian John Zizioulas does not have a social ontology because a truly social ontology cannot begin with an individual entity, even if it is an intrinsically related being.[349]

The relations of origin must be subordinate to the relations of equality.[350] The intention of the Cappadocian Fathers and John of Damascus, says Bracken, was to begin with the plurality of relational entities and then inquire into the ground or source of their dynamic interrelation. This insures the perfect and total equality of the persons, and avoids any intimation of subordination.

347. Bracken, *What Are They Saying about the Trinity?* 52; Bracken, *Christianity and Process Thought,* 107; Bracken, *God: Three Who Are One,* 73–74, 76, 78, 103, 115, 125; Bracken, "The Holy Trinity, Part I," 179; Bracken, "Subsistent Relation," 197; Bracken, "Energy Events and Fields," 163.

348. Bracken, *Christianity and Process Thought,* 55; Bracken, *God: Three Who Are One,* 20, 24, 49, 71–72. Cf. St. Thomas Aquinas, *ST* 1a.29.4.

349. See Bracken, "Trinity: Economic and Immanent," 16–17, 16 n. 19; Bracken, review of *The Promise of Trinitarian Theology,* 322; Bracken, review of *God for Us,* 559; and Bracken, review of *The Father's Spirit of Sonship: Reconceiving the Trinity,* by Thomas G. Weinandy, *Theological Studies* 57 (June 1996): 384.

350. Bracken, "Trinity: Economic and Immanent," 16; Bracken, "Process Philosophy and Trinitarian Theology—II," 84.

The Distinction between the Divine Persons and the Divine Nature

Sometimes referencing the old truism that the persons are only notionally or logically distinct, Bracken otherwise explicitly and forcefully asserts a distinction between the divine essence and persons. If God's nature is "to be" existentially, as when Thomas says God's essence is existence itself, then the personal entitative reality of God must be the subject of the unlimited Act of Being. This introduces a distinction between God as a being existentially and the divine nature, similar to the usual distinction between the essence and the existence of finite created beings. If the distinction between the divine essence and persons is not real and if creatures have their being by participation in God's being, then all finite entities must be the same entity as God. A distinction between the divine essence and persons is the only way to preserve the distinction between God as a being and creaturely finite beings so central to theism and panentheism.[351]

This means the Supreme Being as an entity is not infinite, as Thomas claims. Thomas's confusion of God's nature or infinite eternal activity with the entitative reality of God the Supreme Being results in this error.[352] Thomas should distinguish between "being" as God's underlying nature and the "Supreme Being" as an instantiation of the activity of existing.[353]

When Elizabeth A. Johnson says God and creatures do not both share some *tertium quid* called "being," which she says is a common misunderstanding of participated being, Bracken asks why the misunderstanding is common. He suggests that the misunderstanding reveals an insight into what is true, especially since the principle of analogy requires that entities in comparison have at least something in common.[354] He even claims that Johnson herself, following Thomas, implicitly distinguishes between person and nature in God. The terminology of "subsistent being" distinguishes between God as the uncreated subsistent subject of the

351. Bracken, "The Issue of Panentheism," 210–11; Bracken, *God: Three Who Are One,* 77, 89, 103–4; Bracken, "Response to Elizabeth Johnson's 'Does God Play Dice?'" 721.

352. Bracken, *The Divine Matrix,* 29–30, 43.

353. Ibid., 29, 43; Bracken, "An Example of Western Theology," 43.

354. Bracken, "Response to Elizabeth Johnson's 'Does God Play Dice?'" 721–22; Bracken, "The Issue of Panentheism," 210.

Act of Being and the Act of Being itself as God's essence, which implies a real distinction between the subsistent subject of the Act of Being (the divine person[s]), and Being itself (the divine nature).

A potential objection to applying the essence-existence distinction to God as it applies to finite realities is that it makes the divine persons finite, because essence limits the act of existence (*esse* or being) in finite realities. Bracken even says only the divine nature is infinite since it alone is absolutely formless and undifferentiated, while the persons are determinate entities limited in their relationships to each other and all created entities, and are therefore finite.[355] Yet he says that, as subsistent activities or enduring subjects of the divine act of existence, the three persons share in the potential infinity of the divine act of existence, which is the capability of further actualization in never-ending existence and activity.[356] At any given moment each divine person is infinite by being the subject of the never-ending principle of activity, but is also finite by exercising existence and activity differently from the other persons and all creatures.[357]

Another potential problem with distinguishing between the divine essence and persons is a loss of the persons' full divinity since they are secondary or subordinate to the divine essence. Bracken even says that God's incommunicable attributes, discussed in theology proper or *De Deo uno*, apply more properly to the divine essence than to the persons.[358] He addresses this problem by once again saying essence and persons are equiprimordial, just as societies and their members are equiprimordial.[359]

The Divine Persons as Subsistent Relations

St. Thomas characterizes the divine persons as subsistent relations. Relations between individual created beings are accidents and therefore distinguishable from the substances of the beings themselves, but in God relations are identical with the divine nature itself. They are subsistent relations.[360] Subsistent relation means the being or actuality of the individ-

355. Bracken, *The Divine Matrix*, 138–39.

356. Ibid., 37; Bracken, "*Ipsum Esse Subsistens*," 291.

357. Bracken, *The Divine Matrix*, 65, 145 n. 8.

358. Ibid., 43.

359. Ibid., 108–9; Bracken, *The One in the Many*, 205; Bracken, "Non-Duality," 145; Bracken, review of *The Three-Personed God*, 427.

360. St. Thomas Aquinas, *ST* 1a.29.4.

ual persons as really distinct from each other subsists in their relations. For Thomas, following Western trinitarianism, the only real distinctions in God are relationships of opposition.[361] Since there is no opposition between the concepts of nature and person, each divine person is really identical with the divine essence, so that the fullness of the Godhead is in each person.[362] Since there is real opposition between the concepts of Fatherhood and Sonship, and between the concepts of active spiration (breathing forth of the divine love) and passive spiration (divine love itself), there are real personal distinctions between the divine persons who are, respectively, subsistent Fatherhood, subsistent Sonship, and subsistent Love.[363]

Bracken takes issue with this presentation. Limiting subsistent relation to the divine persons only is an instance of wrongly making God an exception to, rather than the chief exemplification of, metaphysical principles.[364] By explaining the Trinity as subsistent relations but not applying subsistent relations to all entities universally, Thomas unwittingly consigned the Trinity to being an appendage to philosophical theology.[365] The process worldview maintains that God is not an exception to, but chiefly exemplifies, the metaphysical principles. Therefore it must extend the concept of subsistent relation to all entities beyond just the divine persons.[366]

As with his revisionist view of the Act of Being, Bracken believes his own process understanding of the Trinity comports with Thomas Aquinas's exposition of the Trinity.[367] The idea of subsistent relations entails complete equality, avoiding subordinationism, because each person relies on the others for its identity and there is no logical or temporal priority of persons. The Father could not be the Father without the coexistence of

361. Ibid., 1a.28.3. The classical axiom is *"In Deo omnia sunt unum, ubi non obviat relationis oppositio,"* used in the Fourth Lateran Council.

362. St. Thomas Aquinas, *ST* 1a.29.4. See also, St. Augustine, *De Trinitate* 8.1.8.

363. St. Thomas Aquinas, *ST* 1a.28.3–4, 1a.36.1, and 1a.36.4.

364. Bracken, *God: Three Who Are One,* 21, 84–85; Bracken, "Subsistent Relation," 190.

365. Bracken, *God: Three Who Are One,* 21; Bracken, review of *Theism, Atheism and the Doctrine of the Trinity: The Trinitarian Theologies of Karl Barth and Jürgen Moltmann,* by W. Waite Willis Jr., *Theological Studies* 49 (September 1988): 550.

366. Bracken, "Subsistent Relation," 189, 199.

367. Bracken, "Subsistent Relation," 188–204; Bracken, *Society and Spirit,* 177 n. 4; Bracken, *The Divine Matrix,* 43.

the Son, and vice versa. Nor could the Father and Son exist in a love relationship without the Spirit.[368] Bracken is adamant that only the relations of origin distinguish the persons, so without these relations there would be no distinctions in God.[369]

As already explained, Bracken reinterprets the Act of Being to be implicit activity, or the creativity of process metaphysics. Regarding the subsistent relations that are the divine persons, Bracken criticizes Thomas and his followers for understanding these relations as fixed entities (nouns) instead of as ongoing activities (verbs).[370] The divine persons as subsistent relations are interrelated subjects of one and the same activity, the divine nature, which is an ongoing conversion of potentiality to actuality.[371] At any time each divine person is a specific actualization of the divine act of existence for that moment. The subsistent relations are instantiations of both the perpetual activity of interrelation and the ongoing process of becoming.[372] Emphasizing the activity of the subsistent relations, Bracken describes the Father as the act of "Father-ing" and the Son as the act of "Son-ing."[373]

Perichoresis and Subsistent Relations as Foundation for a New Ontology

In addition to applying subsistent relations to all of reality, Bracken sees *perichoresis* as revelatory of the same metaphysical reality: beings are such only in relationships. Subsistent relations and *perichoresis* capture the metaphysical insight that relations are constitutive of the reality of things rather than accidental to their reality.[374] This metaphysical claim is virtually equivalent to the internal relations in Whitehead, who had said the Cappadocian Fathers' *perichoresis* or the mutual immanence and in-

368. Bracken, "Trinity: Economic and Immanent," 17.

369. Bracken, *The Triune Symbol,* 30; Bracken, *The Divine Matrix,* 35–36; Bracken, *Christianity and Process Thought,* 55.

370. Bracken, *Society and Spirit,* 177 n. 4; Bracken, *God: Three Who Are One,* 84.

371. Bracken, *The Divine Matrix,* 26; Bracken, *"Ipsum Esse Subsistens,"* 290.

372. Bracken, "Panentheism from a Process Perspective," 97 n. 9; Bracken, *The Divine Matrix,* 43.

373. Bracken, *Society and Spirit,* 177 n. 4.

374. Bracken, *God: Three Who Are One,* 69–72; Bracken, "Trinity: Economic and Immanent," 14; Bracken, "Concluding Remarks," in *Trinity in Process,* 221; Bracken, "Philosophical Foundations," 57–58; Bracken, "Intersubjectivity," 393.

terpenetration of the divine persons signaled a new metaphysical insight beyond Plato. Those fathers, however, never carried over this insight with respect to God to the world of creation, which is just what Whitehead advocated.

Since the same metaphysical principles applying to divine reality must also apply to creaturely reality, Whitehead's internal relations, epitomized in the ideas of subsistent relations and *perichoresis*, must govern our understanding of the relations of the divine persons to one another, of creatures to God, of creatures to one another, and even the interpretation of the divine and human natures in Jesus. *Perichoresis* and subsistent relations are applicable to all entities without exception, not just the divine persons.[375] With the Trinity as the archetype and created realities as ectypes, every actual entity is a subsistent relation, or exists in and for itself only insofar as it is intrinsically related to other existents.[376] From all of this Bracken concludes that Thomas himself, with his subsistent relations, was unwittingly on the verge of a process understanding of reality.[377]

Trinitarian "Relations of Origin" and "Relations of Opposition"

In an early work Bracken is critical of the traditional idea of "relations of origin" as what defines the three divine persons.[378] In later works, though, he reinterprets what he sees as valuable and legitimate in the traditional doctrine.[379] He unequivocally says the Father, Son, and Holy Spirit hold everything in common except the unique personhood each possesses by its relationship to the others.[380] Each divine person possesses a distinct subjectivity only by the "absolute contradictory self identity" emergent through a dynamic relationship of opposition to the other two subjectivities.[381] This is the same as Thomas's statement that each divine

375. Bracken, *God: Three Who Are One,* 24; Bracken, review of *The History of the Triune God,* 766; Bracken, "Subsistent Relation," 190, 195 n. 18, 199; Bracken, "Concluding Remarks," 221.

376. Bracken, "Creativity," 113; Bracken, "Philosophical Foundations," 52, 58–59; Bracken, "Subsistent Relation," 188–204; Bracken, "The Theology of God of Elizabeth A. Johnson," 31–32 n. 31; Bracken, *Christianity and Process Thought,* 10–12; Bracken, *God: Three Who Are One,* 70–72.

377. Bracken, *Society and Spirit,* 177 n. 4.

378. Bracken, *What Are They Saying about the Trinity?* 78–79.

379. Bracken, *The Divine Matrix,* 36.

380. Bracken, *The Triune Symbol,* 30.

381. Bracken, *The One in the Many,* 127. The terminology comes from Kitaro Nishida.

person is a subsistent relation individually defined by its relation of opposition to the others.[382]

A difference, however, is that traditionally the relations of opposition are relations of origin, but Bracken reinterprets the opposition to consist in the opposition of mutually exclusive subjectivities, not in the opposite poles of origin resulting in opposed relationships. He draws attention away from the relations as relations of *origin*. This focus on mutual opposition of peer personalities better eliminates the implication of hierarchy and inequality entailed by relations of origin.[383] Instead of a "noun-oriented" (substantial) approach, a "verb-oriented" (processive) approach connotes shared feeling, movement and life, and not fixed structures and hierarchy.[384]

Whiteheadian Process Categories in Bracken's Doctrine of the Trinity

In a famous passage Whitehead delineates "four creative phases in which the universe accomplishes its actuality." These involve principles of potentiality, provisional or current actuality, and an entelechy or ultimate actuality, to which Bracken seeks to correlate the Father, Son, and Spirit respectively.[385] As the source of initial aims for all entities, the Father is the first phase: conceptual origination, God's mental pole, primordial nature, or potentiality. As the means by which every actual occasion receives its initial aim from the Father, the Son is the second phase: provisional actuality. The Son is also the third phase: God's physical pole, consequent nature or perfected actuality. By responding to the Father's aim and joining itself to the Son in the Son's own "Yes" to the Father's offer, the actual entity relates itself, more or less perfectly, with the society of all other occasions in union with the Son. As the bond of love between the Father and the Son, the Holy Spirit is the fourth phase: the movement back to the Father from the world's individual occasions in God's superject nature, which allows the Father to supply new aims for the future.

382. Ibid., 127–28, citing St. Thomas Aquinas, *ST* 1a.29.4.

383. Bracken, "The Theology of God of Elizabeth A. Johnson," 34; Bracken, review of *The Father's Spirit of Sonship*, 384.

384. Bracken, *God: Three Who Are One*, 85.

385. Bracken, "Process Philosophy and Trinitarian Theology," 217–30; Bracken, "Process Philosophy and Trinitarian Theology—II," 83–96; Bracken, "Panentheism from a Process Perspective," 102; cf. Whitehead, *Process and Reality*, 350–51 (532).

In correlating the persons to the four creative phases, the names of the persons are important, because the persons play different roles vis-à-vis each other. The Father is the Primal Cause or Originator for their joint existence as one God. The Son is the One Originated or the Primal Effect. The Spirit as bond of love between Father and Son is the Primordial Condition for the interaction between the Primal Cause and the Primal Effect in the Godhead.

The Unity of the Three Persons' Roles in Whitehead's "Four Phases"

Once again to preempt any charges of tritheism, Bracken says these roles essentially overlap and all three persons play a part in each role. It is not only one person involved in each phase. The divine persons are just different ways of being the subject of the infinite Act of Being, which identifies them in the closest possible way, as explained above. The unity is drawn even closer in that all three participate in God's primordial nature, consequent nature, and superjective nature, but in different ways.[386] All three pervade the extensive continuum and effect the events taking place in the continuum. All three are energized each moment by creativity to constitute themselves and the divine community, and to aggregate to themselves all finite occasions brought into existence in that moment.[387] The three persons co-constitute the objective unity of a single structured society or divine field of activity with multiple dimensions.

Bracken even invokes the classical doctrine of "appropriations," though in a modified fashion.[388] Traditionally all three effect each divine activity outside of God *(opera ad extra)* even though each activity is associated with, or "appropriated" to, only one person. Bracken says that while all three participate in the primordial, consequent, and superject natures of God, we can especially relate each person to one of the phases. While associating all three persons with each role, Bracken does make aspects of each role unique to one person, though. All three survey the vast realm of possibilities in their common field of activity but only the Father

386. Bracken, *Society and Spirit,* 133; Bracken, *The Divine Matrix,* 43, 63, 154–55, 154 n. 45; Bracken, *God: Three Who Are One,* xiv, 24; Bracken, "Process Philosophy and Trinitarian Theology—II," 91; Bracken, "Panentheism from a Process Perspective," 101.

387. Bracken, *Society and Spirit,* 134.

388. Bracken, *The Divine Matrix,* 63, 154 n. 45; Bracken, *Society and Spirit,* 133; Bracken, "Process Philosophy and Trinitarian Theology—II," 85, 87–88, 91.

decides which possibility is appropriate for that moment of their common history. All three share in the consequent nature, but only the Son decides to actualize the possibility chosen by the Father. All three share in the superjective nature but the Spirit alone decides to execute the Son's decision, and in this way perpetuates the common life in the community of the three divine persons.

The Trinity and the "Cosmic Society"

The ontogenetic matrix that is God's nature is not only constituted by the divine persons and their dynamic relations, but is further structured by the presence and activity of all of the finite actual occasions. The divine persons and all creatures together in perpetual interrelation constitute the ever-growing cosmic society within the force field made by creativity and the extensive continuum.[389] God and the world of finite entities together are a cosmic community. The world is a structured society of subsocieties incorporated into the divine society, so there is one all-comprehensive field of activity for the events, divine and created, taking place.[390]

God is primary in the cosmic society. The cosmic society is first generated through the interplay of the divine persons, and necessarily depends on the ongoing cooperation of the three persons exercising their respective roles in Whitehead's "four phases" outlined above.[391] Every moment the persons by their dynamic interrelatedness co-constitute and sustain a democratically organized structured society, their reality as one God.[392] They also co-constitute a structured field of activity for the whole of creation.[393] The field or society proper to creation is smaller and more constrained than the field or society proper to the divine persons.[394] All sub-

389. Bracken, *The Divine Matrix,* 60, 61–62, 64; Bracken, *The One in the Many,* 11; Bracken, *Christianity and Process Thought,* 8–10, 54–56; Bracken, *God: Three Who Are One,* 78–80, 104, 118; Bracken, "Philosophical Foundations," 57; Bracken, "Panentheism from a Process Perspective," 103–4; Bracken, "Spirit and Society," 255 n. 6.

390. Bracken, *The Divine Matrix,* 58; Bracken, *Christianity and Process Thought,* 9–10, 54–56, 71, 107; Bracken, *God: Three Who Are One,* 78–79; Bracken, "The Issue of Panentheism," 214; Bracken, "Creativity," 118; Bracken, "Panentheism from a Process Perspective," 106; Bracken, "Whitehead," 104–6, 109 n. 22.

391. Bracken, *Society and Spirit,* 124–25.

392. Bracken, "The World," 96–97.

393. Bracken, "Energy Events and Fields," 163.

394. Bracken, *Society and Spirit,* 148–49; Bracken, *God: Three Who Are One,* 78–79.

societies and their actual occasions in the world comprise the created world, which is an enormous but still finite field. The myriad subsocieties of actual occasions in the world together structure the field of activity proper to the cosmos as a whole. This huge but finite field is itself incorporated into the more comprehensive field proper to the divine persons in their dynamic interrelations.[395]

At the same time, finite creatures do contribute to the ongoing generation of the cosmic society. Finite occasions and the fields they constitute are included in the field of activity proper to the three divine persons.[396] The ontogenetic matrix of creativity plus the extensive continuum is generated through the interplay of divine persons with one another and with their creatures.[397]

The entire cosmic society composed of both divine and creaturely subsocieties is "ultimate reality," or the whole to which all parts contribute.[398] The divine persons alone do not constitute ultimate reality, but the divine persons *plus* all creatures. Only the cosmic society composed of both the three divine persons and their creatures is ultimate reality, since it alone endures. The divine persons are not ultimate reality since they perish and appear anew each moment. The divine persons compose a subsociety, even if the most important subsociety, of ultimate reality as a whole. This is true panentheism: the ontological independence of the divine persons and their creatures distinct from each other but together co-constituting a common world.[399]

Bracken appropriates the traditional Christian doctrine of God's independence by saying God is ontologically independent from the world in terms of the world's origin. Speaking of the doctrine of free or contingent creation, he says the connection between the divine field of activity and the

395. Bracken, "Panentheism from a Process Perspective," 102; Bracken, "The Issue of Panentheism," 214.

396. Bracken, *The Divine Matrix,* 64; Bracken, *Christianity and Process Thought,* 10; Bracken, *God: Three Who Are One,* 74, 78–80, 116.

397. Bracken, "Intersubjectivity," 397; Bracken, review of *The Promise of Trinitarian Theology,* 322; Bracken, "Panentheism from a Process Perspective," 103–5, 106; Bracken, "The Theology of God of Elizabeth A. Johnson," 30, 30–31 n. 30; Bracken, *The Divine Matrix,* 62–65; Bracken, *God: Three Who Are One,* 103–4, 115–16.

398. Bracken, *Society and Spirit,* 148–49; Bracken, *The One in the Many,* 147; Bracken, *God: Three Who Are One,* 104, 105 n. 33.

399. Bracken, *Society and Spirit,* 149–50; Bracken, "Panentheism from a Trinitarian Perspective," 19.

world as a field of activity is not necessary, and that God does not emerge from the field of activity proper to the world, but rather the world emerges from the divine society.[400] This does not mean, however, that God is absolutely necessary and independent and that only creation is contingent. Since all finite actual entities contribute to the cosmic field of activity, the world affects and changes God, which is a central concern of process metaphysics. Since at every moment finite occasions respond to the Father's initial aim in union with the Son through the power of the Spirit, finite occasions structure not only the world of finite creation but also add richness and diversity to the communitarian life of the divine persons.[401]

Here every subject shapes the evolving universal society. The divine persons determine the basic pattern of the universal society's form from moment to moment but finite entities introduce genuine novelty and change into the divine life: the Father's aims become more complex, the Son's response is qualitatively richer, and the Spirit's work is more nuanced, "all because of the presence of created finite entities within the structured society which is the divine life."[402]

The net effect of his idea of this cosmic society, says Bracken, is a greater emphasis on the social character of reality than either Whitehead or Hartshorne ever envisioned. Whitehead and Hartshorne guarantee a degree of social character in that every actual occasion influences and is influenced by every other occasion in the world process. Bracken adds pervasive sociality in the objective order of things of the cosmic society, which the individual occasion and its contemporaries co-constitute here and now and which will survive their passing away.[403]

Eschatology and the Trinity

Bracken's trinitarianism not only affects the God-world relationship, but is also his vision of final eschatological reality. God's ultimate aim is to bring all finite beings into the fullness of the divine life. From the beginning creation has been heading toward union with the Trinity.[404] Here

400. Bracken, "Supervenience," 148–49; Bracken, *Christianity and Process Thought,* 9; Bracken, *God: Three Who Are One,* 79, 104, 105 n. 33.

401. Bracken, *The Divine Matrix,* 64.

402. Bracken, "Authentic Subjectivity," 299.

403. Bracken, "Panentheism from a Process Perspective," 103–4, 106.

404. Bracken, *The Triune Symbol,* 88–89; Bracken, *Christianity and Process Thought,* 8, 38.

he borrows from Teilhard de Chardin. The world as an ever-expanding cosmic society of finite existents who enjoy subjective immortality with the three divine persons is close to Teilhard's *Pleroma,* or the recapitulation of all things in Christ.[405] As for Teilhard, Jesus Christ is Bracken's eschatological Omega Point.

All creation is destined for incorporation into the reality of the Son. The "Body of Christ" is not only the Church, but is in all of creation, the future reality of which the Eucharist adumbrates. Christ as the center of creation and point at which the world unites in response to the Father's initial aims is the ultimate locus of the world's eschatological unity. The fulfillment of this unity, however, has been deferred until the *Parousia.* Along with Jesus eventually all of creation and all humanity will experience a transfiguration of their physical being. Quoting Romans 8:22–23, Bracken says all creation will survive in a transformed state. The unity of everything in Christ and the incorporation of all humanity into an all-inclusive community including the Trinity will no longer be matters of faith, but actualities visible to all.[406]

Inasmuch as his revisions of Whitehead's system advocate the ontological reality of societies as well as the subjective, not merely objective, immortality of actual entities in God's consequent nature, there will be great continuity between the "new creation" and the old. Physical reality will be transformed into the divine life but maintain the same pattern and structure of its existence in the physical world at the point of its actuality.[407] Jesus will always remain unique, however, by being one person with the eternal Son of God. Human beings and all of creation, insofar as they are one with Jesus in his transformed humanity, will one day also share in the process of the divine life in a way unimaginable right now.[408]

Bracken and the Problem of the One and the Many

Having explored Bracken's philosophical theology, we can now examine his attempts to solve the problem of the one and the many. With process metaphysics from its beginnings, Bracken deals with this problem at

405. Bracken, *Society and Spirit,* 161.

406. Bracken, *The Triune Symbol,* 10, 23, 123–24, 174, 181; Bracken, *Christianity and Process Thought,* 8, 38.

407. Bracken, "Intersubjectivity," 399.

408. Bracken, *The Triune Symbol,* 56; Bracken, *Christianity and Process Thought,* 113–14.

length and suggests that his system provides the best solution. Bracken's own treatment of the problem of the one and the many falls within the context of how process thinkers in general understand and try to solve this problem.

Process Thinkers on the Problem of the One and the Many

From its incipience, Anglo-American process thought has addressed the problem of the one and the many and has suggested that process metaphysics best solves the problem compared to other proposals.

Whitehead says the problem of metaphysics is reconciling fluency with permanence, or of explaining how to retain fluency in what is essentially actual and how to retain permanence in what is essentially changing. He also describes the problem as that of the multiplicity of the actual entities in the world attaining a unity, and the overarching unity—which for Whitehead is in God—retaining the multiplicity of the world. Here he conceptually relates permanence with unity, and fluency with multiplicity in an attempt to attain continuity with novelty.

For Whitehead the "one" does not stand for the integral number one but the singularity of an actual being or entity. The word "many" means disjunctive diversity or different actual entities, and presupposes the term "one," which denotes each of the actual entities in disjunctive diversity. Both one and many are essential to our concept of a "being," "entity," or "thing."

Other process thinkers understand the one and the many in ways similar to Whitehead.[409] Donna Bowman says the problem involves balancing permanency and fluency in mutual requirement, so that "neither can be reduced to a principle that stands over against some other independent principle and that could conceivably explain all phenomena without recourse to its opposite."[410] There must be an "eternal balance between the one and the many." We must explain the world process without beginning and ending with the one, "with the many scattered in between as

409. See Ivor Leclerc, *Whitehead's Metaphysics: An Introductory Exposition* (New York: Macmillan, 1958), 210–11; Victor Lowe, "Alfred North Whitehead: Introduction," in *Classic American Philosophers*, ed. Max H. Fisch, 395–417 (New York: Appleton-Century-Crofts, 1951), 400–402; Suchocki, *God, Christ, Church*, 31, 83, 214; Marjorie Hewitt Suchocki, "Spirit in and through the World," in *Trinity in Process*, 188; Bowman, *The Divine Decision*, 103, 108.

410. Bowman, *The Divine Decision*, 101.

a more or less inevitable middle step," but we must also explain the process without beginning and ending with "the many only in their distinction from each other."[411]

While process thinkers typically agree that the problem of the one and the many involves stasis and flux, with reflections on the problem since the Presocratics, they also associate other pairs of juxtaposed ideas with the one and the many. They say the problem of the one and the many involves accounting for seemingly opposed aspects of categorical reality, which they express as pairs of ideas, the poles of which pairs have affinities with one another. These include but are not limited to: becoming and being, potentiality and actuality, infinite and finite, complexity and simplicity, time and eternity, particularity and universality, concretion and abstractness, matter and form, physical and mental, accident and substance, relativity and absoluteness, contingency and necessity, freedom and causality, and subjectivity and objectivity.

For instance, Hartshorne and Ogden say the one and the many are reconciled in the dipolar view of God as both absolute and relative.[412] Criticizing classical theism, Hartshorne says ultimate reality must balance the terms in some of the pairs just iterated in addition to relativity and absoluteness. Classical theism's monopolarity, described earlier, fails to do this. God must have both internal and external relations, potentiality and actuality, complexity and simplicity, concreteness and abstractness, mutability and immutability, temporality and eternality.

With Whitehead, some speak of reconciling determinism and novelty, associating causality with unity and absoluteness, and associating freedom with plurality and relativity.[413] God's necessary features are absolute

411. Ibid., 101, 214.

412. Charles A. Hartshorne, *Reality as Social Process: Studies in Metaphysics and Religion* (Glencoe, Ill.: Free Press, 1953), 116, 120–23; Hartshorne, *The Divine Relativity: A Social Conception of God* (New Haven, Conn.: Yale University Press, 1967), 61; Hartshorne, *Man's Vision of God and the Logic of Theism,* 2nd ed. (Hamden, Conn.: Archon Books, 1964), 17–18, 46, 109–110, 121, 125, 182; Hartshorne, *A Natural Theology for Our Time* (LaSalle, Ill.: Open Court, 1967), 20–21; Hartshorne, *Creative Synthesis and the Philosophic Method* (LaSalle, Ill.: Open Court, 1970), 52–53, 82–84, 167–70; Schubert M. Ogden, *The Reality of God and Other Essays* (New York: Harper & Row, 1966), 48, 59–61, 65.

413. See Alfred North Whitehead, *Religion in the Making* (New York: Macmillan, 1926; reprint, New York: New American Library, 1974), 108–9, 111; Whitehead, *Process and Reality,* 150 (228), 244 (373); Whitehead, *Symbolism, Its Meaning and Effect* (New York: Macmillan, 1927; reprint, New York: Fordham University Press, 1985), 86–87; Ford, *The Lure of God,*

because they obtain regardless of the actualization or non-actualization of certain possibilities. God's contingent features are relative, since they depend on the actualization of certain possibilities by the free choices of actual entities, some of which possibilities are mutually exclusive in actuality.[414] Process thinkers also speak of reconciling the mental and physical, which they sometimes correlate to epistemological rationalism and epistemological empiricism respectively.[415]

Bracken's Conception of the Problem of the One and the Many

Bracken says the problem of the one and the many is "how the many are likewise one without ceasing to be themselves as discrete individuals."[416] He judges the success of proposed solutions by how well they avoid the extremes of "making the one ultimately the real to the exclusion of the many," and "making the many ultimately real, to the exclusion of one" so any real solution must explain "how Ultimate Reality must be irreducibly both one and many at the same time."[417]

Criticizing classical theism, Bracken speaks of an "implicit totalitarianism in the classic understanding of *the one and the many,* because the one is transcendent of the many and orders the many both to one another and to itself."[418] Traditionally the one was understood as a transcendent entity giving unity and order to the empirical many, where the one could be the Form of the Good, Being, or God, depending on the philosophical context.[419] Since the many derive their unity not from their relationships with one another but from their common relationship to the transcendent one, there is an asymmetry, which doesn't solve the problem.[420]

There is an insoluble dilemma in classical approaches to the one and

---

65–66; Bowman, *The Divine Decision,* 85, 90–91; and John F. Haught, *God after Darwin: A Theology of Evolution* (Boulder, Colo.: Westview Press, 2000), 102–3.

414. Ford, *The Lure of God,* 26–27.

415. Whitehead, *Religion in the Making,* 99, 102–7, 118; Hartshorne, *Man's Vision of God,* 60–61, 64; Bracken, *God: Three Who Are One,* 63, 111–19.

416. Bracken, "Philosophical Foundations," 53, 55.

417. Bracken, "Non-Duality," 140.

418. Ibid.

419. Bracken, "Trinity: Economic and Immanent," 17.

420. Bracken, "An Example of Western Theology," 73–74.

the many. To be truly all-inclusive the one must be infinite, since finitude implies limitation by another entity and hence plurality. If the transcendent one is infinite then the many do not really exist. If the many really do exist then the one is not infinite and is just one among the many, even if of a higher order.[421] This relates to a similar dilemma he sees in the choice between monism and dualism. Monism absorbs the empirical many into the unity of the one or infinite, while dualism implicitly makes the infinity of the one finite by juxtaposing it to the finite. A real solution must involve non-duality that includes "the mutual implication of the one in the many and the many in the one."[422]

In sum, Bracken sees the problem as the tendency to make *either* the one *or* the many metaphysically ultimate to the exclusion of the other. The problem is explaining how ultimate reality is both one and many, without reducing either to mere appearance and actual non-existence. Any adequate solution must account for how "Ultimate Reality must be irreducibly both one and many at the same time."[423]

Four main features of process thought in general in addition to his theology in particular adequately solve the problem of the one and the many, in Bracken's view. First, the actual entity's concrescence resolves the problem. Second, his revised version of Whiteheadian structured societies solves the problem. Third, his understanding of creativity's relationship to concrete entities solves the problem. Fourth, his unique process view of the Trinity solves the problem. Finally, he proposes several miscellaneous ways the problem can be resolved.

The Concrescence of the Actual Entity

The actual entity's concrescence exhibiting the ultimate metaphysical principle is frequently cited as the paradigmatic case of how Whitehead solves the problem of the one and the many.[424] In a new entity's concres-

421. Bracken, "Non-Duality," 142.

422. Bracken, *The Divine Matrix,* 76; Bracken, "Non-Duality," 146. See Bracken's discussion of Panikkar's commentary on the Brahmic *mahāvākya* ("Great Saying") and the relationship between *atman* and *Brahman* in Upanashadic Hinduism (Bracken, *The Divine Matrix,* 79–84).

423. Bracken, "Non-Duality," 140.

424. The ultimate metaphysical principle is the "creative advance from plurality to unity, as, in every new moment, 'the many become one and are increased by one.'" Whitehead, *Process and Reality,* 21 (31–32). See Leclerc, *Whitehead's Metaphysics,* 210–11; Lowe, "Alfred

cence the many, which are the actual entities from the universe of one moment ago, or "disjunctive diversity," become one, or add one more entity to the many superject entities of the universe.

Bracken, too, says the actual entity's concrescence solves the problem of the one and the many, but specifies a difference.[425] When Whitehead says creativity is the ultimate principle he means creativity makes each occasion a microcosm of the macrocosm.[426] Bracken argues that Whitehead's dictum that each actual entity "repeats in microcosm what the universe is in macrocosm" reveals how every entity has as part of its common element of form the basic configuration of the entire universe from a moment ago.[427] In this element of form the entity "repeats" the universe from a moment ago. Since all actual entities prehend the universe as it was a moment ago, they share the same element of form, which is the basis for their unity as a universal society in the present moment. As the means by which all actual entities co-constitute the cosmic society, creativity "effects at one and the same time the unity of the universe and the unification or self-constitution of each of its member actual entities."[428]

Bracken's Revised Whiteheadian Societies

Not surprisingly, societies are central in Bracken's solutions to the problem of the one and the many. As explained earlier, Bracken believes most process thinkers are imbalanced on the side of the many by making actual entities primordial and societies derivative. On the other hand he criticizes Royce for making the human society a supraindividual person with a life and self of its own, which overrides the individuality of its members. Bracken urges that society be *equiprimordial* with actual entities, saying equiprimordiality is a sine qua non for any adequate solution to the problem of the one and the many.

Part of the problem is giving either the empirical many or the tran-

---

North Whitehead: Introduction," 400–402; Suchocki, *God, Christ, Church,* 31, 83, 214; Bowman, *The Divine Decision,* 108, 214; Robert C. Neville, *Creativity and God: A Challenge to Process Theology* (New York: Seabury, 1980), 36–40.

425. Bracken, *The Triune Symbol,* 45.

426. Bracken, "Process Philosophy and Trinitarian Theology—II," 87; Bracken, "An Example of Western Theology," 42. Cf. Whitehead, *Process and Reality,* 215 (327).

427. Bracken, "An Example of Western Theology," 42.

428. Bracken, "Process Philosophy and Trinitarian Theology—II," 87. See also Bracken, "Subsistent Relation," 192, and "Philosophical Foundations," 56–57.

sempirical one ultimate preeminence and explanatory power, while not balancing both and affirming both equally. For Bracken actual entities retain their individual identities even when they simultaneously become a new reality, a society by their intrinsic relatedness to one another through the common element of form.[429] The bona fide ontological reality of the society means the member entities are simultaneously one new ontological reality but at the same time many discrete actual entities. Since actual entities always remain themselves with their own individual ontological integrity yet constitute a new reality or society, they are both the many and the one simultaneously.[430]

Also, the one society is present in its many member entities through its common element of form. The whole society as it existed one moment ago exists in each of its parts. At the same time these same parts, through their individual prehensions of that earlier whole, find themselves related by a common element of form, which now constitutes a new whole or the society coming into being in the present moment.[431] The one is in the many and the many in the one.

Bracken on Creativity and Actual Entities

Bracken says the relationship between creativity and actual entities is yet another approach to resolving the problem of the one and the many. This touches on the problems of logocentrism and onto-theology in classical theism. Bracken agrees with Heidegger that classical metaphysics tries to ground the empirical many in the transcendent one understood as an entity or actual being, and so prematurely identifies the unity of being with the Supreme Being, or God. Classical theism is logocentric because it makes the transcendent one control the relation of the empirical many to one another through their conjoint relation to the one as a transcendent individual entity. This makes the transcendent one ultimate at the expense of the ontological reality, integrity, and independence of the created many.[432]

429. Bracken, "Process Philosophy and Trinitarian Theology—II," 94; Bracken, review of *Process Catholicism*, 179.

430. Bracken, "Philosophical Foundations," 54–55; Bracken, "Ecclesiology," 302; Bracken, *The Divine Matrix*, 52–69; Bracken, *The One in the Many*, 109–30, 157–78; Bracken, *God: Three Who Are One*, 78.

431. Bracken, "Subsistent Relation," 192; Bracken, review of *Process Catholicism*, 179.

432. Bracken, *Society and Spirit*, 151–52; Bracken, "An Example of Western Theology," 41;

Many process thinkers replicate the classical problem of relating the transcendent one to the immanent many. This is because the unity of the many finite actual entities only obtains in the superordinate one, where God as the transcendent actual entity prehends every finite entity in God's consequent nature. Derrida and deconstructionists could easily construe the idea that God's consequent nature gives objective unity to the universe as logocentrism. Confusing God's experience of the unity and objectivity of the world process of a moment ago with the still developing world in the present repeats the error of making "ontological objectivity . . . synonymous with God's understanding of the reality."[433]

Bracken claims to avoid logocentrism by denying that the unity of the God-world relationship is found in a transcendent entity, the Supreme Being. Instead unity is found in a transcendent activity, the divine nature. Creativity, not God as the Supreme Being, is the one in the many actual entities it empowers to be and exist in their own right.[434] Creativity is not an abstraction from the fact of concrescence but the Act of Being that constitutes both the entitative reality of God and the ongoing reality of creation.[435] Unity subsists not in the fact that all finite entities are related to God, but rather in how all entities, including God as the Supreme Being, participate in the common principle or act of existence. If the one were an entity or existent, then either it would be just one of the many or it would be outside or above the process. If the former, it would be one more entity needing unification with all other entities. If the latter, either monism similar to that of Advaita Vedanta, or dualism, must obtain.[436]

The *Logos* or ontological principle of unity for the cosmic process is not located in a transcendent entity, but in transcendent activity.[437] There is no single focal point for understanding the cosmic society. The *Logos* is distributed equally among all its members, divine and creaturely, in their dynamic interrelation to each other. It is never concentrated in strictly one reality since even the community of divine persons shares in the

---

Bracken, *The One in the Many,* 37 n. 65, 103; Bracken, "Trinity: Economic and Immanent," 17; Bracken, "Authentic Subjectivity," 297 n. 19.

433. Bracken, *Society and Spirit,* 152; Bracken, *The One in the Many,* 98; Bracken, "An Example of Western Theology," 42; Bracken, "Authentic Subjectivity," 296–97, 297 n. 19.

434. Bracken, "Non-Duality," 141–42; Bracken, "An Example of Western Theology," 42; Bracken, *The One in the Many,* 194.

435. Bracken, "Subsistent Relation," 199.

436. Bracken, "Non-Duality," 142, 143–44.

437. Bracken, *The One in the Many,* 101–4.

common principle of existence and activity. Within creation, the *Logos* is distributed equally among a society's members, since through in their dynamic interrelation they equally constitute a society's unity.

In Bracken's view of societies, creativity, or the unifying principle or the one, arises out of the interplay of the many actual entities. The one *Logos* or creativity emerges out of the many and concomitantly is the source or ground for their constitution. Neither the one nor the many opposes itself to the other as logically or temporally prior, as in the classical logocentric, onto-theological view where the transcendent one is the source of the many and their unity.[438]

Even in the Trinity the one is not prior to the many. God's unity does not preexist the persons, nor do the persons preexist their unity as one God. The one, or creativity or the divine nature, subsists only in the many, or the three divine persons, which also co-constitute the whole, but in and only through their dynamic interrelationships.[439] Creativity or the divine nature is coexistent with the divine persons as the conjoint principle of their existence and activity, and through their dynamic interrelation the divine persons provide a reason for creativity to exist.[440] Even though the persons co-constitute the divine nature or creativity, the persons cannot exist except in virtue of creativity or the divine nature. The one and the many are equiprimordial in the Trinity.[441]

Also, because creativity is an activity immanent in actual entities enabling them to exist as distinct individuals it must, by definition, operate differently in each entity.[442] This makes creativity paradoxically both the principle of otherness or separateness between entities and the principle of unity between them. It is the principle of sameness since it is the Act of Being providing unity to the entire system of the universe at any moment. Yet, this is not the sameness of a transcendent entity, only the sameness of an immanent activity. If creativity is immanent in all crea-

438. Bracken, *Society and Spirit,* 152; Bracken, *The Divine Matrix,* 126.

439. Bracken, "Subsistent Relation," 191; Bracken, "Philosophical Foundations," 55–56; Bracken, *God: Three Who Are One,* 73–74, 104.

440. Bracken, "Panentheism from a Trinitarian Perspective," 25–26; Bracken, *The One in the Many,* 205.

441. Bracken, *The One in the Many,* 128; Bracken, *God: Three Who Are One,* 76–78, 84–85, 103, 115, 125; Bracken, "Non-Duality," 145.

442. Bracken, "Whitehead," 95; Bracken, "An Example of Western Theology," 42; Bracken, "Panentheism from a Trinitarian Perspective," 27.

tures rather than transcendent to them, then creativity must be understood as "from below," an *underlying* principle, rather than "from above," and therefore not logocentric.[443]

Bracken's Social Trinitarianism

Bracken further offers his unique process trinitarianism as yet another way to resolve the problem of the one and the many.[444] The one creativity or divine nature unifying the many actual entities not only unifies the world but also the community of the three divine persons. The one is the Godhead or divine nature common to all three persons, the principle whereby the divine persons exist both by themselves and in dynamic interrelation.[445]

Bracken's view of societies as structured fields of activity solves the problem of threeness and oneness in trinitarian theology. Fields can overlap while substances cannot. Being coterminous, the three divine subsocieties completely overlap and so are really identical in a way that two substances cannot be. In God the many are really identical with the one. Also, there is identity between the one and the many because the divine field of activity exists only by the dynamic interrelatedness of the persons, and the persons continue to relate to one another in the same way because of the structural patterns already resident within the field.[446]

Although he retains a distinction between the divine persons and the divine essence, at points Bracken will use the classical truism that the persons and nature are only notionally distinct, not really distinct, and assert the equiprimordiality of the one and the many in the Trinity. The co-constitution and equiprimordiality of the one nature and the many persons, and the lack of a real distinction between the divine field of activity and its constituent actual occasions, lead Bracken to conclude that the one and the many are truly identical in his trinitarian theology.[447]

443. Bracken, *The One in the Many,* 84; Bracken, "Whitehead," 94–95; Bracken, "An Example of Western Theology," 42; Bracken, "Process Philosophy and Trinitarian Theology—II," 87; Bracken, "Subsistent Relation," 192; Bracken, "Philosophical Foundations," 56–57.

444. Bracken, "Process Philosophy and Trinitarian Theology—II," 93; Bracken, "Philosophical Foundations," 5, 53.

445. Bracken, "Non-Duality," 144.

446. Bracken, "The World," 99.

447. Ibid.; Bracken, "Philosophical Foundations," 55; private interview with Joseph A. Bracken, November 22, 2003.

Finally, as ultimate reality the Trinity is the archetype for equiprimordiality of the one and the many in all levels of reality.[448] Not only humans but *all* created entities are the *Imago Dei.*

As in the Trinity, reality at all levels of existence and activity is "invariably both one and many at the same time," so that "the many and the one are not distinct from one another," and that "the one and the many are fully interdependent."[449] The Trinity as the exemplar of the equiprimordiality of the one and the many is thus the foremost instance of the axiom that God is not an exception to the metaphysical principles but rather their chief exemplification.[450]

Other Ways Bracken Approaches the Problem

At various points Bracken uses other aspects of process thought in general and his own system in particular to approach the problem of the one and the many. For instance, the unity of process balances the one and the many better than the unity of substance because, although both admit functioning totalities greater than the sums of their parts, a substance reduces its parts to a level of negligibility. In contrast, process retains the ontological integrity of the parts in the process while still indicating there is one whole, namely the process. The parts create something bigger than themselves, the whole process, but the parts must remain fully actual in order to do so. In a substance, though, the parts are not actual since they are not substances in their own right so long as they remain parts of still another substance.[451]

By balancing continuity with discontinuity, process philosophy re-

448. Bracken, *The Triune Symbol,* 46; Bracken, *God: Three Who Are One,* 121, 124–25; Bracken, "The Issue of Panentheism," 215; Bracken, "Panentheism from a Process Perspective," 105 n. 21; Bracken, "Panentheism from a Trinitarian Perspective," 27; Bracken, *The One in the Many,* 4, 37 n. 65, 128; Bracken, "Trinity: Economic and Immanent," 12, 22; Bracken, "The Holy Trinity, Part I," 177, 179; Bracken, "Process Philosophy and Trinitarian Theology—II," 94; Bracken, "Creativity," 113; Bracken, "Subsistent Relation," 188–204; Bracken, "The Theology of God of Elizabeth A. Johnson," 31–32 n. 31; Bracken, "Philosophical Foundations," 52, 57, 58–59; private interview with Bracken, November 22, 2003.

449. Bracken, "Non-Duality," 146.

450. Bracken, "Trinity: Economic and Immanent," 15; Bracken, "The Divine *Pleroma,*" *Chicago Studies* 26, no.1 (April 1987): 32; Bracken, "The Theology of God of Elizabeth A. Johnson," 29, 21–32; Bracken, "Process Philosophy and Trinitarian Theology—II," 95; Bracken, *Christianity and Process Thought,* 10–12.

451. Bracken, "Process Philosophy and Trinitarian Theology," 222–23.

solves the problem of the one and the many yet another way. There is discontinuity in how the universe is never exactly the same from moment to moment, since new entities and combinations of entities in societies emerge. There is continuity because the new entities emerging are heavily conditioned by the past, by their prehensions of past actual entities in their immediate societies, and by the cosmos as a whole.[452] Also, the self-determining decision of an actual entity makes it discontinuous from all other actual entities, but the extensive continuum unites all entities in continuity.[453]

From within his own system Bracken argues that the divine or ontogenetic matrix balances continuity and discontinuity. The divine matrix is both ever-the-same and ever-new. It is the enduring substrate for the dynamic relationships of the divine persons to one another and for the relationships of the divine persons to all of their creatures since the beginning of the universe. There is no fundamental change in the basic structure of the divine field of activity since it is constituted by the permanent relationships of the divine persons to one another. However, the details of the divine matrix perpetually change as new events take place in the lives of the three divine persons and in the world, generating newness and hence discontinuity.[454]

Bracken says the intersubjectivity of actual entities also solves the problem of similarity and difference. Referencing Levinas, Bracken agrees that intersubjectivity strongly privileges alterity over sameness.[455] There is still a dialectical relationship between otherness and sameness even in intersubjectivity. For Levinas, persons regularly bridge the infinity separating them as different subjects through language and other modes of communication. In a similar vein, actual entities are discrete in their private subjective concrescences but are not entirely disconnected because they are united via the extensive continuum and prehensive causality.

Also regarding intersubjectivity, Bracken argues for the equiprimordiality of intersubjectivity and objective reality, subjectivity, and objectivity.

452. Bracken, "Essential and Existential Truth," 72; Bracken, *Christianity and Process Thought*, 22–23.

453. Bracken, "Whitehead," 91; Bracken, *Christianity and Process Thought*, 80.

454. Bracken, "Intersubjectivity," 399.

455. Bracken, *The One in the Many*, 79–80, 109 n. 2, 110; Bracken, *Christianity and Process Thought*, 70–71; Bracken, "Whitehead," 91.

The reformed subjectivist principle and internal relations mean that any being in existence results from processes of subjectivity, private and public. Objective reality is the result of sustained intersubjectivity. Yet this intersubjectivity at any time presupposes an established objective state of affairs created by the interplay of earlier objective actual entities. Intersubjectivity and objectivity thus mutually condition one another, grounding each other from a different perspective.[456]

Bracken also urges that Whitehead's ultimate category of creativity in the concrescence of actual entities represents the best balance of causality and freedom. Although heavily conditioned by its environment of predecessor entities in its immediate society and in the universe as a whole, the actual entity ultimately through its own free decision effects its own self-constitution. This means creativity is the source of necessity and order on the one hand, but the source of freedom and novelty on the other.[457]

Conclusion

Joseph A. Bracken's philosophical process theology deserves careful attention as one of the most rigorous, systematic, and consistent presentations of process theology. With a formidable command of the history of Western philosophy and theology, Bracken synthesizes Whiteheadian modern process metaphysics with what he considers permanently relevant in classical metaphysics. In handling traditional as well as cutting-edge thought, Bracken bears kinship with Leibniz centuries before him. In addition to process metaphysics, he culls resources from Aristotle, St. Thomas, Schelling, Royce, Heidegger, and contemporary theologians and philosophers.

Bracken's process theology is important as it seeks to remediate the potential problems with pure Whiteheadian metaphysics. He raises important criticisms of other process thinkers and shows how his system addresses problems. Bracken revises traditional interpretations of Whiteheadian creativity so as to explain how creativity can be an ultimate cause or reason if it is only an abstraction, and how God is related to creativity, a vital question for Christian process theology.

Bracken argues that the Whiteheadian structured society cannot be a

456. Bracken, *The One in the Many,* 207; Bracken, "Authentic Subjectivity," 290–303.

457. Bracken, "Philosophical Foundations," 58, 59; Bracken, "Trinity: Economic and Immanent," 19 n. 27; Bracken, *Christianity and Process Thought,* 23.

mere derivative notion of the nexus category, but must be emphasized as much as or equiprimordially with actual entities in order to avoid the pitfalls of atomism. This rethinking of the Whiteheadian society makes process metaphysics a more consistent social ontology, improves upon Hartshorne's panentheism, and allows Bracken to construct perhaps the most comprehensive process doctrine of the Trinity yet to appear.

Bracken's combination of field-theory in philosophy of science with Whiteheadian societies improves the process theology that is already more conducive to the religion and science dialogue than much classical theology.

Among contemporary process thinkers Bracken spends the most time addressing the perennial problem of the one and the many. Explaining the problem to be "how ultimate reality must be irreducibly both one and many at the same time," he advances both the common process response to this problem and the unique contributions coming from his specific version of process metaphysics. The next chapter will begin my analysis and critique of the solutions proposed for the problem of the one and the many by process thinkers in general and Bracken in particular, in light of what I call the problem of mutual ultimate causality.

CHAPTER 3

The Problem of the One and the Many

The Creator-Creature Distinction

Process thought has been challenged on many counts and from many quarters, including those assuming a more or less classical theistic view of God. I will not rehearse these evaluations here but rather will focus on evaluating process solutions to the specific problem of the one and the many. This will highlight what I see to be a major shortcoming in process metaphysics.

Before analyzing process solutions to the problem, I will suggest a reason for its genesis and difficulty in process thought. One of Whitehead's central axioms is that "God is not to be treated as an exception to all metaphysical principles, invoked to save their collapse. He is their chief exemplification."[1] This is consciously opposed to a major feature of most understandings of the Creator-creature distinction in classical Western monotheism. I suggest that denying this key aspect of the Creator-creature distinction as classically conceived, either explicitly or implicitly, both generates and makes insoluble the problem of the one and the many.

Here I will introduce why I believe this by analyzing process thinkers' responses to the problem of the one and the many. In the final chapter I will discuss how the classical theistic understanding of the difference between God and the world—which difference God both establishes and is, as Karl Rahner says[2]—may obviate the felt need to try to reconcile the various dialectical poles encountered in categorical reality.

1. Alfred North Whitehead, *Process and Reality: An Essay in Cosmology,* corrected ed., ed. David Ray Griffin and Donald W. Sherburne (New York: Free Press, 1978; originally published by Macmillan, 1929), 343 (p. 521 in 1929 edition).

2. Karl Rahner, *Foundations of Christian Faith,* trans. William Dych (New York: Seabury, 1978; reprint, Crossroad, 1999), 62.

From a classical theistic perspective, the dialectical poles frequently associated with the problem of the one and the many are an inherent aspect of finite, created being, which is the only content of our categorical knowledge. These categorical oppositions observed in finite beings are a function precisely of their finitude, which may be expressed in many kinds of incompleteness. One classical and fundamental expression of this is the distinction between essence and existence. No finite being's essence can ever be identical with its existence for multiple reasons, such as that a finite entity's essence both preexists and endures beyond the actual existence of that entity as possibility. No finite being's essence is identical with its existence, so there is always the polarity of essence (possibility) and existence (actuality) in any actually existing finite entity. This also means the actual existence, actuality, or being *(esse)* of any finite being depends on a metaphysically unique entity that alone possesses existence or being essentially, or possesses self-existence or aseity. Finite or created entities in this view inherently and of necessity exist under the situation of an original estrangement or split in their very beings.

From this perspective the problem of the one and the many for process thinkers arises from trying to account for all of reality, including ultimate reality, solely in the context where this bifurcation between the two poles obtains, without reference to a transcendent realm where the estrangement of essence and existence does not obtain. Whitehead's axiom that the same metaphysical principles must apply to all of reality, God included, precludes any exception to the metaphysical principles, including any exception to existential bifurcation. God is the same type of being as categorical beings, and so the estrangement or polarity is utterly ubiquitous.

If ultimate reality is the same kind of being as categorical being, then the split between the terms of the various pairs observed in categorical reality becomes a pressing problem. To be truly ultimate an ultimate explanatory principle must account for itself and everything else, without presupposing, causally or notionally, anything else. In process discussions of the problem of the one and the many, the various pairs observed in categorical reality explain and presuppose each other. If they are not really identical, so that the distinction between them is either only notional or apparent, then there is a problem of causal or logical anteriority or priority. If the poles are going to explain all of reality solely in terms of themselves as categorical beings then they must be somehow reconciled in a way that fully and really identifies them.

The identity I mean here is the logical principle of identity. The terms of the poles must be really identical in every way so as to really be the same thing. Ultimate causality cannot have antecedent causes or parts, which is one of the reasons for the classical doctrine of divine simplicity. Ultimate reality must be simple because an ultimate reality composed of parts or reliant on antecedent causes implies some thing or things more ultimate than itself. If the ultimate explanatory principle is truly ultimate, then the poles can be predicated of it only notionally or symbolically, not literally and really, as are the divine attributes in classical theism's divine simplicity. This also bears on discussions of analogical predication, which I will briefly address below.

Because they are finite creatures in the classical theistic view, the terms of the various pairs are not identical. In dealing with any pair neither term can account for the other entirely and without reference to its opposite term. This, I suggest, is what process thinkers are faced with in the problem of the one and the many. I will call this "the problem of mutual ultimate causality." This is the problem of trying to make the terms in the poles causally or logically account for one another when they are not really (logically) identical, as are the classical theistic divine attributes.

Affirming a real distinction between the terms of the poles but trying to make the terms causally account for one another, process thinkers are faced with the problem of making the terms of the pairs really identical while at the same time denying this real identity. If the terms of the poles are not really identical, then one of them of necessity must be logically, causally, and/or temporally antecedent to the other, and hence the real cause of the other, without that other being a necessary condition of the one that is logically, causally, and/or temporally antecedent.

Again, because two discrete things cannot fully cause each other is one reason for the classical theistic doctrine that ultimate reality is not composed of parts. The two terms of each of the various pairs observed in categorical reality cannot be really identical precisely because they are aspects of finite creation. Philosophically speaking, the necessity and ineluctability of an exception to the principles of the metaphysics of proportionate being is what classical theistic analyses like St. Thomas's five ways attempt to demonstrate.[3]

3. By "proportionate being" here and elsewhere I mean Lonergan's technical use of the term as "being proportionate to our knowing," being "as it lies within … the domains of

Attestations to the Problem of Mutual Ultimate Causality

Diverging in many other ways, a variety of thinkers draw attention to the problem of mutual ultimate causality, or trying to explain all of reality in terms of the metaphysics of proportionate being. In diverse ways they all indicate an inability of each of the terms of the dialectical poles encountered in categorical reality to fully explain both itself and its opposite together, without reference to a transcendent being that is the exception to the metaphysics of categorical being.

Niebuhr argues that analyses of reality always culminate in contradictions necessitating a transcendent source of meaning, which he says is God. Some dialectical poles he notes include: chaos and order, irrationality and rationality, time and eternity, freedom and nature, novelty in history and historical continuity, progress and regress, and negation (or judgment) and fulfillment.[4] Immanent thought systems focusing on either term in these and other dialectical pairs run aground on the problem of the other term's impinging from without and being inexplicable by the first term only. Niebuhr calls this the "negative proof" for the radically transcendent, or God.[5] Exposing these immanent systems as inadequate, he offers the God of the Christian confessions as the transcendent source of meaning, which he calls the "positive proof" for God.[6] Through symbolism, biblical and theological thought attempts to express the "supra-rational truth"

---

man's outer and inner experience," and being that is "to be known by human experience, intelligent grasp, and reasonable affirmation" (Bernard J. F. Lonergan, *Insight: A Study of Human Understanding*, 5th rev. ed. [Toronto: University of Toronto Press, 1992], 676, 663, 416). By "common sense" here and throughout I mean the type of metaphysical investigation just defined as metaphysics of "proportionate being."

4. See Reinhold Niebuhr, *The Nature and Destiny of Man*, 2 vols. (New York: Scribner's, 1941–43), 1:29, 1:76, 1:91, 1:124, 1:164; 1:260, 2:37–38; 2:216–17, 2:129–33, 2:148–49; 2:169, 2:212, 2:215, 2:264, 2:286–7, 2:316; Niebuhr, *Faith and History: A Comparison of Christian and Modern Views of History* (New York: Scribner's, 1949), 15, 17–18, 20, 33, 36, 49, 55, 57, 85, 198, 215; Niebuhr, *Beyond Tragedy* (New York: Scribner's, 1937), 4, 14, 220–21; Niebuhr, *The Self and the Dramas of History* (New York: Scribner's, 1955), 41–42, 104, 204, 242; and Niebuhr, "Between Two Cities," *Christian Scholar* 43 (Summer 1960): 141.

5. Niebuhr, *The Nature and Destiny of Man*, 1:131, 1:165; Niebuhr, *Faith and History*, 32–33, 138, 152, 164.

6. Niebuhr, *The Self and the Dramas of History*, 241; Niebuhr, *Faith and History*, 152, 165–67.

of the transcendent Creator God, as in the doctrine of creation *ex nihilo,* which reveals the limits of immanent rationality and categories.[7]

Neo-Calvinist Cornelius Van Til assiduously argues that when metaphysics ignores the Creator-creature distinction it lapses into dialectical thought in which the two terms of the various dialectical pairs cannot be reconciled and cannot account for one another.[8] Rousas Rushdoony speaks of how departing from the transcendent God "drift[s] into dialectical thought."[9] Gunton judges the problem of the one and the many to be largely the result of a "theology of immanence" that attempts to displace the transcendent Creator God.[10]

Neville analyzes the problem of the one and the many in similar ways. His fundamental criticism of process theology is that it denies what theology has traditionally meant by the metaphysical distinction between God and the world, or the Creator-creature distinction. He alleges that any metaphysics ignoring the transcendent creator God while claiming to "unify the many" really surreptitiously makes the many or the one ultimate to the exclusion of the other.[11]

Tillich attributes what he sees as certain dialectical poles in categorical existence to a sort of "split" that occurs in finite categorical reality.[12]

7. Niebuhr, *The Nature and Destiny of Man,* 1:12, 1:53, 1:76, 1:86, 1:127, 1:166, 1:253, 1:293, 2:240, 2:312; Niebuhr, *The Self and the Dramas of History,* 61, 104; Niebuhr, *Beyond Tragedy,* 4–7, 9, 23–24; Niebuhr, *Faith and History,* 33, 46, 101–6, 237; Niebuhr, "The Truth in Myths," in *Faith and Politics,* ed. Ronald H. Stone (New York: Scribner's, 1953), 17–18. See also Robert D. Knudsen, "Symbol and Myth in Contemporary Theology, with Special Reference to the Thought of Paul Tillich, Reinhold Niebuhr, and Nicolas Berdyaev" (S.T.M. diss., Union Theological Seminary, New York, 1952), 36–39.

8. Cornelius Van Til, *The Defense of the Faith* (Phillipsburg, N.J.: Presbyterian & Reformed, 1967), 25–28; Van Til, *Psychology of Religion* (Philadelphia: Presbyterian & Reformed, 1961), 49ff; Van Til, *Christianity and Barthianism* (Phillipsburg, N.J.: Presbyterian & Reformed, 1962; rev. ed., 1965), 261.

9. John Rousas Rushdoony, "The One and the Many Problem," in *Jerusalem and Athens: Critical Discussions on the Theology and Apologetics of Cornelius Van Til,* ed. E. R. Geehan, 339–48 (Phillipsburg, N.J.: Presbyterian & Reformed, 1980), 347.

10. Colin E. Gunton, *The One, the Three and the Many: God, Creation and the Culture of Modernity* (Cambridge: Cambridge University Press, 1993), 36. See also 18, 33–41, 142, 213–14.

11. Robert C. Neville, *God the Creator: On the Transcendence and Presence of God* (Albany: State University of New York Press, 1992), 43.

12. John Dillenberger believes that while Tillich and Rahner did not influence one another, they bear patent similarities. For both of them, ontological, and hence analogical,

Dependent on and distinct from God, finite existents entail a polarity of being and non-being. He specifies four "categories" (time, space, causality, and substance), which as forms of finitude contain both an affirmative and a negative element through their double relation to both being and non-being. These categories reveal the "polarity of being and non-being," or the positive and negative, in all finite beings.[13] Analysis of the duality in these categories prepares the way for the theological question, the question of God.

In addition, Tillich specifies "ontological elements" with a similar polar character opening them to the threat of non-being: individuation and participation, dynamics and form, and freedom and destiny.[14] In every element "each pole is limited as well as sustained by the other one," and while "a complete balance between them presupposes a balanced whole," nonetheless "such a whole is not given" because of their finitude, which places the poles in tension.[15]

Perhaps my own construal, that finite existents not being the source of their own existence experience an existential condition of an admixture of being and non-being, is closest to Tillich's. Tillich's understanding of this existential split seems like the traditional insight that finite, categorical, created beings have a bifurcation between their essence and existence so that their existence is not necessary, as is God's.

The Problem of Mutual Ultimate Causality in General

The problem of mutual ultimate causality in one sense means each of the two terms in the various pairs of ideas associated with the problem of the one and the many presupposes its opposite term, so ultimately neither term can fully account for the other and itself together. This is sort of a metaphysical version of the logical error of begging the question. What is intended to be explained is already presupposed in the act of explaining.

---

thinking dominates, and for both the proper analysis of reason drives us to its boundary, to horizons lying beyond but not contradicting reason (John Dillenberger, "Contemporary Theologians and the Visual Arts," *Journal of the American Academy of Religion* 53, no. 4 [1985]: 600)

13. Paul Tillich, *Systematic Theology*, 3 vols. (Chicago: University of Chicago Press, 1951–63), 1:192–93.

14. Ibid., 1:176–77, 1:182–83, 1:186, 1:198–200, 1:200–201.

15. Ibid., 1:198.

If the sum of reality, including ultimate reality, is subject to the same metaphysical principles applicable to finite or categorical reality, and if unity and plurality are ultimate explanatory principles beyond which there is nothing more fundamental,[16] then unity and plurality must either each possess a type of aseity or be really identical and only notionally distinct. Process thinkers deny the latter, and I argue that due to the problem of mutual ultimate causality they cannot embrace the former. Categorical unity, if truly ultimate, should by itself and without reference to plurality causally account for categorical plurality, but it presupposes that plurality. Similarly, categorical plurality, if truly ultimate, should by itself and without reference to unity causally account for categorical unity, but it already presupposes that unity.

A reason for the connection between divine simplicity and aseity in classical theism is the fact that what is not simple does not possess being entirely from itself alone. Conversely, creatures in classical theism depend for their existence on both other finite causes and ultimate reality, which as first cause supplies being or the act of existence *(esse)*. If the terms of the various dialectical pairs are considered finite existents, or even principles of finite existence, the fact that they cannot explain their opposed term without presupposing that term is itself a manifestation of the fact that, as finite and created, they are not self-subsistent.

On dipolar accounts, the terms of the pairs are expressly denied the nature of ultimate reality distinct from created entities, as understood in classical theism, because they are subject to the same metaphysical principles as all entities in reality. If the terms of each dialectical pair are considered categorical entities, they will not possess the Act of Being *(esse)* solely from themselves. Put another way, their essence is not identical with their act of existence. This is why each term of the various pairs mentioned in connection with the problem of the one and the many implies the other term, which it is intended to explain.

Although process thinkers typically say God is somehow different from all other actual entities, they expressly abide by the axiom that "God is not to be treated as an exception to all metaphysical principles, invoked to save their collapse. He is their chief exemplification." Admitting

16. In his categoreal scheme, Whitehead places in the category of the ultimate "many and one," along with "creativity," and the category of the ultimate is presupposed in all of the other categories. (Whitehead, *Process and Reality,* 20–22 [30–32]).

a difference between God and other existents does not imply the types of metaphysical differences between God and the world in classical theism. When all of reality inclusive of ultimate reality shares the same metaphysical principles so as to deny the classical theistic Creator-creature distinction, the ultimate or ultimates will causally depend on something else, making them at best penultimate or penultimates.

I suggest that denying God "as an exception to all metaphysical principles" is thus problematic. Putting it this way may be inadequate for classical theism, however, because this implies a point classical theism denies. God is not an exception to principles of categorical metaphysics precisely because God is not *within* categorical metaphysics.

The problem of the one and the many might arise, then, from doing metaphysics solely from an analysis of proportionate being. If each term or pole of the dialectical pairs observed in categorical reality must explain its opposite without presupposing or implying it, the problem seems insoluble. Categorical reality cannot explain itself. It cannot give itself existence. Classical theism affirms the existence of a being qualitatively different from all other existents, one of which differences is that this being is "its own reason" or "self-caused."[17] There is nothing "prior to" or "outside of" God that must be assumed as a condition of the possibility of God's existence. God has no parts or causes. Nothing other than God is implied in the fact of God's existence.[18]

Many observe how the two terms of these various pairs are mutually interdependent, requiring one another. They say each term of these polar pairs requires and presupposes its opposite, so that no term alone can account by itself for itself, its polar opposite, and all of reality.

Discussing Plotinus, Michael F. Wagner concludes that even though

17. St. Thomas would describe God as *ratio sui* but avoid the term *causa sui* because of his strict adaptation of Aristotelian causality. The expression that God is *causa sui* is more characteristic of the Franciscan school, and was later adopted by some who saw themselves in the Thomist tradition. *Causa sui* has become a commonplace expression for the concept of God's aseity in classical theism, however (e.g., Martin Heidegger, *Identity and Difference*, trans. Joan Stambaugh [New York: Harper & Row, 1969], 56, 72).

18. Brian Leftow explains this important point of classical theism when he writes: "It is part of the ordinary theist's concept of God that no regress of true explanations can go past God's existence, i.e., that when one has traced some phenomenon back to the fact that God exists, one can go no further" (Brian Leftow, "Is God an Abstract Object?" *Nous* 24 [1990]: 585).

Plotinus ended up prioritizing unity, he theoretically realized that the universals (unity) and particulars (plurality) are mutually dependent on one another.[19] Varisco observed: "Unity and multiplicity imply each other, so that the one is impossible without the other, and exists only in the other."[20] Explaining pragmatism, James says: "Oneness and the manyness are absolutely co-ordinate here," so that "neither is primordial or more essential or excellent than the other."[21] In his critical monism, Macintosh says: "The one is immanent in the many, and yet transcendent of the many; the many are immanent in the one, and yet in a sense beyond it."[22]

Process thinkers similarly relate a mutual co-dependence of the one and the many. Whitehead's idea of coherence says that "opposed elements stand to each other in mutual requirement. . . . [T]he fundamental ideas . . . presuppose each other so that in isolation they are meaningless."[23] He further says that "the term 'many' presupposes the term 'one,' and the term 'one' presupposes the term 'many,'" so that it is impossible to conceive pure unity without the presupposing multiplicity and it is impossible to conceive pure multiplicity without presupposing unity.[24] As discussed, Bracken speaks of the "mutual implication of the one in the many and the many in the one." Process thinkers thus say that the two poles presuppose each other but that together, though subject to the same metaphysical principles as the rest of reality, they account for all of reality. I disagree. Denying a qualitative metaphysical difference between ultimate reality and the rest of reality, I believe, both precipitates and makes insoluble the problem of the one and the many.

19. Michael F. Wagner, "Plotinus' World," *Dionysius* 6 (1982): 16–17.

20. Bernardino Varisco, *Know Thyself,* trans. Guglielmo Salvadori (London: George Allen & Unwin, 1915), 154.

21. William James, *Pragmatism: A New Name for Some Old Ways of Thinking,* ed. Bruce Kuklick (Indianapolis: Hackett, 1981), 65.

22. Douglas C. Macintosh, *Theology as an Empirical Science* (New York: Macmillan, 1919), 258.

23. Whitehead, *Process and Reality,* 348–49 (529). See also 3 (5).

24. Whitehead, *Process and Reality,* 21 (31); Charles A. Hartshorne, *Man's Vision of God and the Logic of Theism,* 2nd ed. (Hamden, Conn.: Archon Books, 1964), 213; Marjorie Hewitt Suchocki, *God, Christ, Church: A Practical Guide to Process Theology* (New York: Crossroad, 1982), 155.

Specific Examples of the Problem of Mutual Ultimate Causality

I will now try to show how the problem of mutual ultimate causality arises when doing metaphysics solely on the categorical level. A rudimentary inspection of the metaphysics of proportionate being reveals the problem of mutual ultimate causality in categorical unity and plurality. Any collection of categorical entities is a plurality or many. Yet the concept of many here presupposes many entities, each of which is a unity or a one. On another level of analysis the intellect can classify this collection of finite beings, however loose and however many entities it contains, as itself one larger entity. We even speak of *a* plurality. The many categorical entities in any plurality under consideration must be unified in some way, or else they would be entirely disparate and inconceivable as together in any way. Many argue that knowledge depends on the unity of commonalities between otherwise different, particular elements of reality.[25] Ontologically, a plurality of entities presupposes the unity of each entity in the plurality, and epistemologically, knowledge of many similar particulars presupposes the unity of a universal.

Conversely, any one categorical existent can be analyzed in terms of its parts. Because a finite entity does not have self-existence it relies on other entities, parts, and causes to achieve its unity as a limited instance of the Act of Being. Prior to possessing actuality any one being is in potentiality in which its many parts come together to form a whole. This means any categorical instance of unity, or a finite one, presupposes plurality or many.[26] Paradoxical mutual implication of unity and plurality appears in the process understanding of the actual entity. On the one hand an actual entity can be analyzed in terms of its genetic or composite "parts," but on the other hand it is "indivisible," "non-temporal," does not "move," and does not undergo "change."[27]

A further feature of the metaphysics of proportionate being is the dis-

25. "All knowledge is through some likeness" (St. Thomas Aquinas, *Summa contra gentiles* 1.42.3).

26. "[P]rior to all multitude we must find unity. But there is multitude in every composite" (St. Thomas Aquinas, *Summa contra gentiles* 1.18.8).

27. Clarke notes this apparent inconsistency. See Bowman L. Clarke, "God and Time in Whitehead," *Journal of the American Academy of Religion* 48 (December 1980): 563–79.

tinction between being and becoming. Any categorical being comes into being through a process of becoming so that being presupposes becoming. However, there is no such thing as pure becoming, only becoming that presupposes beings coming together to form another being. So in the categorical realm becoming presupposes entities with being, and all observable entities possessing being presuppose their own process of becoming. Becoming and being presuppose each other.

Another dialectical pair raised in discussions of the problem of the one and the many is stasis and flux. Although Heraclitus identified ultimate reality with flux or chaos, commentators have noted how he was compelled to introduce a law of reason and static order, which he called *Logos.* Although Parmenides identified ultimate reality with stasis and claimed that change is illusory, he was obliged to introduce a spiritual principle of flux that he called *"Eros."*[28]

It is difficult to avoid at least the tacit presupposition of stasis and stability in the observation of flux, because change is only conceivable by contemplating some *thing* as changing, within a moment, however puncticular and minute, of identity and stasis.[29] Change is conceptually possible only by envisioning discrete moments wherein the entity experiencing change possesses self-identity. Kierkegaard, and Moltmann echoing him, makes this point regarding Plato's time as "the moving image of eternity."[30] Every discrete moment between the transitions of flux must be conceived as a static moment of timelessness, or as eternity in one

28. Heraclitus, *Fragments* 1–2, 50, 72, in Philip Wheelwright, ed., *The Presocratics* (New York: Macmillan, 1966), 69, 74, 79; *Testimonies* 10, 15–17, 24 in ibid., 81, 84–87; Parmenides, *Testimonies* 8, 10, 11, 15–16, 18, in ibid., 102–4; Vergilius Ferm, *First Adventures in Philosophy* (New York: Scribner's, 1936), 246; and Rudolph Bultmann, *Primitive Christianity: In Its Contemporary Setting,* trans. Reginald H. Fuller (Philadelphia: Fortress Press, 1980), 122.

29. Tillich responds to the historical relativism that denies the possibility of an ontological or theological anthropology by showing how change presupposes stability, something that stays the same and hence can be identified as having changed. He says: "Human nature changes in history. Process philosophy is right in this. But human nature changes in *history.* The structure of a being *which has history* underlies all historical changes. This structure is the subject of an ontological and a theological doctrine of man" (Tillich, *Systematic Theology,* 1:167).

30. Jürgen Moltmann, *Theology of Hope: On the Ground and the Implications of a Christian Eschatology,* trans. James W. Leitch (London: SCM Press, 1967), 29, citing Kierkegaard, *The Concept of Dread,* chapter 3; Jürgen Moltmann, *The Coming of God: Christian Eschatology,* trans. Margaret Kohl (Minneapolis: Fortress Press, 1996), 285. Cf. Plato, *Timaeus* 37D.

sense of the word. Whitehead saw this tension, and said that while societies are enduring objects they are composed of smaller parts, actual entities, which allow them to undergo change across time and space.

Some critics of process thought raise the difficulty that we must posit a moment, however minute and imperceptible, of static self-identity of the entity in process.[31] In describing God as a succession of actual occasions, Cobb and Hartshorne ask how many occasions of experience would occur for God in a second, to which Cobb replies: "The answer is that it must be a very large number, incredibly large to our limited imaginations."[32] Ascribing to God a number of occasions of experience in one second too high for us to conceive, Cobb still holds that God experiences discrete moments of experience involving a moment of static self-identity.

Agreeing with Newton's claim that a portion of space cannot move, Whitehead explains actual entities as comparable to "regions of space," which means that they "cannot move," "do not change," and have "no history." They experience an "internal adventure of becoming," but since the actual appearance or "satisfaction" of an entity is also its end, it does not "move."[33] Yet, it seems difficult to say there is nothing until the actual entity attains static actuality in its satisfaction. Saying the entity has an internal adventure of becoming betrays a sort of identity of the entity with its final, actual product before its satisfaction. The entity is already considered some *thing*, and is referred to as such, while it is still undergoing an "internal adventure of becoming" before it attains satisfaction. Even if the entity does not exist in any sense during its concrescence, one must still posit its antecedent parts, the actual entities from one moment

31. See Tillich, *Systematic Theology*, 1:181; and Millard Erickson, *Christian Theology* (Grand Rapids, Mich.: Eerdmans, 1985), 53.

32. John B. Cobb Jr., "A Whiteheadian Doctrine of God." in *Process Theology and Christian Thought*, ed. Delwin Brown, Ralph E. James, Jr., and Gene Reeves, 215–43 (New York: Bobbs-Merrill, 1971), 226–27; Charles A. Hartshorne, "Whitehead's Idea of God," in *The Philosophy of Alfred North Whitehead*, ed. Paul A. Schilpp, 545–46 (New York: Tudor, 1951).

33. Whitehead, *Process and Reality*, 80 (124–25); Whitehead, *Adventures of Ideas* (New York: Macmillan, 1933; reprint, Free Press, 1967), 204. Lowe explains Whitehead's rejection of change for actual entities as a result of his rejection of "substance-accident" ontology. Since actual entities are "events" and not "substances," they do not have an underlying substratum that does not change (substance) and properties that alter without changing their identities (accidents), both of which are necessary for "change," strictly speaking (Victor Lowe, "Whitehead's Metaphysical System," in *Process Philosophy and Christian Thought*, 10).

ago coming together in the concrescence of the new entity. If there is no movement or change in those parts from potentiality to actuality, from dispersion to union, then it seems impossible that the new actual entity would become actual.

Either way it appears that categorical unity, actuality, being, and stasis presuppose antecedent plurality, potency, becoming, and motion.[34] Similarly, becoming, change, and motion presuppose prior unities of beings that are in some sense static. Like the problem of conceptually apprehending uninformed prime matter apart from a unifying form, it seems impossible to conceive of a process of pure flux without any static unities moving within the flux. It seems impossible to think of, speak of, and identify flux without the assumption of some sort of stasis.

Further, referring to flux in general as the constant element of all experience assumes something constant, consistent, unifying, and static, namely flux. If one claims that nothing is constant except change, one at least admits that change is a constant. The supposition of some sort of

34. In the wake of the philosophical criticisms of time by the absolute idealists (e.g., J. M. E. McTaggart, "The Unreality of Time," *Mind* 17 [1908]: 457–74), which bear striking similarities to the arguments of the Eleatics, along with the emergence of relativity theory in physics, there are now two basic views of "time." The older view that time has some objective existence and that events have the objective properties of being "past," "present," or "future" is called the "A-theory" or "three-dimensional" view of time. The newer view, called the "B-theory," "four-dimensional" theory, or "worm" theory of time, holds that all events of the universe exist simultaneously and that tense is only relative. On the newer view, time does not exist. What we call time is really just the differences in properties of an entity between one "segment" of the static universal "worm" containing the entity in its various stages, and other segments that contain the entity with different properties. The "past," "present," and "future" tenses are only relative. The newer theory finds support in relativity theory, but the older theory finds support in our seemingly inexorable conscious experience of a "present" moment and of "flow." Many physicists, who have not been trained in analytic philosophy, adopt the newer theory, while contemporary analytic philosophers continue to debate the strengths and weaknesses of the two views. Indeed, the question is not so much about the objective existence of "time" as about the objective existence of "change," as time has often been described as a mere measurement of change. The scientist and philosopher J. J. C. Smart has likened this debate on time to the old debate between Heraclitus and Parmenides, associating the adherents of the "A-theory" and "B-theory" with Heraclitus and Parmenides respectively (J. J. C. Smart, "Time and Becoming," in *Time and Cause,* ed. Peter van Inwagen, 1–15 [Dordrecht: Reidel, 1980], 1). For an analytic philosophical argument for the "A-theory," see William Lane Craig, *The Tenseless Theory of Time* (Boston: Kluwer Academic, 2000). For an analytic philosophical argument for the "B-theory," see D. H. Mellor, *Real Time II* (New York: Routledge, 1998).

stasis is unavoidable, simply because flux must be some thing with consistent features and distinguishable from nothingness.[35]

Parmenides says the ultimately real is stasis alone, which is known only by rational thought, and that *Eros,* or changes between polarities like "hot and cold" and "fire and water," appears as an erroneous opinion subsequent to sense experience. Summarily one can, with warrant, question the claim that the experience of change is illusory. More important, it seems that rational thought presupposes distinctions, and thus plurality and therefore change. Indeed, the elements of priority and causality in logical progression for finite intellects imply temporal succession. One could thus say the Eleatic deduction from the premises that "nothing comes from nothing" and "there is something" to the conclusion that only being, stasis, and unity are real seems self-defeating, because change, progression, distinction, and plurality are all implied as conditions of the possibility of such a deduction. In this case those who deny the objective reality of flux, becoming, change, and plurality rely on the realm they call "opinion" (the realm of progression, change, distinction, and plurality) in arriving at what they call "knowledge" (that only stasis, stability, and unity are real).[36]

Related to the problem of mutual ultimate causality in categorical flux and stasis is the mutual implication of time and eternity. It is very difficult to conceive of eternity as anything other than "arrested temporal succession."[37] Conceiving of eternity presupposes temporality because

35. This is Bracken's point when he redefines immutability and ascribes it to the ontogenetic matrix. John Haught makes an observation to this effect regarding discussions of primordial chaos in contemporary cosmogonies, even referencing the Presocratic *eros* and *logos:* "The distinction between eros and logos, however, is problematic for both logical and scientific reasons. Logically speaking, a sheer primordial eros must in some sense be distinguishable from sheer meaninglessness (or maximum entropy). Otherwise we could not make a solid case for its actual presence in nature. But if nature from the beginning possessed an eros that oriented it toward inwardness, then it must have been *patterned* in a way that would distinguish it conceptually from sheer chaos. In that case logos (intelligible structuring) would be prior to, or at least co-originative with, eros after all" (John F. Haught, *God after Darwin: A Theology of Evolution* [Boulder, Colo.: Westview Press, 2000], 183).

36. In addition to the Eleatics these would include the neo-Hegelian absolute idealists and many contemporary physicists, who have denied the reality of change, flux, and becoming.

37. Moltmann, *Theology of Hope,* 29, citing Kierkegaard, *The Concept of Dread,* chapter 3; and Moltmann, *The Coming of God,* 285.

we can conceive of eternity only as a lack of time. We speak of eternity as timelessness. On the other hand, time as the realm of progression, change, and distinction assumes a changeless, static, and undifferentiated realm. A linear succession of moments in relation to one another is comprehensible only within a higher static frame of reference transcending the flow of discrete moments in time and thereby unifying them. In order to retain self-identity, this static collection of moments must be timeless or eternal.

In addition to the elements of experience discussed by the Presocratics, there are certain pairs of terms based on Aristotle that arise in discussions of the one and many, and that likewise presuppose one another. In various medieval philosophies based on Aristotle a finite essence limits the infinite act of existence or being. A finite essence provides ontological and noetic unity to a finite being in its act of existence, for which reason essence is associated with unity. Yet a finite essence relies for its identity in part on its distinction from other essences, which thereby implies a plurality of essences. One categorical essence presupposes a plurality. Conversely, the plurality of categorical essences differentiated by how they each circumscribe a finite instance of the act of existence presupposes the unity of each essence in the plurality. This unity of each of the essences is necessary in order that each essence may be something truly distinct from the others. A plurality of categorical essences presupposes unity.

Similarly, a substance is an essence in the act of existence in a particular being. The idea of substance specifies what stays the same across time and space, while the idea of accident denotes what changes without altering the being as "this" particular being. While the substance unifies because of its finite essence, it also presupposes distinction from the many other finite substances. Contemporary relational ontologies are partly based on this fact. A relation implies at least more than one, or plurality.

A fact neglected by many who criticize substance ontologies and advocate relational-process event ontologies, though, is that whether one uses "substance" or any other term something is required to identify the unities of the individual identifiable entities in relation across time and space and in their various relationships. This unifying, enduring, continuous part of each entity in relation is classically called its "substance." Relations are between things, which can be considered spatially, temporally, or logically solitary unities by themselves, "before" they enter into relations and even while they exist in relations. Similarly, events or processes presuppose *things* that both make events and change possible and are undergoing change themselves.[38] So the many relations, events, and changes presuppose one unifying component, classically called substance. Again, plurality implies unity.

Another pair of terms in many metaphysical systems borrowing from Aristotle, such as Thomism, is potency and act. One can even observe a mutual implication of potentiality and actuality viewed strictly within categorical metaphysics, without reference to Thomism's theism. Finite beings in actuality have causes and are composed of parts, which mean they do not possess existence from themselves or simplicity. Their actuality presupposes the potentiality of many causes and parts coming together, with the one actual being as the final goal of potency. Potency is implied in every finite being in act. Also, once in actual existence, any one categorical being relies on the plurality of its many parts and causes for its existence, because it is not self-caused. Any one categorical being in actuality presupposes many parts and causes. In the categorical realm, unity implies plurality and actuality implies potency.

Potency involves the working of causes and the coming together of parts to form one whole, a telic being in its act of existence. Yet, the many causes and parts in potency are themselves unified, actual wholes. Each cause or part is a being in actuality. In potency, then, there is no pure plurality without unity. Each of the parts and causes are themselves already one unitary being in actuality. In the categorical realm plurality implies unity and potency implies actuality.

The problem of mutual ultimate causality is also seen in epistemology, which is inextricably bound up with ontology. One dialectical pair here is the universal and the particular. Rational deduction moves from the one universal to the many particulars. A syllogism begins with known universal premises, like "all humans are mortal," which provide knowledge

38. "Substance points to something underlying the flux of appearances, something which is relatively static and self-contained. . . . The problem of substance is not avoided by philosophers of function or process, because questions about that which *has* functions or about that which *is* in process cannot be silenced. The replacement of static notions by dynamic ones does not improve the question of that which makes change possible by not (relatively) changing itself. Substance as a category is effective in any encounter of mind and reality; it is present whenever one speaks of some*thing*" (Tillich, *Systematic Theology,* 1:197).

about many particulars in that universal, like "Socrates is mortal." Empirical induction moves from many particulars to the one universal. We observe and know many particulars, and based on their similarities we see a universal applying to each of these many similar beings we already knew as particular entities.

With respect to epistemic causes a deduction's starting point presupposes induction, and induction's starting point presupposes deduction. A universal presupposes particulars and particulars presuppose the universal. Universals come from induction from particulars, so that the premises in any syllogism were arrived at through empirical induction.[39] Yet, identifying particulars with which to begin induction presupposes knowledge of the universal to which the particulars belong. How can one identify a particular as a member of the genus being considered without a universal to recognize the similarity? How can a particular be known without a form?[40]

Closely related to this is the problem of uninterpreted "brute facts." All data are theory-laden in that paradigms and interpretative grids determine what is "seen," so that a posteriori knowledge of the particular presupposes the a priori.[41] This can be seen in the post-Kantian gravitation away from "naïve realism" toward "critical realism,"[42] wherein subjective a priori categories inform and determine in part what data are perceived. For hermeneutics, recognition of "pre-understanding" results in the "hermeneutical spiral." In interpretation the objective text or communication does not impose itself upon the interpreter in an intractable objectivity,

39. This fact can be seen pragmatically in what Edward Schillebeeckx calls the "refractoriness" or "resistance" of reality, which means that our theories, hypotheses, and models encounter new objective particulars through experiences that force us to change our general theories. See, Edward Schillebeeckx, *Christ: The Experience of Jesus as Lord,* trans. John Bowden (New York: Crossroad, 1980; reprint, 1999), 34–36.

40. Regarding the medieval philosophical distinction between first and second intentions, the first intention *(intentio objectiva)* is associated with the particular object, for instance, "animal" applies to that particular object like Fuzzy the Rabbit or Socrates. The second intention *(intentio formalis)* is the generic concept, species, or form, like "rabbit" or "human being."

41. Thomas S. Kuhn, *The Structure of Scientific Revolutions,* 3rd ed. (Chicago: University of Chicago Press, 1996), 111–13; Wolfhart Pannenberg, *Basic Questions in Theology,* 2 vols., trans. George H. Kelm (Philadelphia: Fortress Press, 1970–71), 2:39.

42. See, Martin Heidegger, *Being and Time,* trans. John Macquarrie and Edward Robinson (New York: Harper & Row, 1962), 190–91.

but its reception is in part shaped and determined by the a priori subjective categories of the interpreter. Yet there is an objective element that over time modifies the interpreter's pre-understanding, so that the process of interpretation involves mutual interplay between the subjective interpreter and the objective text or communicator. There is a "circular movement" but still progress, which is compared to a "spiral." One can say that the answer to a question is a function of that question, and the pre-understanding that produced that particular question is in turn confirmed, modified, or replaced by that answer.[43]

An epistemological problem of mutual ultimate causality also arises in the question of whether theory or practice is logically and temporally prior in theology. Setting a precedent for many liberation and political theologies, Gustavo Gutiérrez defined theology as "critical reflection on praxis (in light of the Word of God or in light of faith)," in such a way that depicts it as a secondary moment to praxis.[44] On the other hand, Leslie Newbigin criticizes Langdon Gilkey's assertion that praxis must always precede theory and reflection, because insofar as practical action is intentional it presupposes what "theoretical" beliefs about means and ends must be implied in intentionality.[45]

The problem of the mutual ultimate causality of the universal and the particular also arises in a question of contemporary philosophical and theological anthropology: Is there a "universal" human nature and a "universal" human experience? A focus on the differences between languages, cultures, and contexts mitigates such a universality. Yet, recognizing the differences between humans in their natures and experiences presupposes that we can identify them all as *humans,* by something similar and common to all of them.[46] Thus even some who focus on the differences between human experiences and natures, or focus on individu-

43. Schillebeeckx, *Christ,* 33–34, 50–55; Schillebeeckx, "Towards a Catholic Use of Hermeneutics," in *God the Future of Man,* trans. N. D. Smith (New York: Sheed & Ward, 1969), 7–8.

44. Gustavo Gutiérrez, *A Theology of Liberation: History, Politics, and Salvation. 15th Anniversary Edition* (Maryknoll, N.Y.: Orbis, 1988), xxix, xxxii, 5–8, 41.

45. Leslie Newbigin, "Religion for the Marketplace," in *Christian Uniqueness Reconsidered: The Myth of a Pluralistic Theology of Religions,* ed. Gavin D'Costa, 135–48 (Maryknoll, N.Y.: Orbis, 1990), 144–46.

46. For instance, John Cobb, who repeatedly speaks of the importance of the details and the particular, and is always careful to guard against the loss of content involved in

al particular "existing" human beings instead of universalizing essences, speak of "anthropological constants," "existentials" of human existence "distinguishing them [humans] essentially from everything else that exists," "shared or common experiences," and "unifying constants," like the phenomenon of language itself, among all the different types of individual human beings.[47] On the other hand, any one universal about humanity relies on and presupposes many empirically observed antecedent particular existents classified as humans.[48]

The problem of mutual ultimate causality emerges in analyses of free agency, both anthropologically and in theology proper. Do agents constitute their nature through their free decisions, as some existentialists say, or are agents' free actions determined, at least in part, by their antecedent natures or essences? In the doctrine of God, questions arise about what it means to say that God "wills his nature" and questions of modality arise regarding whether God "could have" or "could not have" willed his essence, or aspects of his essence, differently. These debates arise by asking whether freedom or nature is logically and/or temporally anterior. On the one hand, free agency presupposes a being with a nature that already exists and can make free choices. On the other hand, free choices bring about changes in that being, thus in a sense constituting and determining its nature. The freedom of a being that exercises free agency presupposes the being's essence, but the being's essence presupposes the freedom that affects and in a sense co-constitutes its nature with each exercise of will.

---

abstractions, nevertheless, says that an analysis of anything whatsoever necessitates using abstractions (John B. Cobb Jr., *The Structure of Christian Existence* [Philadelphia: Westminster Press, 1967], 22).

47. See, for instance, James H. Cone, *A Black Theology of Liberation. Twentieth Anniversary Edition* (Maryknoll, N.Y.: Orbis, 1990), 87; Paul F. Knitter, *Jesus and the Other Names: Christian Mission and Global Responsibility* (Maryknoll, N.Y.: Orbis, 1996), 36; and Josiah Royce, *The Problem of Christianity* (New York: Macmillan, 1918; reprint, Chicago: University of Chicago Press, 1968), 238–39. Although he speaks of existentials that distinguish humans "essentially" from other things, Cone expressly concurs with Sartre's dictum that "existence precedes essence," and generally believes that universalizing and classifying humans "essentially" has been and is used for oppressive purposes (Cone, *A Black Theology of Liberation*, 84–85).

48. In a very real sense, "the concrete human being must be the point of departure of any phenomenological analysis of human existence," and "there is no essence or universal humanity independent of persons in . . . concreteness " (ibid., 84).

Mutual Ultimate Causality in Process Solutions

Having explained what I call the problem of mutual ultimate causality, I now turn to process solutions, exemplified in Bracken, to the problem of the one and the many. I believe these exhibit the problem of mutual ultimate causality because of the univocal predication to ultimate reality of the finite, categorical, proportionate, metaphysical principles applicable to created beings alone in classical metaphysics.

If neither the one nor the many is ultimate in the sense of exhaustively explaining both itself and its opposite, we can ask whether it is really possible for an adequate solution to the problem of the one and the many to show how "ultimate reality must be irreducibly both one and many at the same time," as Bracken claims and other process thinkers intimate. If the one or the many always presupposes, logically and/or temporally, its opposite, then it cannot be the ultimate causal explanation of both itself and its opposite. In addition, if a process treatment of the problem of the one and the many thereby fails to reach a truly ultimate reality solely in terms of the principles of categorical or proportionate being, according to Whitehead's axiom denying that God is an exception to the metaphysical principles, then there is corroboration for my thesis that the problem of the one and the many arises from a neglect of a central feature of the Creator-creature distinction as classically conceived.[49] I hope to show how

49. It is important to note that some theologians who may disagree with certain terms of classical theism, as Paul Tillich does with *actus purus* (Tillich, *Systematic Theology*, 1:246), may in some ways be affirming in content or materially the same things, like the fact that unity and non-composition are necessary for divine self-sufficiency, aseity, and independence. While wanting to predicate of God *symbolically* the poles of his "ontological elements," like dynamics and form, Tillich nonetheless warns that "some thinkers . . . emphasize the dynamics in God and . . . depreciate the stability of dynamics in pure actuality. They try to distinguish between two elements in God, and they assert that, in so far as God is a living God, these two elements must remain in tension," claiming that "the basic error of these doctrines is their metaphysical-constructive character. They apply the ontological elements to God in a nonsymbolic manner, and are driven to religiously offensive and theologically untenable consequences" (p. 247). Tillich emphasizes the necessity of predicating these ontological elements to God *symbolically,* and the reality of their being "united" in God: "If the element of form in the dynamics-form polarity is applied symbolically to the divine life, it expresses the actualization of its potentialities. The divine life inescapably unites possibility with fulfillment. Neither side threatens the other, nor is there a threat of disruption. In terms of self-preservation one could say that God cannot cease to be God.

both a process treatment of the problem of the one and the many and the concomitant problem of mutual ultimate causality are of a piece, both resulting from trying to account for all of reality solely on the principles of categorical metaphysics, without exception, where the metaphysical differences between ultimate reality and the rest of the world are of degree only, and not of kind.[50]

Mutual Ultimate Causality in the Concrescence Solution

A paradigmatic process solution to the problem of the one and the many, also used by Bracken, is Whitehead's statement that "the many become one and are increased by one" in the actual entity's concrescence. Concrescence explains how "the many are likewise one without ceasing to be themselves as discrete individuals," which any adequate solution must do, in Bracken's view.

Every new actual entity in concrescence is a microcosm of the one macrocosmic universal society. Because each actual entity in a society prehends the same objective universe that existed a moment ago, the prehensions of all concrescing entities involve a common element of form, the form of the universe as a whole as it existed a moment ago. When the many of the antecedent universe become one in the new actual entity, the one and the many are identical. Bracken cites here as a corollary the Thomistic doctrine of subsistent relations, where each person of the Trinity is identical with the divine nature, while remaining distinct from the others.

An initial problem here is the appeal to the doctrine of subsistent relations, which means to say that the divine persons are identical with the divine nature "concomitantly," to use predicates derived from creatures

His going-out from himself does not diminish or destroy his divinity. It is united with the eternal 'resting in himself'" (ibid.).

50. In various ways, process thinkers do admit important distinctions between God and the world, although not in terms of God's qualitative exemption from the metaphysics of categorical reality and proportionate being. Bracken, for example, tries to preserve the doctrine of God's free creation of the world, but at the same time he expressly denies the types of metaphysical distinctions (what Whitehead calls "exceptions") that apply to God in classical theism.

Admission of a type of difference between God and the world is by no means necessarily equivalent to an admission of the metaphysical differences between God and the world affirmed by classical theism, any more than admission of any real differences between finite, categorical realities is necessarily an admission of metaphysical differences between them.

in time. The divine relations are not identical with the divine substance from a "moment ago," and in fact for classical theists God transcends time as its Creator. Each person in the Godhead is identical in every way with the whole "eternally present" divine nature. Each person or relation is identical with the entire divine essence that exists *now.*

Corresponding to this is how on Bracken's account the unity of the many actual entities *now* is not the one macroscopic whole that exists now, but the unity of the one whole from a moment ago. Their unity is not the unity of the now since only the previous whole (universe from a moment ago) exists in each part (actual entity) that now is. The many that become one are the many objective actual entities from a moment ago, but the one in which they are unified is an actual entity in the present.[51] Since the many becoming one are never coterminous they are never, strictly speaking, identical. Bracken says any adequate solution to the problem of the one and the many must demonstrate how ultimate reality is "irreducibly both one and many at the same time." In the solution he proposes here, the many and the one existing at the same moment are never fully and really identical. If the many and the one that are contemporaneous are not identical, but ultimate reality is "irreducibly" each of them "at the same time," either there are really two ultimate realities, which Bracken does not admit, or he has failed to demonstrate how ultimate reality is "both one and many at the same time."

In terms of the problem of mutual ultimate causality, the fact that the many and the one are never temporally and really identical, as in the logical principle of identity, means that they imply one another. The unity or oneness of the universe in the currently concrescing actual entity presupposes a moment of prior plurality, the many discrete actual entities that achieved satisfaction a moment ago. The many disparate actual entities in concrescence in the present moment presuppose the unity of the universe from a moment ago, and not a current, contemporary unity.[52] The

51. Bracken himself qualifies his comparison between Whiteheadian concrescence and the trinitarian doctrine of subsistent relations by speaking of the "minor precisions added by Whitehead in line with his presupposition that prehensions are always of past (rather than contemporary) entities" (Joseph A. Bracken, "Subsistent Relation: Mediating Concept for a New Synthesis?" *Journal of Religion* 64 [April 1984]: 192). See also Bracken, "Authentic Subjectivity and Genuine Objectivity," *Horizons* 11 (Fall 1984): 297–98.

52. Bracken expressly agrees with Whitehead's affirmation that the concrescence of actual entities in the present is "private," which means that actual entities undergoing con-

one of the present presupposes the many of the past, and the many of the present presuppose the one of the past, while the one and the many of the present are never identical.

Mutual Ultimate Causality in the Creativity Solution

Bracken believes the question of how the unity of all created societies and the cosmic society is grounded in the unity of the divine Selfhood is a basic question regarding the relationship of the one to the many. He believes classical theism errs in grounding the empirical many in the transcendent one of the actual Supreme Being who is God, and links this to Heidegger's critique of "onto-theology" and postmodern critiques of "logocentrism." In his estimation, much of process theism is susceptible to the same criticisms.

Bracken avoids this difficulty in resolving the problem of the one and the many by grounding the unity of the God-world relationship in the transcendent activity, not entity, of creativity. The divine nature, not God as the supreme entitative being, is the one that gathers the many divine and created entities into a higher unity by empowering them to exist in every moment. As with his other proposed solutions, Bracken says that the one creativity and the many entitative realities are equiprimordial. Creativity or the divine nature is the ground and source of all finite, determinate actualities, including the three divine persons as three societies of actual occasions. Yet the one emerges out of the dynamic interplay of the many with one another, first and foremost in the *perichoretic* relations of the trinitarian persons. Neither the one nor the many is "over," "against," "prior," or "antecedent," logically or temporally, to its opposite. The one emerges out of the many and the one is the source of the many, coevally.

---

crescence contemporaneously do not influence one another. See Bracken, "Subsistent Relation," 192; and Bracken, "Authentic Subjectivity," 297–98. In two places he experiments with a modification of the "private" concrescence of actual entities that would allow contemporary actual entities undergoing concrescence at the same time to indirectly influence each other (Bracken, "Substance—Society—Natural System: A Creative Rethinking of Whitehead's Cosmology," *International Philosophical Quarterly* 25 [1985]: 6; Bracken, "Intersubjectivity and the Coming of God," *Journal of Religion* 83, no. 3 [July 2003]: 389). This, however, does not become a dominant feature of his thought nor does it enter into his discussions of how the concrescence of the actual entity addresses the "problem of the one and the many," which explanations follow the standard "private" concrescence understanding, in accordance with Whitehead.

This account seems to exhibit the problem of mutual ultimate causality, however, because whatever is causally dependent and presupposes something else can only be a penultimate explanation, not a truly primordial one in the sense of being absolutely first. Creativity's emergence out of the many actual entities seems to imply causally and presuppose logically the actuality of the many. Conversely, creativity as the ground and source for the many actual entities seems to imply causally and presuppose logically the reality of the one. If there is a real plurality of ultimates and the simplicity of ultimate reality is denied, it seems difficult to avoid the problem of mutual ultimate causality.

Closely related to Bracken's creativity solution for the problem of the one and the many is the pair flux and stasis. Saying that metaphysics should prioritize becoming over being, Bracken attributes to creativity or the divine nature aspects typically associated with plurality and flux, like movement or non-stasis, energy, dynamism, process, vitality, change, otherness, and potentiality. These are the opposite of static, realized actuality. He criticizes classical metaphysics for viewing ultimate reality as one static, individual substance instead of a plurality of many individuals in relationships, and defines "process in the most generic sense as a dynamic unity in totality of functioning parts or members."[53]

While claiming that the divine matrix is the perpetual source of novelty and as infinite has the indeterminacy and potency of non-being (non-actuality), Bracken also says at points that the extensive continuum is "eternal and unchanging," and, "though involved in the becoming of every actual occasion (both finite and infinite), it does not itself become since it is simply the *wherein* of all becoming."[54] Since the divine nature as the perpetual underlying activity of the universe is the only eternally enduring reality, and since it is ever the same in what it does in every transient entity, it has consistency, stasis, sameness, and unity, according to Bracken.

This affirmation that ultimate reality is both the becoming of flux and the stasis of immutability appears to be another manifestation of

53. Joseph A. Bracken, *The Triune Symbol. Persons, Process and Community* (Lanham, Md.: University Press of America, 1985), 20. See also Bracken, *Christianity and Process Thought: Spirituality for a Changing World* (Philadelphia: Templeton Foundation Press, 2006), 80.

54. Joseph A. Bracken, *Society and Spirit: A Trinitarian Cosmology* (London: Associated University Press; Selinsgrove, Pa.: Susquehanna University Press, 1991), 130–31.

the problem of mutual ultimate causality. This is because, as explained above, the stasis and flux in categorical reality observed by a commonsense metaphysics of proportionate being imply one another causally and logically. One cannot say with Heraclitus παντα ρει ("everything flows") without assuming this state of affairs is a static constant,[55] and if it were not then by definition not everything changes and there is some stasis after all.

Another potential difficulty with Bracken's creativity solution to the problem of the one and many revolves around his attempt to abide as closely as possible to Whitehead's ontological principle: only that which is referable to the decision of an actual entity is actual, and therefore capable of being a reason for anything. Creativity, the extensive continuum, and societies are not identical with actual entities in Whitehead's metaphysics, and Bracken likewise denies them actuality. In order to give them explanatory power and make them "of consequence," though, he makes them a sort of *tertium quid* between Whiteheadian actual entities and nothingness.[56]

This has drawn criticism from Whiteheadians who consider this view somewhat heterodox. For most Whiteheadians creativity is only a conceptual abstraction from individual actual entities and their processes, so that creativity has no ontological status in any sense.[57] Andrew Reck criticizes Bracken for admitting that creativity is not an entity but also attributing to creativity a different "mode of being" and making it identical with God's nature, which is a "reification" of creativity, according to Reck.[58] He levels a similar charge against Bracken's view of the extensive continuum. For Whitehead the extensive continuum is neither a catego-

55. On this point regarding process thought in general, Paul Tillich comments: "It would become absurd if it [process philosophy] tried to dissolve the structure of process into a process. This simply would mean that what we know as process has been superseded by something else, the nature of which is unknown at present. In the meantime, every philosophy of process has an explicit or implicit ontology which is aprioristic in character" (Tillich, *Systematic Theology*, 1:167).

56. The classical maxim that "to be is to act," and the corollary description of being as "actuality," means to "be of consequence" or "be a reason," and does not originally connote "activity," motion, or movement.

57. John B. Cobb Jr., *A Christian Natural Theology* (Philadelphia: Westminster Press, 1965), 203–14; Donald Sherburne, *A Whiteheadian Aesthetic* (New Haven, Conn.: Yale University Press, 1961), 20–21.

58. Andrew J. Reck, "God as the Ultimate Meaning Is the *Primordial* Source of All Mean

ry nor a hypostasized space-time being of a different type than an actual entity, but only a derivative notion referring to the potentialities of actual entities to be related to one another.

Bracken has no qualms with attributing to creativity some sort of existence, albeit different from that of an actual entity. He argues creativity must be conceived monistically because for creativity to be ongoing it must be numerically one rather than many. Creativity must be a single foundational activity at work in all self-constituting actual occasions rather than simply a descriptive term or empirical generalization for all particular activities of self-constitution, which are discrete. When creativity is presented as simply a descriptive principle rather than a metaphysical absolute, there is no explanation for why such a perpetuating process should exist in the first place. Bracken's hypostatization of creativity while simultaneously denying that it is an entity shows, however, that his prioritization of flux, becoming, potentiality, and indeterminacy still cannot avoid being in terms of actuality, unity, and causality.

Mutual Ultimate Causality in the Revised Whiteheadian Societies Solution

Bracken revises Whiteheadian societies in ways similar to how he revises Whitehead's creativity. He also says that societies are ontological actualities in some sense while denying that they are actual entities, the sole existents in Whitehead's system. Although Bracken avoids predicating the word "entity" to societies, he still attributes to them a level of existence and activity usually connoted by the word entity. In his affirmation of some ontological status for societies, he is admitting that the type of unity associated with being as a transcendental predicate does not obtain only on the level of the many entities, but is also external to them in the larger wholes of societies. Bracken proposes this revised understanding of societies as a solution to the problem of the one and the many in several related ways.

First, in a society "the many are likewise one without ceasing to be themselves discrete individuals," which is one of Bracken's criteria for any adequate solution to the problem. In his explanation actual entities retain their individual identity even when they become a new reality, a so-

ings: A Comment on Joseph A. Bracken's Presentation of the Ultimate Ground in Whitehead's Philosophy of Becoming," *Ultimate Reality and Meaning* 16 (March–June 1993): 138.

ciety, through their intrinsic relatedness to one another through the society's common element of form. In a society actual entities are discrete individuals, or many. At the same time, because of the common element of form, the society's member actual entities are one. In this way, according to Bracken, actual entities in societies are both one and many at the same time.

The problem of mutual ultimate causality seems to emerge here because, on Bracken's own account, a society's actual entities are never logically or really identical with the society. A causal and explanatory problem of priority arises when two really distinct things are both sufficient and necessary conditions, causally and/or logically, for each other's ontological reality. It would seem that a society and its member entities must be really identical in terms of the logical principle of identity if they are to be truly ultimate.

One way logical identity is lacking is that it is only through their intrinsic relationships with one another through the society's form that the member actual entities are one. The many actual entities' unity with the one society presupposes the society as a separate ontological reality represented by a form by which the member actual entities are unified, which is discrete from the entities themselves. Bracken follows Whitehead, however, in saying that the society's common element of form presupposes, and is in some sense dependent on, the member actual entities. The one society is logically and ontologically distinct from its member entities if only because Bracken distinguishes between actual entities as the only things that are entities, and societies as structured fields of activity or forms with a type of ontological reality, but not that of an entity. So the one society and many members imply and presuppose each other for their own realities.

A second way in which the many members are not really identical with the one society is that the individual entities are united by the form of the society that existed one moment ago, not the form of the society coming to be in the present. Because Whitehead maintained that actual entities never prehend their contemporaries, but only past (now superject) actual entities, the transmission of macroscopic wholes had to be linked to the past form and not to the present form. Even though in two places Bracken perfunctorily proposes a type of indirect causality contemporary actual entities may have on one another, with respect to the transmission of societal form he always sides with the standard view that it is the past societal form that unites the member actual entities undergoing concrescence in the present moment. Since present actual entities are not identical with the form of the contemporary society but that from one moment ago, the many are never really logically identical with the one.

Bracken also urges the equiprimordiality of societies and actual entities in his system as a solution to the problem of the one and the many. The many actual occasions prior to the society generate the society's common element of form, and at the same time the society's one common element of form is prior to and determinative of the concrescence and constitution of the society's member entities. On the one hand, the one society as a whole depends on the many actual entities as a prior given, which in different ways generate, sustain, and modify the society as it exists across time and space. By prehending the society's common element of form from a moment ago the actual entities undergoing concrescence in the present moment co-constitute the society in the present. While actual entities only "directly" produce themselves, they "indirectly" produce the society, according to Bracken, and through their collective agencies the many actual entities maintain the ontological unity of the society over time. Yet, he says, the one society exercises causal determination on its many member entities and the manner in which they exist. The society shapes, conditions, and causally affects its constituent actual entities. Also, the society's member actual entities would not exist with the same form over time unless they prehended the same society, and the society transmits its formal structure from one generation of actual entities to the next. Of a piece with this equiprimordiality of societies and actual entities for Bracken is the relationship of the societal laws to the member entities. Following Whitehead, Bracken maintains that every society has laws dominating and structuring the society. He says the society's laws are in the society as a whole, determining the constitution of the society's member actual entities, but are also in the actual entities, determining the constitution of the societal form as a whole.

Once again, though, the question arises as to whether what is truly metaphysically primordial can rely on and presuppose still something else that in some sense both possesses ontological reality and is ontologically distinct from it. On Bracken's account, the existence of the one society presupposes the many actual entities, while the existence of the many actual entities presupposes the one society. If the many actual entities generate, sustain, modify, and determine the laws of the one society, it would seem that the society's existence, sustenance, and changing presuppose the actual entities as already existing. Conversely, if the society contributes to the existence of its member entities by making them members of *this* society and by transmitting to them the societal form and laws, it would seem the existence of the actual entities as the particular entities that they are presupposes the society as an ontological reality. How can the one common element of form or structured field of activity be the context for the new concrescent actual entities if they themselves produce this common element of form or field? How can the society exist before the actual entities but then be the product of these entities? How can the actual entities exist before the society but at the same time be the product of this society?

Another facet of this same difficulty is that the actual entities and the societal form come into existence and perish moment by moment. Preserving the Whiteheadian priority of actual entities, Bracken says the societal form does not exist apart from its member actual entities. The one societal form exists only in the interrelation of the subjectivities of the many member entities. For this reason, just as the actual entities come into being and perish in each successive moment, so, too, the societal form perishes and comes into being anew. At the same time, however, Bracken says the societal form is the necessary context, environment, or place for the emergence of the next generation of occasions, according to Whitehead's claim that while actual entities come and go without ever experiencing change, societies alone endure across time and undergo change.[59] The new member entities undergoing concrescence in every

59. It should be noted that Bracken goes beyond what Whitehead means here. Whitehead only meant to acknowledge that while individual actual entities come and go, never experiencing endurance and change across time, the societal form that comes into being and perishes in each moment has a type of persistent identity across successive moments of time. He also never said that the societal form itself affects the generation of new member entities. Rather, he said the new member entities all prehend "analogous conceptual feelings" of the same eternal object that represents the antecedent nexus of the society's actual entities from a moment ago (Whitehead, *Process and Reality,* 251–53 [384–87]). Bracken's elevation of the society to an ontological reality in its own right allows him to ascribe to the societal form a type of direct causality on newly concrescing member entities.

moment presuppose the societal form as a causal factor in their constitution.

Regarding mutual ultimate causality, both the many actual entities and the one societal form are temporal and contingent, coming into existence and perishing in each new moment. At the same time, the new member entities coming into existence presuppose the society as their context of generation, and the new societal form coming into existence presupposes those very same member actual entities in its coming into existence. This problem could perhaps be alleviated if Bracken said that the newly concrescing entities prehend the societal form from the now objective superject member entities from a moment ago, but he does not say this. He specifically says that the new entities undergoing concrescence in the present are what regenerate the societal form. How can something no longer in existence be the necessary cause of one of its own necessary causes?

In summary, the mutual co-constitution of the society's many member actual entities and the one overall society from moment to moment, or the equiprimordiality of the one society and the many actual entities, seems to evidence the problem of mutual ultimate causality. Here what is the condition of the possibility of a particular reality seems to reciprocally assume the particular reality that it causally explains as one of the conditions of the possibility of its own existence.

Mutual Ultimate Causality in the Trinitarian Solution

As explained, for Bracken the triune God exemplifies all of the metaphysical principles applying to reality everywhere else in the cosmos, in accordance with Whitehead's axiom that "God is not to be treated as an exception to all metaphysical principles, invoked to save their collapse. He is their chief exemplification." In this way the Trinity is the archetypal way in which Bracken's philosophical process theology addresses the problem of the one and the many.

I've described the problem of mutual ultimate causality as explicable in part by the fact that systems exhibiting this problem posit multiple ultimates, which presuppose and causally rely on each another. I've also contrasted this to the classical theistic claim that ultimate reality, in order to be truly ultimate, must be one, simple, and possess aseity. For classical theism, analogically speaking, God is the only "being" the essence of which is the act of existence *(esse)*. God is being or existence itself, and so necessarily exists and possesses aseity. God does not require anything else, either causally speaking or in terms of the impartation of *esse*, to exist. God is the "uncaused cause," his "own reason" *(ratio sui)*, "self-causing" *(causa sui)*, and "self-moving," although these very terms must be understood analogically and not univocally.

As discussed earlier, Bracken posits a distinction between God as the one "divine nature," and God as the "Supreme Being." God as the divine nature is creativity plus the extensive continuum, or energy, potentiality, indeterminate and infinite activity, or "being" as the activity of a verb, not a noun. God as the Supreme Being is an entitative reality, determinate being or noun, which includes the divine persons as three societies of subsocieties who arise, like all entities, out of the divine matrix or divine nature. The relationship between the divine nature and the divine persons is the paragon of the metaphysical principles applying univocally to all of reality.

If the problem of mutual ultimate causality carries any force, however, then the hiatus between the divine essence and the divine persons in Bracken's theology proper would make God or ultimate reality the preeminent expression of how categorical beings cannot account for their existence solely by reference to themselves or from themselves alone. In traditional parlance, the essence of no categorical, finite created being is ever identical with its existence. As possibilities, categorical, finite, created essences require something else in order to have actual existence. In order to actually exist, all finite created beings require the Act of Being *(esse)*, which they do not contain in themselves. Bracken's claim that metaphysical principles apply to God in a way differing only in degree and not in kind from the way they apply to categorical beings would then both precipitate the problem of the one and the many and make it insoluble because of the problem of mutual ultimate causality.

Similar to his explanation of the relationship between the one and the many in societies and member entities, for Bracken the divine persons perpetually generate the divine matrix or divine nature by their ongoing activity of interrelating, but at the same time the divine nature is the context out of which the three divine persons continually emerge in each new moment. Bracken does try to maintain the closest possible relationship between the divine nature and the divine persons by not assigning either an ontological priority. Despite their mutual co-constitution, neither the one divine nature nor the many persons has ontological reality first, above, before, or prior, to the other; they are equiprimordial. However, he does affirm a real distinction between them, or at least that the traditional "notional" distinction between them is "rooted in reality," which is very important for all of his philosophical theology—including his solutions to the problem of the one and the many. Expressly keeping the two distinct seems to make each rely on the other for its ontological reality. This again raises the question of logical and/or temporal priority. If the one divine matrix is truly distinct from the three divine persons, and if each presupposes the other for its ontological reality, then it appears difficult to avoid the problem of mutual ultimate causality.

Questions might even arise as to whether Bracken's trinitarian solution to the problem of the one and the many satisfactorily meets his own criterion for any adequate solution: it must demonstrate how "the many are likewise one without ceasing to be themselves as discrete individuals."

First, Bracken likens the fact that any one society exists in each of its many member actual entities to the doctrine of subsistent relations in the Trinity. As mentioned, most trinitarians who are classical theists, including St. Thomas, do not view the divine nature as a whole, of which the divine persons are parts. Each person is fully and exhaustively the divine nature. Nor do they view God as in time so that there could be a temporal succession of moments in which the divine persons would be identical with the divine nature from a moment ago. Yet, even if the divine persons were parts constituting a whole, and even if God were experiencing a temporal succession of moments, the identity between the one divine society and the many divine persons would never be absolutely identical in terms of the logical principle of identity because of the time element. Only the previous whole from one moment ago would exist in the parts now; the many persons would never be identical with the one divine nature simultaneously.

A second way in which the one nature and the many persons do not seem really identical lies in Bracken's distinction between the discrete private subjectivities of the three persons and their objective common prehension of the divine society's societal form. Bracken claims his revision of Whiteheadian metaphysics best balances the subject-object dialectic, which he relates as an epistemological expression of the problem expressed metaphysically in reconciling the one and the many. Whitehead was preoccupied with the actual entity subjectively prehending the past universe and coming to be, so he did not really address the ontological state of affairs transcending all subjectivity, which we call "objective reality." For Bracken the structured society is the key to including objectivity in Whiteheadian thought, because the societal form from one moment ago becomes the "object" of every subjective actual occasion in the present that is prehending it.

Despite the real objectivity of the common element of form, this form is the result of the prior subjectivity of the individual actual entities, corresponding to Whitehead's axiom that "objectivity follows upon subjectivity." Bracken explicitly applies this to the Trinity by saying that the Godhead's objective unity is the common element of form derived from the divine persons' prehensions of what they were as a society of persons one moment ago.

A potential problem emerges from this idea that divine unity comes from the three persons' prehending the same objective reality of their society a moment ago. While saying the common element of form prehended anew each moment by the three divine persons is "perfectly uniform," "in every respect the same," and an "indivisible reality," he qualifies this identity by saying that the three forms prehended by each of the divine persons are *subjectively* different, or from "different standpoints," even though they are *objectively* the same. Bracken says his own metaphysics necessitates that the divine persons be finite in some sense because they are related to, and hence different from, one another. Since the divine persons are true subjects, each with discrete activities of knowing and willing, and since finite subjects do not have infinite knowledge, they have different subjective perspectives. Hence, although the persons objectively prehend the same common element of form of the divine society or nature, they do so from different subjective standpoints. The discrepancies between the societal forms prehended by each of the three divine persons subjectively detract from the claim that the many can be really one, as in the principle of identity. This is so apart from the problem that there is a temporal hiatus between the one societal form from a moment ago and the prehension of that form in the present moment.

A third way in which the one divine nature and the many divine persons do not seem really identical is apparent when Bracken says the persons in community have a higher "unity and greater actuality than would be theoretically possible for each of them as individual persons." If the axiom derived from a common-sense metaphysics of proportionate being, "the whole is greater than the sum of the parts," applies to Bracken's understanding of the relationship between the one divine society and the three divine persons, then the one is not truly identical with the many.

In summary, Bracken's solutions to the problem of the one and the many based on his unique process theological reconstruction of a social Trinity seem to fall short of his own criteria for an adequate solution, and appear to run aground on the problem of mutual ultimate causality. First, there seems to be lacking the full identify of the one and the many in the way he says it is necessary for an adequate solution to this problem. Second, as the preeminent epitome of all metaphysical principles, and not an exception to them, his Trinity encounters the difficulties of making the categorical, created one and the many presuppose each other, or the problem of mutual ultimate causality.

Mutual Ultimate Causality in the Various Other Solutions

Here I will briefly explain why I believe that the problem of mutual ultimate causality might also surface in some of the remaining miscellaneous ways in which Bracken argues that process thought in general, and his process philosophical theology in particular, provide adequate solutions to the problem of the one and the many.

First, he says the unity provided by process or creativity strikes a better balance between the one and the many than the unity provided by the classical idea of substance. Both substance and process allow for functioning totalities greater than the sum of their parts, but substance makes the parts negligible. Process, in contrast, maintains the ontological integrity of the parts in process but still comprises the process as one whole, so that the many parts are just as real as the one whole.

I see a potential twofold problem with this solution. First, the parts and the whole are never identical, similar to the lack of full identity between societies and member entities, and the divine nature and the divine persons in which "the whole is greater than the sum of the parts." Second, the whole process implies the parts for its identity precisely as one functioning totality greater than its parts, and the parts imply the whole for their identity precisely as parts of the one larger functioning totality. The two mutually presuppose one another logically, if not temporally, in such a way that neither by itself can account for both itself and the other.

Bracken also discusses the balancing of continuity and discontinuity, similarity and contrast. The process universe has discontinuity because in each new moment the world is never exactly the same as new actual entities and societies perpetually emerge. At the same time there is continuity because the new entities and societies are heavily conditioned by the past through their prehensions of past actual entities, societies, and the whole universe. Also in process metaphysics contemporary actual entities are distinct from one another but at the same time the extensive continuum is an underlying unity, similarity, and commonality.

Again one might ask whether this solution meets Bracken's own criteria for an adequate solution to the problem of the one and the many. Although balancing discontinuity and continuity, it never demonstrates how they are really identical, according to the criteria that an adequate explanation must show "how Ultimate Reality must be irreducibly both one and many at the same time" and "how the many are likewise one without ceasing to be themselves as discrete individuals." Are discontinuity and continuity somehow ontologically identified in addition to being balanced? In terms of the problem of mutual ultimate causality, this solution does not explain how discontinuity and continuity are identical to the point that the reality of one does not presuppose the other as something different from itself. The discontinuities of emergent actual entities and societies in the ontogenetic matrix presuppose the underlying unity of the ontogenetic matrix; however, the discontinuous, discrete actual entities and societies are the "location" of the ontogenetic matrix, which cannot "exist" apart from actual entities.

Bracken also explains a balance between flux and stasis. In the perpetual process of change and novelty generated by creativity there is continual flux. In the ontogenetic matrix composed of creativity and the extensive continuum there is one unchanging substrate for perpetual generation of, and the dynamic relationships between, the divine persons and all created entities. The divine matrix is ever the same, and thus in a sense is static and one. As in his discussion of the balance between discontinuity and continuity, here stasis and flux are not really identical. The appearance of new entities and societies characteristic of the matrix itself is not the same as the repetition of the consistent process whereby this happens.

Beyond this, my earlier analysis of the problem of mutual ultimate causality in attempts to make either categorical flux or categorical stasis ultimate may apply here. Change or creativity presupposes some *thing* that is changing. This *thing* also must remain in some sense the same across the change in order for there to be a change, similar to the way in Aristotelian metaphysics a substance stays the same while its accidents change. Discontinuity presupposes some form of continuity whereby there can be knowledge of the discontinuity, or else there would be complete disparity and no intelligible basis for comparison. Every contrast presupposes a deeper similarity. Hence flux presupposes stasis.

Conversely, the continuity or "ever-the-same" nature of the divine matrix presupposes creativity, change, and discontinuity precisely for its identity as that which stays the same. The one feature by which the extensive continuum and creativity are identified as such across time is precisely the continual but consistent process and change involving novelty. Thus the stasis presupposes the flux.

Another variation on the problem of the one and the many discussed by Bracken is the dialectic between subjectivity and objectivity. The intersubjective aspect of Whiteheadian metaphysics entails a scenario where subjectivity and objectivity "mutually condition one another, with each serving as the ground for the other from a different perspective."[60] Here he offers an equiprimordiality of subjectivity and objectivity akin to the equiprimordiality of the one and the many in Whiteheadian societies, and ultimately in the Trinity.

The problem of mutual ultimate causality might arise in the explanation of the mutual conditioning of subjectivity and objectivity. According to the dictum that "objectivity follows upon subjectivity," Bracken says objective existential beings result from the public and private processes of the subjectivity of actual entities. At the same time, the experience of subjectivity presupposes an established objective state of affairs. This is the objective world created by the subjective experiences of the actual entities that achieved satisfaction in the previous moment.

60. Joseph A. Bracken, *The One in the Many: A Contemporary Reconstruction of the God-World Relationship* (Grand Rapids, Mich.: Eerdmans, 2001), 207. See also Bracken, *Christianity and Process Thought*, 70–71.

The difficulty is that subjectivity presupposes an antecedent objective state of affairs, but objectivity follows from, and presupposes, an antecedent act of subjectivity. Subjectivity and objectivity presuppose each another and rely upon one another to take place or exist. Once again the question of logical, if not temporal, priority arises. There seems to be either an infinite regress or the admission that at some point either subjectivity or objectivity becomes an exception to the metaphysical principles of relationality and dependence. If the latter, either subjectivity or objectivity at some point becomes an exceptional "first cause," which is either initially caused by something other than the partner upon which it subsequently depends, or it is self-causing. In either case there seems to be an exception to the metaphysical principles.

Bracken also discusses balancing the dialectic between freedom and causality in reference to the problem of the one and the many. Whitehead's ultimate explanatory principle of creativity instantiated in every actual entity balances causality and freedom. In its concrescence the actual entity is both conditioned by its predecessor superject actual entities along with God's initial aim, and freely determines its own actual existence by making decisions. Once again, I suggest that upon closer analysis the appeal to the balancing of freedom and causality in the actual entity's concrescence does not solve the problem of the one and the many, but rather evidences the problem of mutual ultimate causality.

On the one hand, it is only subjective freedom that results in actual entities that can be subsequent causes. On the other hand, in the Whiteheadian cosmos freedom presupposes the limitation of infinite possibility by an antecedent objectivity of actualities (actual entities as superjects), which thereby become causal factors in the next moment of decision. Thus the question arises as to whether freedom can at some point exist prior to objective actualities as causes limiting infinite possibility, or whether there can be some objective actuality to limit infinite possibility prior to any subjective act of freedom.

This apparent need to ultimately prioritize and make independent either freedom or causality is related to a problem that arises in the Whiteheadian description of the actual entity's concrescence itself. Typically, for an experiencing subject to exercise freedom, the existence of that free agent as an actual being is presupposed, but Whitehead and process thinkers do not admit the existence of the actual entity until it freely decides its actuality. However, if the free decision belongs to the selfsame entity and not some other external cause, then the selfsame entity must in some sense exist antecedently, at least logically if not temporally. As Victor Lowe has noted, "Many philosophers consider Whitehead's doctrine of a self-creating experiencer unintelligible."[61] Edward Pols and Robert C. Neville also argue against the free self-creative character of Whiteheadian actual entities along these lines.[62] That the freedom of the agent presupposes the agent as its cause, and that the agent as cause presupposes the self-constituting freedom of the agent in Whiteheadian thought, seems to be an instance of the problem of mutual ultimate causality.

Theologically, this question of whether either freedom or causality must ultimately be prioritized leads to the problem addressed by Bracken and others of making sense out of God's freely determining God's "nature," yet making decisions "according to this nature," and thereby remaining consistent.[63] Eschatologically it leads to the difficulty of explaining how the future can be genuinely open but at the same time there is proleptic knowledge of a certain final triumph of good over evil.[64]

A Possible Objection by Bracken to the Mutual Ultimate Causality Critique

There is a way Bracken could object to my critique of mutual ultimate causality in his system. In several places Bracken asserts a type of mutual causation between cause and effect so that the cause is simultaneously the effect of the effect, which in turn thus becomes its cause. He gives some evidence to support this but never develops this view of causation in more detail, explains how it is better than rival alter-

61. Lowe, "Whitehead's Metaphysical System," 7–8.

62. Robert C. Neville, *Creativity and God: A Challenge to Process Theology* (New York: Seabury, 1980), 9–10; George R. Lucas explains Pols's criticism in George R. Lucas, *Two Views of Freedom in Process Thought: A Study of Hegel and Whitehead* (Missoula, Mont.: Scholars Press, 1979), 3–40.

63. Joseph A. Bracken, "The Holy Trinity as a Community of Divine Persons, Part I," *Heythrop Journal* 15 (1974): 180–81; Bracken, "Toward a New Philosophical Theology Based on Intersubjectivity," *Theological Studies* 59 (1998): 708–9; Bracken, "Intersubjectivity and the Coming of God," 393; Bracken, "Philosophical Foundations of Human Rights: A Process Approach," *Cogito* 1, no. 1 (March 1983): 58, 73 n. 12.

64. Bracken, *The Triune Symbol,* 88, 106 nn. 10–11, 159–61. He says: "Not the collective power of evil, but rather the collective power of good in the end will prevail" (Bracken, *Christianity and Process Thought,* 138).

natives, or defends it against objections. Here I will present Bracken's claims about the mutual causality of what have traditionally been understood as cause and effect, his supporting evidence, and my responses. Discussing Leonardo Boff's doctrine of the Trinity, Bracken says Boff is

> consciously moving away from the traditional understanding of cause and effect within classical metaphysics, in which the cause always preexists the effect, to a "processive and dynamic metaphysics," in which cause and effect come into existence at the same time and are mutually interdependent.[65]

In the same place, discussing Mary Daly's claim that we should shift our understanding of God and being from noun-oriented to verb-oriented, he says that a verb/activity approach to God and being will ultimately change how one understands the workings of causes and effects:

> Within the static noun-oriented approach to reality, causes and effects are inevitably separate from one another in time and sometimes also in space, with the cause always existing prior to the effect. The effect is then dependent upon the cause for its own subsequent existence. Within a more dynamic verb-oriented approach to reality, causes and effects are not separated in time and space but always linked together as ongoing interdependent realities. The effect has as much influence on the cause as the cause has on the effect. Neither is superior to the other since both codetermine what actually happens.[66]

Thus Bracken makes a broad appeal to process metaphysics as entailing a mutual co-determination of causes and effects. He similarly criticizes traditional metaphysical approaches that view God and the world as objects in external cause-effect relationships instead of as intersubjective and interdependent subjects of experience.[67]

Bracken also refers to the doctrines of *perichoresis, circumincessio,* and subsistent relations, in which the divine persons are mutually and intrinsically constituted in their discrete beings by their mutual relations to one another. They model causality differently than efficient causality, and so support the idea of causes and effects mutually constituting one another.[68]

65. Joseph A. Bracken, *God: Three Who Are One* (Collegeville, Minn.: Liturgical Press, 2008), 76. Here Bracken is discussing Leonardo Boff, *Trinity and Society,* trans. Paul Burns (Maryknoll, N.Y.: Orbis, 1988), 141–46.

66. Bracken, *God: Three Who Are One,* 85–86.

67. Joseph A. Bracken, "Response to Elizabeth Johnson's 'Does God Play Dice?'" *Theological Studies* 57 (December 1996): 722.

68. Bracken, *The One in the Many,* 184; Bracken, *God: Three Who Are One,* 69–73, 86

In some earlier works Bracken explicates what he sees as the common claim of some Oriental traditions that causes and effects mutually constitute one another. He refers to Adi Shankara, the ninth-century Advaita Vedanta ("non-dualist" self-realization school) philosopher, who said that all plurality is an illusion and every apparently discrete entity, including the human self *(atman),* is really identical with the one indescribable ultimate reality, or *Brahman.*[69] He similarly invokes Acharya Nāgārjuna, the second-century founder of the Mādhyamaka (middle way) school of Mahayana Buddhism. Specifically, he cites Nāgārjuna's doctrines of dependent co-origination *(pratītyasamutpāda)* and emptiness *(śūnyatā)* to support the view that neither cause nor effect is ontologically prior to the other, but that they arise and cease to be in mutual interdependence.[70] Finally, he cites a passage in the Chuang Tzu (pronounced "Zhuang-zi"), which he sees as the Daoist equivalent of dependent co-origination in Mādhyamaka Buddhism:

> There is nothing that is not the "that" and there is nothing that is not the "this." Things do not know that they are the "that" of other things; they only know what they themselves know. Therefore, I say that the "that" is produced by the "this" and the "this" is also caused by the "that." This is the theory of mutual production.[71]

Two other points to support the view that causes and effects mutually cause one another are "supervenience" in contemporary discussions of the mind-body problem, and recent "holistic web of belief" epistemologies.[72]

---

n. 9, 104; Bracken, "Trinity: Economic and Immanent," 13–14. He also briefly mentions how St. Thomas saw a mutual equality of cause and effect in self-contained activities, like the act of seeing (*Summa theologiae* 1.85.2), but laments how "with respect to transient activity where the actor and the thing acted upon are separate realities, Aquinas followed Aristotle in giving ontological priority to the cause over the effect" (Bracken, *God: Three Who Are One,* 86 n. 9).

69. Joseph A. Bracken, *The Divine Matrix: Creativity as Link Between East and West* (Maryknoll, N.Y.: Orbis, 1995), 86–89; Bracken, "Non-Duality and the Concept of Ultimate Reality," *Ultimate Reality and Meaning* 19 (1996): 142.

70. Bracken, *The Divine Matrix,* 97–98.

71. The *Chuang Tzu,* in *A Source Book in Chinese Philosophy,* trans. and comp. Wing-tsit Chan, 182–83 (Princeton, N.J.: Princeton University Press, 1963), quoted in Bracken, *The Divine Matrix,* 122.

72. Bracken, *The One in the Many,* 164 n. 15. See also ibid., 147–50; Bracken, "Supervenience: Two Proposals/Supervenience and Basic Christian Beliefs," *Zygon* 36 (2001): 140,

Supervenience says that higher-order mental properties and processes emerging from lower-order physical properties and processes, such as consciousness, can have effects on the lower-order physical properties and processes that originate them. Also referred to as "top-down" causality, supervenience clearly entails the claim that what is itself an effect (e.g., consciousness) of a cause (e.g., the physical organ of the brain) can exercise causal power on its original cause.

Beginning with W. V. O. Quine and others, human beliefs have been modeled on "webs" or "nets," where every belief depends on every other belief, bar none, so that there are no privileged foundational beliefs possessing a sort of Cartesian certainty, immune from conditioning by other beliefs.[73] Others developed an independent criterion of "coherence," or how consistent any given web of beliefs is on its own terms, as a way to vindicate certain systems of belief as superior to others, apart from the older, common-sense criterion that beliefs are true based on *adæquatio rei et intellectus*.[74] The web-of-belief epistemological model can support the view that causes and effects are interdependent and mutually condition one another inasmuch as beliefs affecting other beliefs can be construed in terms of causality.

A Response to Bracken's Mutual Determination of Cause and Effect

A casual reading of Bracken's examples of causes and effects that are not unilateral but rather mutually co-constitutive might seem to invalidate the criticism of mutual ultimate causality. If it is possible for a cause to produce an effect while at the same time the effect produces the cause, then Bracken would have a highly plausible rejoinder to my criticism. On closer analysis I believe there are serious problems both with Bracken's claim that causes and effects mutually cause one another and with the ways he uses his sources to buttress this claim.

146; Bracken, *The One in the Many,* 161–62, 164 n. 15, 147–50, 170, 186–90, 187 n. 32; Bracken, "Revising Process Metaphysics in Response to Ian Barbour's Critique," *Zygon* 33 (September 1998): 405.

73. See W. V. O. Quine, "Two Dogmas of Empiricism," in *From a Logical Point of View,* 20–46 (Cambridge, Mass.: Harvard University Press, 1953), 42; and W. V. O. Quine and J. S. Ullian, *The Web of Belief,* 2nd ed. (New York: Random House, 1978).

74. See, for instance, Alasdair MacIntyre, *Three Rival Versions of Moral Enquiry: Encyclopaedia, Genealogy, and Tradition* (Notre Dame, Ind.: University of Notre Dame Press, 1989).

First, Bracken spends practically no time developing the details of this view of causality, explaining why it is superior to other theories of causality, or defending his own view against potential objections. Discussions of the metaphysics of causation in contemporary analytic philosophy focus on many issues that arise when contemplating causality. These include questions of the types of "things" that are related in causal relationships or causal *relata* (e.g., events, facts, states of affairs, situations, aspects, tropes), the number of causal *relata* in any given causal relationship (e.g., "cause" and "effect" only or the inclusion of possible causal alternatives and/or possible different effects), whether causal relations are tied to facts, whether they are in space and time, whether causes and effects are individuated as events or processes (granularity), what differentiates causal relations in terms of the connection of causes and effects from two things that lack a causal connection, and whether temporal direction is the basis for causal direction. Amid the multifarious positions on causality today there are none, however, that assume, defend, or address as a potential rival position the claim that what we call "effects" cause what we call their "causes."[75]

Two aspects of current philosophical discussions of causality that are germane to assessing Bracken's view regard the connection between causal *relata* and whether causal direction is based on temporal direction. The various positions on the connection between causes and effects essentially reduce to the question of whether there is some causal "glue" in reality, by which causes exert some power on their effects so as to produce them, or whether what we describe as causality is really a mental imposition on the bare facts that one thing follows another with a degree of regularity, but with no necessary connection. The former is the standard or traditional view based on a common-sense investigation of categorical reality or proportionate being. Hume is famous for at least raising the latter view, if not being bold enough to actually embrace it.[76] Yet modernity's

75. Jonathan Schaffer, "The Metaphysics of Causation," *The Stanford Encyclopedia of Philosophy* (Winter 2007 edition), ed. Edward N. Zalta, http://plato.stanford.edu/entries/causation-metaphysics/.

76. "We may define a cause to be an object followed by another, and where all the objects, similar to the first, are followed by objects similar to the second. Or, in other words, where, if the first object had not been, the second never had existed" (David Hume, *Enquiry Concerning Human Understanding,* section 7, part 2). There is debate as to whether Hume was merely raising doubt as to the reality of a "causal glue" in the world because of its non-

tacit nominalism coupled with the twentieth-century positivist suspicion of anything that is not empirically observable has led to the elevation of the "Humean regularity view" as a serious contender among contemporary causal theories.[77] Even when they incorporate the findings of contemporary physics, neither of these two positions in general, nor any of their diverse particular incarnations, claims that what we call the effect is just as much a cause of its own cause as its cause is cause of that effect.

The question of direction in causality is about whether or not the temporal order is the causal order, because it is possible to conceive that something in the future causes something in the past. The denial that causal direction depends upon temporal direction is based on imaginable scenarios like time travel based on relativity theory, futures seen by a clairvoyant influencing the present, and older theories of backwards causation in physics that no longer hold credence today. There are also debatable examples in which cause and effect might occur simultaneously, which would also preclude the necessity of temporal order for causality.[78] Yet, as with the debates about causal connection, discussions about the necessity of the temporal direction for causal direction never involve the claim that an effect causes its causes. In the conceivable situation of something in the future causing something in the present, it is never a situation in which the present effect of the future event is also the cause of the future event in some sort of bidirectional way. The direction is still unidirectional, and the question only involves whether or not the directional experience of time's flow from past to present to future is necessary to ground causal direction. The same can be said for examples of "simultaneous causation," which does not mean that cause and effect cause each other simultaneously, but only that the unidirectional causality does not presuppose temporal directionality.

---

empirical nature or whether Hume himself adopted this regularity view, denying a metaphysical basis for causation.

77. Bertrand Russell, W. V. O. Quine, and others popularized this view in the twentieth century. The "counterfactual view," which analyzes causal talk in terms of counterfactual statements such as "If the first thing (what we call the 'cause') had not existed, then the second thing (what we call the 'effect') would not have," was developed by David Lewis and others in order to overcome problems with the Humean regularity view. See Peter Menzies, "Counterfactual Theories of Causation," *The Stanford Encyclopedia of Philosophy* (Winter 2008 edition), ed. Edward N. Zalta, http://plato.stanford.edu/entries/causation-counterfactual/.

78. See Schaffer, "The Metaphysics of Causation," section 2.2, "Direction."

Regarding Bracken's claims that "cause and effect are mutually interdependent," that the "effect has as much influence on the cause as the cause has on the effect," and that "neither is superior to the other since both codetermine what actually happens," contemporary analytic philosophers might easily object that these claims destroy the very notions of "cause," "effect," and "causality" in general. For one, it seems built into the very notion of a cause that it somehow "brings about" its effect in a way in which it would be just a mistake to talk of an effect "bringing about" its cause. Second, it is inconceivable that something nonexistent can cause something, which in turn is a necessary reason for its own existence. While unidirectional causality independent of temporal direction may be conceivable, bidirectional causality in the strong, traditional sense of the word "cause," as that which is responsible, at least in part, for the existence of the effect, is inconceivable. This is because it seems to involve a metaphysical version of logical question-begging even more problematic than logical question-begging because it involves questions of actual existence and not merely statements or concepts.

As for the examples Bracken evinces, some important ones are the statements and ideas of some Oriental religious and philosophical thinkers. First, as mentioned earlier, some criticize Bracken's discussions of Eastern traditions for being overly general and ignoring the radical particularities of, and differences between, those traditions. Perhaps only specialists in those traditions could say whether the Chuang Tzu meant to affirm something like the dependent co-origination of the Mādhyamaka Buddhist tradition, let alone whether either of these two traditions affirm that effects cause their causes in the same way that causes cause those same effects.

It is probably better to say that Adi Shankara's unqualified non-dualism is a monism obliterating all distinctions between cause and effect, which are only illusory. There is a mutual determination of cause and effect precisely because they are identical, which means that there really is no notion of causality in the traditional sense. Bracken is clearly not a monist or a pantheist, though, and asserts the distinct individual ontological integrity of mutually co-constitutive causes and effects, whether they are member actual entities and their societies, or the divine nature and the divine persons. Any notion of causality is ultimately obviated in a radically monistic metaphysics that denies the reality of distinct, individual entities. The issue of causality arises immediately, though, as soon as genuine ontological plurality is admitted.

In discussing Buddhist doctrines of dependent co-origination and emptiness, Bracken admits they presuppose a universal, objective, necessary, and invariable causality, but faults them for jettisoning the deeper question of the nature of cause and effect.[79] In addition, one could argue that when Nāgārjuna extended these two doctrines from discussions about the self or *atman* (or no-self or *anatman*) to all realities metaphysically, there was a paradigm shift denying causes and effects entirely since all things without exception are empty. This is perhaps the meaning of the characteristically paradoxical statement of Nāgārjuna cited by Bracken that no existents have arisen "from themselves, from another, from both, or from a non-cause."[80]

Regarding supervenience, top-down causation, and holistic web-of-beliefs epistemologies, these theories never claim that effects cause the existence and activity of their causes. Supervenience and top-down causality do not assert that the properties and processes of the mind cause the physical brain, but only that the mind as an "effect" of the physical brain exerts a type of causal influence back upon body. It is certainly true that an effect, which owes its existence and activity to its causes, exercises a type of influence back upon its causes. An engine in an automobile, for instance, generates heat as an effect that affects the engine, which is its original cause. In some cases, without proper cooling and lubrication, engine heat can cause the engine that produced it to malfunction or cease functioning altogether. Yet it seems inconceivable that engine heat is as much responsible for the existence and activity of the mechanical engine as the engine is responsible for the existence and activity of the heat it generates. The fact that effects influence their causes in many ways is very different from claiming that the effect is responsible for the existence and activity of its causes, in the way Bracken asserts.

In distinction to Bracken, Whitehead accepts the basics of Aristotle's four causes (material, efficient, formal, and final).[81] In fact, while never

79. Bracken, *The Divine Matrix*, 93–94.

80. Ibid., 97–98. Interestingly, the *Mādhyamaka* doctrine of the emptiness of all categorical entities seems related to the Thomistic point that while finite, creaturely secondary causes are involved in the causation of other finite, creaturely beings, no finite entity has self-subsistence or being/*esse* from itself.

81. See, for instance, Bracken, *The One in the Many*, 15, 22.

denying efficient causes Whitehead consciously intended to also bring back teleological causes in the wake of their denial in much modern philosophy and scientific method, which stressed efficient causality alone.[82] Whitehead clearly, repeatedly, and unequivocally affirms the efficient causality of past actual entities, or superjects, upon presently concrescing actual entities in addition to affirming that the subjective aim of the entity experiencing concrescence currently is that particular entity's final cause in the Aristotelian sense.[83] For Whitehead past actual entities, or their "objectifications" as superjects, are efficient causes of actual entities undergoing concrescence in the present.[84] The present actual entity is not, however, an efficient cause of the existence and activity of the past actual entities that are its own efficient causes. Whitehead's description of an entity's subjective aim as a final cause may lead to the illusion that the effect, which comes later, is a cause of its own cause. But Whitehead is not saying the final cause itself reciprocally causes the past efficient causes, or past actual entities. He is only claiming that the present actual entity is the product of at least two distinct types of causes: effi-

82. "His [Aristotle's] philosophy led to a wild overstressing of the notion of final causes during the Christian middle ages; and thence, by a reaction, to the correlative overstressing of the notion of 'efficient causes' during the modern scientific period. One task of a sound metaphysics is to exhibit final and efficient causes in their proper relation to each other. The necessity and the difficulty of this task are stressed by Hume in his *Dialogues Concerning Natural Religion*" (Whitehead, *Process and Reality,* 84 [128–29]). See also ibid., 344 (522–23). Donna Bowman writes: "The balance between teleological explanations for reality, and explanations in which the cause precedes and produces the effect, marks the process system consistently" (Bowman, *The Divine Decision,* 83–84).

83. He says: "The 'objectifications' of the actual entities in the actual world, relative to a definite actual entity, constitute the efficient causes out of which *that* actual entity arises; the 'subjective aim' at 'satisfaction' constitutes the final cause, or lure, whereby there is determinate concrescence; and that attained 'satisfaction' remains as an element in the content of creative purpose. There is, in this way, transcendence of the creativity; and this transcendence effects determinate objectifications for the renewal of the process in the concrescence of actualities beyond that satisfied superject" (Whitehead, *Process and Reality,* 87 [134]).

84. "A simple physical feeling is an act of causation. The actual entity which is the initial datum is the 'cause,' the simple feeling is the 'effect,' and the subject entertaining the simple physical feeling is the actual entity 'conditioned' by the effect. This 'conditioned' actual entity will also be called the 'effect.' All complex causal action can be reduced to a complex of such components. Therefore simple physical feelings will also be called 'causal' feelings" (Whitehead, *Process and Reality,* 236 [361]); and "according to this account, efficient causation expresses the transition from actual entity to actual entity; and final causation expresses the internal process where by the actual entity becomes itself" (ibid., 150 [228]).

cient causes in terms of the past actual entities and a final cause in terms of its own subjective aim.[85]

Whitehead also explicitly argues against the regularity view of Hume and the category understanding of causality of Kant, both of which see causal efficacy as an interpolation by the mind on the raw data of experience, which lacks any "causal glue." Contra Hume and Kant, Whitehead argues for the direct empirical perception of causal efficacy that is not a mental idea brought to experience, and argues for a primitivist account of causal powers inherent in reality apart from the mind.[86] He asserts with Locke the reality of objective causal powers so that past actual entities exercise objective transeunt causality on entities currently undergoing concrescence.[87]

Bracken is, of course, aware of and discusses Whitehead's notion of causal efficacy, in which superject entities are efficient causes in the constitution of present actual entities. He wants to stress, however, that for Whitehead the actual entity is in the first place the agent of its own self-constitution or primarily active, and only secondarily the effect of causal activity or passive, which is the opposite of traditional Aristotelian metaphysics.[88] Yet even with these emphases on how Whitehead differs from Aristotle, Whitehead clearly does not abandon the standard notions that past causes exercise efficient causality on present effects, and that effects are never causes of the existence and activity of their causes.

In summary, while Bracken says in various places that causes and ef-

85. A simpler example to demonstrate this distinction would be how an idea or perception of the future entity, not the future entity itself because it does not yet exist, can causally influence a human agent now. The idea of the future reality is distinct from the future reality itself.

86. Alfred North Whitehead, *Symbolism, Its Meaning and Effect* (New York: Macmillan, 1927; reprint, Fordham University Press, 1985), 39–46.

87. "What is felt subjectively by the objectified actual entity is transmitted objectively to the concrescent actualities which supersede it. In Locke's phraseology the objectified actual entity is then exerting 'power,' that is, exercising transeunt causality upon those subsequent actual entities" (Whitehead, *Process and Reality,* 58 [91]).

88. Bracken, *The One in the Many,* 22, 57–58, 60–61. Lewis Ford describes how Whitehead "revolutionized" the understandings of subject and object. For Whitehead the efficient causes of the past become the passive objects, and the present subjective actual occasion the effect that is active. In the usual understanding the past causes are the active subjects and the present effects are the passive objects. See Lewis S. Ford, *The Lure of God: A Biblical Background for Process Theism* (Philadelphia: Fortress Press, 1978), 6.

fects are mutually responsible for each other's existence and activity, he mostly just makes this claim without rigorously justifying or defending it. This position has never seriously been entertained in discussions of causality in contemporary philosophy, including Whiteheadian philosophy, perhaps because the core idea is incoherent, if not inconceivable. It seems to destroy the very notion of causality. The various sources Bracken periodically marshals in support do not, on closer examination, seem to justify the strong claims Bracken needs to support his position.

Conclusion

Beginning with an explanation of what I call the problem of mutual ultimate causality, this chapter went on to adduce others who see a similar problem in ultimate metaphysical explanations. I explained this problem in general discussions of the problem of the one and many going back to the Presocratics, and then raised the question of this problem in Bracken's various solutions to the problem of the one and the many. In each case the solution seems to try to have one of the two terms in a particular conceptual pair associated with the problem of the one and the many account for the other term without supposing or implying the other term supposedly being accounted for. I also attempted to demonstrate how, even on his own terms, Bracken's various solutions to the problem of the one and the many seem to fail, and the problems with Bracken's idea that causes and effects mutually constitute each other's existence and activity.

I now turn to an argument for how the metaphysical distinction between God and the world as understood by classical theists, which includes the fact that the world as a whole cannot explain itself but derives its existence from God, might be the only way to avoid the problem of the one and the many. I contend that the problem of the one and the many arises from attempting to make categorical unity and plurality, which are finite and not self-subsistent, ultimate reality.

CHAPTER 4

Classical Theism and the Problem of the One and the Many

Process Thinkers and the Creator-Creature Distinction

I have argued that process thought in general and Bracken's theology in particular simultaneously generate the so-called problem of the one and the many and are unable to solve it, because they relegate metaphysics, including the metaphysics of ultimate reality, to principles that have classically been understood as applying to created reality only. Before examining how classical theism might respond to the problem of the one and the many with reference to the distinction between finite and transcendent being, or the Creator-creature distinction, I will point to ways in which it appears that process thinkers themselves do not avoid this distinction.

Whitehead's axiom that the same metaphysical principles applicable to all other existents must apply to God may well be a defining feature of process theology. Metaphysically, God is quantitatively but not qualitatively different from all other beings. Whitehead criticized the Church Fathers because "they made no effort to conceive the World in terms of the metaphysical categories by means of which they interpreted God, and they made no effort to conceive God in terms of the metaphysical categories which they applied to the World."[1] For Whitehead, God's "actuality at once exemplifies and establishes the categoreal conditions."[2]

Process theologians follow Whitehead in affirming that the same meta-

1. Alfred North Whitehead, *Adventures of Ideas* (New York: Macmillan, 1933; reprint, Free Press, 1967), 169.

2. Alfred North Whitehead, *Process and Reality: An Essay in Cosmology,* corrected ed., ed. David Ray Griffin and Donald W. Sherburne (New York: Free Press, 1978; originally published by Macmillan, 1929), 343 (p. 522 in 1929 edition).

physical categories applying to the world apply to God, and vice versa, so that there is no qualitative difference between God and the world exempting God from the metaphysical principles of categorical reality.[3] Regarding theological language, process theologians generally criticize the traditional doctrine of analogical predication, modifying it or repudiating it entirely, and frequently aver that language about God and all other entities is strictly univocal.[4]

Critics of process theology have found its lack of a metaphysical distinction between God and other entities, and its proclivity toward univocal predication, to be major shortcomings. In an incisive analysis, Huston Smith criticizes, among other things, process theology's "stunted ontology" that does not recognize God's radical incomprehensible transcen-

3. Charles A. Hartshorne, *The Divine Relativity: A Social Conception of God* (New Haven, Conn.: Yale University Press, 1967), xv; Schubert M. Ogden, *The Reality of God and Other Essays* (New York: Harper & Row, 1966), 175–77; Donna Bowman, *The Divine Decision: A Process Doctrine of Election* (Louisville, Ky.: Westminster/John Knox Press, 2002), 168–70; Joseph A. Bracken, "The Theology of God of Elizabeth A. Johnson," in *Things New and Old: Essays on the Theology of Elizabeth A. Johnson,* ed. Phyllis Zagano and Terrence W. Tilley, 21–38 (New York: Crossroad, 1999), 29, 31–32; Bracken, *God: Three Who Are One* (Collegeville, Minn.: Liturgical Press, 2008), 21, 24, 74, 84–85, 121; Bracken, "Images of God Within Systematic Theology," *Theological Studies* 63, no. 2 (June 2002): 368–69; Bracken, "Subsistent Relation: Mediating Concept for a New Synthesis?" *Journal of Religion* 64 (April 1984): 188–204; Bracken, "Process Philosophy and Trinitarian Theology—II," *Process Studies* 11 (Summer 1981): 95; Bracken, "Trinity: Economic and Immanent," *Horizons* 25 (Spring 1998): 15.

4. Charles A. Hartshorne, "The Idea of God—Literal or Analogical?" *Christian Scholar* 39 (1956): 136; Hartshorne, *Man's Vision of God and the Logic of Theism,* 2nd ed. (Hamden, Conn.: Archon Books, 1964), 174–205; Hartshorne, *The Divine Relativity,* 17–18, 31–35; Hartshorne, *The Logic of Perfection and Other Essays in Neoclassical Metaphysics* (LaSalle, Ill.: Open Court, 1962), 133–47; Ogden, *The Reality of God,* 174–75; Schubert M. Ogden, "What Sense Does It Make to Say, 'God Acts in History'?" *Journal of Religion* 43 (January 1963): 8–10; Bowman, *The Divine Decision,* 169–70. Process modifications of analogical predication typically involve understanding the *difference* between God and other entities as quantitative only, and not qualitative. Thus in explaining how "analogy" involves difference as well as similarity, Ogden refers to how Whitehead says that God is not simply *an* exemplification of metaphysical principles, but is their "*chief*" exemplification. That is, God's being the *chief exemplification* is how God is different from all other entities, which are only exemplifications of metaphysical principles (Ogden, *The Reality of God,* 175 n. 23). Ogden similarly reinterprets the traditional *analogia entis* to mean that the concepts in which we think and speak of God apply to God eminently, which is not the case for all other existents (ibid., 58–59).

dence, its "waning metaphysical spirit" that gives up the search for the ultimate and contents itself with a penultimate, and its "flawed exegesis" that applies predicates to God in too univocal a fashion.[5] Even the more sympathetic David Tracy, who finds much merit in process metaphysics' views of religious language, urges that the more univocal theories of the process thinkers must be tempered with the "negative" and equivocal aspects of how concepts and words apply to God in classical theism.[6]

I suggest that no metaphysics beginning with the metaphysics of finite categorical reality can avoid the necessity of transcendent being as its condition of possibility. This argument is perhaps most famously enshrined in St. Thomas's "five ways," and has been more recently couched in post-Kantian philosophy by transcendental Thomists. Although the term "exception" is perhaps inadequate given classical theism's view of God, what Whitehead and process thinkers mean by an exception to categorical metaphysical principles seems ultimately unavoidable.

The Whiteheadian view of God as an actual entity exhibits some important exceptions to the principles applicable to all other actual entities. These include that God is non-temporal, God has a type of aseity different from the self-causation of finite actual entities, God is a modified version of Aristotle's Unmoved Mover, God's process of concrescence is the reverse of that of all other actual entities, and God can even be construed as infinitely actual in distinction from the finite actuality of other actual entities. Just as God's immutability is the opposite of creaturely mutability in classical theism, some of these assertions about God in Whiteheadian thought seem to be the opposite of what is predicated of all finite entities, thus lending credence to the claim that some exceptions are necessary in order to account for certain fundamental elements of the metaphysical system, as well as to give the system consistency.

First, for Whitehead God is a non-temporal actual entity, which distinguishes God from all other actual entities,[7] and which primarily means

5. Huston Smith, "Has Process Theology Dismantled Classical Theism?" *Theology Digest* 35 (1988): 302–18.

6. David Tracy, *Blessed Rage for Order: The New Pluralism in Theology* (New York: Seabury Press, 1975), 179, 181; Tracy, *The Analogical Imagination: Christian Theology and the Culture of Pluralism* (New York: Crossroad, 2000), 439–40 n. 7.

7. Whitehead, *Process and Reality*, 6–7 (10–11), 32 (48), 39–40 (63–64), 46 (73). Lewis Ford employs this aspect of Whitehead's doctrine of God to retain a type of "timelessness" in the God of process theism, as in the classical theistic conception of God. He calls this the

that God is exempt from the perpetual perishing all other actual entities undergo.[8] While all actual entities are finite in Whitehead's metaphysics because actuality involves finitude, by God's ascertainment of all of the eternal objects, which are only potentially infinite, God may be construed as in fact actually infinite.[9]

God is also unique because God provides God's own subjective aim, while all other actual entities receive their initial aim from God and modify it as their subjective aim. While all actual entities are *causa sui* in that they constitute their final actuality through their own decisions, the fact that God does not derive God's initial aim from elsewhere as do all other entities is a type of aseity akin to that ascribed to God in classical theism, which differentiates God from all other existents.[10]

In denying the efficient causality that some associate with Aristotle's Unmoved Mover, Whitehead does appropriate the Unmoved Mover in ways he sees as more faithful to Aristotle's intention. Explaining God's initial aim to creatures, he quotes Aristotle's *Metaphysics,* saying that an Unmoved Mover is possible just as the objects of desires and thoughts move the desirer or thinker without themselves moving.[11] God is thus a type of Unmoved Mover while all other entities are both moved and move.

The Whiteheadian God differs from all other existents in that God's concrescence is, of necessity, exactly and in every way the opposite of the concrescence of all other actual entities: "In every respect God and the World move conversely to each other in respect to their process."[12] This

---

"atemporal" aspect of God, linking it objectively to the Whiteheadian "eternal objects" and subjectively to God's non-temporal decision in God's primordial nature, in which God "creates" both the eternal objects and God's own being in a way similar to, but uniquely different from, the self-creating nature of all other actual entities (Lewis S. Ford, "The Non-Temporality of Whitehead's God," *International Philosophical Quarterly* 13 [1973]: 346–76). See also Ford, *The Lure of God: A Biblical Background for Process Theism* (Philadelphia: Fortress Press, 1978), 40, 102.

8. John B. Cobb Jr., "A Whiteheadian Doctrine of God," in *Process Theology and Christian Thought*, ed. Delwin Brown, Ralph E. James Jr., and Gene Reeves, 215–43 (New York: Bobbs-Merrill, 1971), 223; Bowman, *The Divine Decision,* 170.

9. Ford, "The Non-Temporality of Whitehead's God," 346–76.

10. Whitehead, *Process and Reality,* 344 (522–23).

11. Ibid.

12. Ibid., 349 (529). See also Marjorie Hewitt Suchocki, *God, Christ, Church: A Practical Guide to Process Theology* (New York: Crossroad, 1982), 36–41, 84, 183; Bowman, *The Divine*

difference is required to make the system work and be consistent. Every actual entity except God begins with its physical pole, in which it prehends superject actual entities and an initial aim from God as the data informing its concrescence, and ends with its conceptual pole, in which it has decided or determined its actuality by accepting and rejecting prehensions, and finally attains a satisfaction. God alone begins with the conceptual pole, or God's primordial nature as the envisagement of possibilities, and moves to the physical pole, or God's consequent nature as the concrete realization of those possibilities in actual entities.[13]

For God, permanence is primordial and flux is derived from the world, but for the world flux is primordial and permanence is derived from God. God is primordially one as God is the primordial unity of the relevance of the many potential forms or eternal objects, and in the process God acquires a consequent multiplicity, which the primordial character absorbs into its unity. Conversely, the world is primordially many in the many actual entities with their physical finitude, and in the process the world acquires a consequent unity in a novel actual entity, which is then absorbed into the multiplicity of the primordial character. This means God as "one and many" is such in the way exactly converse to the way that the world is "many and one."[14] God's primordial pole is immutable (immutable eternal objects, possibilities, and God's own subjective aim), while God's physical pole is contingent upon the free acts of creatures. The physical pole of finite actual entities is immutable insofar as the data they receive are set and immutable, but their mental pole is contingent upon their own free responses.[15]

There are yet other ways process theologians see God as fundamentally different from all other entities. Affirming with Tillich that God is the ground of being, Ogden speaks of God as in the "strictest sense necessary" in distinction from all other actual entities. This is because while

---

Decision, 83, 183; and Joseph A. Bracken, *The One in the Many: A Contemporary Reconstruction of the God-World Relationship* (Grand Rapids, Mich.: Eerdmans, 2001), 95. Suchocki notes that while Whitehead used the term "actual entity" to apply to both God and finite reality, he used the term "actual occasion" only when referring to finite reality, because although the dynamics of existence are the same for God and finitude, there is a necessary distinction in how they apply (Suchocki, *God, Christ, Church,* 36, note.).

13. Whitehead, *Process and Reality,* 87 (184), 345 (524), 348 (528–29).

14. Ibid., 348 (529).

15. Bowman, *The Divine Decision,* 183.

every other entity is an actualization of only one among infinite possibilities, and could have actualized a different possibility, God is the ground of being making both all actualities and all potentialities possible.[16]

Daniel Day Williams adds an element of necessity in God that does not subsist in other actual entities. Borrowing from classical metaphysics, he says that while other actual entities constitute their own beings and actualities through their decisions, God has an essence that he "cannot violate" and that "categorically determines" the way God acts on all other entities.[17] Affirming that God is passible, with process thought and contra classical theism, Williams still distinguishes how God is affected by all other entities from the way all other entities are affected by each other and by God. Suffering can threaten the creature's very being but the integrity of God's being is never jeopardized by suffering, due to this inviolable, essential aspect of God.[18]

Similar to Williams, Bracken speaks of types of immutability and impassibility that apply to God but do not apply to other entities. While the divine persons allow themselves to be acted upon by creatures, the intratrinitarian divine life is not "ultimately affected" by what happens in creation, and creation is not "ultimately constitutive" of the being of the divine persons.[19]

For Whitehead and process thinkers, then, there seem to be specific ways in which God is an exception to the metaphysical principles applicable to all other actual entities. These differences in metaphysical principles for process thinkers are certainly not the same as the ways in which God is different from finite categorical beings for classical theists. Nonetheless, it seems that Whitehead and process thinkers are compelled to distinguish God from all other entities by either exempting God from certain metaphysical principles or by altering the ways they apply to God. I see this as evidence that no metaphysical system can avoid some sort of explanatory principle transcendent to the metaphysical principles applicable to finite categorical existents, or at least be complete without such

16. Ogden, *The Reality of God,* 124.

17. Daniel Day Williams, "How Does God Act? An Essay in Whitehead's Metaphysics," in *Essays in Process Theology,* ed. Peter LeFevre, 98–117 (Chicago: Exploration Press, 1985), 107.

18. Daniel Day Williams, *The Spirit and the Forms of Love* (London: James Nisbet, 1968), 167.

19. Joseph A. Bracken, *The Triune Symbol. Persons, Process and Community* (Lanham, Md.: University Press of America, 1985), 87, 101–2.

an explanatory principle. In the terms of transcendental Thomism, this is the condition of the possibility of categorical metaphysics, and theologically speaking this is classical theism's Creator-creature distinction.

Some Common Criticisms of Classical Theism

In contemporary theology and philosophy, classical theism has fallen on hard times. First, critics say that its imposition of Greek philosophical categories on Hebrew and early Christian views of God in scripture is foreign and ill-advised, so that it is both an unfaithful representation of the Judeo-Christian God and a pagan corruption of the "God of Abraham, Isaac, and Jacob," who is not "the God of the philosophers." Second, critics claim classical theism results in a litany of theoretical problems, including those addressed by various process theologians and open theists. Third, critics allege that classical theism spawns a host of practical problems, like the diminution of the meaning and effects of history and creatures, the marginalization of creaturely suffering, and tyranny in the form of hegemonic meta-narratives founded upon classical metaphysical systems.

Regarding the first criticism, process theists and those influenced by them claim their theology faithfully represents the God of the Judeo-Christian scriptures while classical theology imposes the foreign "god" of pagan philosophy upon the God of the Bible.[20] They quickly point out how the biblical God is subject to time and to history, moves from potency to act, is really (not just notionally) related to the world, essentially depends

20. Charles A. Hartshorne, "Is Whitehead's God the God of Religion?" *Ethics* 53, no. 3 (April 1943): 219–27; Hartshorne, "Whitehead's Idea of God," in *The Philosophy of Alfred North Whitehead,* ed. Paul A. Schilpp, 513–59 (Chicago: Northwestern University Press, 1941), 55; Daniel Day Williams, *God's Grace and Man's Hope* (New York: Harper & Brothers, 1949; rev. ed., 1965), 42; Ogden, *The Reality of God,* 66–67, 122; Ogden, "Theology and Philosophy: A New Phase of the Discussion," *Journal of Religion* 44 (January 1964): 1–16; John B. Cobb Jr., *God and the World* (Philadelphia: Westminster Press, 1969), 42, 68, 82; Norman Pittenger, *God in Process* (London: SCM Press, 1967), 14–17, 90, 99–101; Ford, *The Lure of God,* x, 12, 29; Eulalio R. Baltazar, *God within Process* (New York: Newman Press, 1970), 110–14, 127, 130; George Allan, "The Aims of Societies and the Aims of God," in *Process Philosophy and Christian Thought,* ed. Delwin Brown, Ralph E. James Jr., and Gene Reeves, 464–74 (Indianapolis: Bobbs-Merrill, 1971), 469–70; Bowman, *The Divine Decision,* 125, 167–68, 173; John F. Haught, *God after Darwin: A Theology of Evolution* (Boulder, Colo.: Westview Press, 2000), 187–89. Even David Tracy seems to believe that the categories of process thought are more faithful to the limit-language of the Hebrew and Christian scriptures than those of classical theism (Tracy, *The Analogical Imagination,* 160–61, 174, 177–84, 189, 200 n. 89).

in some ways on the world, is mutable, is passible, does not always possess exhaustive foreknowledge of the future, and is limited by creatures' freedom. Classical theists ostensibly resort to fancy explanations contrived to explain away what is patently inconsistent with the God of the Bible, while they themselves supposedly take scriptural depictions of God at their face value.

I believe this first criticism is wrongheaded for several reasons. First—and I cannot argue this at length here—due to the nature of hermeneutics and the appropriation of scripture in theology, all theologians, whether process, open, or classical theists, must inevitably at certain points apply the categories of some philosophical system or other on a "second order" analysis and systematization of the assertions of the texts on the "first order." Decisions about subjectivity's determining being, becoming as prior to being, the nature of cause and effect, the dipolar nature of actual entities, of whom God is the chief exemplification, creativity as the metaphysical ultimate, and other such matters, are by no means gleaned from a prima facie reading of the biblical text.[21] Inasmuch as they use philosophical systems developed during the modern period, some of which were formulated by non-theists and even overtly non-religious individuals, process theologians could also be charged with imposing a god of pagan philosophy onto the God of the Bible.

The second-century apologists and the Church Fathers quickly realized that this employment of philosophy for second-order reflection is a sine qua non for theology. Following the lead of Hellenistic Judaism, they thus employed the great philosophical systems available to them to explain, understand, and defend the Christian faith. The Christian tradi-

21. This point also applies to the various dialectical, neo-orthodox, and postmodern narrative theologies that profess to cast off metaphysics and stick to just what the text "says." Karl Barth, who disliked the use of philosophy in theology, could not avoid the issues taken up by such second-order reflection. A case could be made that Barth was heavily influenced by the Kierkegaardian reaction to Hegel, and Barth does not refrain from making fundamental metaphysical claims like *esse sequitur operari* (Karl Barth, *Church Dogmatics,* ed. G. W. Bromiley and T. F. Torrance [Edinburgh: T & T Clark, 1936–69], 2/1, §28, p. 82). Where in the variegated depictions of God in the Hebrew and Christian scriptures do any of the authors clearly and unequivocally speak of an "infinite qualitative distinction" between time and eternity, and between God and the world? Barth's metaphysical claim that *esse sequitur operari* became the springboard for the work of his eminent interpreter and disciple, Eberhard Jüngel (Eberhard Jüngel, *God's Being Is in Becoming: The Trinitarian Being of God in the Theology of Karl Barth. A Paraphrase,* trans. John Webster [Grand Rapids, Mich.: Eerdmans, 2001]).

tion, from its incipience until the late Middle Ages, thus found philosophy to be a necessary tool, so that the attitudes of those like Tertullian were by far the minority view until the late medieval nominalists, and the Protestant Reformers heavily influenced by them, emerged to facilitate what would become the common but novel view in modernity that philosophy and Christian theology are incompatible.

In light of these considerations, the question is not whether we should employ philosophical and metaphysical systems to systematize scriptural descriptions of God, but rather which of these systems is the most relatively adequate. The merits of various philosophical resources (for example, ancient Greek, modern European) should be discussed, not whether philosophy should be used by Christian theologians, which seems unavoidable.

Hermeneutics has become exponentially more complicated in recent centuries precisely because of the findings of historical criticism. The historical situatedness, the contextual embeddedness, and the genre-laden and extremely diverse nature of the scriptures present formidable, but not necessarily insuperable, challenges to anyone seeking to use scripture in theology. The premodern method of proof-texting simply will not do. Interestingly, we sometimes find process theologians and those influenced by them, such as the open theists, using the Bible in the same proof-texting manner they accuse classical theists of using. Even when not taking the findings of historical criticism into account, second-order systems of philosophy and hermeneutics must be introduced, wittingly or unwittingly, to fit together the many prima facie contradictory statements in scripture, such as: "God is not a man, that He should lie, nor a son of man, that He should change His mind" (Nm 23:19; cf. 1 Sm 15:29, Ez 24:14, and Mal 3:6); and "The Lord changed His mind about the harm which He said He would do to His people" (Ex 32:14; cf. Jer 26:18; Am 7:3–6, Jon 3:10). Also, criticizing classical theists for saying biblical depictions of temporality, change, and limitation in God are mere anthropomorphisms, process theologians and open theists themselves deny the literal nature of references to God having "eyes," "ears," a "righteous right hand," and "length of nostrils," or "sitting on a throne."[22] Even the ostensibly simple process of adjudicating what is literal and what is not literal must move into a "second order" of the text.

22. "Length of nostrils" is a Hebrew idiom for patience, representing the opposite of being easily angered, which is associated with the "flaring of nostrils."

Second, this criticism seems to be based primarily on aspects of ancient Israelite religion and the Hebrew scriptures that existed and were generated before second temple Judaism. Second temple Judaism experienced a significant encounter with Greek philosophy, religion, culture, and language during the Hellenistic period. Many Hellenistic Jews seem to have realized the point I just made: advanced theological reflection necessitates the adoption of second-order philosophical categories. In fact, Jewish religious writings and scriptures generated during the second temple and intertestamental periods reflect an increasing incorporation of Greek religious and philosophical thought.

A fact seemingly ignored by the critics is that the New Testament documents themselves are heavily influenced by Greek philosophy and religion. Whether it is John's *Logos* and metaphysical assertions, Paul's implicit and explicit references to Greek thinkers, Luke-Acts' interaction with and use of Greco-Roman philosophy and religion in its apologetic to the ancient Greco-Roman establishment, or the author of the Epistle to the Hebrews' use of Plato's terminology of "form/idea" and "shadow," the New Testament is heavily informed and influenced by the Hellenistic Judaism from which early Christianity emerged. The warnings against "hollow and deceptive philosophy" and "knowledge falsely so called" come from the later New Testament writings and were aimed specifically against proto-Gnostic Christianity, which employed ancient Greco-Roman philosophy in negative ways. Since the Christian canon includes the New Testament, and the sacred authors therein did not hesitate to employ Greek philosophy at times, it seems that a proper use of Greek philosophy is warranted. For a Christian theologian considering appropriate philosophical categories to employ in theology, it would seem that an important precedent is already set in the Christian scriptures themselves.

Third, while the most ancient writers of the Hebrew scriptures did not employ the categories of Greek philosophy to describe how God is different from creation, they did use the languages and concepts available to them to express the same basic underlying ideas. They seemed to have no reticence in ubiquitously employing what was available to them from their ancient Near Eastern, non Israelite contexts.[23] How can we be certain they would not have availed themselves of certain philosophical par-

23. See, for instance, *The Context of Scripture,* 3 vols., ed. William W. Hallo and K. Lawson Younger (Leiden: Brill, 2003).

adigms, categories, and vocabularies of which they were unaware, had they known of them? To take but one example, that of God being "inside" or "outside/above" time: It is certainly questionable as to whether the ancient Hebrews, and even the early Christians, conceived of time as a kind of "box" that an entity can either be "inside" or "outside" of. Yet it appears they did, in their own ways, try to express that God transcends the limitations we normally associate with time. God transcends the limitations of beginning and end, which characterize all beings created by him.[24] God transcends the limitations of ignorance of the past and of the future,[25] and God transcends the frequently frustrating aspects of temporal existence.[26]

Although these most ancient biblical authors never state overtly and unequivocally that God is "outside of time," "above time," or "timeless," using their own languages and categories for understanding reality they seem to convey in places the idea that God transcends the limitations of time that characterize what it means to be "in time." Similar arguments could be made with respect to the other classical theistic incommunicable attributes of God. As a result of these three considerations, I believe the first general charge—that the God of classical theism does not correspond to the God of biblical revelation, and that classical theism wrongly relies on ancient philosophical categories—is too naïve and simplistic.

Regarding the second general allegation—that classical theism is riddled with theoretical and philosophical problems—astute observers note that classical theism's critics often either do not adequately deal with, or do not even properly consider, the subtle complexities of classical theism.[27] Even Charles Hartshorne has said that philosophy in and after modernity "has often drifted so far from medieval metaphysics as scarcely to

24. See, Dt 32:40, 33:27; Jb 36:26; Pss 9:7, 29:10, 33:11, 93:2, 90:1–2, 102:24–27, 145:13, 146:10; Is 26:4, 57:15; and Lam 5:19. Regarding *B'Reshit* (בְּרֵאשִׁית) (Gn 1:1), James Barr comments: "In general there is a considerable likelihood that the early Christians understood the Genesis creation story to imply that the beginning of time was simultaneous with the beginning of the creation of the world, especially since the chronological scheme takes its departure from that date" (James Barr, *Biblical Words for Time* [Naperville, Ill.: A. R. Allenson, 1962], 75).

25. See, 1 Chr 28:9; Jb 31:4, 34:21; Ps 44:21, 94:9–10, 139:1–4, 147:4–5; Prv 15:3; Is 40:28, 42:9, 44:7, 45:21, 46:10; Jer 17:10, 23:24, 32:19; and Dn 2:28. The common biblical notion of prophecy also assumes God's knowledge of, and even control over, the future.

26. See Pss 33:9–11, 90:4; Prv 16:9, 19:21; and Is 14:26–27, 46:10.

27. Tracy, *The Analogical Imagination,* 83 n. 12.

see what that metaphysics was about."[28] In fact, a very strong case could be made that these critics are responding more to a less robust, less nuanced, less sophisticated, epigonistic form of theism that started to develop in late medieval nominalism through the Protestant Reformation and into the modern period, and not to classical theism at its best. One could similarly argue that many of the specific theoretical problems with classical theism raised by critics are either satisfactorily answered in the classical theism of the High Middle Ages, provided this is properly understood, or are attacks on straw men, due to a lack of understanding.[29]

With respect to the third general criticism, classical theism's supposedly pragmatic ill-effects, one must in all fairness try to discern whether the blame lies in whole, or even in part, with classical theism. In addition, the venerable axiom that *abusus non tollit usum*, if true, makes any attempt to discredit classical theism based on the fact that some have used it to ill-effect impuissant. Practically anything imaginable could be discredited, since practically everything has been abused to some degree, at some time, by someone. Additionally, it does not logically follow that practical negativities resultant from the abuse of certain assertions necessarily prove that those assertions are not true.

Doubtless many contemporary theologians and philosophers find classical theism wanting in the areas just discussed, yet I find their criticisms to be faulty and have briefly tried to show why.

Divine Aseity and the Problem of the One and the Many

Classical theism describes God's transcendence in many ways. Surveying the world of categorical entities that are not self-moving, self-

28. Hartshorne, *Man's Vision of God*, 58.

29. For example, for a good explanation of how Thomism, rightly understood, reconciles exhaustive divine sovereignty and electing grace with real libertarian free will and God's universal salvific will, see Fr. Reginald Garrigou-Lagrange, O.P., *Predestination*, tr. Dom Bede Rose, O.S.B. (Rockford, Ill.: Tan Books and Publishers, 1998; originally *La prédestination des saints et la grace*, 1939). Elizabeth Johnson recently tried to raise and address a few of these misunderstandings in "Does God Play Dice?" *Theological Studies* 57 (1996): 2–18. For a detailed discussion of the differences between "real" classical theism and the forms of theism appearing during modernity that are frequently mistaken for classical theism, see William C. Placher, *The Domestication of Transcendence: How Modern Thinking about God Went Wrong* (Louisville, Ky.: Westminster/John Knox Press, 1996).

causing, in possession of the act of existence by nature (necessarily), necessary, self-measuring, or autotelic has led many to urge that we must posit a unique being, qualitatively different from all of the rest in a metaphysical way, with precisely these distinct qualities.[30]

A central difference between God and all that is not God bearing on my analysis of the problem of the one and the many is that God's essence is God's existence. The most fundamental statement that no being other than God can account for itself is the statement that nothing, save God, includes existence in its essence. Any created essence is possible but not necessarily actual, because existence is not essential to it. An entity's essence never includes the act of existence itself. All finite beings in actual existence presuppose an act of existence (being or *esse*) not contained in their individual essences, and which their individual essences do not supply. In this way there is a split, or lack of identity, between the essence of any finite being and its existence. This is one of the simplest statements of what creaturehood entails.[31]

Empirically speaking, all perceptible beings come into being and perish.[32] In addition, empirical investigation gives explanations in terms of causes but cannot provide an ultimate explanation to Leibniz's celebrated

30. St. Thomas is, of course, a famous example (St. Thomas Aquinas, *Summa theologiae* 1a.2.3). It is important to note that because for Thomas God's existence is God's essence, and God's essence is incomprehensible to created intellects, Thomas's famous "five ways" do not make God's existence clear to us, that is, what God is *(Dei essentia),* but rather only prove the veracity of the statement that God is *(Deus est).*

31. "The only possible explanation for the presence of such finite and contingent beings is that they have been freely given existence by 'Him who is,' and not as parcels of his own existence, which, because it is absolute and total, is also unique, but as finite and partial limitations of what He himself eternally is in his own right. This act whereby 'He who is' causes to exist something that, of itself, is not, is what is called, in Christian philosophy, 'creation.' . . . Between 'Him who is' and ourselves, there is the infinite metaphysical chasm which separates the complete self-sufficiency of His own existence from the intrinsic lack of necessity of our own existence" (Étienne Gilson, *God and Philosophy* [New Haven, Conn.: Yale University Press, 1941; 2nd ed., 2002], 52, 54).

32. Since every categorical being comes into existence and eventually ceases to exist, while the possibility of its existence, or essence, both predates and postdates its actual existence, no categorical being includes in itself (essentially) the necessity of existence or the Act of Being *(esse).* St. Thomas further argued from this that given an infinite amount of time there would be a time when all possible essences are not in existence simultaneously. Thus, since there are contingent beings in existence now, we must posit a unique being, the essence of which includes its existence, or exists necessarily (St. Thomas Aquinas, *ST* 1a.2.3).

question: "Why there is something rather than nothing?"[33] Science tells us *what* something is, not *why* something is, so the question of why there are any beings, taken singularly or cosmically, is beyond scientific inquiry.[34]

Finite existents further presuppose an infinite act of existence for their own limited acts of existence, because every finite being manifests the act of existence in certain ways determined by its essence, but never in the fully unlimited way of an infinite act of existence.[35] Stated epistemologically in terms of the unity of being and knowing, in apprehending any entity the intellect can conceive of a greater one, which means all finite intelligible realities presuppose an infinite intelligible reality.[36]

Hence in classical theism there are metaphysical differences between the Creator and creatures such that created beings are not self-explaining, due to the hiatus between essence (possibility) and existence (actuality) in all beings that are not God. I have already discussed some of the conceptual pairs observed in the categorical world of finite, created beings often associated with the problem of the one and the many by juxtaposition of their terms. I now propose that the split between the terms of each pair, and the fact that each term presupposes its opposite, resulting in the prob-

33. G. W. Leibniz, *Principles of Nature and Grace, Based on Reason,* §7.

34. See Brian Davies, *Aquinas* (New York: Continuum, 2002), 33–34, 35; and Jonathan L. Kvanvig and Hugh J. McCann, "Divine Conservation and the Persistence of the World," in *Divine and Human Action: Essays in the Metaphysics of Theism,* ed. Thomas V. Morris (Ithaca, N.Y.: Cornell University Press, 1988), 18. Davies also makes the point that scientific inquiry presupposes existence because it abstracts from already existing actual existents or beings *(entia)* (Davies, *Aquinas,* 35).

35. In Thomistic terms, every essence *(essentia)* is a "negative" principle because it limits and determines the infinite positive act of existence *(esse)* (Emerich Coreth, *Metaphysics,* trans. Joseph Donceel [New York: Herder & Herder, 1968], 83–84). This is only a partial or relative, not a full or absolute, negation, because it negates only some but not all determinations of being (ibid., 84). Yet the determinations of Infinite Being negated by the essence are still presupposed in this negation as those determinations from which this particular essence is distinguishing or differentiating itself (ibid., 84–85).

36. St. Thomas Aquinas, *Summa contra gentiles* 1.43.10. This truth is fundamental in transcendental Thomism. See, for instance, Karl Rahner, "The Concept of Mystery in Catholic Theology," in *Theological Investigations,* vol. 4, *More Recent Writings,* trans. Kevin Smyth, 36–73 (Baltimore: Helicon Press, 1966), 51; Rahner, *Foundations of Christian Faith,* trans. William Dych (New York: Seabury, 1978; reprint, Crossroad, 1999), 61–62, 77–78; Coreth, *Metaphysics,* 10–11, 56–66. Also, it is important to note that just because a reality greater than the one being contemplated can always be thought of does not mean that a created intellect can comprehend the infinite intelligible reality toward which it strives.

lem of mutual ultimate causality, is intimately bound up with the split between essence and existence in finite created beings and their absolute dependence upon their Creator.[37] Thus the classical theistic distinction between the Creator and creatures, or the transcendent and the categorical, is central in illuminating the nature of the problem.

If one says all of reality, including ultimate reality, is subject to the same metaphysical principles without exception, then problems of ultimate causal explanations arise that also arise with respect to creatures in classical theism. As discussed, process thinkers often make some distinctions between God and the world, but admitting some differences between God and the world is not the same as acknowledging the types of metaphysical differences classical theists have seen as most important. For classical theists, the metaphysical ways in which God is qualitatively different from all other beings are conclusions necessitated by the fact that no other being can explain itself in terms of its own ontological conditions. Admitting distinctions between God and the world but still applying the same metaphysical principles to God as to the world results, then, in a problem very similar to that of the world explaining itself.

Process thought subjects all of reality, including ultimate reality or God, to the same metaphysical principles. This seems to at once precipitate and render insoluble the problem of the one and the many due to the problem of mutual ultimate causality. Because finite beings cannot exhaustively account for themselves solely in terms of the metaphysical principles applicable to them, the same problem of ultimate causal explanations arises when key metaphysical distinctions between God and the world urged by classical theists are denied. If it is true that all categorical, finite beings cannot account for their own acts of existence, this is true for any one of them taken singularly, any collection of them, or the whole of them taken together as the cosmos. If ultimate reality is bound by the same ontological conditions as all beings that are not ultimate reality, then the seemingly insoluble problem arises of trying to have a creature, a collection of creatures, or all creatures taken together account for their own existence.

37. Robert C. Neville argues extensively that the solution to the problem of the one and the many requires a theory of creation, but his understanding of how the problem is "solved" takes a different direction from my analysis here (Robert C. Neville, *God the Creator: On the Transcendence and Presence of God* [Albany: State University of New York Press, 1992], 8, 15–16, 34, 40–43, 48, 50, 60, 70–71, 94, 157).

The problem of the one and the many arises, then, as dialectical pairs corresponding to the distinction between essence and existence are observed in finite, created beings. As aspects of created being, the juxtaposed terms in each of the pairs are finite and contingent themselves, and upon closer analysis can be seen to imply or presuppose one another so that neither by itself can exhaustively account for both itself and its opposite. As discussed earlier, any given categorical unity, continuity, and similarity presupposes plurality, discontinuity, and difference as already given, and therefore cannot account for this plurality solely by itself *(a se).*[38] Conversely, any incidence of plurality, discontinuity, and dissimilarity among proportionate beings presupposes unity, continuity, and identity as already given, and therefore cannot account for this unity in and of itself *(a se).*[39] Whether logically or causally considered, a categorical many always requires an antecedent one, and a categorical one always requires an antecedent many.

38. Coreth explains that if there is any one finite being, there is the concomitant necessity of the possibility of multiple finite beings, since difference is necessary for the determinations of finite beings (i.e., differences from other determinations of the act of existence or infinite being) (Coreth, *Metaphysics,* 123). For every finite being, the unity of self or self-identity presupposes difference from other finite beings, so that it is one among many. The "inner unity" and "outer unity" of any finite being assumes a plurality of finite beings. Every finite being as one is one in a different way from all other finite beings. In the realm of finite categorical beings, being itself as the element of unity and similarity becomes differentiated, determined, and plural by the determination, and hence diversity, supplied by finite essences. Transcendental Thomism adds to this analysis that underlying the difference of being (similarity) plus essence (difference), between finite beings in a multiplicity, there must be a presupposed unity without the duality of being and essence. This is Being itself, whose essence it is to Be—i.e., God (ibid., 124–25).

39. Coreth explains several ways in which multiplicity presupposes unity. Every multiplicity presupposes a unity (of the individual), since every multiplicity is composed of individuals identical with themselves but different from each other. Multiplicity presupposes unity also because multiplicity is constituted by multiple individuals considered *together* (i.e., as *one* group). Multiplicity further presupposes unity in the multiplicity itself, because members of a multiplicity must have something in common, in order for them to be grouped together. Without this unity there would only be completely disparate, unrelated individuals, and being itself is the most common feature among all members of any given multiplicity (Coreth, *Metaphysics,* 123–24).

Analogical Predication and the Limitations of Conceptualizing God

Two essential elements of many forms of classical theism bearing on this discussion of the problem of the one and the many and the problem of mutual ultimate causality are God's incomprehensibility and analogical predication. For much of classical theism no created intellect can comprehend God, but created intellects can know certain things about God in a manner according to the mode of knowing of created intellects. Since God's essence is incomprehensible in itself, all of our thought and speech about God comes of necessity from creatures.

A metaphysical investigation into the nature of ultimate reality that does not presuppose a faith commitment from within the context of any given religious tradition may come to the philosophical conclusion that ultimate reality is incomprehensible. Only by supposing a priori, or demanding, that all of reality be comprehensible to the human intellect can one relegate affirmations of the ultimate reality's incomprehensibility to the realm of religious faith. Though one may demand such exhaustive comprehensibility, its possibility, especially in discussions of ultimate reality, is debatable. It is quite conceivable that an investigation into the conditions of possibility of the finite universe leads to the affirmation of a type of being exempt from certain metaphysical principles applicable to categorical reality, and these metaphysical differences may include the belief that this other type of being is incomprehensible. The element of incomprehensibility in this solution to the problem of explaining the necessary conditions for finite reality is a problem only if one demands that all explanations must be fully comprehensible to the human intellect. On the other hand, if one is open to the possibility of ultimate reality's incomprehensibility, then this exception to the metaphysics of the finite categorical realm is not a problem but rather a solution. Although ultimate reality's incomprehensibility is central to various presentations of classical theism, this fact alone does not preclude incomprehensibility from being essential to purely philosophical explanations of ultimate reality.

Analogical predication, on the other hand, is peculiar to classical theism. St. Thomas did not construct a theory of analogical predication, which task was left to later Thomists. He did, however, provide a foundation for analogical predication in his statements on the limitations of our words and concepts of God. A lack of appropriation, lack of understanding, or even neglect of the classical theistic idea of analogical predication can easily lead to the problem of mutual ultimate causality in discussions of God in theology proper.

St. Thomas took the phenomenon of similarities and differences between how we predicate the same word in different instances, most memorably with the example of a "healthy" human, a "healthy" diet, and "healthy" urine, as his starting point.[40] The concept of "health" is predicated in different but related ways, namely the object of health, a cause of health, and a sign of health, to different subjects. This was not his ending point, however. Because we know what the subjects are, we can understand what the predicate means in each case. Since we do not and cannot understand the "essence" of God, there is an extreme lacuna in our understanding of what any predicate means when applied to God. There is also much more negation of how words predicated of creatures apply to God than there is affirmation. This is like saying a prattlenack is healthy where "prattlenack" (a word that I made up) is an organism that cannot be sick, does not have a diet, and does not urinate. There is a connection between what is predicated of God and how the same predicates apply to creatures, though, so that there is not pure equivocation as with the word "leaves" in the phrase "leaves of a tree" and the statement "the car leaves." We cannot understand the connection, however, since we cannot understand God.[41]

This means that there is far more mystery than understanding in how creaturely predicates apply to God. Indeed in classical theism extreme negation and apophaticism are not attenuated by affirmation, as can be seen in the Fourth Lateran Council's (AD 1215) declaration: "Between Creator and creature no similitude can be expressed without implying a greater dissimilitude."[42] Regarding the immediate discussion of the problem of mutual ultimate causality, we must note how St. Thomas said the concept of "causality" is entirely equivocal with reference to God as the "First Cause" in the universal production of being or *esse*.[43]

40. St. Thomas Aquinas, *ST* 1a.13.10.

41. See St. Thomas Aquinas, *ST* 1a.13.3, and *Summa contra gentiles* 1.30.2.

42. Heinrich Denzinger, *Enchiridion symbolorum definitionum et declarationum de rebus fidei et morum*, 34th ed., ed. Adolfus Schönmetzer (New York: Herder, 1965), §806.

43. St. Thomas Aquinas, *Commentary on Aristotle's Physics*, 8.2.974. This has enormous

In addition to this, analogical predication partly arises from aspects of God's nature in classical theism. Lacking potency, component parts, and causes, God is entirely simple.[44] Everything in God is one except the terms in the relations of opposition for trinitarian classical theists. God has no other distinctions *in se,* but our finite intellects seeking to know God impose distinctions on our conceptions of God in accordance with their finite limitations. Since our words about God, and the concepts about God that they signify, come from our knowledge of God's creatures, they do not properly and fully signify the divine essence.[45] We can know God only from creatures, and so can know God only as far as creatures represent God, which always fall short of God's supereminent perfections.[46]

Our intellect forms ideas proportional to the perfections flowing from God to creatures, and while these perfections in God are indivisibly united and simple, in creatures they are divided and multiplied. For each perfection represented by creatures there is one infinite perfection represented by many discrete finite creatures exhibiting that perfection differently; so, too, the many different ideas in our intellect correspond to the one, altogether simple, indissolubly unified God. Ultimately "in God" all things signified by our words are synonymous, but for us they are not synonymous because they signify that one thing under many different aspects in our created intellects. As God's perfections are unified in God but divided among God's creaturely effects, so, also, any ideas we hold of God's perfections are distinct, because they come only through knowledge of God's creaturely effects.[47]

Because God's perfections are multiplied among creatures, and because all knowledge of God comes from creatures, we can think of God only in terms of the division and multiplication of what is really unified and identical in God. This means creaturely limitations affect our concepts of God, which further means that the problem of mutual ultimate causality attends us at every step in our thinking about and speaking about God. The dialectical tension between the terms in the pairs associated with the problem of the one and the many, coupled with improp-

---

consequences for the potency of modern criticisms (à la Hume and Kant) of the classically theistic arguments for God's existence.

44. St. Thomas Aquinas, *ST* 1a.3.7; *Summa contra gentiles* 1.18.1–8.

45. St. Thomas Aquinas, *ST* 1a.13.1.

46. Ibid., 1a.13.2.

47. Ibid., 1a.13.4–5.

er univocal predication of these terms to God and creatures, results in enigmatic intellectual puzzles in theology proper. These include such questions as Does God's nature determine what God chooses, or does God determine God's nature by an act of will? Why did God create one state of affairs instead of countless other possible ones? Are there certain structures of existence to which God is bound, or does God determine all structures of existence? Are there certain eternal moral principles to which God is bound or does God determine all moral principles (Plato's *Euthryphro* dilemma)? Is God abstract or concrete, impersonal or personal? Does one divine substance or multiple subsistent relations in community unify the Trinity?

We cannot comprehend divine simplicity but can still affirm it as incomprehensible mystery. We cannot conceive of a being the essence of which is to exist but can still affirm this of God in inscrutable transcendent mystery. In the same way we can affirm that the split between the dialectical pairs observed in categorical reality is not "in God," even though God is incomprehensible to our finite intellects. The two terms in the dialectical pairs associated with the problem of the one and the many are separated in finite existence, corresponding to the hiatus between essence and existence in categorical existence, but the terms are identical in God, corresponding to the identity of God's essence and existence. Whether by philosophical investigation into the conditions of the possibility of finite reality, or by religious belief in revelation about God's nature, we can justifiably hold that God infinitely transcends our predications and ideas.[48] These predications and ideas derive from creatures and so perforce contain the creaturely distinction of possessing a dialectical split between what is unified in God.[49]

48. As St. Thomas says: "All affirmations we can make about God are not such that our minds may rest in them, nor of such sort that we may suppose God does not transcend them" (St. Thomas Aquinas, *De divinibus nomnibus* 1.2). Regarding what he calls the divine "accommodation" to human modes of speech and thought, John Calvin, borrowing from St. John Chrysostom, writes: "For who even of slight intelligence does not understand that, as nurses commonly do with infants, God is wont in a measure to 'lisp' in speaking to us? Thus such forms of speaking do not so much express clearly what God is like as accommodate the knowledge of him to our slight capacity. To do this he must descend far beneath his loftiness" (John Calvin, *Institutes of the Christian Religion*, trans. Ford Lewis Battles, ed. John T. McNeill [Philadelphia: Westminster Press, 1960], 1.13.1, p. 121).

49. Paul Tillich notes: "When applied to God, superlatives become diminutives. They

If God *in se* were the preeminent exemplification of creaturely ontology, then God would also possess the highest degree of existential splitting of the two poles observed in categorical reality. As Rahner says, absolute being must not be thought of as the "highest and most perfect factor in this world."[50] God is not a being "alongside" or "above" other beings, because the ground of being cannot be found within the totality of beings, and is thus of an entirely different order.[51] Not an object or element in the world, God is instead the transcendental precondition of the world, beyond all immanent categories, ontology, and logic, which means God's transcendence is ultimately indefinable.[52] Indeed, traditional Christian faith has held that the essence of God remains incomprehensible even in the beatific vision.[53]

Many contradictions in, and criticisms of, classical theism arise from applying the metaphysics of created, finite categorical reality to God. We cannot but think of God in terms of these insoluble tensions because of our mode of knowing God. If we remember that by definition and on its own terms classical theism says that all knowledge of God comes through creatures, that our concepts and words about God never correspond to God univocally, and that God is incomprehensible to finite intellects, we may be well on the way to seeing some of the inadequacies of the contemporary criticisms of classical theism.

The Unity of the Poles of the Categorical Pairs in God

In closing I would like to comment on several ways in which the terms or poles of several of the pairs observed in categorical reality are identical in God. There is no opposition between the terms because they are identical. God's essence is God's existence, God's being is God's acting, God's

place him on the level of other beings while elevating him above all of them" (Paul Tillich, *Systematic Theology,* 3 vols. [Chicago: University of Chicago Press, 1951–63], 1:235).

50. Karl Rahner, "Christology in the Setting of Modern Man's Understanding of Himself and of His World," in *Theological Investigations*, vol. 11, *Confrontations 1*, trans. David Bourke, 215–29 (New York: Seabury, 1974), 222–25.

51. Tillich, *Systematic Theology,* 1:172, 205, 235–36.

52. Rahner, *Foundations of Christian Faith,* 62–64, 74.

53. St. Thomas Aquinas, *ST* 1a.12.7. Karl Barth similarly says that all mysteries of the world can eventually cease to be mysteries for man, but "God is always a mystery" (Barth, *Church Dogmatics,* 1/1, §8, 321).

nature is God's will, and the one divine essence is identical with each of the three divine persons. In terms of the problem of mutual ultimate causality it can be said that there is no such problem in God, since the juxtaposed poles are really identical, and hence truly mutually causally ultimate.

As discussed, for classical theism a defining qualitative distinction between God and creatures is that God's essence is God's existence.[54] Perhaps the most fundamental split in creaturehood is between essence and existence.[55] All creatures are possible, but none of them are unconditionally necessary. They are conditionally necessary when they do actually exist,[56] but they are not necessary by their own nature, and hence never unconditionally necessary.

For a variety of reasons, classical theists argue that there must be a metaphysically unique entity, God, the very essence of which is to exist, in order to account for categorical reality. The essences of creatures do not contain within themselves the act of their existence, but receive their existence from God. Since no empirically observable entities have always existed, none of them necessarily exist, but must "borrow" their existence, as something distinct from themselves, from elsewhere. One can deny the existence of any empirically encounterable essence without logical contradiction, and since essences can be thus conceived without contradiction as possibly non-existent, the question of why they do exist arises. The fact that no empirically observable categorical entities are necessary by nature means that not one of them contains within itself the sufficient conditions for its existence. When it does exist it does so neces-

54. St. Thomas Aquinas, *ST* 1a.3.4; *Summa contra gentiles* 1.21.1–6, 1.22.1–11; Friedrich Schleiermacher, *The Christian Faith,* 2nd ed., ed. H. R. Mackintosh and J. S. Stewart (Berlin: Martin Redeker, 1830–31; Edinburgh: T & T Clark, 1989; reprint, 1997), 1, §50, 3, p. 199, 1, §54, 4, pp. 218–19; Tillich, *Systematic Theology,* 1:205, 236, 248; Louis Berkhof, *Systematic Theology* (Grand Rapids, Mich.: Eerdmans, 1936–38; new ed., 1996), 58.

55. This is true in Catholic and many Protestant presentations. For instance, the Reformed theologian Herman Bavinck says God's aseity is presented as God's first incommunicable attribute, because we use divine aseity "to designate God as God, and to distinguish him from all that is not God" (Herman Bavinck, *Doctrine of God* [Grand Rapids, Mich.: Eerdmans, 1951], 125).

56. Emerich Coreth calls this the "Principle of Ontic Identity," which says that "insofar as a being is, it is necessarily," and notes that whenever a being is, it is so unconditionally, yet the fact that it requires a positive unconditional ground makes its existence a "conditional unconditionally" (Coreth, *Metaphysics,* 95–96).

sarily, but that necessity cannot come from its own essence. Since no categorical being is its own sufficient condition, the necessity of any and all categorical entities must come from some unique being that is not contingent, but necessary, and can give existence to contingent beings.

The qualitative metaphysical difference between God and contingent created beings can also be stated with respect to causality. All categorical entities are involved in a causal nexus, being both the reasons for other beings and having other entities as their own reasons. Since no categorical essence includes existence, existence as a primary cause of any entity's actuality must come from elsewhere. It cannot come from itself because it does not yet exist. It cannot come from any of its categorical causes, since they, too, possess existence as one of their causes *ad extra* and not contained in their own essence. The phenomenon of causality, then, leads to positing a unique being, the essence of which is the pure act of existing, the essence of which is not to be "this and that" but rather "to be" itself. "Being" itself never slips into non-being. This unique being, or God, therefore does not exist in the way that created, categorical beings exist.[57]

A dialectical tension associated with the problem of the one and the many and entailing the problem of mutual ultimate causality arises in the question of whether a being first exists and then acts, or whether it is in action itself that a being constitutes itself. Surveying the realm of categorical beings, some ask whether beings exist and act as they do because of what they are, or whether they are what they are because of how they exist and act. This leads to debates between substance ontologies and existential ontologies. In theological and philosophical anthropology, this dialectic manifests itself in debates between compatibilist and libertarian views of free will.

Because we can ask whether a creature's essential features, like a hu-

57. For this reason Paul Tillich said God does "not exist" (Tillich, *Systematic Theology,* 1:236–37), but his meaning has been misunderstood. Saying "it is as atheistic to affirm the existence of God as to deny it. God is being-itself, not *a* being" (ibid., 1:237), and "in God there is no difference between essence and existence. . . . God does not exist" (ibid., 1:205), he is using existence in the sense of what I am calling categorical existence. Central for Tillich, as with classical theism in general, is the claim that "the being of God cannot be understood as the existence of a being alongside others or above others" (ibid., 1:235). John Hick clarified this by indicating that when Tillich says God does not exist he means God does not exist in the way creatures do. He is simply trying to express a distinction between God's necessary and unconditional being and contingent beings (John H. Hick, "The Idea of Necessary Being," *Princeton Seminary Bulletin* 54, no. 2 [November 1960]: 11–21).

man being's intellect and will, precede and inform its being and acting, and because our concepts and words about God come from creatures, we ask questions about the priority of nature/action/will with respect to God. In thinking about God we predicate essential features like omniscience, omnipotence, and omnibenevolence to God, and since we can conceive of God only by means of creatures, we naturally ask whether God's essential features determine God's actions.[58]

Discussions of the freedom-and-necessity dialectic regarding God often involve asking whether God is entirely free in what God does (unlimited), or is determined by something antecedent to and limiting God's will. The former can take the form of a nominalist view of God's nature as pure unfettered will, or of Cartesian expatiations about whether logical, mathematical, and geometrical truths are contingent and not necessary. The latter can take the form of a divine nature dictating what and how God can choose, or of abstract objects, universals, or forms existing eternally alongside of God.[59]

Questions of causal and logical priority in creatures result from the contingent and dependent nature of creatures. We can ask about what constitutes a being in the act of existence, what follows from the being in existence, whether beings act because of their essences or in part generate their essences by their acts of existing, all because of their finite, composite, and contingent natures. These dilemmas discussed in relation to God are obviated for classical theism in light of the doctrines of God as *actus purus,* divine simplicity, and God's atemporality.

Various classical theists claim God is neither complex nor composed of parts, God is not material, God's essence is the act of existence, God is infinite, and God is not limited to created time but is eternal. For these reasons they also affirm that God is *actus purus:* God is the pure Act of Being, with no admixture of potency, potentiality, or non-being.[60] God's

58. The immediate discussion is informed by, and highly indebted to, Hugh J. McCann, "Divine Power and Action," in *The Blackwell Guide to Philosophy of Religion,* ed. William E. Mann (Oxford: Basil Blackwell, 2004), 20–47, and W. E. Mann, "Divine Simplicity," *Religious Studies* 18 (1982): 451–71.

59. See Alvin C. Plantinga, *Does God Have a Nature?* (Milwaukee: Marquette University Press, 1980). Plantinga's answer bears a suspicious resemblance to a pure Platonism, replete with the horde of "Ideas" or "Forms."

60. St. Thomas Aquinas, *ST* 1a.8.1, 1a.20.1; *Summa contra gentiles* 1.16 1–7, 1.17.7, 1.43.6; Francis Turretin, *Institutes of Elenctic Theology,* trans. George Musgrave Giger, ed. James

nature involves no unrealized potency or potentiality, but is fully realized in God's act of existence. God just is what God does, and this "doing" is not temporal or logical, which would involve some movement, becoming, and transition from potency to act. We cannot conceive of this because all creatures are admixtures of potency and act, move from potency to act, come into being, and perish. Yet classical theists affirm this of God even though it is beyond our ken.

God as *actus purus* is of a piece with the classical theistic doctrine of divine simplicity. Simplicity denies any type of composition or parts in God, since that would imply something antecedent and more fundamentally real than God.[61] Becoming involves a plurality of parts or causes in potency coming together to the emergence of the unitary entity in its act of existence or actuality. Thus St. Thomas argues that there is no composition in God because there is no potentiality in God.[62] While created intellects can conceive of God's perfections only as diverse, different, and disparate, they are ultimately all identical in God. Classical theology speaks of God's aseity, eternality, infinity, immutability, impassibility, omnipotence, omniscience, omnipresence, omnibenevolence, love, righteousness, holiness, justice, mercy, and so on. At the same time classical theists affirm that in God all of these are really one and identical, and that distinctions between the attributes are only notional, in our intellects. Because God is always incomprehensible to finite intellects, the concept of divine simplicity is beyond our intellectual grasp. Classical theists nevertheless affirm it, always knowing that we can never fully understand this mystery.

Inextricably bound to God as *actus purus* and divine simplicity in classical theism is the claim that God transcends time as its Creator. Time is a created effect, so God is neither "inside" time nor subject to temporality, and all discrete moments of time in creation are simultaneously present to God in eternity.[63] God's "activity" transcends time but our crea-

T. Dennison Jr., vol. 1, *First through Tenth Topics* (Leiden: Batavor, 1696; Phillipsburg, N.J.: Presbyterian & Reformed, 1992), 1.3.7, pp. 191–92; and Tillich, *Systematic Theology,* 1:203, 280.

61. St. Thomas Aquinas, *ST* 1a.3.1–8; Turretin, *Institutes of Elenctic Theology,* 1.3.7, pp. 191–94, 1.3.11, pp. 204–6; Schleiermacher, *The Christian Faith,* 1, §51, 1, p. 201; 1, §53, 2, p. 206; 1, §54, 4, p. 218; 1, §56, 1, pp. 229–31; Berkhof, *Systematic Theology,* 62–63.

62. St. Thomas Aquinas, *Summa contra gentiles,* 1.18.2.

63. St. Augustine, *Confessions,* trans. Henry Chadwick (New York: Oxford University

turely experiences of the results of God's activity are temporally indexed according to the mode of existence of creation in time.[64]

The fact that God is pure act, utterly simple, and atemporal means that in God there is no composition, neither in essence and existence, nor in potency and act, nor in substance and attribute. Not only is there no real distinction between substance and accidental attributes in God, there is not even a real distinction between God's substantial attributes and the divine substance. This, along with the fact that God transcends time, means God does not exist substantially prior to God's actions, as do creatures. God is substantially identical with the action in which God's attributes are manifested. Since God is simple, eternal, *actus purus,* God has no nature, goodness, or desires determining God's actions, as creatures do: God just is what God does.[65]

For classical theism, then, debates over whether God wills and acts because of what God is, or whether God is what God is because of what God wills and acts are wrongheaded; they cannot apply to God. The problem we have with God's aseity comes from our projecting the ontological structure of created, finite, categorical beings onto God. It makes no sense to speak of an entity conferring existence on itself, because this assumes the entity has some sort of existence before it confers existence on itself. Though this objection holds for temporal created categorical beings, and as such raises interesting questions from another quarter about the world's ability to account for itself, it does not hold for the God of classical theism. While God wills and is the sole source of God's existence, God does not "bring God's self into existence" in any way conceivable to us. God transcends time, so there is no temporal or logical mo-

Press, 1992), 11.1.1, p. 221, 11.4.6–11.8.10, pp. 224–27; St. Thomas Aquinas, *ST,* 1a.14.13; *Summa contra gentiles* 1.66.7; Calvin, *Institutes of the Christian Religion,* 1.13.18, pp. 142–43; Turretin, *Institutes of Elenctic Theology,* 1.3.10, pp. 202–4; Schleiermacher, *The Christian Faith,* 1, §52, 1–2, pp. 203–6; Charles Hodge, *Systematic Theology,* 3 vols. (New York: Scribner's, 1871–73; reprint, Grand Rapids, Mich.: Eerdmans, 1997), 1:385–90; Berkhof, *Systematic Theology,* 69; John H. Wright, "Divine Knowledge and Human Freedom: The God Who Dialogues," *Theological Studies* 38, no. 3 (1977): 474–77.

64. Kvanvig and McCann, "Divine Conservation and the Persistence of the World," 23, 46. Kvanvig and McCann also argue that God's creation of the world did not take place "in time," and took "no time," because the transition from nothing to something did not involve a change in anything, as nothing existed yet (ibid., 19–20).

65. McCann, "Divine Power and Action," 16, 18–19, 31.

ment prior to God's act of existence whereby God wills God's existence.[66] Another way of saying this is that finite beings are composed of parts, two of which are their essence and the Act of Being, but since God is absolutely simple, God's existence cannot be a logically or temporally prior part of God, which means that God's essence must be God's existence.[67]

The question of whether God's willing is determined by God's nature or some other antecedent ontological structures, or whether God is so entirely free that God determines those structures, does not apply to God for classical theism. God as timeless, simple, *actus purus* means that there is neither a moment prior to which God wills so that God's essence or nature determines God's deciding, nor is there a moment subsequent to God's willing which results in God's essence or nature as the consequence of God's act of willing. As *actus purus,* God has no antecedent nature, goodness, or desires determining God's actions, as creatures do, but just is what God does. Nor does God's act of will contribute to or determine God's nature consequently.[68] God freely and without any cause wills his own being, essence, and goodness,[69] but does so necessarily, not with the "non-necessity" with which he wills all other things.[70] Thus Paul Tillich speaks of the ontological elements of "freedom and destiny," split in finite

66. McCann says that "necessary being is more difficult, for while there is plenty of reason for thinking God has this trait, we do not really understand it. This much, however, can be said: to tie God's necessary existence to an eternal act of will with which he is in fact identical would not involve our saying that God confers existence on himself, in the sense of bringing himself into existence. That would not be possible for a timeless God" (ibid., 32).

67. St. Thomas Aquinas, *Summa contra gentiles* 1.22.8.

68. "The import of that claim [i.e., God is *actus purus*] is that there is no potentiality in God, that the attributes he exemplifies do not consist in dispositions to behave in various ways, but instead are fully realized in what he is and does" (McCann, "Divine Power and Action," 28). See also ibid., 16, 18–19, 26–28.

69. St. Thomas Aquinas, *Summa contra gentiles* 1.73.1–5, 1.80.1–6; *ST* 1a.19.3, 1a.19.5, 1a.19.10; Barth, *Church Dogmatics,* 1.1 §12, p. 434.

70. St. Thomas Aquinas, *Summa contra gentiles* 1.81.1–7; *ST* 1a.19.4. Regarding all things other than God's self, since the divine will is eternal and immutable, a mode of necessity, which Thomas calls "necessity of supposition," obtains regarding all that God wills other than God's self. Due to God's sovereign freedom. which is moved by no other cause, God's willing of all things other than God is not "absolutely necessary" (St. Thomas Aquinas, *Summa contra gentiles* 1.83.1–5). That God "cannot will the impossible" is taken with respect to what God has willed by the necessity of supposition, not with respect to absolute necessity considered "prior" to what he freely chooses to will, and which therefore becomes necessary by supposition (ibid., 1.84.1–2).

existence, but identical in God.[71] In a way utterly incomprehensible to us, in transcendent sovereign freedom God even wills God's act of willing.[72] If God is truly God, then there can be no forms, universals, or abstract objects "outside" of God by which God is defined and which are part of God's "nature."

Further, if the venerable Aristotelian axiom that "actuality precedes possibility" is true, then there are no possibilities "before" God acts, because possibilities suppose beings but there are none, and also because there is no "before" for God. Modality, possibility, and temporality are all God's effects, not contexts in which God operates in God's knowing, acting, and willing.[73] Questions about whether there are any things to which or by which God is bound in God's acting and creating, or whether everything is possible as in Cartesian universal possibilism and forms of nominalism, can arise only by assuming that God is subject to some sort of temporal succession as God moves from multiple possibilities to choosing and effecting the one thing God decides to actualize. In creating, God does not choose between various pre-defined possibilities, even an infinite number of possibilities.[74] In creating, God simultaneously creates the possibilities; they appear only with God's act of creation, not temporally or logically prior to it.

From another perspective, since God is the first cause of everything

71. "God is called 'free,' but he is free not in arbitrariness but in an absolute and unconditional identity with his destiny, so that he himself is his destiny, so that the essential structures of being are not strange to his freedom but are the actuality of his freedom. In this way, although the symbols used for the divine life are taken from the concrete situation of man's relationship to God, they imply God's ultimacy, the ultimacy in which the polarities of being disappear in the ground of being, in being-itself" (Tillich, *Systematic Theology*, 1:244). See also ibid., 1:248–49.

72. "For His will wills itself and other things by one and the same act" (St. Thomas Aquinas, *Summa contra gentiles* 1.82.9). See also McCann, "Divine Power and Action," 31–32.

73. St. Thomas explains this with reference to how there is no potency in the divine will: "Mutability, similarly, is not required. For, if there is no potentiality in the divine will, God does not thus prefer one of the opposites among His effects as if He should be thought as being in potency to both, so that He first wills both in potency and afterward He wills in act; rather, He wills in act whatever He wills, not only in relation to Himself but also in relation to His effects" (St. Thomas Aquinas, *Summa contra gentiles* 1.82.7).

74. McCann calls this ill-advised approach the "deliberational model" of God's willing and freedom in creation (McCann, "Divine Power and Action," 14–17, 22–26, 29). If true, this has enormous implications for discussions of possible worlds and the problem of evil in modern and contemporary philosophy.

by providing all things with the Act of Being *(esse)* directly and without intermediate causes, there is nothing, not even intermediate possibilities, between God and what God creates directly. God requires no causal means to bring about anything, as do creaturely causes, because God's causation is direct and unmediated. Any mediated causes would themselves require the Act of Being *(esse),* which God alone can provide. So God directly creates everything other than God, including alternative possibilities.[75]

For our part, we can conceive of and predicate to God's knowing, acting, and willing only from what we know of God's effects. This means we can think and speak of God's one, eternal, simple Act of Being only in terms of temporal succession, mediate causation, potency and alternative possibilities, and all other ontological structures of finite created existence. As we do so, we must realize this is not how "it really is" for God. We must ultimately acknowledge that it is wrongheaded to ask questions about whether God "could have" or "could not have" willed God's self to be, or to act, a certain way. Likewise, discussion of "possible worlds" God could have or could not have created with respect to God's existence and action is also misguided.

Another dialectical polarity associated with the problem of the one and the many and the problem of mutual ultimate causality is that between abstract impersonality and particular personhood. This is itself a variation on the tension between universality and particularity, and arises in discussions of theology proper. Surveys of classical theism and the various metaphysical ultimates in systems of Western philosophy frequently lead to the criticism that the "God of the philosophers" is an impersonal abstraction devoid of personhood. What concrete content is there in an infinite, eternal, immutable Act of Being?

A common-sense analysis of proportionate being and epistemologies resulting from such analysis often reveal an inverse and mutually exclusive relationship between universality and particularity. Going up the ladder of abstraction removes the particularities unique to any given existent. Similarities obtained by abstracting universals are at the expense

75. Philosophically, God's causality upon creatures as direct and unmediated is the only way of avoiding an infinite regress in attempts to explain causality (Kvanvig and McCann, "Divine Conservation and the Persistence of the World," 47–48, n. 26; Hugh J. McCann, "The Author of Sin?" unpublished manuscript, 3–4).

of differences and particularities. The highest abstraction for finite categorical beings is sometimes said to be "being" itself. Here all differences disappear and all things are subsumed under this all-encompassing, abstract category. The pure unity of being without variety or difference of any kind seems valueless. This is such that some remark with Hegel that abstract being itself, because it tells us nothing definite, is virtually indistinguishable from non-being.[76]

The God of classical theism is not an impersonal abstraction devoid of personhood, however. Quoting Justin Martyr, Étienne Gilson notes that in addition to being "*That* which is," the God of Moses and of biblical faith is "*He* who is," and that while the former does not necessarily include the latter, the latter includes the former, and much more.[77] As with other pairs of concepts juxtaposed and mutually exclusive from the observation of categorical reality, the ideas of absolute and person seemingly cannot be identical in any meaningful way for us. The God of classical Christian theism, though, is reputedly both absolute and personal. "He who is" is not a principle or abstract concept. Philosophically speaking, God is the concrete universal that we can never comprehend or adequately speak of.[78]

Rahner explains how God is not impersonal despite all of the problems we might have in ascribing personhood to God. Creaturely personhood cannot be derived from something impersonal, because the impersonal only gives rise to the impersonal, while only the personal gives rise to the personal. God's personhood must be analogous to, yet completely transcendent to, human personhood. God cannot be conceived as a human, or even as an angelic person, no matter how great. So the statement "God is a person" must be left open to the "ineffable darkness of mystery." Christian faith must confess God as the "Absolute Person," who stands in absolute freedom in relation to everything else, including human persons.[79]

76. Hartshorne, *Man's Vision of God*, 212–13.

77. Gilson, *God and Philosophy*, 42, quoting Justin Martyr, *Hortatory Address to the Greeks*, chapter 22. See also Hodge, *Systematic Theology*, 1:391–93.

78. Paul Tillich indicates that in subsuming God under the subject-object scheme runs into various absurdities in our interpretation of God, although the subject-object structure of finite beings is itself grounded in the divine life (Tillich, *Systematic Theology*, 1:278–79).

79. Rahner, *Foundations of Christian Faith*, 74–75.

Important in regard to God as both absolute and personal is the doctrine of the Trinity. Tillich presented the doctrine of the Trinity as the balance between the concrete personalism toward which man strives in his ultimate concern, and the absolute element toward which man strives in that same concern.[80] He notes how trinitarian faith has nothing to do with what he calls the "trick question" of how one can be three and three be one. The doctrine of the Trinity is not a quantitative, but rather a qualitative claim about God. It is an attempt to affirm that in God, the living God no less, "the ultimate and the concrete are united"; it is about the "unity between ultimacy and concreteness in the living God."[81]

Saying both "God is Absolute" and "God is Person" is not a heretical view of the Trinity in the form of a reversion to Modalistic Monarchianism (Sabellianism). Insofar as the one divine will and the one divine intellect are identical with the divine essence, and intellect and will are personal properties, it can be said that God is substantially personal.[82] As the rational nature signified by the word "person" is a creaturely perfection and God's essence contains every perfection, it is fitting to apply, by way of eminence, the word "person" to God.[83] In defending the claim that "person" signifies relation in God, St. Thomas does say a subsistent relation or hypostasis in God is identical with the divine nature itself. Thus he allows "person" to signify the divine essence indirectly when expressed by way of hypostasis, and he even says that "person" signifies the divine essence directly insofar as the essence is the same as the hypostasis.[84] Replying to the objection that because we say there are "three persons" in God, where "person" signifies a being subsisting in intellectual nature, we must then also say that there are "three Gods," St. Thomas says that what is meant by the word "person" when we say " three persons" is the adjective "personality" or personal property, not essence or na-

80. Tillich, *Systematic Theology,* 1:221, 1:228.

81. Ibid., 1:228.

82. St. Thomas says God's intellect or act of understanding is God's substance and so one, not multiple (*ST* 1a.14.4.). The divine will, which follows the divine intellect, is also identical with the one divine act of existence (ibid., 1a.19.1.).

83. St. Thomas Aquinas, *ST* 1a.29.3.

84. Ibid., 1a.29.4. He also says Boethius's definition of a "person" as "an individual substance of a rational nature" does not contradict "person" signifying relation in God, because God with respect to his one individual, incommunicable substance includes the idea of relation (ibid., 1a.29.4.).

ture. He bases this on his distinction that what is predicated of God substantively *(substantive)* must be predicated of the persons in the singular, while what is predicated of God adjectivally *(adiective)* must be predicated of the three persons in the plural.[85]

Although there is a valid social analogy for the Trinity compatible with tradition, certain contemporary social trinitarians predicate the personal properties of intellect and will to the three divine persons both plurally and substantially, as if in God there were three different "subjectivities" in the modern sense of the word "person." Some social trinitarians even accuse Barth and Rahner of Sabellianism, claiming their doctrines of God are inimical to trinitarian faith. This is because they thought it wise to avoid denoting as "persons" what they call the three "modes of being" or "subsistences" in God because of the connotations of the modern word "person," and because they deny that the doctrine of the Trinity means that there are three distinct "personalities" or "subjectivities" in God.[86]

I cannot defend this here, but the tortured history of the use of the word "person" in Western trinitarian theology seems to reveal that the intention of orthodoxy was never to claim that there are three distinct substantial (nominative, not adjectival) "centers of consciousness" or "subjectivities" in God. In its Occidental presentations and arguably even in its Oriental presentations, the doctrine of the Trinity intends to affirm non-identical relations of opposition in God, which are each identical with the divine substance but not separate subjectivities in God.[87]

85. St. Thomas Aquinas, *ST* 1a.39.3.

86. See, for instance, Jürgen Moltmann, *The Trinity and the Kingdom: The Doctrine of God,* trans. Margaret Kohl (Minneapolis: Fortress Press, 1993), 145; Catherine Mowry LaCugna, *God for Us: The Trinity and the Christian Life* (San Francisco: HarperCollins, 1991), 253–54; Joseph A. Bracken, *What Are They Saying about the Trinity?* (New York: Paulist Press, 1979), 12–13; Bracken, *Christianity and Process Thought: Spirituality for a Changing World* (Philadelphia: Templeton Foundation Press, 2006), 69; and Bracken, "The Holy Trinity as a Community of Divine Persons, Part II," *Heythrop Journal* 15 (1974): 258, 260. Even those not affiliated with the trend toward social trinitarianism have made similar criticisms regarding Rahner's suggested substitution of "persons" with "distinct modes of subsistence." See Walter Kasper, *The God of Jesus Christ,* trans. Matthew J. O'Connell (New York: Crossroad, 1984), 288; Engelbert Gutwenger, S.J., "Zur Trinitätslehre von Mysterium Salutis II," in *ZKTh* 90 (1968): 328; and William J. Hill, *The Three-Personed God: The Trinity as a Mystery of Salvation* (Washington, D.C.: The Catholic University of America Press, 1982), 144–45, 179, 215, 254–55.

87. See Marc A. Pugliese, "Is Karl Rahner a Modalist?" *Irish Theological Quarterly* 68 (Fall 2003): 229–49.

Some social trinitarians seem to say that there are three substantial centers of consciousness, intellects, and will in God. While by definition a person possesses self-consciousness, a person is not identical with self-consciousness, and each of the divine persons possesses the one infinite self-consciousness of God. Indeed the Western tradition has associated the procession of the *Logos* in the Trinity with the moment of divine self-knowledge, and the procession of the Holy Spirit with the moment of willing, predicated to God as one divine subject.[88]

This identity of absoluteness and personality leads to the examination of how a final dialectical tension seen in the categorical realm of creation does not obtain in the transcendent Creator God. Although the doctrine of the Trinity was not originally intended to be a resolution of the problem of the one and the many, some contemporary theologians see the Trinity as a locus from which to address the problem of the one and the many. With respect to historical theology, the doctrine of the Trinity developed out of the early Church's attempt to reconcile its self-understanding as heir to Hebrew monotheism with the experience of God's salvation in the historic person Jesus of Nazareth, and in the ongoing work of the Holy Spirit. Though second temple Jewish developments, like the *Logos* theology of Alexandrian Judaism and Johannnine theology in the New Testament, prepared the way for understanding and formulating the doctrine of the Trinity, the doctrine's emergence was arguably eminently practical.

With these caveats, some Christian theologians wrestling with the problem of the one and the many have found a ready resource in the doctrine of the Trinity. Associating the divine substance with universality and the three persons with particularity, David S. Cunningham claims the mystery of the Trinity "reconciles oneness and difference."[89] Colin Gunton speaks of the Trinity as "preserving in dynamic interrelation" and giving "due weight to both one and many, to both particular and universal, to both otherness and relation," and he proposes adding "*perichoretic* relation" to the traditional transcendental predicates of be-

88. St. Augustine's psychological model for the Trinity is well known, articulated in *De trinitate,* but adumbrated in the *Confessions.* See, St. Augustine, *Confessions* 13.11.12. It is often forgotten, however, that in both places he stresses the inadequacy of this analogy, focusing on the radical transcendence of the mystery of the Trinity.

89. David S. Cunningham, *These Three Are One: The Practice of Trinitarian Theology* (Oxford: Blackwell Publishers, 1998), 9, 69, 158, 197.

ing of unity, truth, and goodness.[90] Others interpret the Trinity as resolving the problem of the one and the many because it claims that each of the persons is really identical with the divine essence, so that in God the many are identical with the one in ways that can never obtain in non-divine reality.[91] Bracken himself, of course, offers one of the most sophisticated presentations of how the doctrine of the Trinity bears on the problem of the one and the many.

In closing I would like to offer my own reflections on how the doctrine of the Trinity might speak to discussions of the problem of the one and the many in ways consonant with the rest of my argument. I have suggested that the problem of the one and the many and the concomitant problem of mutual ultimate causality arise from collapsing metaphysics into cosmogony, and developing the metaphysics of ultimate reality without an adequate account of the Creator-creature distinction. Just as God's essence and existence are identical, God's being and doing are identical, God's nature and willing are identical, and God is at once a person and an absolute. None of these can be said properly and literally of creatures. So, too, the doctrine of the Trinity identifies in God what is disparate in finite categorical, creaturely reality.

A central element of the mystery of the Trinity, which dogma affirms but which we cannot comprehend, is that in God each of the three relations that are the divine persons is really identical with the divine essence but is also really distinct from the other relations.[92] Any distinction we might

90. Colin E. Gunton, *The One, the Three and the Many: God, Creation and the Culture of Modernity* (Cambridge: Cambridge University Press, 1993), 6–7; ibid., 13, 36, 140–41, 149–59, 163–66, 190–91, 200, 212. After citing Gregory of Nazianzus—"No sooner do I conceive of the one than I am illumined by the splendour of the Three; no sooner do I distinguish them than I am carried back to the one" (Gregory of Nazianzus, *Oration* 40.41)—Gunton says, "The interesting point about Gregory is that that is precisely what we find: a dynamic dialectic between the oneness and the threeness of God of such a kind that the two are given equal weight in the processes of thought. Thinking about God denies his mind rest in either unity or plurality, Parmenides or Heraclitus" (Gunton, *The One, the Three and the Many,* 149–50).

91. Cornelius Van Til, *A Survey of Christian Epistemology* (Philadelphia: Presbyterian & Reformed, 1969), 219; Van Til, *An Introduction to Systematic Theology* (Philadelphia: Presbyterian & Reformed, 1974), 23; Van Til, *Common Grace and the Gospel* (Philadelphia: Presbyterian & Reformed, 1972), 7–8, 64; Van Til, *Psychology of Religion* (Philadelphia: Presbyterian & Reformed, 1961), 49ff.; Van Til, *Defense of the Faith,* 41.

92. St. Thomas Aquinas, *ST* 1a.28.2–3; Calvin, *Institutes of the Christian Religion,* 1.13.19–20, pp. 143–45, 1.13.25, pp. 153–54; Turretin, *Institutes of Elenctic Theology,* 1.3.27, p. 278.

make between the essence and the persons is only notional, not real, but at the same time in God there are real distinctions between the real relations of opposition.[93] Further, the relations in God are not merely accidental determinations of the one divine substance, but are subsistent relations.

This leads to the seeming impossibility that the three relations that subsist are identical with the same thing, the divine substance, but not identical with one another. It is true that the divine relations are, by definition, neither absolute nor entities.[94] Therefore, the dogma *does not claim* that three absolute entities are each identical with another absolute entity but are not identical with each other. Yet, that the relations are not accidents but are real and subsistent with the reality and subsistence of the divine essence lands our finite intellects in the same realm of inscrutability.

Another facet of this same mystery is, as Fortman observes, that while each person is really identical with the divine essence, each person is involved in active or passive generation and/or active or passive spiration, but the divine essence is not.[95] The mutually opposed relations constituting the persons are unique to each of the persons, and not predicated of the divine substance. The Father alone possesses paternity in relative opposition to the Son, who alone possesses filiation, and the Father and the Son together possess active spiration in relative opposition to the Holy Spirit, who alone possesses procession or passive spiration. None of these mutually opposed relations, however, can be predicated to the absolute divine essence. Still, the divine substance and each of the relations are really identical, and only notionally distinct. Being identical with the divine substance, the persons are absolutely simple, transcending the category of composition. Thus the divine paternity, filiation, spiration, and procession are not attributes that could obtain in a finite created being. We can think about and name these notions only according to the mode of our intellects, which we know only through created things, and our intellects cannot apprehend the divine simplicity.[96]

93. St. Thomas Aquinas, *ST,* 1a.28.2–3.

94. By "entity" here I mean a substantial, determinate being (derived from the Latin "*ens*" so that there are not three "*entes*" in God). As St. Thomas points out, when speaking of the relations in God we can use the word *res* ("thing") in the plural, but when speaking of God's absolute substance we use the word *res* in the singular (ibid., 1a.39.3.3).

95. Edmund J. Fortman, *The Triune God: A Historical Study of the Doctrine of the Trinity* (Grand Rapids, Mich.: Baker, 1972), 200.

96. St. Thomas Aquinas, *ST* 1a.32.2. In addition to the four relations of paternity, filia-

In these ways we affirm what we cannot conceive: the three divine persons are really identical with the divine essence but really distinct from one another. The distinction between absolute and relative subsistence notwithstanding, because the relations are real and subsistent we still affirm that three subsistent relations are identical with the same reality of the divine essence, but are not identical with each other. This, and not some apparent numerical impossibility, where "one is three and is one" at the same time, is at the heart of the mystery of the Trinity.[97]

Only in the infinitely transcendent, incomprehensible God can we say, without full understanding, that what we know and speak of as the one and the many from finite categorical created reality are truly identical in ways that can never be so in creation. In a way, the doctrine of the Trinity does say that in God the many are the one and the one is the many.[98] Admitting all the while the inadequacy of our words and concepts, the classical doctrine of the Trinity, predicated on the theology of classical theism, affirms the identity of the one and the many in a way that limiting metaphysics to the realm of categorical ontology cannot. I propose, then, that only by giving up the Whiteheadian restriction of God to the metaphysical principles of categorical reality, and by letting God truly be God, does it seem that we can truly find in God, according to our own finite mode of understanding, "the mutual implication of the one in the many and the many in the one."

---

tion, spiration, and procession, St. Thomas adds the Father's inascibility to the notions, but notes that this is not a relation of opposition (ibid., 1a.33.3).

97. Barth, *Church Dogmatics,* §9 1.1, pp. 367–68. Here Barth gives a litany of "great problems besetting the doctrine of the Trinity," one of which is "How can three such relations be the essence and yet not be the same as each other, but indissolubly distinct from one another?" (ibid.). He says one of the "great problems" involved in the doctrine of the Trinity is "how can 3 really be 1, and 1 really be 3?" and also states something that the dogma denies when he asks: "How can an essence produce itself and then in a 2-fold way be its own product?" (ibid.). The Fourth Lateran Council (A.D. 1215) expressly denied that the divine essence generates, or is generated, or proceeds, instead saying that only the divine persons are involved in generation, being generated, and processions.

98. The Fourth Lateran Council also denied that God is a quaternity, saying that the one supreme, incomprehensible, and ineffable reality is "Father, Son, and Holy Spirit," "at the same time the three persons taken together and singly." The "One is the many" in that the one divine essence is not some fourth, overarching abstraction unifying the three, but subsists in and only in the three. See also Calvin, *Institutes of the Christian Religion,* 1.13.19, pp. 143–44; 1.13.25, pp. 154–55; and Berkhof, *Systematic Theology,* 88.

CHAPTER 5

Conclusion

Thorough treatment of the genesis and features of process metaphysics is necessary to understand its meaning and significance, the challenges it poses, and its widespread influence, even among those who are not process thinkers. Like the classical Western metaphysics to which it responds, process metaphysics is frequently misunderstood, marginalized, and even summarily dismissed. This book aims at understanding and informed analysis.

Process thought appeared as a reconstruction of the perennial task of systematically addressing the ever-present ultimate limit questions of the great philosophical and religious traditions, but in a way that seriously reckons with the significant theoretical and practical developments of the modern period. Modernity secularized philosophy and emancipated it from long-standing authoritative traditions. The turn to the subject prioritized epistemology over ontology, with enormous implications for philosophical and theological method. The success of the scientific method, coupled with a supreme confidence in reason for answering all of humanity's questions, similarly had enormous consequences for philosophy and theology. Not the least of these was questioning the entire metaphysical project. A new humanism elevated the importance of human existence and activity to heights unseen for over a millennium. Globalization, which began with the age of exploration and has brought a world full of diversity much closer together, brought a hitherto unseen sense of plurality and radical alterity in the midst of interdependent relationships. The nineteenth century's turn to history, which particularized and relativized much that was previously seen as eternal, universal, and absolute, had a monumental impact on philosophy and theology. The paradox of how the largest strides in human knowledge and manipulation of the world in history could also result in the grossest, most horrendous atrocities of history introduced yet another important factor into the intellectual milieu of the early twentieth century, especially in the wake of the First World War.

Process metaphysics thus emerged as an attempt to continue the great task of philosophy and religion in serious consideration of all of these modern developments. While on the one hand incorporating with utmost seriousness the developments of the modern period, process thinkers on the other hand demonstrate with puissance that metaphysics is a necessary and unavoidable project, and that the great questions of philosophy and religion demand as much attention as ever. The roots of process metaphysics go back to the *philosophia perennis* of the Western intellectual tradition, but are more proximately found in modern philosophy. They are most immediately found in late-nineteenth- and early-twentieth-century thinkers who were reckoning with all that had transpired theoretically and practically in the several centuries prior. Although many consider Alfred North Whitehead to be the father of process metaphysics, he heavily depended on his immediate philosophical and scientific predecessors, as we have seen.

Process theology developed with Whitehead's disciples, most notably with Charles Hartshorne, as a serious rethinking of Christian theology in the light of the considerations addressed by Whitehead's metaphysics. Process theologians held that modernity could not be ignored, and that philosophy and religion had to be transposed to a modern key to present themselves as plausible and satisfactory to modern man. Theology had to reconcile itself with modern science and modern epistemic canons of rationality that were replacing older authoritative traditions and appeals to mystery. Process theologians judged older Judeo-Christian monotheism as tried in the fires of modernity and found woefully wanting.

Problems with classical theism appeared at many levels, including those of rational consistency, compatibility with modern philosophy, reconciliation with the findings of modern science, and practical relevance in the lives of modern religious persons. For these reasons process theology has influenced a spectrum of theologians who would not identify themselves as process thinkers. These range from those working within classical Magisterial Protestant traditions, like Moltmann and Pannenberg, to conservative evangelicals in the open theism movement.

Process metaphysics has had a more limited impact in Roman Catholic theology. Joseph A. Bracken, S.J., however, develops perhaps the most thoroughgoing, robust, and innovative synthesis of process thought and the Roman Catholic intellectual tradition. Bracken stands out as the Catholic thinker who has produced perhaps the most sophisticated combination of Catholic theology and process theology. He exemplifies in our time the great Catholic tradition of grappling with the best philosophy of a given age while drawing on time-honored Christian philosophical and theological sources. He thus works to understand how long-standing Christian doctrines can be understood in a process-relational metaphysical framework. Few process theologians have developed as careful and consistent a doctrine of the Trinity from a process perspective as has Bracken, which alone commends him to process theologians. With capacious erudition, Bracken incorporates a sweeping array of sources as he undertakes this project, including classical Greek thought, Thomism, modern philosophy, German idealism, Anglo-American idealism, existentialism, philosophy of science, social philosophy, and even postmodern thought.

Intramurally, Bracken argues that his rethinking of some central concepts of Whiteheadian metaphysics solves more adequately certain problems plaguing process thought. These include formulating the most viable panentheistic analogy, constructing a genuinely trinitarian process theology, avoiding postmodern charges of logocentrism, laying a surer foundation for interreligious dialogue, finding the most common ground for the religion-and-science debates, and resolving the problem of the one and the many. For all of these reasons, among contemporary process thinkers Bracken merits special attention.

Beginning with its nineteenth-century antecedents and through its incipience, process metaphysics has addressed itself to the ancient problem of the one and the many, of change and stasis, seeing it as the central problem of metaphysics. Core elements of process thought developed as express responses to the problem of the one and the many, and almost all process thinkers directly engage this problem. Process theologians have found classical theism's privileging of Being over becoming, actuality over potentiality, stasis over change, eternality over temporality, immutability over mutability, impassibility over passibility, absoluteness over relativity, unity over plurality, simplicity over complexity, and objectivity over subjectivity as serious failures to adequately resolve the problem of the one and the many, and as crippling liabilities, especially in our modern and contemporary contexts. Striving for an adequate resolution to the problem of the one and the many is a centerpiece of Bracken's thought.

Hence this book has tried to accomplish several things. I have tried to provide an introduction to the significance, challenges, and implications of process metaphysics for philosophy and theology today. Beginning with its immediate antecedents in the modern period and more specifically the nineteenth century, I have provided an exposition of the genesis of process metaphysics with special attention to Whitehead's process-relational philosophy and the process theology that emerged from it. I have explained features of process metaphysics that developed out of, and in response to, the theoretical and practical developments of the modern period. I gave special attention to perceived problems with Western metaphysics and the forms of classical theism. In doing so I paid particular attention to how, from the first, process metaphysics has represented a modern attempt to engage the inveterate problem of the one and the many.

After describing Whiteheadian process philosophy and theology, I analyzed in detail the important system developed by Joseph A. Bracken, S.J. This system incarnates all of the concerns, challenges, and implications of process metaphysics, not the least of which is assiduous engagement with the problem of the one and the many. Bracken truly epitomizes, on so many counts, the very best of the process-relational project.

I then turned to analyzing process metaphysics in general and Bracken's system in particular from the perspective of classical theism. Classical theism is as often misunderstood and unappreciated as the process metaphysics that responds to it. While many challenges and criticisms can be, and have been, posed to process metaphysics from the perspective of classical theism, my analysis focused on one of process thought's most significant features: the insistence that ultimate reality not be treated as an exception to the metaphysics principles invoked to save them from collapse, but rather as their chief exemplification. This directly bears on what classical theism has construed as the Creator-creature distinction. I try to bring this criticism to bear on the way process metaphysics handles the problem of the one and the many. In doing so I offer my own understanding of the problem of the one and the many from a classical theistic perspective, and propose how classical theism might address this problem.

I argue that the problem of the one and the many in its many particular instantiations arises from collapsing metaphysics into cosmology and denying, either implicitly or explicitly, the essence of the distinction between God and the world as articulated in the various versions of classical theism. I have tried to show that all attempts to make the two terms of any of the dialectical pairs of juxtaposed aspects of categorical reality, or creation in classical theism, ultimate explanatory principles so that each term is either identical with its opposite, or exhaustively accounts for both itself and its opposite, fail in the final analysis. This is because of what I call the "problem of mutual ultimate causality," or the fact that each term in each of these pairs already assumes and implies its opposite.

Another way of expressing this is that all attempts to account for all of reality, including ultimate reality, solely in terms of the metaphysical principles applicable to all that is not God in classical theistic explanations are doomed to fail. As finite, complex, dependent, and lacking self-subsistence, any given part of creation cannot exhaustively account for itself, let alone any other part of creation. In the case of these dialectical pairs associated with the problem of the one and the many, any term of any given pair cannot account for itself, let alone its opposite. I propose that this leads to the inevitable conclusion that it is impossible to avoid the positing of a being qualitatively different from the world in that it possesses self-existence. I also tried to show how process theologians diverge from their axiom that "God is not to be treated as an exception to all metaphysical principles, invoked to save their collapse. He is their chief exemplification."

As diverse thinkers throughout history have concluded, a metaphysical analysis of categorical reality can certainly lead to the conclusion that there must be something "exempt" from the metaphysical principles to which categorical realities are bound precisely in order to provide the condition of the possibility of categorical reality. Intimately bound up with this is the possibility that not only may ultimate reality be utterly different metaphysically from the rest of reality, but that it may also be incomprehsible to finite intellects, contra the demands for ultimate reality's exhaustive rational apprehension in much modern philosophy and theology. These have been the constant contentions of classical theism.

What I call the problem of mutual ultimate causality thus is a function of how these aspects of categorical reality are creatures, which for classical theism means among other things that they possess neither aseity nor simplicity in the way that God as ultimate reality does. I have urged that a central distinction between ultimate reality or God and the rest of reality or creation is how God does not have the existential split between essence and existence characteristic of created entities. This existential split is the primordial example of how none of the terms in the dialectical pairs observed in categorical reality or creation can ever exhaustively account for themselves or their opposites without falling into the problem of mutual ultimate causality.

I ended my analysis by showing how, based on the differences in metaphysical principles applicable to categorical reality/creatures and to ultimate reality/God, classical theism avoids the problem of mutual ultimate causality with respect to ultimate reality. With the identity of God's essence and existence as the paradigmatic example of the identity of the terms of the various dialectical pairs, I tried to explain how classical theism affirms the real identity, in terms of the logical principle of identity, of some of these pairs in God.

Now, although there are many possible critiques of process metaphysics from a classical theistic perspective, and despite my own critique, process metaphysics deserves the careful attention of all theologians and philosophers today. Process thought is one of the most sophisticated responses to the many developments of the modern period, has immediate relevance and specific contributions to all contemporary theological and philosophical projects, and offers incisive challenges that all working in theology and philosophy must address. Process thought may be one of the best attempts at a metaphysics of categorical reality in light of the theoretical and practical developments of the modern period.

It is my hope that this work has brought to the fore the meaning, significance, implications, and challenges of process metaphysics for the ongoing work of philosophy and theology in our day.

Bibliography

Works of Joseph A. Bracken, S.J.

A Theory of Property according to John Locke. M.A. thesis, Loyola University, 1960.

Review of *Der Akt-Charakter des Seins, Der: Eine spekulative Weiterfuhrung der Seinslehre Thomas v Aquins,* by Heinrich Beck. *Theological Studies* 27, no. 4 (1966): 716–17.

Freiheit: Wesen und Wirklichkeit: Eine Interpretation der Freiheitsschrift und anderer Werke von F. W. J. Schelling im Lichte eines bestimmten Denkmodells. Ph.D. diss., Albert-Ludwigs-Universitat zu Freiburg i. Br., 1967.

Review of *Begriff und Systematik der Abstraktion,* by Erhard Oeser. *Theological Studies* 31 (December 1970): 776–78.

Review of *Menschwerdung Gottes,* by Hans Küng. *Theological Studies* 31 (December 1970): 767–69.

"Toward a Grammar of Dissent." *Theological Studies* 31 (September 1970): 437–59.

Review of *Auf dem Weg zu einem neuen Gottesverständnis: Die Gotteslehre des J B Hirscher als Antwort auf das säkularisierte Denken der Aufklärungszeit,* by Karl Frielingsdorf. *Theological Studies* 32 (December 1971): 7.

Review of *The Future of Philosophical Theology,* ed. Robert A. Evans. *Theological Studies* 32 (December 1971): 742–43.

"Alienation and Reconciliation in the Judaeo-Christian Experience." In *Alienation,* edited by William Christian Bier, 3–9. Bronx, N.Y.: Fordham University Press, 1972.

Freiheit und Kausalität bei Schelling. Symposion; philosophische Schriftenreihe, 38. Freiburg i. Br.: K. Alber, 1972.

Review of *The Church in an Age of Revolution, 1789 to the Present Day,* by Alexander Roper Vidler. *Theological Studies* 33 (June 1972): 387.

Review of *Glaubenseinheit und Lehrentwicklung bei Johann Adam Möhler,* by Hans Geisser. *Theological Studies* 34 (March 1973): 165–67.

Review of *Protestant Thought in the Nineteenth Century, Volume 1: 1799–1870,* by Claude Welch. *Theological Studies* 34 (June 1973): 328–30.

"The Holy Trinity as a Community of Divine Persons." *Heythrop Journal* 15 (1974): 166–82, 257–70.

Review of *David Friedrich Strauss and His Theology,* by Horton Harris. *Theological Studies* 35 (December 1974): 761–62.

"Freedom and Causality in the Philosophy of Schelling." *New Scholasticism* 50 (Spring 1976): 164–82.

"Salvation: A Matter of Personal Choice." *Theological Studies* 37 (September 1976): 410–24.

"Schelling's Positive Philosophy." *Journal of the History of Philosophy* 15 (July 1977): 324–30.

"Process Philosophy and Trinitarian Theology." *Process Studies* 8 (Winter 1978): 217– 30.

"Trinity and World Process." In *Proceedings of the Catholic Theological Society of America,* 203–28. New York: Catholic Theological Society of America, 1979.

What Are They Saying about the Trinity? New York: Paulist Press, 1979.

"Process Philosophy and Trinitarian Theology—II." *Process Studies* 11 (Summer 1981): 83–96.

"Ecclesiology and the Problem of the One and the Many." *Theological Studies* 43 (June 1982): 298–311.

"Philosophical Foundations of Human Rights: A Process Approach." *Cogito* 1, no. 1 (March 1983): 51–73.

Review of *Hegel's Concept of God,* by Quentin Lauer. *Theological Studies* 44 (June 1983): 331–32.

"Authentic Subjectivity and Genuine Objectivity." *Horizons* 11 (Fall 1984): 290–303.

"Essential and Existential Truth." *Philosophy Today* 23 (Spring 1984): 66–76.

"An Example of Western Theology Taking Modernity Seriously: 'Process Theology.'" In *Different Theologies, Common Responsibility: Babel or Pentecost?* edited by Clause Geffré, Gustavo Gutiérrez, and Virgil Elizondo, 40–45. Concilium 171. Edinburgh: T & T Clark, 1984.

"Subsistent Relation: Mediating Concept for a New Synthesis?" *Journal of Religion* 64 (April 1984): 188–204.

"The Trinity as Interpersonal Process." *Ecumenical Trends* 13, no. 7 (July–August 1984): 97–99.

"Faith and Justice: A New Synthesis—The Interface of Process and Liberation Theologies." *Process Studies* 14 (Summer 1985): 73–75. (Originally delivered at a conference at Xavier University, Cincinnati, October 1983.)

Review of *Bibliotheca Trinitariorum, V 1. Theological Studies* 46 (December 1985): 753.

Review of *Evil and Evolution: A Theodicy,* by Richard W. Kropf. *Horizons* 12 (Fall 1985): 399.

Review of *The Holy Spirit,* by Alasdair I. C. Heron. *Horizons* 12 (Spring 1985): 180.

Review of *In Search of Deity: An Essay in Dialectical Theism,* by John Macquarrie. *Theological Studies* 46 (December 1985): 720–21.

Review of *Omnipotence and Other Theological Mistakes,* by Charles Hartshorne. *Horizons* 12 (Spring 1985): 181.

Review of *The Three-Personed God: The Trinity as a Mystery of Salvation,* by William J. Hill. *Journal of Religion* 65 (July 1985): 426–27.

Review of *When a Person Dies: Pastoral Theology in Death Experiences*, by Robert L. Kinast. *Theological Studies* 46 (June 1985): 396.

Editor of a special issue on process theology. *Process Studies* 14 (Summer 1985): 73–141.

"Substance—Society—Natural System: A Creative Rethinking of Whitehead's Cosmology." *International Philosophical Quarterly* 25 (1985): 3–13.

The Triune Symbol. Persons, Process and Community. College Theology Society Studies in Religion 1. Lanham, Md.: University Press of America, 1985.

"The Two Process Theologies: A Reappraisal." *Theological Studies* 46 (1985): 115–28.

"God's Historicity: Trinitarian Perspectives." In *Process Theology and the Christian Doctrine of God*, ed. Santiago Sia, 65–73. Petersham, Mass.: St. Bede's Publications, 1986.

"Process Perspectives and Trinitarian Theology." In *Word and Spirit 8: Process Theology and the Christian Doctrine of God*, edited by Santiago Sia, 51–64. Petersham, Mass.: St. Bede's Publications, 1986.

Religion & Public Life: The Role of Religious Bodies in Shaping Public Policy. Cincinnati, Ohio: Xavier University, 1986.

Review of *Bruno, or On the Natural and the Divine Principle of Things*, by Friedrich von Schelling. *Process Studies* 15, no. 1 (Spring 1986): 70–71.

Review of *Divine Impassibility: An Essay in Philosophical Theology*, by Richard E. Creel. *Theological Studies* 47, no. 4 (December 1986): 707–8.

Review of *Essays in Process Theology*, by Daniel D. Williams. *Theology Today* 42 (January 1986): 561–62.

"Spirit and Society: A Study of Two Concepts." *Process Studies* 15 (Winter 1986): 244–55.

"The Divine *Pleroma*." *Chicago Studies* 26, no.1 (April 1987): 25–36.

Review of *Community: A Trinity of Models*, by Frank G. Kirkpatrick. *Theological Studies* 48, no. 1 (March 1987): 199–201.

Review of *The Logic of Theology*, by Dietrich Ritschl. *Theological Studies* 48 (December 1987): 741–44.

Review of *On Theology*, by Schubert M. Ogden. *Theological Studies* 48 (December 1987): 741–44.

Review of *The Science of Theology*, by Gillian R. Evans. *Theological Studies* 48 (December 1987): 741–44.

Review of *The Unchanging God of Love: A Study of the Teaching of St. Thomas Aquinas on Divine Immutability in View of Certain Contemporary Criticisms of this Doctrine*, by Michael J. Dodds. *Theological Studies* 48, no.2 (June 1987): 356–58.

"Testimony and Intersubjectivity: A Process-oriented Approach to Revelation." *Philosophy and Theology* 2 (Fall 1987): 35 43.

"Cultural Pluralism as a Metaphysical Issue." In *Philosophy and Culture*, vol. 2, edited by Venant Cauchy, 505–9. Montreal: Montmorency, 1988.

Review of *Anselmian Explorations: Essays in Philosophical Theology*, by Thomas V. Morris. *Theological Studies* 49 (June 1988): 382–83.

Review of *Natürliche Theologie: Grundriss philosophischer Gotteserkenntnis,* by Heinrich Beck. *Theological Studies* 49 (March 1988): 201–2.
Review of *The Possibility of an All-Knowing God,* by Jonathan L. Kvanvig. *Theological Studies* 49 (March 1988): 202–3.
Review of *Religion and Radical Empiricism,* by Nancy Frankenberry. *Horizons* 15 (Spring 1988): 203–4.
Review of *Theism, Atheism and the Doctrine of the Trinity: The Trinitarian Theologies of Karl Barth and Jürgen Moltmann,* by W. Waite Willis Jr. *Theological Studies* 49 (September 1988): 549–550.
"Energy Events and Fields." *Process Studies* 18 (Fall 1989): 153–65.
Review of *The End of Evil: Process Eschatology in Historical Context,* by Marjorie Hewitt-Suchocki. *Horizons* 16 (Spring 1989): 198–99.
Review of *The Reality of Time and the Existence of God: The Project of Proving God's Existence,* by David Braine. *Theological Studies* 50 (March 1989): 175–76.
Jesuit Spirituality from a Process Perspective. St. Louis, Mo.: Seminar on Jesuit Spirituality, 1990.
Review of *God and the Processes of Reality: Foundations of a Credible Theism,* by David A. Pailin. *Theological Studies* 51 (June 1990): 354–55.
Review of *The Incarnation of God: An Introduction to Hegel's Theological Thought as Prolegomena to a Future Christology,* by Hans Küng. *Journal of the American Academy of Religion* 58 (Spring 1990): 128–30.
Review of *The Trinitarian Faith: The Evangelical Theology of the Ancient Catholic Church,* by Thomas F. Torrance. *Theological Studies* 51 (September 1990): 522–24.
"The World: Body of God or Field of Cosmic Activity?" In *Charles Hartshorne's Concept of God,* edited by Santiago Sia, 89–102. Dordrecht, Netherlands: Kluwer Academic Publishers, 1990.
"*Ipsum Esse Subsistens:* A Subsistent Being or Subsistent Activity? A Search for URAM in Systematic Theology." *Ultimate Reality and Meaning* 14 (December 1991): 279–92.
Review of *Behind the Masks of God: An Essay toward Comparative Theology,* by Robert C. Neville. *Theological Studies* 52 (September 1991): 598–99.
Review of *Buddhist Emptiness and Christian Trinity: Essays and Explorations,* by Roger Corless and Paul F. Knitter. *Theological Studies* 52 (June 1991): 381–83.
Review of *The Emptying God: A Buddhist-Jewish-Christian Conversation,* ed. John B. Cobb Jr., and Christopher Ives. *Theological Studies* 52 (June 1991): 381–83.
Review of *God's Power Traditional Understandings and Contemporary Challenges,* by Anna Winters-Case. *Horizons* 18 (Fall 1991): 326–27.
Review of *Theology and Dialogue: Essays in Conversation with George Lindbeck,* edited by George A. Lindbeck and Bruce Marshall. *Journal of Ecumenical Studies* 28, no. 3 (Summer 1991): 496–97.
Society and Spirit: A Trinitarian Cosmology. London: Associated University Press; Selinsgrove, Pa.: Susquehanna University Press, 1991.

"The Issue of Panentheism in the Dialogue with the Non-believer." *Studies in Religion/Sciences-religieuses* 21, no. 2 (1992): 207–18.
"Our Life in God: Learning to Accept Acceptance." Keenan Lecture Series, 1992. Unpublished.
Review of *God for Us: The Trinity and Christian Life*, by Catherine Mowry-LaCugna. *Theological Studies* 53 (September 1992): 558–60.
Review of *The History of the Triune God: Contributions to Trinitarian Theology*, by Jürgen Moltmann. *Theological Studies* 53 (December 1992): 765–66.
Review of *The Promise of Trinitarian Theology*, by Colin E. Gunton. *Horizons* 19 (Fall 1992): 321–22.
Review of *Can Christ Become Good News Again?* by John B. Cobb Jr. *Journal of Religion* 73 (April 1993): 272–73.
Review of *Divine Infinity in Greek and Medieval Thought*, by Leo Sweeney. *Theological Studies* 54 (June 1993): 365–66.
Review of *Eternity and Time's Flow*, Robert C. Neville. *Theological Studies* 54 (December 1993): 751–52.
"Creativity and the Extensive Continuum as the Ultimate Ground in Alfred North Whitehead's Philosophy of Becoming." *Ultimate Reality and Meaning* 16 (March–June 1993): 110–19.
Review of *Mysticism and New Paradigm Psychology*, by John E. Collins. *Journal of Ecumenical Studies* 30 (Summer–Fall 1993): 475.
Review of *The Numinous Universe*, by Daniel Liderbach. *CTNS Bulletin* 13 (Winter 1993): 28–29
Review of *Systematic Theology, Volume 1*, by Wolfhart Pannenberg. *Horizons* 20 (Fall 1993): 355–56.
"Whiteheadian Creativity, the Tao, and the Thomistic Act of Being." *Pacifica* 6 (June 1993): 179–88.
"Proposals for Overcoming the Atomism Within Process-Relational Metaphysics." *Process Studies* 23 (Spring 1994): 10–24.
Review of *God as Trinity: Relationality and Temporality in Divine Life*, by Ted Peters. *Journal of Religion* 74 (October 1994): 575–76.
Review of *Hellfire and Lightning Rods: Liberating Science, Technology, and Religion*, by Frederick Ferre. *CTNS Bulletin* 14 (Summer 1994): 17–19.
Review of *The One, the Three and the Many: God, Creation and the Culture of Modernity*, by Colin E. Gunton. *Horizons* 21 (Fall 1994): 361–62.
The Divine Matrix: Creativity as Link Between East and West. Faith Meets Faith: An Orbis Series in Interreligious Dialogue. Maryknoll, N.Y.: Orbis, 1995.
"Panentheism from a Trinitarian Perspective." *Horizons* 22 (Spring 1995): 7–28.
Review of *The Becoming of Time: Integrating Physical and Religious Time*, by Lawrence W. Fagg. *CTNS Bulletin* 15 (Fall 1995): 1–17.
Review of *Christ and the Spirit: Spirit Christology in Trinitarian Perspective*, by Ralph Del-Colle. *Horizons* 22 (Fall 1995): 304.
Review of *Gottesbegriff und Geschichtsphilosophie in der Sicht Schellings*, by Wilhelm G. Jacobs. *Journal of Religion* 75, no. 3 (July 1995): 426–27.
Review of *Trinity and Process: A Critical Evaluation and Reconstruction of Harts-*

horne's Di-Polar Theism towards a Trinitarian Methaphysics, by Gregory A. Boyd. *Horizons* 22 (Spring 1995): 138–39.

"Non-Duality and the Concept of Ultimate Reality." *Ultimate Reality and Meaning* 19 (1996): 140–47.

"Response to Elizabeth Johnson's 'Does God Play Dice?'" *Theological Studies* 57 (December 1996): 720–30.

Review of *Evidence of Purpose: Scientists Discover the Creator,* by John Marks Templeton. *CTNS Bulletin* 16 (Winter 1996): 16–17.

Review of *The Father's Spirit of Sonship: Reconceiving the Trinity,* by Thomas G. Weinandy. *Theological Studies* 57 (June 1996): 384.

Review of *The Hindu Connection: Roots of the New Age,* by A. R. Victor Raj. *Theological Studies* 57 (June 1996): 389–90.

Review of *Modern Trinitarian Perspectives,* by John Thompson. *Theology Today* 52 (January 1996): 532.

Review of *Theologie aus asiatischen Quellen: der theologische Weg Choan-Seng Songs vor dem Hintergrund der asiatischen ökumenischen Diskussion,* by Karl H. Federschmidt. *Religious Studies Review* 22 (October 1996): 340.

Review of *Theo-Monistic Mysticism: A Hindu-Christian Comparison,* by Michael Stoeber. *Horizons* 23 (Fall 1996): 364–65.

"Concluding Remarks." In *Trinity in Process: A Relational Theology of God,* edited by Joseph A. Bracken, S.J., and Marjorie Hewitt Suchocki, 215–24. New York: Continuum, 1997.

"Panentheism from a Process Perspective." In *Trinity in Process: A Relational Theology of God,* ed. Joseph A. Bracken, S.J., and Marjorie Hewitt Suchocki, 95–113. New York: Continuum, 1997.

Review of *Anthology of World Scriptures,* by Robert E. Van Voorst. *Horizons* 24 (Spring 1997): 127.

Review of *A Broader Vision: Perspectives on the Buddha and the Christ,* by Richard H. Drummond. *Journal of Ecumenical Studies* 34 (Spring 1997): 269.

Review of *The Fire in the Equations: Science, Religion and the Search for God,* by Kitty Ferguson. *CTNS Bulletin* 17 (Summer 1997): 18–19.

Review of *The Trinity in a Pluralistic Age: Theological Essays on Culture and Religion,* ed. by Kevin J. Vanhoozer. *Theology Today* 54 (October 1997): 400–404.

Review of *The Truth of Broken Symbols,* by Robert C. Neville. *Theological Studies* 58 (June 1997): 365–67.

"Infinity and the Logic of Non-Dualism." *Hindu-Christian Studies Bulletin* 11 (1998): 39–44.

"The Metaphysical Grounding for a Multi-Term Approach to Human Nature." *American Journal of Philosophy and Theology* 19 (Spring 1998): 241–53.

Review of *The Christian Doctrine of God: One Being, Three Persons,* by Thomas F. Torrance. *Horizons* 25 (Spring 1998): 119–20.

Review of *Das Gottesproblem 1, Das: Gott und Unendlichkeit in der neuzeitlichen Philosophie,* by Philip Clayton. *Theological Studies* 59 (March 1998): 148–50.

Review of *Persons in Communion: An Essay on Trinitarian Description and Human Participation with Special Reference to Volume One of Karl Barth's Church Dogmatics,* by Alan J. Torrance. *Horizons* 25 (Spring 1998): 119–20.
Review of *The Trinity,* by Karl Rahner. *Horizons* 25 (Spring 1998): 117–19.
"Revising Process Metaphysics in Response to Ian Barbour's Critique." *Zygon* 33 (September 1998): 405–14.
"Toward a New Philosophical Theology Based on Intersubjectivity." *Theological Studies* 59 (1998): 703–19.
"Trinity: Economic and Immanent." *Horizons* 25 (Spring 1998): 7–22.
Review of *The Triune Creator: A Historical and Systematic Study,* by Colin E. Gunton. *Horizons* 26, no. 2 (1999): 381–82.
"The Theology of God of Elizabeth A. Johnson." In *Things New and Old: Essays on the Theology of Elizabeth A. Johnson,* edited by Phyllis Zagano and Terrence W. Tilley, 21–38. New York: Crossroad, 1999.
"Prehending God in and through the World." *Process Studies* 29 (2000): 4–15.
Review of *God After Darwin,* by John Haught. *Horizons* 26, no. 1 (2000): 196–98.
Review of *The God of Evolution: A Trinitarian Theology,* by Denis Edward. *Horizons* 26, no. 1 (2000): 196–98.
Review of *Process Catholicism: An Exercise in Ecclesial Imagination,* by Robert L. Kinast. *Process Studies* 29, no. 1 (Spring–Summer 2000): 177–79.
Review of *Trinity and Truth,* by Bruce D. Marshall. *Theological Studies* 61, no. 4 (2000): 764–65.
"Absolute Nothingness and the Divine Matrix." *The International Journal for Field-Being* 1 (2001).
The One in the Many: A Contemporary Reconstruction of the God–World Relationship. Grand Rapids, Mich.: Eerdmans, 2001.
Review of *Prozesstheologie: zu ihrer Würdigung und kritischen Erneuerung,* by Roland Faber. *Theological Studies* 62, no. 3 (September 2001): 628–29.
Review of *Varieties of Transcendental Experience: A Study in Constructive Postmodernism,* by Donald L. Gelpi. *Horizons* 28, no. 1 (Spring 2001): 130–31.
"Supervenience: Two Proposals/Supervenience and Basic Christian Beliefs." *Zygon* 36 (2001): 137–52.
"Images of God within Systematic Theology." *Theological Studies* 63, no. 2 (June 2002): 362–73.
Review of *Der gottbezogene Mensch: eine systematische Untersuchung zur Bestimmung des Menschen und zur "Selbstverwirklichung" Gottes in der Anthropologie und Trintätstheologie Wolfhart Pannenbergs,* by Franz-Joseph Overbeck. *Theological Studies* 63, no. 1 (March 2002): 180–82.
Review of *New Maps for Old: Explorations in Science and Religion,* by Mary Gerhart. *Interpretation* 56, no. 2 (April 2002): 226.
"Whitehead and the Critique of Logocentrism." In *Process and Difference: Between Cosmological and Poststructuralist Postmodernisms,* edited by Catherine Keller, 91–110. Albany: State University of New York Press, 2002.
"Intersubjectivity and the Coming of God." *Journal of Religion* 83, no. 3 (July 2003): 381–400.

"The Body of Christ—An Intersubjective Interpretation." *Horizons* 31 (2004): 7–21.
"Divine Providence and Human Freedom: A Second Look." *Theoforum* 35 (2004): 301–16.
Review of *Gottes Klarheiten: Eine Neuinterpretation der Lehre von Gottes "Eigenschaften,"* by Wolf Kroetke. *Theological Studies* 65, no. 1 (March 2004): 228.
"Bodily Resurrection and the Dialectic of Spirit and Matter." *Theological Studies* 66 (2005): 770–82.
"The End of Evil." In *World without End,* edited by Joseph A. Bracken, 1–11. Grand Rapids, Mich.: Eerdmans, 2005.
"Subjective Immortality in a Neo-Whiteheadian Context." In *World without End: Christian Eschatology from a Process Perspective,* edited by Joseph A. Bracken, 72–90. Grand Rapids, Mich.: Eerdmans, 2005.
Editor, *World without End: Christian Eschatology from a Process Perspective.* Grand Rapids, Mich.: Eerdmans, 2005.
Christianity and Process Thought: Spirituality for a Changing World. Philadelphia: Templeton Foundation Press, 2006.
"Of Particles and Fields." *Theology and Science* 5, no. 1 (2007): 47–56.
"Space and Time from a Neo-Whiteheadian Perspective." *Zygon* 42, no. 1 (March 2007): 41–47.
God: Three Who Are One. Engaging Theology: Catholic Perspectives. Collegeville, Minn.: Liturgical Press, 2008.
"A. N. Whitehead and My Search for a Fully Consistent Social Ontology." Unpublished manuscript, 2009.
"Dependent Co-Origination, the Trinity and the God–World Relationship." Available from the Center for Process Studies, 1325 North College Avenue, Claremont, Calif. 91711.
Joseph A. Bracken and Marjorie Hewitt Suchocki, eds. *Trinity in Process: A Relational Theology of God.* New York: Continuum, 1997.
Sears, Robert T., and Joseph A. Bracken. *Self-Emptying Love in a Global Context: The Spiritual Exercises and the Environment.* Eugene, Ore.: Cascade Books, 2006.

Secondary Sources

Alexander, Samuel. *Space, Time, and Deity.* 2 vols. London: Macmillan, 1920.
Allan, George. "The Aims of Societies and the Aims of God." In *Process Philosophy and Christian Thought,* edited by Delwin Brown, Ralph E. James Jr., and Gene Reeves, 464–74. Indianapolis: Bobbs-Merrill, 1971. (Originally published in the *Journal of the American Academy of Religion* 35, no. 2 [June 1967]: 149–58.)
Anonymous. Review of *The Divine Matrix: Creativity as Link between East and West: Creativity of East and West,* by Joseph A. Bracken. *Irénikon* 68, no. 3 (1995): 444.
Augustine. *Expositions of the Book of Psalms.* Translated by A. Cleveland Coxe.

Nicene and Post Nicene Fathers 8. Christian Literature Publishing, 1888; reprint, Peabody, Mass.: Hendrickson, 1995.
———. *Augustine: Earlier Writings.* Edited by John H. S. Burleigh. The Library of Christian Classics, Ichthus Edition 6. Philadelphia: Westminster Press, 1953.
———. *The Trinity.* Translated by Stephen McKenna. The Fathers of the Church 18. Washington, D.C.: The Catholic University of America Press, 1963.
Bakewell, Charles M. *Source Book in Ancient Philosophy.* New York: Scribner's, 1907.
Baltazar, Eulalio R. *God within Process.* New York: Newman Press, 1970.
Barbour, Ian G. "Teilhard's Process Metaphysics." *Journal of Religion* 49, no. 2 (April 1969): 136–59.
———. *Myths, Models, and Paradigms: A Comparative Study in Science and Religion.* New York: Harper & Row, 1974.
———. *Religion in an Age of Science.* San Francisco: Harper & Row, 1990.
———. *Religion and Science: Historical and Contemporary Issues.* San Francisco: Harper & Row, 1997.
Barr, James. *Biblical Words for Time.* Naperville, Ill.: A. R. Allenson, 1962.
Barth, Karl. *Church Dogmatics.* Edited by G. W. Bromiley and T. F. Torrance. Edinburgh: T & T Clark, 1936–69.
Basinger, David. *The Case for Free Will Theism: A Philosophical Assessment.* Downers Grove, Ill.: InterVarsity Press, 1996.
Bavinck, Herman. *Doctrine of God.* Grand Rapids, Mich.: Eerdmans, 1951.
Bergson, Henri. *Time and Free Will.* Translated by F. L. Pogson. London: Swan Sonnenschein, 1910.
———. *Creative Evolution.* Translated by Arthur Mitchell. New York: Henry Holt, 1911.
———. *Matter and Memory.* Translated by Nancy Margaret Paul and W. Scott Palmer. London: Swan Sonnenschein, 1911.
———. *Mind-Energy.* Translated by H. Wildon Carr. London: Macmillan, 1920.
———. *The Two Sources of Morality and Religion.* Translated by R. Ashley Audra and Cloudesley Brereton. New York: Doubleday, 1935.
Berkhof, Louis. *Systematic Theology.* Grand Rapids, Mich.: Eerdmans, 1936–38; new ed., 1996.
Bosanquet, Bernard. *The Essentials of Logic.* London: Macmillan, 1895.
———. *The Principle of Individuality and Value.* London: Macmillan, 1912.
———. *The Value and Destiny of the Individual.* London: Macmillan, 1913.
Bowman, Donna. *The Divine Decision: A Process Doctrine of Election.* Louisville, Ky.: Westminster/John Knox Press, 2002.
Bowne, Borden Parker. *Metaphysics: A Study in First Principles.* New York: Harper & Brothers, 1882.
———. *Personalism.* New York: Houghton Mifflin, 1908.
Boyd, Gregory A. *Trinity and Process: A Critical Evaluation and Reconstruction of Hartshrone's Di-Polar Theism towards a Trinitarian Metaphysics.* New York: Peter Lang, 1992.

———. "The Self-Sufficient Sociality of God: A Trinitarian Revision of Hartshorne's Metaphysics." In *Trinity in Process: A Relational Theology of God*, edited by Joseph A. Bracken, S.J., and Marjorie Hewitt Suchocki, 73–94. New York: Continuum, 1997.

———. *God of the Possible: A Biblical Introduction to the Open View of God.* Grand Rapids, Mich.: Baker, 2000.

Bradley, F. H. *The Principles of Logic.* Honolulu: University Press of the Pacific, 1883.

———. *Essays on Truth and Reality.* Oxford: Clarendon Press, 1914.

———. *Appearance and Reality.* London: George Allen & Unwin, 1916.

Brightman, Edgar Sheffield. *The Problem of God.* New York: Abingdon, 1930.

Broad, C. D. *The Mind and Its Place in Nature.* London: Kegan, Paul, Trench and Trubner, 1923.

Brugger, Walter. "*Das Mitsein. Eine Erweiterung der scholastischen Kategorienlehre.*" *Scholastik* 21 (1956): 370–83.

Buber, Martin. *I and Thou.* Translated by Walter Kaufmann. New York: Scribner's, 1970.

Bultmann, Rudolph. *Primitive Christianity: In Its Contemporary Setting.* Translated by Reginald H. Fuller. Philadelphia: Fortress Press, 1980.

Caird, Edward. *The Evolution of Religion.* 2 vols. Glasgow: James Maclehose, 1893.

Calvin, John. *Institutes of the Christian Religion.* Translated by Ford Lewis Battles. Edited by John T. McNeill. The Library of Christian Classics 20–21. Philadelphia: Westminster Press, 1960.

Case-Winters, Anna. *God's Power: Traditional Understandings and Contemporary Challenges.* Louisville, Ky.: Westminster/John Knox Press, 1990.

Chan, Wing-tsit, trans. and comp. *A Source Book in Chinese Philosophy.* Princeton, N.J.: Princeton University Press, 1963.

Christian, William. *An Interpretation of Whitehead's Metaphysics.* New Haven, Conn.: Yale University Press, 1959.

Clarke, Bowman L. *The Philosophical Approach to God: A Contemporary Neo-Thomist Perspective.* Winston-Salem, N.C.: Wake Forest University Publications, 1979.

———. "God and Time in Whitehead." *Journal of the American Academy of Religion* 48 (December 1980): 563–79.

Clayton, Philip. "Pluralism, Idealism, Romanticism: Untapped Resources for a Trinity in Process." In *Trinity in Process: A Relational Theology of God*, edited by Joseph A. Bracken, S.J., and Marjorie Hewitt Suchocki, 117–45. New York: Continuum, 1997.

———. Foreword to *The One in the Many: A Contemporary Reconstruction of the God–World Relationship*, by Joseph A. Bracken, S.J. Grand Rapids, Mich.: Eerdmans, 2001.

Cobb, John B., Jr. "Whitehead's Philosophy and a Christian Doctrine of Man." *The Journal of Bible and Religion* 32, no. 3 (July 1964): 209–20.

———. *A Christian Natural Theology.* Philadelphia: Westminster Press, 1965.

———. *The Structure of Christian Existence.* Philadelphia: Westminster Press, 1967.

———. *God and the World.* Philadelphia: Westminster Press, 1969.

———. "A Whiteheadian Christology." In *Process Philosophy and Christian Thought,* edited by Delwin Brown, Ralph E. James Jr., and Gene Reeves, 382–98. New York: Bobbs-Merrill, 1971.

———. "A Whiteheadian Doctrine of God." In *Process Theology and Christian Thought,* edited by Delwin Brown, Ralph E. James Jr., and Gene Reeves, 215–43. New York: Bobbs-Merrill, 1971.

———. *Beyond Dialogue: Towards a Mutual Transformation of Christianity and Buddhism.* Philadelphia: Fortress Press, 1982.

———. "Overcoming Reductionism." In *Existence and Actuality: Conversations with Charles Hartshorne,* edited by John Cobb and Franklin Gamwell, 149–64. Chicago: University of Chicago Press, 1984.

———. "Response to Ted Peters." *Dialog* 30 (Summer 1991): 241–45.

———. "The Relativization of the Trinity." In *Trinity in Process: A Relational Theology of God,* edited by Joseph A. Bracken, S.J., and Marjorie Hewitt Suchocki, 1–22. New York: Continuum, 1997.

———. *Transforming Christianity and the World: A Way beyond Absolutism and Relativism.* Edited by Paul F. Knitter. Maryknoll, N.Y.: Orbis, 1999.

Cobb, John B., Jr., and Christopher Ives, eds. *The Emptying God: A Buddhist-Jewish-Christian Conversation.* Maryknoll, N.Y.: Orbis, 1990.

Cobb, John B., Jr., and Clark H. Pinnock. *Searching for an Adequate God: A Dialogue between Process and Free Will Theists.* Grand Rapids, Mich.: Eerdmans, 2000.

Cobb, John B., Jr., and David Ray Griffin. *Process Theology: An Introductory Exposition.* Louisville, Ky.: Westminster/John Knox Press, 1976.

Collingwood, R. G. *The Idea of History.* Oxford: Clarendon Press, 1946; reprint, New York: Oxford University Press, 1967.

Collins, James. *A History of Modern European Philosophy.* Milwaukee: Bruce, 1954.

Cone, James H. *A Black Theology of Liberation. Twentieth Anniversary Edition.* Maryknoll, N.Y.: Orbis, 1990.

Copleston, Frederick, S.J. *Religion and the One: Philosophies East and West.* Gifford Lectures. London: Search Press, 1982.

Coreth, Emerich. *Metaphysics.* Translated by Joseph Donceel. New York: Herder & Herder, 1968.

Cousins, Ewert. "A Theology of Interpersonal Relations." *Thought* 45 (1970): 69–70.

, ed. *Hope and the Future of Man.* London: Teilhardian Center for the Future of Man, 1973.

Craig, William Lane. *The Tenseless Theory of Time.* Boston: Kluwer Academic Publishers, 2000.

Crowley, Aleister. *Magick: Book 4, Liber Aba.* 2nd rev. ed. Edited by Mary Desti, Leila Waddell, and Hymenaeus Beta. Newburyport, Mass.: Weiser Books, 1998.

Cunningham, David S. *These Three Are One: The Practice of Trinitarian Theology.* Challenges in Contemporary Theology 2. Oxford: Blackwell, 1998.

Daly, Mary. *Beyond God the Father: Toward a Philosophy of Women's Liberation.* Boston: Beacon Press, 1973.

Davies, Brian, O.P. *Aquinas.* New York: Continuum, 2002.

Denzinger, Heinrich. *Enchiridion symbolorum definitionum et declarationum de rebus fidei et morum.* 34th ed. Edited by Adolfus Schönmetzer. New York: Herder, 1965.

Dewart, Leslie. *The Foundations of Belief.* New York: Herder & Herder, 1969.

Dillenberger, John. "Contemporary Theologians and the Visual Arts." *Journal of the American Academy of Religion* 53, no. 4 (1985): 599–615.

Driesch, Hans. *The Science and Philosophy of Organism.* 2 vols. London: Adams and Charles and Black, 1908.

———. *The History and Theory of Vitalism.* Translated by C. K. Ogden. New York: Macmillan, 1914.

———. *The Problem of Individuality.* London: Macmillan, 1914.

Edington, A. S. *The Nature of the Physical World.* Cambridge: Cambridge University Press, 1928.

Erickson, Millard. *Christian Theology.* Grand Rapids, Mich.: Eerdmans, 1985.

Faber, Roland. "Trinity, Analogy, and Coherence." In *Trinity in Process: A Relational Theology of God,* edited by Joseph A. Bracken, S.J., and Marjorie Hewitt Suchocki, 147–71. New York: Continuum, 1997.

Ferm, Vergilius. *First Adventures in Philosophy.* New York: Scribner's, 1936.

Fetz, Reto Luzius. "Creativity: A New Transcendental?" In *Whitehead's Metaphysics of Creativity,* edited by Friedrich Rapp and Reiner Wiehl, 189–208. Albany: State University of New York Press, 1990.

Feuerbach, Ludwig. *The Essence of Christianity.* Translated by George Eliot. New York: Harper & Row, 1957.

Fiddes, Paul S. *The Creative Suffering of God.* Oxford: Clarendon Press, 1988.

Ford, Lewis. "Boethius and Whitehead." *International Philosophical Quarterly* 8, no. 1 (March 1968): 63–67.

———. "The Non-Temporality of Whitehead's God." *International Philosophical Quarterly* 13 (1973): 346–76.

———. "Process Trinitarianism." *Journal of the American Academy of Religion* 43, no. 2 (June 1975): 199–213.

———. *The Lure of God: A Biblical Background for Process Theism.* Philadelphia: Fortress Press, 1978.

———. *The Emergence of Whitehead's Metaphysics 1925–29.* Albany: State University of New York Press, 1984.

———. "Inclusive Occasions." In *Process in Context: Essays in Post-Whiteheadian Perspectives,* edited by Ernest Wolf-Gazo, 107–36. Bern: Peter Lang, 1988.

———. "Contingent Trinitarianism." In *Trinity in Process: A Relational Theology of God,* edited by Joseph A. Bracken, S.J., and Marjorie Hewitt Suchocki, 41–68. New York: Continuum, 1997.

Fortman, Edmund J. *The Triune God: A Historical Study of the Doctrine of the Trinity.* Grand Rapids, Mich.: Baker, 1972.

Fredericks, James L. Review of *The Divine Matrix: Creativity as Link between East and West: Creativity of East and West,* by Joseph Bracken. *Theological Studies* 57 (March 1996): 189.

Gadamer, Hans-Georg. *Truth and Method.* Translated and edited by Garrett Barden and John Cumming. New York: Crossroad, 1984.

Garrigou-Lagrange, Reginald, O.P. *Predestination.* Translated by Dom Bede Rose, O.S.B. Rockford, Ill.: Tan Books, 1998. Originally *La prédestination des saints et la grace,* 1939.

Gilkey, Langdon. *Maker of Heaven and Earth: The Christian Doctrine of Creation in Light of Modern Knowledge.* Garden City, N.Y.: Anchor Books, 1965.

Gilson, Étienne. *God and Philosophy.* New Haven, Conn.: Yale University Press, 1941; 2nd ed., 2002.

Green, Thomas Hill. *Prolegomena to Ethics.* Edited by A. C. Bradley. Oxford: Clarendon Press, 1883.

Griffin, David Ray. "Whitehead's Philosophy and Some General Notions of Physics and Biology." In *Mind in Nature. Essays on the Interface of Science and Philosophy,* edited by John B. Cobb Jr. and David Ray Griffin, 122–34. Washington, D.C.: University Press of America, 1977.

———. "A Naturalistic Trinity." In *Trinity in Process: A Relational Theology of God,* edited by Joseph A. Bracken, S.J., and Marjorie Hewitt Suchocki, 23–43. New York: Continuum, 1997.

———. *Deep Religious Pluralism.* Philadelphia: Westminster/John Knox Press, 2005.

Gunton, Colin E. *The One, the Three and the Many: God, Creation and the Culture of Modernity.* Cambridge: Cambridge University Press, 1993.

———. *The Promise of Trinitarian Theology.* 2nd ed. Edinburgh: T & T Clark, 1997.

Gutiérrez, Gustavo. *A Theology of Liberation: History, Politics, and Salvation. 15th Anniversary Edition.* Maryknoll, N.Y.: Orbis, 1988.

Gutwenger, Engelbert, S.J. "*Zur Trinitätslehre von Mysterium Salutis II.*" *Zeitschrift für katholische Theologie* 90 (1968): 325–28.

Haldane, J. S. *Mechanism, Life and Personality.* London: John Murray, 1913.

———. *The Sciences and Philosophy.* London: Hodder and Stoughton, 1929.

Hallow, William W., and K. Lawson Younger, eds. *The Context of Scripture.* 3 vols. Leiden: Brill, 2003.

Hallman, Joseph M. *The Descent of God: Divine Suffering in History and Theology.* Minneapolis: Fortress Press, 1991.

Halper, Edward C. "One over Many." In *The Cambridge Dictionary of Philosophy,* 2nd ed., edited by Robert Audi. Cambridge: Cambridge University Press, 1999.

Hamilton, Peter. "Proposals for a Modern Christology." In *Christ for Us Today,* edited by Norman Pittenger, 154–75. London: SCM Press, 1968.

Haring, Ellen S. "The Ontological Principle." *The Review of Metaphysics* 16 (Summer 1962): 3–13.

Harrington, Wilfrid J. *The Tears of God: Our Benevolent Creator and Human Suffering.* Collegeville, Minn.: Liturgical Press, 1992.

Harrison, Paul. "Unity and Diversity: The One and the Many." *Time Magazine,* December 12, 1996.

Hartshorne, Charles A. *The Philosophy and Psychology of Sensation.* Chicago: University of Chicago Press, 1934.

———. "Redefining God." *The New Humanist* 7 (July–August 1934): 8–15.

———. "The Compound Individual." In *Philosophical Essays for Alfred North Whitehead,* edited by F. S. C. Northrop, 193–220. New York: Russell & Russell, 1936.

———. "The New Pantheism." *The Christian Register,* February 20, 1936, 119–20.

———. "Whitehead's Idea of God." In *The Philosophy of Alfred North Whitehead,* edited by Paul A. Schilpp, 513–59. Chicago: Northwestern University, 1941.

———. "Is Whitehead's God the God of Religion?" *Ethics* 53, no. 3 (April 1943): 219–27.

———. *Reality as Social Process: Studies in Metaphysics and Religion.* Glencoe, Ill.: Free Press, 1953.

———. "The Idea of God—Literal or Analogical?" *Christian Scholar* 39 (1956): 131–36.

———. *The Logic of Perfection and Other Essays in Neoclassical Metaphysics.* LaSalle, Ill.: Open Court, 1962.

———. "The Logic of Panentheism." In *Philosophers Speak of God,* edited by Charles Hartshorne and William L. Reese, 499–514. Chicago: University of Chicago Press, 1963.

———. "Whitehead's Novel Intuition." In *Alfred North Whitehead: Essays on His Philosophy,* edited by George L. Kline, 18–26. Englewood Cliffs, N.J.: Prentice-Hall, 1963.

———. *Man's Vision of God and the Logic of Theism.* 2nd ed. Hamden, Conn.: Archon Books, 1964.

———. *Anselm's Discovery.* LaSalle, Ill.: Open Court, 1965.

———. "The Dipolar Conception of Deity." *The Review of Metaphysics* 21, no. 2 (December 1967): 273–89.

———. *The Divine Relativity: A Social Conception of God.* New Haven, Conn.: Yale University Press, 1967.

———. *A Natural Theology for Our Time.* LaSalle, Ill.: Open Court, 1967.

———. *Creative Synthesis and the Philosophic Method.* LaSalle, Ill: Open Court, 1970.

———. "Philosophical and Religious Uses of 'God.'" In *Process Theology,* edited by Ewert H. Cousins, 101–19. New York: Newman Press, 1971.

———. *Aquinas to Whitehead: Seven Centuries of Metaphysics of Religion.* Milwaukee: Marquette University Press, 1976.

———. *Omnipotence and Other Theological Mistakes.* Albany: State University of New York Press, 1984.

Hartshorne, Charles A., and William Reese, eds. *Philosophers Speak of God.* Chicago: University of Chicago Press, 1953.

Hasker, William. *God, Time, and Knowledge.* Ithaca, N.Y.: Cornell University Press, 1989.

———. *Providence, Evil and the Openness of God.* New York: Routledge, 2004.

Haught, John F. *God after Darwin: A Theology of Evolution.* Boulder, Colo.: Westview Press, 2000.

Havrilak, Gregory. "Karl Rahner and the Greek Trinity." *St. Vladimir's Seminary Theological Quarterly* 34 (1990): 61–77.

Heidegger, Martin. *Being and Time.* Translated by John Macquarrie and Edward Robinson. New York: Harper & Row, 1962.

———. *Identity and Difference.* Translated by Joan Stambaugh. New York: Harper & Row, 1969.

———. "The End of Philosophy and the Task of Thinking." In *The End of Philosophy,* translated by Joan Stambaugh, 55–73. New York: Harper & Row, 1973.

———. "Metaphysics as History of Being." In *The End of Philosophy,* translated by Joan Stambaugh, 19–26. New York: Harper & Row, 1973.

———. "Who Is Nietzsche's Zarathustra?" In *Nietzsche,* edited and translated by David Farrell Krell, 211–32. San Francisco: HarperCollins, 1991.

Hick, John H. "The Idea of Necessary Being." *Princeton Seminary Bulletin* 54, no. 2 (November 1960): 11–21.

Hill, William J., O.P. *The Three-Personed God: The Trinity as a Mystery of Salvation.* Washington, D.C.: The Catholic University of America Press, 1982.

Hocking, William Ernest. *The Meaning of God in Human Experience.* New Haven, Conn.: Yale University Press, 1912.

———. *Human Nature and Its Remaking.* New Haven, Conn.: Yale University Press, 1918.

———. "Fact, Field, and Destiny: Inductive Elements of Metaphysics." *The Review of Metaphysics* 11 (1957–58): 531–34.

Hodge, Charles. *Systematic Theology.* 3 vols. New York: Scribner's, 1871–73; reprint, Grand Rapids, Mich.: Eerdmans, 1997.

Hodgson, Leonard. *The Doctrine of the Trinity.* New York: Scribner's, 1944.

Holt, Edwin B., Walter T. Marvin, William Pepperell Montague, Ralph Barton Perry, Walter B. Pitkin, and Edward Gleason Spaulding. *The New Realism: Coöperative Studies in Philosophy.* New York: Macmillan, 1912.

James, William. *A Pluralistic Universe.* London: Longmans and Green, 1901.

———. *Some Problems of Philosophy.* London: Longmans and Green, 1911.

———. *Pragmatism: A New Name for Some Old Ways of Thinking.* Edited by Bruce Kuklick. Indianapolis: Hackett, 1981.

Johnson, Elizabeth A. "Does God Play Dice?" *Theological Studies* 57 (1996): 2–18.

———. *She Who Is: The Mystery of God in Feminist Theological Discourse.* 2nd ed. New York: Crossroad, 1997.

Jones, Judith A. *Intensity: An Essay in Whiteheadian Ontology.* Nashville: Vanderbilt University Press, 1998.

Jüngel, Eberhard. *God's Being Is in Becoming: The Trinitarian Being of God in the Theology of Karl Barth. A Paraphrase.* Translated by John Webster. Grand Rapids, Mich.: Eerdmans, 2001.

Kane, Robert. *A Contemporary Introduction to Free Will.* New York: Oxford, 2005.

Kasper, Walter. *The God of Jesus Christ.* Translated by Matthew J. O'Connell. New York: Crossroad, 1984.

Kaufman, Gordon D. *Systematic Theology: A Historicist Perspective.* New York: Scribner's, 1968.

Klein, Jacob. *Greek Mathematical Thought.* Cambridge, Mass.: MIT Press, 1968.

Knitter, Paul F. *Jesus and the Other Names: Christian Mission and Global Responsibility.* Maryknoll, N.Y.: Orbis, 1996.

Knudsen, Robert D. "Symbol and Myth in Contemporary Theology, with Special Reference to the Thought of Paul Tillich, Reinhold Niebuhr, and Nicolas Berdyaev." S.T.M. diss., Union Theological Seminary, New York, 1952.

Kuhn, Thomas. *The Structure of Scientific Revolutions.* 2nd ed. Chicago: University of Chicago Press, 1970.

Kvanvig, Jonathan L., and Hugh J. McCann. "Divine Conservation and the Persistence of the World." In *Divine and Human Action: Essays in the Metaphysics of Theism,* edited by Thomas V. Morris, 13–49. Ithaca, N.Y.: Cornell University Press, 1988.

LaCugna, Catherine Mowry. *God for Us: The Trinity and the Christian Life.* San Francisco: HarperCollins, 1991.

Laszlo, Ervin. *An Introduction to Systems Philosophy: Toward a New Paradigm of Contemporary Thought.* New York: Gordon & Breach, 1972.

———. *The Systems View of the World: The Natural Philosophy of the New Developments in the Sciences.* New York: Braziller, 1972.

Leclerc, Ivor. *Whitehead's Metaphysics: An Introductory Exposition.* New York: Macmillan, 1958.

———. "Review of 'An Interpretation of Whitehead's Metaphysics,' by W. A. Christian." *Journal of Philosophy* 57, no. 4 (1960): 138–43.

———. *The Nature of Physical Existence.* New York: Humanities Press, 1972.

———. *The Philosophy of Nature.* Washington, D.C.: The Catholic University of America Press, 1986.

Lee, Bernard J., S.M. "An 'Other' Trinity." In *Trinity in Process: A Relational Theology of God,* edited by Joseph A. Bracken, S.J., and Marjorie Hewitt Suchocki, 191–214. New York: Continuum, 1997.

Lefebure, Leo D. Review of *The Divine Matrix: Creativity as Link Between East and West: Creativity of East and West,* by Joseph Bracken. *New Theology Review* 10, no. 1 (1997): 121.

Leftow, Brian. "Is God an Abstract Object?" *Nous* 24 (1990): 581–98.

Leibniz, Gottfried Wilhelm. *Monadology.* Edited by Nicholas Rescher. Pittsburgh, Pa.: University of Pittsburgh Press, 1991.

Levinas, Emmanuel. *Totality and Infinity: An Essay on Exteriority.* Translated by Alphonso Lingis. Pittsburgh, Pa.: Duquesne University Press, 1969.

Lewis, David. "New Work for a Theory of Universals." *Australasian Journal of Philosophy* 61 (1983): 343–77.

Lindbeck, George. *The Nature of Doctrine: Religion and Theology in a Postliberal Age.* Philadelphia: Westminster Press, 1984.

Loeb, Jacques. *The Dynamics of Living Matter.* New York: Columbia University Press, 1906.

———. *The Mechanistic Conception of Life: Biological Essays.* Chicago: University of Chicago Press, 1912.

Lonergan, Bernard J. F. *Insight: A Study of Human Understanding.* 5th rev. ed. *Collected Works of Bernard Lonergan,* vol. 3. Edited by Frederick E. Crowe and Robert M. Doran. Toronto: University of Toronto Press, 1992.

Loomer, Bernard. "The Size of God." *American Journal of Theology & Philosophy* 8, nos. 1–2 (1987): 20–51.

Lowe, Victor. "Alfred North Whitehead: Introduction." In *Classic American Philosophers,* edited by Max H. Fisch, 395–417. New York: Appleton-Century-Crofts, 1951.

———. *Understanding Whitehead.* Baltimore: John Hopkins University Press, 1962.

———. "Whitehead's Metaphysical System." In *Process Philosophy and Christian Thought,* edited by Delwin Brown, Ralph E. James Jr., and Gene Reeves, 3–20. New York: Bobbs-Merrill, 1971.

Lucas, George R. *Two Views of Freedom in Process Thought: A Study of Hegel and Whitehead.* Missoula, Mont.: Scholar's Press, 1979.

Macintosh, Douglas C. *Theology as an Empirical Science.* New York: Macmillan, 1919.

———, ed. *Religious Realism.* New York: Macmillan, 1931.

MacIntyre, Alasdair. *Three Rival Versions of Moral Enquiry: Encyclopaedia, Genealogy, and Tradition.* Notre Dame, Ind.: University of Notre Dame Press, 1989.

Mann, W. E. "Divine Simplicity." *Religious Studies* 18 (1982): 451–71.

Masson, Robert. "Analogy and Metaphoric Process." *Theological Studies* 62 (September 2001): 571–96.

McCabe, Lorenzo D. *Divine Nescience of Future Contingencies a Necessity.* New York: Philips and Hung, 1882.

———. *The Foreknowledge of God.* Cincinnati: Cranston and Stowe, 1887.

McCann, Hugh J. "Divine Power and Action." In *The Blackwell Guide to Philosophy of Religion,* edited by William. E. Mann, 26–47. Oxford: Basil Blackwell, 2004.

———. "The Author of Sin." Unpublished manuscript.

McCann, Hugh J., and Jonathan L. Kvanvig. "The Occasionalist Proselytizer: A Modified Catechism." In *Philosophical Perspectives,* vol. 5, *Philosophy of Religion,* edited by J. E. Tomberlin, 587–615. Atascadero, Calif.: Ridgeview, 1991.

McDougall, William. *Body and Mind.* London: Methuen, 1911.

———. *Modern Materialism and Emergent Evolution.* London: Methuen, 1934.

McFague, Sallie. *The Body of God: An Ecological Theology.* Minneapolis: Fortress Press, 1993.

McInerny, Ralph M. *Aquinas and Analogy.* Washington, D.C.: The Catholic University of America Press, 1996.

McTaggart, J. M. E. "The Unreality of Time." *Mind* 17 (1908): 457–74.

———. *The Nature of Existence.* 2 vols. Cambridge: Cambridge University Press, 1921.
McWilliams, Warren. *The Passion of God: Divine Suffering in Contemporary Protestant Theology.* Macon, Ga.: Mercer University Press, 1985.
Meland, Bernard. *The Realities of Faith.* New York: Oxford University Press, 1962.
———. *Fallible Forms and Symbols: Discourses on Method in a Theology of Culture.* Philadelphia: Fortress Press, 1976.
Mellor, D. H. *Real Time II.* New York: Routledge, 1998.
Menzies, Peter. "Counterfactual Theories of Causation." *The Stanford Encyclopedia of Philosophy.* Winter 2008 edition. Edited by Edward N. Zalta. http://plato.stanford.edu/entries/causation-counterfactual/.
Moltmann, Jürgen. *Theology of Hope: On the Ground and the Implications of a Christian Eschatology.* Translated by James W. Leitch. London: SCM Press, 1967.
———. *The Crucified God: The Cross of Christ as the Foundation and Criticism of Christian Theology.* Translated by R. A. Wilson and John Bowden. San Francisco: Harper & Row, 1974.
———. *The History of the Triune God: Contributions to Trinitarian Theology.* Minneapolis: Fortress Press, 1991.
———. *God in Creation: A New Theology of Creation and the Spirit of God.* The Gifford Lectures 1984–85. Translated by Margaret Kohl. Minneapolis: Fortress Press, 1993.
———. *The Trinity and the Kingdom: The Doctrine of God.* Translated by Margaret Kohl. Minneapolis: Fortress Press, 1993.
———. *The Coming of God: Christian Eschatology.* Translated by Margaret Kohl. Minneapolis: Fortress Press, 1996.
Montague, William Pepperell. "Professor Royce's Refutation of Realism." *Philosophical Review* 11 (1902): 43–55.
Morgan, C. Lloyd. *Instinct and Experience.* 2nd ed. London: Methuen, 1913.
———. *Emergent Evolution.* London: Williams and Norgate, 1923.
———. *Life, Mind and Spirit.* London: Williams and Norgate, 1923.
Murray, John Courtney. *The Problem of God: Yesterday and Today.* New Haven, Conn.: Yale University Press, 1964.
Neville, Robert C. *Creativity and God: A Challenge to Process Theology.* New York: Seabury, 1980.
———. *God the Creator: On the Transcendence and Presence of God.* Albany: State University of New York Press, 1992.
———. *The Highroad around Modernism.* Albany: State University of New York Press, 1992.
Newbigin, Leslie. "Religion for the Marketplace." In *Christian Uniqueness Reconsidered: The Myth of a Pluralistic Theology of Religions,* edited by Gavin D'Costa, 135–48. Maryknoll, N.Y.: Orbis, 1990.
Niebuhr, Reinhold. *Beyond Tragedy.* New York: Scribner's, 1937.
———. *The Nature and Destiny of Man.* 2 vols. New York: Scribner's, 1941–43.

———. *Faith and History: A Comparison of Christian and Modern Views of History.* New York: Scribner's, 1949.
———. "The Truth in Myths." In *Faith and Politics,* edited by Ronald H. Stone, 17–18. New York: Scribner's, 1953.
———. *The Self and the Dramas of History.* New York: Scribner's, 1955.
———. "Between Two Cities." *Christian Scholar* 43 (Summer 1960): 141.
Nishitani, Keiji. *Religion and Nothingness.* Translated by Jan Van Bragt. Berkeley: University of California Press, 1982.
Noble, Edmund. *Purposive Evolution: The Link between Science and Religion.* New York: Henry Holt, 1926.
Nobo, Jorge Luis. *Whitehead's Metaphysics of Extension and Solidarity.* Albany: State University of New York Press, 1986.
———. "Experience, Eternity, and Primordiality." *Process Studies* 26 (1997): 171–204.
O'Donnell, John J. *Trinity and Temporality: The Christian Doctrine of God in Light of Process Theology and the Theology of Hope.* New York: Oxford University Press, 1983.
———. "The Trinity as Divine Community: A Critical Reflection upon Recent Theological Developments." *Gregorianum* 69, no. 1 (1988): 5–34.
———. *The Mystery of the Triune God.* New York: Paulist Press, 1989.
Ogden, Schubert M. "What Sense Does It Make to Say, 'God Acts in History'?" *Journal of Religion* 43, no. 1 (January 1963): 8–10.
———. "Theology and Philosophy: A New Phase of the Discussion." *Journal of Religion* 44, no. 1 (January 1964): 1–16.
———. *The Reality of God and Other Essays.* New York: Harper & Row, 1966.
———. "On the Trinity." *Theology* 83 (1980): 97–102.
Padgett, Alan G. *God, Eternity, and the Nature of Time.* New York: St. Martin's Press, 1992; reprint, Eugene, Ore.: Wipf & Stock, 2000.
Pannenberg, Wolfhart. "The Revelation of God in Jesus of Nazareth." In *Theology as History.* New Frontiers in Theology 3, 101–33. New York: Harper & Row, 1967.
———. *Basic Questions in Theology.* Translated by George H. Kelm. 2 vols. Philadelphia: Fortress Press, 1970–71.
———. *Introduction to Systematic Theology.* Grand Rapids, Mich.: Eerdmans, 1991.
———. *Systematic Theology.* 3 vols. Translated by Geoffrey W. Bromiley. Grand Rapids, Mich.: Eerdmans, 1991–98.
Parker, Thomas. "The Political Meaning of the Doctrine of the Trinity: Some Theses." *Journal of Religion* 60 (1980): 165–84.
Paulsen, Friedrich. *Einleitung in die Philosophie.* Berlin: Hertz, 1892.
Peacocke, Arthur. *Theology for a Scientific Age: Being and Becoming—Natural, Divine, and Human.* Revised edition. Minneapolis: Fortress Press, 1993.
Peters, Ted. *God as Trinity: Relationality and Temporality in the Divine Life.* Louisville, Ky.: Westminster/John Knox Press, 1993.
Pinnock, Clark H. *Most Moved Mover: A Theology of God's Openness.* Grand Rapids, Mich.: Paternoster/Baker Academic, 2001.

Pinnock, Clark, Richard Rice, John Sanders, William Hasker and David Basinger. *The Openness of God: A Biblical Challenge to the Traditional Understanding of God.* Downers Grove, Ill.: InterVarsity Press, 1994.

Pittenger, W. Norman. *The Word Incarnate: A Study of the Doctrine of the Person of Christ.* New York: Harper & Brothers, 1959.

———. *God in Process.* London: SCM Press, 1967.

———. *God's Way with Man.* London: Hodder and Stoughton, 1969.

———. *The Historic Faith and a Changing World.* New York: Oxford University Press, 1969.

———. *Christology Reconsidered.* London: SCM Press, 1970.

———. *The Christian Church as Social Process.* London: Epworth Press, 1971.

———. *The Holy Spirit.* Philadelphia: Pilgrim Press, 1974.

———. *The Divine Triunity.* Philadelphia: United Church Press, 1977.

Placher, William C. *The Domestication of Transcendence: How Modern Thinking about God Went Wrong.* Louisville, Ky.: Westminster/John Knox Press, 1996.

Plantinga, Alvin C. *Does God Have a Nature?* Milwaukee: Marquette University Press, 1980.

Powell, Samuel M. "A Trinitarian Alternative to Process Theism." In *Thy Nature & Thy Name Is Love: Wesleyan and Process Theologies in Dialogue,* edited by Bryan P. Stone and Thomas Jay Oord, 143–67. Nashville: Abingdon, 2001.

Power, William L. "The Doctrine of the Trinity in Whitehead's Metaphysics." *Encounter* 45, no. 4 (Fall 1984): 287–302.

Pringle-Pattison, Andrew Seth. *Hegelianism and Personality.* London: William Blackwood and Sons, 1887.

———. *The Idea of God in the Light of Recent Philosophy.* New York: Oxford University Press, 1917.

Pugliese, Marc A. "Is Karl Rahner a Modalist?" *Irish Theological Quarterly* 68 (Fall 2003): 229–49.

Quine, W. V. O. "Two Dogmas of Empiricism." In *From a Logical Point of View,* 20–46. Cambridge, Mass.: Harvard University Press, 1953.

Quine, W. V. O., and J. S. Ullian. *The Web of Belief.* 2nd ed. New York: Random House, 1978.

Rahner, Karl. "The Concept of Mystery in Catholic Theology," translated by Kevin Smyth. In *More Recent Writings,* 36–73. Theological Investigations 4. Baltimore: Helicon Press, 1966.

———. "The Theology of the Symbol." In *Theological Investigations.* Vol. 4, More Recent Writings. Translated by Kevin Smyth, 221–52. Baltimore: Helicon Press, 1966.

———. *Spirit in the World.* Translated by William Dych, S.J. New York: Herder and Herder, 1968.

———. *The Trinity.* Translated by Joseph Donceel. New York: Herder and Herder, 1970.

———. "Christology in the Setting of Modern Man's Understanding of Himself and of His World." In *Theological Investigations.* Vol. 11, Confrontations 1. Translated by David Bourke, 215–29. New York: Seabury, 1974.

———. *Foundations of Christian Faith.* Translated by William Dych. New York: Seabury, 1978; reprint, New York: Crossroad, 1999.

Reck, Andrew J. "God as the Ultimate Meaning Is the Primordial Source of All Meanings: A Comment on Joseph A. Bracken's Presentation of the Ultimate Ground in Whitehead's Philosophy of Becoming." *Ultimate Reality and Meaning* 16 (March–June 1993): 137–39.

Reese, William L., and Eugene Freeman, eds. *Process and Divinity.* LaSalle, Ill.: Open Court, 1964.

Reeves, Gene, and Delwin Brown. "The Development of Process Theology." In *Process Philosophy and Christian Thought,* edited by D. Brown, R. E. James Jr., and G. Reeves, 21–64. Indianapolis: Bobbs-Merrill, 1971.

Rice, Richard. *The Openness of God: The Relationship of Divine Foreknowledge and Human Free Will.* Nashville: Review & Herald Publishers, 1979.

———. "Divine Foreknowledge and Free-Will Theism." In *The Grace of God and the Will of Man,* edited by Clark H. Pinnock, 121–39. Minneapolis: Bethany House Publishers, 1989.

Ricoeur, Paul. *Fallible Man.* Chicago: Regnery, 1965.

Royce, Josiah. *The Religious Aspect of Philosophy: A Critique of the Bases of Conduct and of Faith.* Boston: Houghton Mifflin, 1885.

———. *The Conception of Immortality.* Boston: Houghton Mifflin, 1900.

———. *The World and the Individual.* New York: Macmillan, 1901.

———. *The Problem of Christianity.* New York: Macmillan, 1918; reprint, Chicago: University of Chicago Press, 1968.

Royce, Josiah, et al. *The Conception of God: A Philosophical Discussion Concerning the Nature of the Divine Idea as a Demonstrable Reality.* New York: Macmillan, 1897.

Ruether, Rosemary Radford. *Woman and Redemption: A Theological History.* Minneapolis: Fortress Press, 1998.

Rushdoony, John Rousas. "The One and the Many Problem." In *Jerusalem and Athens: Critical Discussions on the Theology and Apologetics of Cornelius Van Til,* edited by E. R. Geehan, 339–48. Phillipsburg, N.J.: Presbyterian & Reformed, 1980.

Russell, Bertrand. *A History of Western Philosophy.* New York: Simon and Schuster, 1945.

Sanders, John. "God as Personal." In *The Grace of God and the Will of Man,* edited by Clark H. Pinnock, 165–80. Minneapolis: Bethany House Publishers, 1989.

———. *The God Who Risks: A Theology of Providence.* Downers Grove, Ill.: InterVarsity Press, 1998; 2nd rev. ed., 2007.

Schaffer, Jonathan. "The Metaphysics of Causation." *The Stanford Encyclopedia of Philosophy.* Winter 2007 edition. Edited by Edward N. Zalta. http://plato.stanford.edu/entries/causation-metaphysics/.

Scharlemann, Robert P. *The Being of God: Theology and the Experience of Truth.* New York: Seabury, 1981.

Schoonenberg, Piet. "God or Man: A False Dilemma." In *The Christ,* translated by D. Couling, 13–49. New York: Seabury, 1971.

Schillebeeckx, Edward. "Towards a Catholic Use of Hermeneutics." In *God the Future of Man.* Translated by N. D. Smith, 1–49. New York: Sheed and Ward, 1969.

———. *Christ: The Experience of Jesus as Lord.* Translated by John Bowden. New York: Crossroad, 1980; reprint, 1999.

Schleiermacher, Friedrich. *The Christian Faith.* 2nd ed. Edited by H. R. Mackintosh and J. S. Stewart. Berlin: Martin Redeker, 1830–31; Edinburgh: T & T Clark, 1989; reprint, 1997.

Sherburne, Donald. *A Whiteheadian Aesthetic.* New Haven, Conn.: Yale University Press, 1961.

Smart, J. J. C. "Time and Becoming." In *Time and Cause,* edited by Peter van Inwagen, 3–15. Dordrecht: Reidel, 1980.

Smith, Huston. "Has Process Theology Dismantled Classical Theism?" *Theology Digest* 35 (1988): 302–18.

Spencer, Herbert. *First Principles.* 3rd ed. London: Williams & Norgate, 1870.

Spinoza, Baruch. *Ethics.* Translated and edited by G. H. R. Parkinson. New York: Oxford University Press, 2001.

Stone, Bryan P., and Thomas Jay Oord, eds. *Thy Nature and Thy Name Is Love: Wesleyan and Process Theologies in Dialogue.* Nashville: Kingswood Books, 2001.

Stump, Eleonore. *Aquinas.* New edition. New York: Routledge, 2005.

Suchocki, Marjorie Hewitt. *God, Christ, Church: A Practical Guide to Process Theology.* New York: Crossroad, 1982.

———. *The End of Evil: Process Eschatology in Historical Context.* Albany: State University of New York Press, 1988.

———. "Spirit in and through the World." In *Trinity in Process: A Relational Theology of God,* edited by Joseph A. Bracken, S.J., and Marjorie Hewitt Suchocki, 173–93. New York: Continuum, 1997.

———. *The Fall to Violence: Original Sin in Relational Theology.* New York: Continuum, 1999.

———. *Divinity and Diversity: A Christian Affirmation of Religious Pluralism.* Nashville: Abingdon Press, 2003.

Teilhard de Chardin, Pierre. *The Appearance of Man.* Translated by J. M. Cohen. London: Collins, 1965.

———. *The Divine Milieu.* New York: Harper & Row, 1965.

———. *The Future of Man.* Translated by Norman Denny. New York: Harper & Row, 1969.

———. *The Activation of Energy.* Translated by René Hague. London: Collins, 1970.

———. *Christianity and Evolution.* Translated by René Hague. London: Collins, 1971.

Temple, William. *Nature, Man and God.* London: Macmillan, 1934.

Thomas Aquinas. *Summa theologiae.* Translated from the Latin by the Fathers of the English Dominican Province. New York: Benziger, 1947.

———. *Summa contra gentiles. Book One: God.* Translated by Anton C. Pegis, F.R.S.C. New York: Doubleday, 1955; Notre Dame, Ind.: University of Notre Dame Press, 1975.

———. *Exposition of Dionysius on the Divine Names.* The Pocket Aquinas. Edited by Vernon J. Bourke. New York: Simon & Schuster, 1960.

Thornton, Lionel. *The Incarnate Lord.* London: Longmans Green, 1928.

Tillich, Paul. *Systematic Theology.* 3 vols. Chicago: University of Chicago Press, 1951–63.

Torrance, Thomas F. *The Trinitarian Faith.* Edinburgh: T & T Clark, 1988.

Tracy, David. *Blessed Rage for Order: The New Pluralism in Theology.* New York: Seabury Press, 1975.

———. *The Analogical Imagination: Christian Theology and the Culture of Pluralism.* New York: Crossroad, 2000.

Tugendhat, Ernst. *Ti kata tinos: eine Untersuchung zu Struktur und Ursprung aristotelicher Grundbegriffe.* Freiberg i. Br.: Karl Alber Verlag, 1958.

Turretin, Francis. *Institutes of Elenctic Theology.* 3 vols. Edited by James T. Dennison Jr. Translated by George Musgrave Giger. Leiden: Batavor, 1696; Philipsburg, N.J.: Presbyterian & Reformed, 1992.

Van Til, Cornelius. *Psychology of Religion.* Philadelphia: Presbyterian & Reformed, 1961.

———. *Christianity and Barthianism.* Phillipsburg, N.J.: Presbyterian & Reformed, 1962; rev. ed., 1965.

———. *The Defense of the Faith.* 3rd ed. Phillipsburg, N.J.: Presbyterian & Reformed, 1967.

———. *A Survey of Christian Epistemology.* Philadelphia: Presbyterian & Reformed, 1969.

———. *Common Grace and the Gospel.* Philadelphia: Presbyterian & Reformed, 1972.

———. *An Introduction to Systematic Theology.* Philadelphia: Presbyterian & Reformed, 1974.

Varisco, Bernardino. *The Great Problems.* Translated by R. C. Lodge. London: George Allen, 1914.

———. *Know Thyself.* Translated by Guglielmo Salvadori. London: George Allen & Unwin, 1915.

von Brück, Michael. *The Unity of Reality: God, God-Experience, and Meditation in the Hindu-Christian Dialogue.* Translated by James V. Zeitz. New York: Paulist Press, 1991.

von Herder, Johann Gottfried. *Ideen zur Philosophie der Geschichte der Menschheit (1784–91).* 10 vols. Edited by Martin Bollacher et al. Frankfurt am Main: Deutscher Klassiker Verlag, 1985–.

von Schelling, Friedrich Wilhelm Joseph. "Letter to Hegel, February 4, 1795." In *Sämtliche Werke.* 14 vols. Edited by K. F. A. Schelling. Stuttgart, 1856.

Wagner, Michael F. "Plotinus' World." *Dionysius* 6 (1982): 16–17.

Wallack, Bradford. *The Epochal Nature of Process in Whitehead's Metaphysics.* Albany: State University of New York Press, 1980.

Ward, James. *Naturalism and Agnosticism.* 2 vols. London: Adam and Charles Black, 1906.

———. *The Realm of Ends or Pluralism and Theism.* Cambridge: Cambridge University Press, 1911.

Watson, John. *Christianity and Idealism.* Glasgow: James Maclehose, 1897.

Weatherson, Brian. "The Problem of the Many." *The Stanford Encyclopedia of Philosophy.* Fall 2004 edition. Edited by Edward N. Zalta. http://plato.stanford.edu/ archives/fall2004/entries/problem-of-many/.

Welker, Michael. "Christian Theology: Which Direction at the End of the Second Millennium." In *The Future of Theology: Essays in Honor of Jürgen Moltmann,* edited by Miroslav Volf, Careman Krieg, and Thomas Kucharz, 73–88. Grand Rapids, Mich.: Eerdmans, 1999.

———. *Creation and Reality.* Minneapolis: Fortress Press, 1999.

Westphal, Merold. *Overcoming Onto-Theology: Toward a Postmodern Christian Faith.* New York: Fordham University Press, 2001.

Wheelwright, Philip, ed. *The Presocratics.* New York: Macmillan, 1966.

Whitehead, Alfred North. *The Concept of Nature.* Cambridge: Cambridge University Press, 1920.

———. *The Principle of Relativity.* Cambridge: Cambridge University Press, 1922.

———. *An Enquiry Concerning the Principles of Natural Knowledge.* 2nd ed. Cambridge: Cambridge University Press, 1925 (originally 1919).

———. *Science and the Modern World.* New York: Macmillan, 1925; reprint, Free Press, 1967.

———. *Religion in the Making.* New York: Macmillan, 1926; reprint, New American Library, 1974.

———. *Symbolism, Its Meaning and Effect.* New York: Macmillan, 1927; reprint, Fordham University Press, 1985.

———. *The Function of Reason.* Princeton, N.J.: Princeton University Press, 1929.

———. *Adventures of Ideas.* New York: Macmillan, 1933; reprint, Free Press, 1967.

———. *Nature and Life.* Cambridge: Cambridge University Press, 1934.

———. *Modes of Thought.* Cambridge: Cambridge University Press, 1938.

———. *Essays in Science and Philosophy.* New York: Philosophical Library, 1947.

———. *The Aims of Education.* New York: American Library, 1949.

———. *Dialogues of Alfred North Whitehead as Recorded by Lucien Prince.* New York: Mentor Books, 1956.

———. *Process and Reality: An Essay in Cosmology.* Corrected ed. Edited by David Ray Griffin and Donald W. Sherburne. New York: Free Press, 1978.

Wieland, Wolfgang. *Schellings Lehre von der Zeit.* Heidelberg: Winter Verlag, 1956.

Williams, Daniel Day. *God's Grace and Man's Hope.* New York: Harper & Brothers, 1949; revised edition, 1965.

———. *The Spirit and the Forms of Love.* London: James Nisbet, 1968.

———. "How Does God Act? An Essay in Whitehead's Metaphysics." In *Essays in Process Theology*, edited by Peter LeFevre, 98–117. Chicago: Exploration Press, 1985.

Williams, Ronald L. "The Two Types of Christology: A Neoclassical Analysis." *Journal of Religion* 49, no. 1 (January 1969): 18–40.

Wilcox, John R. "A Monistic Interpretation of Whitehead's Creativity." *Process Studies* 20, no. 3 (Fall, 1991): 162–74.

Wright, John H. "Divine Knowledge and Human Freedom: The God Who Dialogues." *Theological Studies* 38, no. 3 (1977): 474–77.

Zizioulas, John. *Being as Communion: Studies in Personhood and the Church.* Crestwood, N.Y.: St. Vladimir's Seminary Press, 1985.

Zwingli, Huldrych. *On Providence and Other Essays.* Edited by William John Hinke. Philadelphia: Heidelberg Press, 1922; reprint, Eugene, Ore.: Wipf & Stock, 1999.

Index

The One, the Many, and the Trinity: Joseph A. Bracken and the Challenge of Process Metaphysics was designed and typeset in Minion by Kachergis Book Design of Pittsboro, North Carolina. It was printed on 60-pound House Natural Smooth and bound by Sheridan Books of Ann Arbor, Michigan.